Philosophical Finesse

Philosophical Finesse

Studies in the Art of Rational Persuasion

Martin Warner

CLARENDON PRESS · OXFORD
1989

Oxford University Press, Walton Street, Oxford OX2 6DP
Oxford New York Toronto
Delhi Bombay Calcutta Madras Karachi
Petaling Jaya Singapore Hong Kong Tokyo
Nairobi Dar es Salaam Cape Town
Melbourne Auckland
and associated companies in
Berlin Ibadan

Oxford is a trade mark of Oxford University Press

Published in the United States
by Oxford University Press, New York

British Library Cataloguing in Publication Data
Warner, Martin, 1940–
Philosophical finesse: studies in the art of rational
persuasion.
1. Rational argument
I. Title
168
ISBN 0-19-824455-X

Library of Congress Cataloging in Publication Data
Warner, Martin.
Philosophical finesse: studies in the art of rational persuasion
Martin Warner.
Bibliography: p.   Includes index.
1. Reasoning.   2. Philosophy, Ancient.   3. Bible. O.T. Job—
Criticism, interpretation, etc.   4. Pascal, Blaise, 1632–1776.
5. Hume, David, 1711–1776.   6. Nietzsche, Friedrich Wilhelm,
1844–1900.   I. Title.
BC177.W347 1989   121—dc19   88-38799
ISBN 0-19-824455-X

Photoset by Rowland Phototypesetting Ltd
Bury St Edmunds, Suffolk

Printed and bound in
Great Britain by Biddles Ltd,
Guildford and King's Lynn

For Veronica
emblematic of finesse

Acknowledgements

My intellectual debts are normally noted later where appropriate. There remain certain general ones which should be acknowledged here: above all to Rick Gekoski and William Righter, my dialectical partners over many years; also to my colleagues in the Department of Philosophy at Warwick, who have given assistance in diverse ways, and to the Department's invaluable Staff Seminar from which I have learnt much; also to anonymous readers for the Clarendon Press who have helped me to express myself with greater finesse.

I am grateful to Peter Larkin for substantial library assistance, and to the University of Warwick for the generous provision of sabbatical leave in the course of what has turned out to be an extended project.

I also thank certain copyright holders for permitting me to quote extensively from the following editions and translations: Cambridge University Press for use of R. Hackforth's translation of Plato's *Phaedo*; The National Council of the Churches of Christ in the USA for use of the *Revised Standard Version* of the Bible; Thomas Nelson and Sons for use of N. Kemp Smith's edition of Hume's *Dialogues Concerning Natural Religion*; Penguin Books for use of A. J. Krailsheimer's translation of Pascal's *Pensées*, all the quotations from which are reproduced by permission of Penguin Books Ltd; Random House for use of W. Kaufmann's translations of works contained in *Basic Writings of Nietzsche*; The Viking Press for use of W. Kaufmann's translations of works contained in *The Portable Nietzsche*.

M.M.W.

Contents

On a huge hill,
Cragged and steep, Truth stands, and hee that will
Reach her, about must, and about must goe;
And what th' hills suddennes resists, winne so.

(Donne, 'Satyre III', ll. 79–82)

οἰκτρὸν ἂν εἴη τὸ πάθος, εἰ ὄντος δή τινος ἀληθοῦς καὶ
βεβαίου λόγου καὶ δυνατοῦ κατανοῆσαι, ἔπειτα διὰ τὸ
παραγίγνεσθαι τοιούτοις τισὶ λόγοις, τοῖς αὐτοῖς τοτὲ μὲν
δοκοῦσιν ἀληθέσιν εἶναι, τοτὲ δὲ μή, μὴ ἑαυτόν τις αἰτιῷτο
μηδὲ τὴν ἑαυτοῦ ἀτεχνίαν, ἀλλὰ τελευτῶν διὰ τὸ ἀλγεῖν
ἅσμενος ἐπὶ τοὺς λόγους ἀφ' ἑαυτοῦ τὴν αἰτίαν ἀπώσαιτο καὶ
ἤδη τὸν λοιπὸν βίον μισῶν τε καὶ λοιδορῶν τοὺς λόγους
διατελοῖ, τῶν δὲ ὄντων τῆς ἀληθείας τε καὶ ἐπιστήμης
στερηθείη.

(Plato, *Phaedo*, 90c–d)

I

Philosophical Reasoning: The Disposition to Geometrize

1. Rival Philosophical Models

God, we are told, always geometrizes;[1] philosophers have repeatedly attempted to emulate him, with unfortunate results.

Of course, few philosophers have been expressly committed to the geometric model as their paradigm for philosophical reasoning, but the fact that several of the leading figures of the seventeenth-century revolution in philosophy were so committed has had disproportionate influence. Indeed, Descartes's discarding of "those weapons of the schoolmen, probable syllogisms" in favour of a method of philosophizing designed to "attain a certitude equal to that of the demonstrations of Arithmetic and Geometry"[2] represented a decisive shift in philosophers' conception of their own activity, the consequences of which are still working themselves out. Both the "methods of proof" available to "the geometrical mode of writing" enumerated by Descartes ((1), ii, 'Reply to Objections II', 48), the analytic and the synthetic, have their twentieth-century counterparts, and both give rise to serious difficulties.

Even in the seventeenth century the geometric ideal met resistance—Descartes was immediately countered by Pascal—and such opposition has repeatedly been renewed, but there has also been a recurrent tendency for philosophers to assess the reasoning of such

---

[1] The principal authority is, of course, Plato as quoted by Plutarch (IX, *Table-Talk*, VIII. ii. 718: ἀεὶ γεωμετρεῖν τὸν θεόν). He is seconded by Newton (iii, 'Letter to Bentley', 235): "To make this systeme therefore with all its motions, required a Cause . . . very well skilled in Mechanicks & Geometry." De Quincey (x. 17), apparently drawing on Sir Thomas Browne (18 and 201) renders the Platonic tag "God geometrizes eternally".

[2] Descartes, *Regulae*, i. 5. All quotations from Descartes are given in the Haldane and Ross translation unless otherwise indicated. Descartes reverts to the topic in pt. II of his *Discourse on the Method* (i. 92–3) and at the close of his 'Reply to the Second Set of Objections' (ii. 48–51).

objectors by reference to "geometric" canons—with unflattering results. It is only comparatively recently, for example, that the English-speaking world has accepted such subversives as Pascal and Nietzsche as genuine philosophers. Yet now that the limitations of the assumptions behind those dismissive assessments are becoming increasingly apparent, it is worth exploring the work of such re-calcitrants, without presupposing the methodology of their opponents, in order to evaluate their own conceptions of philosophical reasoning.

Such evaluations require some tact and subtlety. On the one hand, an accurate understanding of a philosopher's arguments is most likely to be achieved if one interprets them within his own preferred model of reasoning, but on the other, to use that model as the primary criterion for evaluation is as likely to involve *petitio* as the more traditional practice of judging them in terms of assumptions he was attempting to combat. Further, interpretation and evaluation cannot always be cleanly separated in the exploration of such texts.

In order to provide a comparatively untendentious vocabulary and set of perspectives for such explorations, Chapter 2 sketches three influential models of philosophical reasoning—developed long before the seventeenth century and the battle lines it has bequeathed to us. These accounts are not wholly alien to the later writers discussed, for the latter make significant use of the leading Classical traditions for their own purposes; indeed, Aristotle's attempt to limit the aspirations of that quasi-geometrizing model of reasoning to which Plato was increasingly drawn has significant parallels with Pascal's critique of the pretensions of Cartesian reason. Nevertheless, the differences are also important; on the one hand, as we shall see, Descartes's reinterpretation of the geometric ideal breaks with an element crucial to all the Classical writers discussed, even at their most "geometric"; on the other, in their methodological discussions his opponents typically draw on conceptions closely related to what is today termed 'authenticity' which have Biblical as well as Classical roots. In subsequent chapters these Classical models can therefore be used both as points of entry and as distancing devices, capable of being themselves modified and improved by reference to the works to which they are applied.

Behind "those weapons of the schoolmen" stands the figure of Aristotle. His writings provide the most systematic and wide-ranging investigations into the ways in which we may distinguish between good and bad reasoning extant from Classical times, and his threefold distinction, discussed in Chapter 2, between 'demonstration', 'dialectic', and 'rhetoric'—with the first two categories providing criteria for assessing philosophical reasoning—proved seminal for most of two millenia. With Descartes, however, the Aristotelian analysis was rejected, and a unified "method" with many of the main features of the old "demonstration" taken as the key to acceptable reasoning in philosophy—with the rider that "the operation is profited but little by those constraining bonds by means of which the Dialecticians claim to control human reason" ((1), 1, *Regulae* ii. 5). Dialectic was characterized by Aristotle as "a process of criticism wherein lies the path to the principles of all inquiries" (1, *Topics*, A. 101b) and, so construed, much of the argumentation I shall be considering will be "dialectical", and the resistance to the geometric model there embodied represent the pressing of the claims of dialectic against the all-engrossing demands of demonstration.

Insistence on this vocabulary could be misleading, however, not only because the term 'dialectic' has kept doubtful company of late, but also because the texts to be studied do not keep strictly to the Aristotelian rules for dialectic—casting, indeed, some doubt on the distinctions they presuppose between dialectic and rhetoric. I have preferred instead to attempt to rehabilitate a term Pascal introduced in a somewhat sketchy fashion to oppose to the geometric mode of reasoning, 'finesse', in part for its very lack of detailed specificity and incrustation of associations, in part for the aptness of Pascal's adumbration, and in part for the overtones of "subtle discrimination" carried by the word today in non-technical contexts. These studies are intended as a contribution towards the analysis and defence of philosophical finesse.

In this capacity they seek to help re-enfranchise a range of voices, procedures, and positions which have long been marginalized by the dominance of the geometric model of philosophical argument. The case-studies point beyond themselves to a conception of philosophy as an activity of interrogation (including self-interrogation) for which the paradigms associated with analysis and system-building are inadequate. But it is a form of interrogation which is centrally concerned with the seeking of truth and for which the fashionable and apparently anti-Cartesian models of "conversation" and even "play" are also inadequate—representing but the reverse side of the same suspect coin.

Behind the disposition to geometrize lies, of course, the desire for "certitude". Descartes himself complains of philosophy "that it has been cultivated for many centuries by the best minds that have ever lived, and that nevertheless no single thing is to be found in it which is not subject of dispute, and in consequence which is not dubious" ((1), i, *Discourse*, 1). The attraction of geometry is precisely that here matters are held to be otherwise. Descartes's complaint and prescription are recurrent; even Kant contrasts the way mathematics early "entered upon the sure path of science" with metaphysics' lack of this "good fortune" so that "ever and again we have to retrace our steps", and seeks to bring the latter to the condition of the former ((1) B. xi–xix).[3] Similar observations have formed a leitmotif within twentieth-century philosophy (for a recent example see Dummett (454–8)), until despair of the goal has led some to radical scepticism about the whole enterprise of philosophy as a truth-seeking activity; reasonable assurance is traded for what the Socrates of the *Phaedo* long ago stigmatized as 'misology', out of frustrated aspiration after "a certitude equal to that of the demonstrations of Arithmetic and Geometry". But while the philosopher's concern to aim at knowledge of the truth rather than opinion about probabilities is both defensible and at least as old as Plato, it remains questionable whether the conceptions of "knowledge" and "certitude" here appropriate are best construed on the model of mathematics.

Chapters 3 to 5 explore five texts which in different ways help to give content to the alternative model I have called 'finesse'. In the case of two of them, the *Phaedo* and Hume's *Dialogues*, commentators have traditionally concentrated on their more "geometric" aspects; while these certainly exist, I shall attempt to show that other elements also play important argumentative roles by drawing particular attention to the way both works take seriously what one of Hume's characters calls "irregular" arguments. The *Phaedo*, indeed, represents an unusually sophisticated Classical enactment

---

[3] Kant, of course, is far from straightforwardly Cartesian in his methodology employing, indeed, a form of "dialectic". However he is not an exponent of finesse; at the heart of his methodology lies a sharp distinction between reason and persuasion which owes much to his conceptualizing of "science" in quasi-mathematical terms. See also ch. 2, n. 54.

of argument using both "regular" (quasi-geometric) and "irregular" means, in a balance lost in the later Platonic dialogues. The Book of Job is paradigmatic for that influential Biblical rejection of conceptions of "Wisdom" which construe it in terms of arguments which Hume was later to term "formal and regular" (Hume (2), *Letters*, i. 155), in favour of the wisdom of the "heart". The *Phaedo* and Job only provide partial adumbrations of "finesse", but Pascal's *Pensées*, the discussion of which represents the pivot of the entire book, do more; they present the "dogmatism" of geometric reason and traditional scepticism as meeting in an intellectual impasse, which can only be resolved by appeal to the "reasons of the heart"—a subtle blend of Classical and Biblical "irregular" arguments, embodying a broader conception of rationality than the Cartesian. Pascal uses this analysis for religious purposes, but Hume and Nietzsche—without falling back on merely geometric canons—provide very different types of secular riposte to the Pascalian religious apologia, which make significant use of "irregular" arguments and have affinities with that broader conception.

Despite their obvious disparities, there is a certain family resemblance between the underlying methodologies of these five works, and the final chapter attempts to draw this out. Chapter 1 sets out the seminal Cartesian version of the geometric model of reasoning, argues that variants of it still play an important role in philosophy today, and sketches a number of recent attempts to make use of non-geometric inferential models to resolve the difficulties to which the geometric one gives rise. Chapter 8 sets out a non-geometric account of rationality—finesse—as it has emerged from the case-studies, attempts to meet some of the obvious objections, and argues that several of the current efforts to resolve philosophical perplexities discussed in Chapter 1 parallel different aspects of philosophical finesse.

The concluding chapter also contains some more positive arguments for taking this rival conception of rationality seriously, but as the notion of a "cumulative argument" plays an important role in finesse, it is appropriate that the main burden of the case for it should depend on the cumulative force of the analyses and assessments of arguments contained in the five main case-studies. Within the limitations appropriate to a work concerned with second-order issues, this book itself represents an attempt to enact at least some aspects of its recommended mode of argument.

Reflexivity also plays a role in the choice of case-studies. Up-holders of the geometric ideal frequently fail to exemplify con-sistently their preferred method; at least in the *Meditations* and *Discourse* Descartes himself employs forms of procedure which have strong affinities with finesse, and even that geometric Ultima Thule, Spinoza's *Ethics*, may not be entirely free of such.[4] Recogni-tion of this has opened the way to contemporary "deconstructive" efforts to undercut the whole philosophic enterprise as inevitably implicated in procedures it *ex officio* disavows. But with exponents of finesse such mismatch of theory and practice is less endemic, and for the sake of clarity I have chosen texts where the method employed is either an (at least partial) enactment of that advocated (Plato, Pascal, Nietzsche) or at least defensible in terms of the author's meta-philosophical position (Hume); the Book of Job resists the very drawing of these distinctions. Given the account of finesse that arises out of these studies, the failure of reflexivity in the Cartesian tradition can be seen not as undermining philosophy as such, but as showing its members often to be better philosophers than their official methodology allows: *Finesse expellas furca, tamen usque recurret.*

2. The Geometric Model

For two centuries the *Port-Royal Logic* dominated the treatment of logic and related issues by most philosophers,[5] and the section on method took its inspiration directly from the work of Descartes and Pascal. Thus although the geometric model of reasoning exerted overt and decisive influence on several other seventeenth-century

---

[4] A similar distinction between practice and theory can be drawn at the level of philosophical commentary. Commentators often highlight "geometric" patterns of argument in the philosophical works they are discussing (such, for example, as Plato's *Phaedo* and Hume's *Dialogues*) through the use of finesse-like hermeneutic procedures. My own studies are intended both to highlight and to exemplify such procedures; given the affinities between finesse and Aristotelian dialectic this project does not, of course, debar me from on occasion using straightforwardly deductive reasoning.

[5] See Kneale (320): "Some features of the *Port-Royal Logic* reflect special interests of Arnauld and Nicole which could not be expected to spread far beyond their own circle; but the general conception of logic which they expounded in this book was widely accepted and continued to dominate the treatment of logic by most philosophers for the next 200 years." The *Logic* was published in 1662; the section on method is pt. 4.

philosophers, from Hobbes to Spinoza, for present purposes it is reasonable to confine attention to the figures behind Arnauld.

Descartes's philosophical method has the advantage of providing a challengingly uncompromising set of criteria for distinguishing between philosophical reasoning which is acceptable and that which is not. It is in the *Regulae ad directionem ingenii* that we find his most sustained discussion. The second "Rule" states that "Only those objects should engage our attention, to the sure and indubitable knowledge of which our mental powers seem to be adequate" ((1), i. 3), and in discussing it Descartes argues that we should "make it a rule to trust only what is completely known and incapable of being doubted"; however, "of the sciences already discovered, Arithmetic and Geometry alone are left, to which the observance of this rule reduces us". He concludes, "not, indeed, that Arithmetic and Geometry are the sole sciences to be studied, but only that in our search for the direct road towards truth we should busy ourselves with no object about which we cannot attain a certitude equal to that of the demonstrations of Arithmetic and Geometry".

In the course of the argument we find that the key to privileged status is deduction: "While our inferences from experience are frequently fallacious, deduction, or the pure illation of one thing from another, though it may be passed over, if it is not seen through, cannot be erroneous when performed by an understanding that is in the least degree rational." As it stands, the contrast being attempted is unclear; arguments based on a particular type of premiss (that of "experience") are contrasted with a particular species of inference. The original latin, however, uses the word '*experientias*', which is a technical term for inductive arguments, thus on the usual—not implausible—reading[6] the contrast involved is that

---

[6] It has recently been argued by Clarke that Descartes's use of '*experientia*', '*deducere*' and related terms is too flexible to bear the weight usually put on them (see s. 3, 8 and app. 1). This is not the place to debate the matter, for it is the way Descartes has been interpreted that is of primary importance for the argument of this book. But even for Clarke Descartes uses 'deduction' to designate reliable inference (69), and the standards set for reliability are remarkably severe. Further, Clarke concedes that "Cartesian method involves an extrapolation . . . of a method which is peculiar to mathematics" in the sense that "analysis and synthesis was originally conceived of as a geometric method" (166). For a scholarly presentation of the more traditional reading see Beck, for whom Cartesian "deduction does come, in the end, to the same thing as the ideally perfect ἀποδεικτικὸς συλλογιομός of Aristotle" (113). Haldane and Ross (i. 4) draw attention to the technical significance of '*experientias*'.

between deductive and inductive arguments. Further, we have seen that Descartes also opposes his preferred deductive inferences to "probable syllogisms" and inferential rules developed by "the Dialecticians". Here, then, we appear to be presented with a model of rationality such that the serious philosophical search after knowledge should be confined within the limits of deductive inference, after the analogy of arithmetic and geometry; probable reasoning (in terms of which Aristotle defined 'dialectic') is inappropriate, inductions from experience are dismissed, and no alternative, if such there be, is admissible as a rival.[7]

Cartesian deduction, glossed as "the pure illation of one thing from another", has its own distinctive features. In opposition to syllogistic, Descartes refuses to separate form and content in reasoning, and deduction is understood in terms of the progress of the mind through successive self-evident steps.[8] As L. J. Beck puts it, "No conclusion must be affirmed as true unless it follows in an uninterrupted sequence of self-evident steps from the initial vision of self-evident data" (47). This is a slight over-simplification, for this quasi-axiomatic vision better represents the "synthetic" method of proof than the "analytic", which is moved rather by the thought that "our beliefs cannot be certain so long as they *imply* or *presuppose* propositions which are uncertain" (Williams (1), 60). Nevertheless, for analysis too deduction is the essential tool, and the fact remains that for Descartes "sure and indubitable knowledge" is the goal

---

[7] Descartes's idiosyncratic use of '*inductio*' can prove a trap for the unwary here. The priority of deduction is laid down under Rule 2, but at Rule 11 we are told that when we are presented with a "complex and involved" deduction "we give it the name of enumeration or induction (*Enumeratio sive Inductio*), because it cannot then be grasped as a whole at the same time by the mind, and its certainty depends to some extent on the memory" ((1), i. 33). Here we are clearly not concerned with inductions from experience, but with a term of art required by Descartes's non-formal analysis of deduction. On the standard reading, "enumeration or induction is essential as an auxiliary to the deductive argument" (Beck, 139), not a rival to it.

[8] The more orthodox conception of deduction as a succession of propositions validated by reference to their form was revived by Leibniz in his ideal of an *Ars Combinatoria* and now stands almost unchallenged. In Descartes ((1), i. 7), the fact that the '*intuitus*' is involved "not only in the enunciation of propositions, but also in discursive reasoning" gives a certain unity to the method by which "sure and indubitable knowledge" is to be reached—a unity undergirded by the notions of 'clarity' and 'distinctness'. But with the adoption of a formal conception of deduction, the appeal to *intuitus* to ground the deductive chains is something of an anomaly, as Leibniz was well aware. Some of our contemporary problems stem from the ways we have combined certain remnants of the Cartesian vision of the place of deduction in philosophy with a broadly Leibnizian conception of its nature.

which, when achieved, makes the synthetic method of proof possible; "synthesis functions after analysis has laid bare the principles,
the self-evident truths" (Beck 176).

It is the method of analysis and synthesis that represents the heart
of Descartes's understanding of the geometric model of reasoning
and the projected *Mathesis Universalis*.[9] Analysis consists in showing "the true way by which a thing was methodically discovered",
whereas synthesis "employs an opposite procedure" with "a long
series of definitions, postulates, axioms, theorems and problems"
((1), ii. 48–9).

The method of analysis begins by positing the problem in all its complexity
and obscurity. The problem is then divided into as many parts as are
thought necessary by a preliminary survey or enumeration. This preliminary survey may have to be repeated on successive parts of the first ordering
or classification until the problem is laid out in its provisional series of
deductions. The deductions follow in the prescribed order of effects to
causes, culminating in the intellectual intuition of the simple self-evident.
The reverse process is followed in synthesis. The result of the synthetic
method is to reproduce the problem as it was posited before the simplifying
process of analysis, but the problem is now seen as a clear and distinct series
of deductive links (Beck, 175).

Although he holds that "it was this synthesis alone that the ancient
Geometers employed in their writings" ((1), ii. 49), Descartes
himself uses both; the *Discourse* and the *Meditations* primarily
exemplify analytic demonstration, the *Principles* and the "Arguments . . . drawn up in geometrical fashion" at the close of the
second set of *Replies* synthetic. But on whichever side the emphasis
lies, account needs to be taken of the other. The double movement
is expounded succinctly in the statement of the fifth Rule:

Method consists entirely in the order and disposition of the objects towards
which our mental vision must be directed if we would find out any truth. We
shall comply with it exactly if we reduce involved and obscure propositions
step by step to those that are simpler, and then starting with the intuitive
apprehension of all those that are absolutely simple, attempt to ascend to
the knowledge of all others by precisely similar steps ((1), i. 14).[10]

---

[9] For a brief but judicious, if dated, examination of the method as practised by the
ancient geometers, see Robinson's 'Analysis in Greek Geometry'. The best recent
full-length study is probably that of Hintikka and Remes.
[10] The best known formulation of this double movement is to be found in the
second and third Rules of the *Discourse* (i. 92).

To the extent that the two elements can in practice be separated, Descartes holds that analysis is "the best and truest method of teaching" ((1), ii. 49), but on this point the *Port-Royal Logic* differs, terming synthesis the 'method of instruction'[11] and characterizing it as "the more important of the two methods" (Arnauld, 302 and 309); behind this disagreement lies the influence of Pascal.

While the latter did not subordinate analysis to synthesis, the aspect of the geometrical model to which he found it worth while to devote his main attention was the synthetic one. In an early letter defending his work on the vacuum, Pascal lays it down as a rule of scientific method that one should never affirm or deny a proposition unless what one claims either of itself appears "so clearly and distinctly to sense or to reason, according as it is subject to one or the other, that the mind cannot doubt its certainty, and this is what we call a *principle* or *axiom*", or else "it be deduced as an infallible and necessary consequence from such principles or axioms" ((7), 365–6). This respect for the ideal of geometric synthesis was exemplified more extensively a decade later, when Pascal articulated the geometric model of human reasoning in his *De l'esprit géométrique*, declaring that "whatever transcends geometry transcends us" ((2), 349).

For Pascal, however, man's chief business is with that which transcends him, thus this apparently extravagant encomium is less unqualified than it looks. Both his agreement and disagreement with Descartes come out in the associated work *De l'art de persuader* which, while upholding the geometric model of reasoning about the natural world, maintains that religious truths need to be approached differently; so far as the latter are concerned,

God alone can put them into the soul, and in whatever way He pleases. I know He has willed they should enter into the mind from the heart and not into the heart from the mind, that He might make humble that proud power of reason, which claims the right to be judge over the things chosen by the will, and that He might cure the infirmity of that will . . . God established

---

[11] Port-Royal terms analysis alternatively the method of 'resolution' or 'invention', and synthesis 'composition' or 'instruction' (Arnauld, 302), the former alternates recalling the *metodo resolutivo* and the *metodo compositivo* of Zabarella, Galileo, and the Paduan School (see Randall). The distinction was something of a commonplace at the time, being paralleled by Ramus' contrast between the 'prudential' and 'natural' methods, and Bacon's opposition of 'probative' to 'magisterial' ones; see Howell (2), ch. 6.

this order above nature and entirely opposed to the order which should be natural to men in natural things. ((7), 440)

Here we have a major break with Cartesianism,[12] and the implications of this doctrine of different orders—together with the associated contrast between "mind" and "heart"—will become pressing when we examine the *Pensées* in Chapter 5. But where the natural order is concerned the procedure Pascal advocates is structurally parallel to that of Descartes, and the "reason" which is said to be inappropriate to supernatural truths has much in common with Cartesian reason.[13] For when we are examining "truths within our reach", we should "never agree to anything but demonstrated truths", and here the correct method

which is simply the management of perfect scientific proofs, consists of three essential parts: defining by clear definitions the terms to be used; laying down evident principles or axioms to prove the matter in question; always mentally substituting in the demonstration, in place of the things defined, their definitions ((7), 442).

Three paragraphs later he refers to this as the "method of geometrical proofs".

Descartes and Pascal, then, maintain that we can know indubitable truths which may serve as axioms for synthetic proofs *more geometrico*, and part of philosophy's ultimate aim (at least, so far as Pascal is concerned, as regards "natural things") is so to reveal the

---

[12] Descartes had distinguished between philosophical and theological argument, but still held that the fundamental theological principles of the existence of God and the immortality of the soul could and should be demonstrated by philosophical argument (see, *inter alia*, his dedication to the *Meditations*). For Pascal such purported demonstrations are worthless.

[13] Although there are strong similarities and structural parallels between the accounts given by Descartes and Pascal of admissible philosophical reasoning, there are also significant differences—some of which support Pascal's insistence on its inherent limitations. Professor Miel's summary brings out the contrast, given the conventional reading of Descartes: "For Descartes, the clearest, most self-evident ideas have their existence in his mind, even if only latently; furthermore they have the status of essences and are the point of departure for the deductive process. But for Pascal, we do not know the nature or essence of these basic terms, only what they designate, and hence nothing can be deduced from them. Further, they are not in Pascal's mind: they result from the interaction of our awareness with the qualities or features of the world in which we find ourselves, qualities we know naturally (by instinct, by the heart) but which our reason can only designate, or assign a name to" (Miel (2), 269–70). The logical chasm between definitions and axioms cuts much deeper in Pascal than in Descartes.

structure of knowledge that it is capable of being laid out in accordance with the synthetic "method of proof". In this sense, the philosopher aims to uncover a system of propositions which are necessary in the sense that they impose themselves on all rational beings, and about which agreement is therefore inevitable. Thus for Descartes,

Whenever two men come to opposite decisions about the same matter one of them at least must certainly be in the wrong, and apparently there is not even one of them who knows; for if the reasoning of the second was sound and clear he would be able so to lay it before the other as finally to succeed in convincing *his* understanding also ((1), i. 3).

In Pascal the Cartesian theory of self-evidence is developed and applied. Self-evidence is thought of as being at one and the same time psychologically compelling for any normal mind and a criterion of the truth of what so imposes itself; logical and psychological considerations are thus run together. The terminus of all proofs is a set of axioms which, being themselves self-evident, have no need of proof:

As we proceed ever further with our investigations, we come of necessity to primitive words which can no longer be defined and to principles so clear that it is no longer possible to find others more clear for their demonstration. . . . Geometry . . . assumes only things clear and invariant by the natural light, and that is why it is perfectly true, nature supporting it in default of discourse ((7), 431–2).

The *Port-Royal Logic* echoes this account:

Some propositions are clear and evident in themselves and need no demonstration; . . . only propositions which are clear and evident can serve as undemonstrated principles of a demonstration. . . . We hold as clear anything which appears so to those who take the trouble to consider things attentively and who are sincere in revealing their innermost convictions (Arnauld, 318).

Thus the fully fledged theory that only geometrical reasoning is acceptable in philosophy seems to be committed to the availability of substantial necessary truths, whose psychological force somehow guarantees their axiomatic status.

3. Problems with the Geometric Model

It was not long before unease was expressed at the extent to which the Cartesian method ran logical and psychological considerations together. Thus Leibniz maintained that demonstrations should "be provided for all axioms which are not primary, without reference to men's opinions about them and without caring whether they agree to them or not" (75). For the primary axioms, however, he fell back on the innateness hypothesis, for without innate "items of knowledge" there would be "no way of achieving actual knowledge of necessary truths in the demonstrative sciences, or of learning the reasons for facts" (86). Indeed, without some such move the geometric model appears to be unable to explicate the status of fundamental postulates and axioms. But there are well-known objections to any such manœuvres and, as much philosophy is concerned with such fundamentals, this casts doubt on any attempt to set the model up as a criterion for assessing the canons of rationality in philosophical argument. As Professor Ryle put it,

Philosophical arguments are not demonstrations of the Euclidean type, namely deductions of theorems from axioms or postulates. For philosophy has no axioms and it is debarred from taking its start from postulates. Otherwise there could be alternative philosophical doctrines as there are alternate geometries (Ryle (2), 'Philosophical Arguments', 196–7).

But although the geometric model involves notorious difficulties, there have been many efforts to rehabilitate various elements of it, and in particular to defend the centrality for philosophy of forms of deductive reasoning analogous to those found in Euclid. The most explicit recent attempt of this sort was provided by Professor Ryle in his Inaugural Lecture cited above, and through his various writings this approach became widely influential. The main thesis is set out early on in the lecture:

My object is to exhibit the logical structure of a type of arguments which are proper to philosophical thinking. It makes no difference whether these arguments are used polemically in controversies between philosophers or peaceably in private philosophical reflection. For arguments are effective as weapons only if they are logically cogent, and if they are so they reveal connexions, the disclosure of which is not the less necessary to the discovery of truth for being also handy in the discomfiture of opponents. . . . A

pattern of argument which is proper and even proprietary to philosophy is
the *reductio ad absurdum*. This argument moves by extracting contradictions or logical paradoxes from its material. It is the object of this discussion
to show how this is possible and why it is necessary (ibid.).

He goes on to distinguish the "weak" *reductio* of Euclid, which sets
out to deduce consequences in conflict with axioms, from the
"strong" *reductio* which "consists in deducing from a proposition or
a complex of propositions consequences which are inconsistent with
each other or with the original proposition". Here we have a model
of philosophical discussion which is deductive and has affinities with
geometry, but seems free from the fundamental difficulty that
besets the Cartesian account.

Although Ryle goes on to remark that "I am not trying to prove
that no other types of argument are proper to philosophy", the
philosophical *reductio* is assigned a crucial role in his *The Concept of
Mind*.

The key arguments employed in this book are . . . intended to show why
certain sorts of operations with the concepts of mental powers and processes are breaches of logical rules. I try to use *reductio ad absurdum*
arguments both to disallow operations implicitly recommended by the
Cartesian myth and to indicate to what logical types the concepts under
question ought to be allocated. I do not, however, think it improper to use
from time to time arguments of a less rigorous sort, especially when it seems
expedient to mollify or acclimatise. . . . If persuasions of conciliatory kinds
ease the pains of relinquishing inveterate intellectual habits, they do not
indeed reinforce the rigorous arguments, but they do weaken resistances to
them (Ryle (1), 8).

This passage is fascinating for a number of reasons. In part it
appears to represent a retreat from the position that "arguments are
effective as weapons only if they are logically cogent", unless it is
also held that an argument can be logically cogent without being
fully "rigorous"; a retreat whose significance will become clear in
later chapters. But in the present context its main interest lies in its
provision of an apparently ready-made criterion for distinguishing
"rigorous" philosophical arguments, which are deductive and probative, from others whose persuasive role is merely "conciliatory".

The distinction involved seems to have close affinities with
Pascal's contrast between "mind" and "heart". If we wish to
persuade through the "mind" we must "convince" by means of
"demonstration"; but, since men are "almost always led into belief

not because a thing is proved but because it is pleasing", it is often expedient to attempt our persuasions through the "heart"—and in this case our aim is to "please" the "will" ((7), 440–1). In Ryle the two methods are not opposed, as often in Pascal, but used in conjunction; demonstrations for the mind are accompanied by more conciliatory efforts to mollify the heart. The distinctions in Pascal and Ryle are not, of course, identical; but their resemblance reinforces the impression that in Ryle's work we are presented with an attempt to rehabilitate a central element of the classic geometric model.

But Ryle's criterion for identifying "rigorous" philosophical arguments is no more successful than Descartes's; indeed, it fails for closely analogous reasons. The major problem with the axiomatic method in philosophy lies with an argument's starting-point; the major problem with Ryle's "strong" *reductio*—setting aside various technical questions which may be raised about its separability from Euclid's "weak" one[14]—lies in its terminus, the claim that a thesis has been shown to be "absurd". For if the test of absurdity is simple self-contradiction, then comparatively few philosophical issues are such that they can be adequately dealt with through this technique alone. Usually a less narrow characterization of "absurdity" is involved, in which case the traditional problems which beset the Cartesian model return.

If 'absurdity' is defined in terms of self-contradiction, the conclusion of any "rigorous" philosophical argument is the negation of a self-contradiction, which is necessary because analytic; but if the necessity need not be analytic then how can we know it to be necessary? Ryle's own reply is that we may safely dismiss a proposition if it can be shown to exhibit a "category mistake", but the allocation of propositions to various categories—and the rules governing predication across categories—are themselves determined by appeals to what is and is not "absurd", thus the whole procedure is open to the charge of circularity. It is worth remarking that Ryle himself closes his main discussion with the question "But what are the tests of absurdity?" (Ryle (2), 'Categories', 184).

---

[14] If any consistent deductive system can be axiomatized, and if valid deductions can only take place within such a deductive system, then any form of *reductio* can be properly represented as involving conflict with axioms. Presumably Ryle would invoke his controversial doctrines about the status of "inference licences" (Ryle (2), "'If', 'So', and 'Because'"", 234–49) in order to resist this conclusion.

Subsequent debate strongly suggests that any such appeal to category or type transgressions as a criterion of absurdity will be similarly circular.[15] Much philosophical discussion, not least in the twentieth century, has, indeed, revolved around arguments about what is or is not absurd. Apart from the problems in the philosophy of mind with which Ryle was concerned, Moore's attempt to refute Idealism, the Logical Positivist assault on metaphysics, and Austin's critique of Phenomenalism all provide prominent examples. Thus the *reductio ad absurdum* appears to provide a less than adequate criterion for assessing the cogency of philosophical arguments.

It could be argued that reliance on the *reductio* has more in common with the synthetic "method of proof" of the geometric model than the analytic, and that it is the latter which has had the greater influence on recent philosophy. Certainly the term 'analysis' has had considerable currency in philosophical self-description, and to the extent that it is understood as involving the reduction of "involved and obscure propositions step by step to those that are . . . absolutely simple" (Descartes (1), i. 14) has obvious affinities with the programme of logical atomism. Two classic articulations of this orientation are Wittgenstein's *Tractatus* and Carnap's *Aufbau*. Carnap, however, came to concede that the strict deductive ideal here was a mirage;

the reduction of higher level concepts to lower level ones cannot always take the form of explicit definitions; generally more liberal forms of concept introduction must be used. . . . Correspondence rules connect the theoretical terms with observation terms. Thus the theoretical terms are interpreted, but this interpretation is always incomplete (Carnap, viii–ix).

Wittgenstein retreated further from the ideal, rejecting the very notion of analytic reduction to simples; "To say that a red circle is *composed* of redness and circularity, or is a complex with these component parts, is a misuse of these words and is misleading" (*Philosophical Remarks*, 302; for a fuller discussion see *Philosophical Investigations*, paras. 39–64). As Ryle remarked of this whole episode, "the ultimates of Logical Atomism took sanctuary in Utopia" (Ryle (3), 10).

A less ambitious programme of analysis was developed by

---

[15] See, for example, Smart (1953), Thompson (1957), Cross (1959), Pap (1960), Passmore (1961) ch. 7, Hillman (1963), Sommers (1965), Odegard (1966), Haack (1) 1968, Strawson (2) 1970, and Mundle (1970) sect. 6.

Moore, which sought to give correct analyses of the meanings of certain types of concept and proposition; sometimes the proposition in question was a deliverance of common sense (Moore (1), 32–59) such that, to use Pascal's words, "the mind cannot doubt its certainty". But this, too, ran into difficulties analogous to those which plagued the *Aufbau*, and in particular encountered the notorious "paradox of analysis"according to which all analysis is either trivial or false; if the *analysandum* and the *analysans* are synonymous no information is conveyed, but if not the information conveyed is incorrect. Moore conceded that "I cannot give any clear solution to the puzzle" (Moore (2), 666; see also 321–42). More recent attacks, inspired by Professor Quine (1), on the relevant notion of "meaning" have further undermined confidence in this form of programme.

Neither the synthetic nor the analytic elements of the classic geometric model, however rehabilitated, seem capable of providing us with a fully satisfactory paradigm for philosophical reasoning, and the fully fledged theory—with axiomatized deduction at its heart—is past saving.

4. The Retreat to Philosophical Neutrality

Some philosophers have drawn radical conclusions from such considerations. If deduction is the only rigorous form of argument, and if neither the self-evidence of axioms nor the absurdity of conclusions nor even the ultimacy of simples may be taken for granted in philosophy, then not all philosophical argument can be rigorous. Dr Waismann, indeed, went further: "Philosophical arguments are not deductive; therefore they are not rigorous; and therefore they don't prove anything" (471). He does not thereby conclude that philosophy is an irrational activity, but rather that it is not concerned with proofs, or "rigour", if these are understood as being essentially deductive;[16] its concern is rather with aiding our understanding by means of examples—and he actually instances Ryle, though

[16] A decade after his Inaugural Lecture, Ryle himself toyed with the thesis that "philosophers do not provide proofs", suggesting that "It is for the powerfulness and originality of his arguments that a philosopher merits the respect of his colleagues. Yet these powerful arguments of his are not rigorous proofs, and they are not unrigorous proofs either" (Ryle (2), 'Proofs in Philosophy', 319–20).

appealing to his "persuasions of conciliatory kinds" rather than to those persuasions which, in his *Concept of Mind*, Ryle himself regarded as decisive:

What do you find in reading Ryle or Wittgenstein? Lots of examples with little or no logical bone in between. . . . Not that the "proofs" proffered are valueless: a *reductio ad absurdum* always points to a knot in thought, and so does an infinite regress. But they *point* only. The real strength lies in the examples (Waismann, 481–2).

The background assumption here, of course, is that only deductive arguments are "rigorous". Philosophers should therefore relegate "rigour" to a subordinate place, and look to other ideals for assessing philosophical discussion.

A good deal of the history of "Anglo-Saxon" philosophy over the past half-century can be seen as a sustained attempt to avoid this conclusion while retaining the background assumption, and the pivot on which the bulk of such attempts have swung has been some version of the formal/empirical dichotomy, often combined with a version of Logical Atomism, of Moorean analysis, or of both. If philosophy can be exhibited as formal, then its arguments are governed by rules which dismiss certain conclusions as absurd and establish certain premises as analytic; the Cartesian ideal of deductive rigour can thereby be attained.

We have already seen some of the difficulties with such endeavours. In their classic forms these programmes maintain that philosophical reasoning does not issue in the discovery of fact, it simply clarifies by "analysis" what in some sense is known already by exploring the implications of propositions established by science or common sense, and all such accounts have the "paradox of analysis" to deal with. But setting this worry aside, it is worth noting that the formal/empirical dichotomy has itself proved problematic, even for those who do not accept the Quinean attack on analyticity. The most influential technique for drawing the necessary distinctions has been the exploitation of some version of the Verification Principle, but the greater the effort that has been expended in trying to develop a version free from objection, the more it has come to seem that the whole exercise is misconceived. The leading popularizer and defender of the Principle in England was for many years Sir Alfred Ayer; it is worth citing his own account of what many have come to regard as the fatal flaw in the whole exercise. In his Oxford

Inaugural Lecture he expresses his doubts whether the Verification Principle

is a wholly effective means of distinguishing questions of analysis or interpretation from questions of fact. The trouble lies with the assumption that it is possible to supply a neutral record of facts, which is free from any taint of theory; a common bedrock for divergent interpretations. But this is highly dubious. It is alleged, for example, that a naïve realist and a follower of Berkeley do not differ with regard to any matter of fact. Whatever they may respectively think that they mean by their perceptual judgements, they accept the same observable states of affairs as showing them to be true. But what are these observable states of affairs? The Berkleian describes them in a way that the naïve realist finds unintelligible: the naïve realist describes them in a way that the Berkleian might regard as begging the question against him. It is common ground, at least for those who accept the verification principle, that in the normal way, when a man sets out to describe what he perceives, he manages to assert something which is true; but what this is may be a matter for dispute. It has been thought that it could first be stated and then analysed; but it would seem that in the very attempt to state it one already commits oneself to some form of analysis.

If this is right, it appears that philosophy does after all intrude upon questions of empirical fact. Once it is established what is to count as a fact, that is, once the criteria are settled, it is an empirical and not a philosophical question whether they are satisfied. But adoption of these criteria implies the acceptance of a given conceptual system, and the appraisal of conceptual systems does fall within the province of philosophy (Ayer, 'Philosophy and Language', 21).

Frequently we find philosophers accepting the main lines of the above argument, but resisting its conclusion by denying that philosophy is concerned with "the appraisal of conceptual systems". The most radical move here is to reject, in Quinean fashion, the formal/empirical dichotomy, and with it the very idea of a "conceptual system" as standardly interpreted (Davidson (1)), though it may be that part of the thrust of Ayer's conclusion could be reformulated in terms of Professor Bernard Williams's account of a "representation of the world" (Williams (1), 64–5).[17] Alternatively, it is often maintained that philosophy is descriptive, bringing

[17] For Davidson (1), the main objection to the idea of a "conceptual scheme" is the aid it gives to conceptual relativism, the doctrine that "reality itself is relative to a scheme: what counts as real in one system may not in another" taken together with the thesis that "there may be no translating from one scheme to another" (5); typically, on these accounts, such schemes are "'incommensurable' . . . The neutral

footnote continued overleaf

out the implications of "our", or a given, conceptual scheme in a purely analytical manner, while avoiding any attempt to "revise the scheme in question or to assess its merits in the light of some other one as misconceived;[18] sometimes appeal is made to our knowledge, as native speakers of a language, of "what we should say" in given circumstances. For a considerable time such suggestions were very fashionable, the underlying presuppositions being elegantly summed up by G. J. Warnock:

We have become familiar enough with the idea that phenomena may be viewed in more than one way, comprehended within more than one theory, interpreted by more than one set of explanatory concepts. It has thus become almost impossible to believe that some *one* way of seeing, some *one* sort of theory, has any exclusive claim to be the *right* way; the notion of 'reality' itself, it would commonly be held, must be given its sense in terms of some particular theory or view, so that the claim that any such theory reveals or corresponds to 'reality' can be given a circular justification which is also open, in just the same way, to quite other views as well (Warnock (1), 144).

[18] Sometimes, though controversially (see ch. 5 n. 12), such a position is attributed to Wittgenstein. It has certain affinities with Collingwood's doctrine of "absolute presuppositions" as discussed in his *An Essay on Metaphysics*. See also Strawson's *Individuals: An Essay in Descriptive Metaphysics*.

---

footnote 17 cont.
content waiting to be organized is supplied by nature". (12) He rejects the notion of "a theory-neutral reality" as a "ground for comparison of conceptual schemes" (17), and argues that "we cannot make sense of" conceptual incommensurability (7). When people differ it may sometimes be reasonable to distinguish between differences of belief and differences of concept, but "no general principle, or appeal to evidence, can force us" to make the allocation either way (20); there is no clear boundary here, thus conceptual differences are as much subject to the arbitrament of truth as differences in belief. Ayer himself, of course, does not regard his use of the notion of a "conceptual system", together with his abandonment of the ideal of "a neutral record of facts" or observation language, as committing him to conceptual relativism. Unlike Warnock, he sees differences between schemes as subject to the arbitrament of truth and falsity; the role of finesse in such arbitrament is a major theme of this book.

It was with an eye to such a possibility that Williams, in his discussion of Descartes, introduced the notion of a "representation of the world (or part of the world)" as comprising a man's "beliefs, . . . experiences of the world, and ways of conceptualising it, which have given rise to those beliefs and are expressed in them". On this account beliefs and concepts, which Davidson insists are yoked together, are both incorporated in a "representation", and Descartes can be seen as attempting to find a fully inclusive or "absolute" representation which is not only fully commensurable with other representations, but capable of discriminating between them in terms of truth and adequacy ((1), 64–5).

Given the deductive model of philosophical argument, some such doctrine of philosophical neutrality or conceptual relativism is very tempting, for it is difficult to see how deduction could arbitrate in a non-circular manner between such theories. Nevertheless, in their practice philosophers frequently ignore it, and sometimes explicitly disavow belief in any such thesis. A certain amount depends, of course, on the scope of the proposed neutrality; if the "conceptual systems" in question are taken to represent particular philosophical theses such as physicalism—an example given by Ayer—not many philosophers are neutral between them. But if the argument for neutrality turns on the lack of any decision procedure available in terms of the deductive model, it is difficult to see why they should be treated any differently from more wide-ranging metaphysical theories. Thus it is not surprising to find that here too philosophical neutrality is often abandoned.

Since Descartes and Pascal the conflict between religious and secular conceptions of reality has provided a leading example of an apparent rivalry between such wide-ranging metaphysical schemes, an example we shall be examining in the chapters on Pascal, Hume, and Nietzsche. One of the most influential recent commentaries on such rivalry, Professor Wisdom's 'Gods', provided an instructive lack of neutrality. The famous parable of the "Invisible Gardener" is introduced to illustrate a typical metaphysical argument, where one man believes, and one does not, that the evidence warrants belief in such a being, "each presenting and re-presenting the features of the garden favouring his hypothesis, that is, fitting his model for describing the accepted fact; each emphasizing the pattern he wishes to emphasize" ((1), 159). On Warnock's terms we should expect to be told that, whatever the strength of the temptation to see the phenomena now in one way and now in another, we should not finally commit ourselves to either. However, Wisdom lays greater stress on certain patterns than on others: 'Feelings of awe before power, dread of the thunderbolts of Zeus, confidence in the everlasting arms, unease before the all-seeing eye . . . we are reminded of how we felt as children to our parents' ((1), 164–5). Not surprisingly, given this emphasis, he comes close to concluding that "we can recognise systems of superhuman, sub-human, elusive beings for what they are—the persistent projections of infantile phantasies". The term 'phantasies' is qualified, but the qualifications adduced point inwards, drawing on psycho-analysis, and interpreted as telling decisively against conceiving of the gods as "mysterious powers outside us". In the sense initially considered there is, it would appear, no gardener—"The kingdom of Heaven is within us" ((1), 166–7). First- and second-order arguments flow together, as analysis of the different conceptual systems gives way to appraisal.[19]

Professor Wisdom himself rejects the deductive model of philosophical reasoning (156–9), and the arguments of his paper do not conform to it. They are much more like the sorts of arguments envisaged by Ayer, in the lecture quoted above, when discussing how one might attempt to appraise conceptual systems. The problem as Ayer sees it is that "so long as it is free from inner contradiction, it is hard to see how any philosophical thesis can be refuted; and equally hard to see how it can ever be proved" (Ayer, 27). He cites the thesis of physicalism, and concludes that if we do not accept the thesis then, in arguing with an adherent, "our only hope . . . is to make the interpretations appear so strained that the assumptions on which they rest become discredited". But arguments of this sort are far removed from the Cartesian model, or any attempted rehabilitation of it. If a philosophical thesis is to be "discredited" it is not by such means as Ryle's "strong" *reductio*, but rather by his "persuasions of conciliatory kinds". Thus Ayer's position turns out to be not far removed from that of Waismann.

5. Extra-Philosophical Models

But if the ideal of deductive rigour proves inadequate for assessing philosophical argument, we are faced with the ancient problem—as old as Plato—of finding criteria for distinguishing between good and bad reasoning in philosophy. And as Descartes looked outside philosophy to geometry for his inspiration, so contemporary philosophers have sought for inferential models developed in other contexts to explicate and assess philosophical arguments.

Professor Quine, for example, has argued that no coherent

---

[19] My debt to Professor Mitchell here is considerable, and not only to his published work. I am particularly grateful to him for allowing me to see some of his unpublished papers, which have influenced my handling of several issues discussed in the text.

distinction can be drawn between formal and empirical enquiries which will bear the weight philosophers have wanted to place on this dichotomy, and that consequently no sharp dividing line can be drawn between philosophy and the empirical sciences (Quine (1), (2), and (3)). In part such a claim can be seen as a rejection of Descartes's dismissal of inductions from experience—and indeed Quine accepts induction as having a significant though limited role to play—but induction by itself cannot do all the work required of it; further, the claim still runs into difficulties even when we interpret it in terms of non-inductivist interpretations of scientific method.

Hume's problem about the justification of induction still haunts philosophers, and even if we are sympathetic towards the more recent attempts to resolve it we are left with further problems. L. J. Cohen summarizes the essential issues helpfully:

Some philosophers have argued that it does not make sense to ask for a justification of induction, because it is analytic that a valid inductive inference is an inference of such-or-such a kind and because there are no standards by reference to which inductive standards could be justified. This argument . . . is refuted by the objection that even if H is analytic we can always ask whether our concepts should be such that it is so. Hence a useful sense imputable to requests for a justification of induction is the question: what is our title to use a term like 'valid' in relation to inductive inference? . . . What analogies are there between valid cases of deductive inference and reputedly valid cases of inductive inference, such that the use of the same word 'valid' in both cases is more than just a homonym? Hume's scepticism about inductive reasoning was based on an argument from disanalogy here: to answer him we must find analogies that he overlooked (Cohen (2), 183).

Cohen's own preference is to explore the logical syntax of a favoured version of inductive support in such a way that it can be mapped on to an appropriate formal system, thereby "unifying the syntax of logical truth and the syntax of inductive support" (207–9). Any particular "set of inductive criteria, or ordered set of experimental tests" in a particular field should themselves be tested by inductive means; it is argued that this procedure is not as viciously circular as it at first appears (192–206). The difficulties of using such a model to rescue philosophical reasoning are clear enough. The closer the analogies with deduction, the more open it is to the problems we have already encountered; the weaker the analogies, the more need to show that the method will apply in those areas of philosophical discussion where the deductive model breaks down. The "ordered set of experimental tests" here envisaged take their place within the context of a particular scientific field of enquiry, yet the "appraisal of conceptual systems" does not at all obviously take place within such a context and, indeed, often seems to be required precisely where experiment cannot help.

Indeed, this is the major problem with most invocations of scientific method—whether or not conceived as inductivist—to solve the problems of philosophical rationality. Where the criteria are settled for assessing experimental results by an overall scientific research programme, or in terms of what Professor Kuhn has called "paradigm", there is little analogy with the problematic philosophical cases. The analogy is much stronger when we come to choice between paradigms (see Mitchell (2), ch. 5), or the assessment of rival research programmes, but it is just here that scientific method is at its least clear, and where specific claims are made for it they tend to weaken the analogy. Indeed, Kuhn denies that a logical account can be given of paradigm choice, for the paradigm itself includes all the available criteria; as there can be neither demonstrative argument here, nor appeal to strict probabilities, the only accounts he sees as available are psychological and sociological ones. But this is the sort of impasse which led philosophers to look for help to the sciences in the first place.

Professor Lakatos took issue with Kuhn's conclusion in the light of a more Popperian methodology in his 'Falsification and the Methodology of Scientific Research Programmes', but the criteria appealed to in order to assess research programmes ultimately turn on the ability of a programme to facilitate certain types of empirically testable predictions; the stronger the appeal to such criteria, the more problematic the application to philosophy. "Conceptual systems" which interpret human knowledge in terms of empirical testing are among those which philosophers are concerned to "appraise", thus the danger of the sort of circularity noted by Kuhn is hardly avoided; and where the systems being compared include contrasting hierarchies of evaluation (as, for example, in Nietzsche's critique of Pascal) the relevance of appeal to such criteria needs to be very carefully explained and defended. Some philosophers, indeed, see the problems attendant on the sort of approach suggested by Lakatos as undermining any "fixed theory of rationality" (Feyerabend, 27).[20]

Behind many of these discussions lies the presupposition that deduction and induction between them exhaust the field of rational argument, but the case for this has never been satisfactorily made out.[21] The assault on such claims has been at the heart of much of Wisdom's philosophizing;

The idea that the justification of a statement must be either of the *inductive* sort . . . or of the *deductive* sort . . . has played a double part in metaphysics. It has encouraged and distorted its growth and also nearly brought about its premature death by hoisting it by its own inadequate petard ((1), 268–9).

Wisdom himself prefers to look to the law courts rather than the empirical sciences for fruitful argumentative models, and others too have found in the law distinctive patterns of rational procedure. Recently Cohen, for example, has argued that there are major difficulties in the way of construing the convergence of circumstantial evidence in terms of the classic probability calculus, with its

---

[20] Thus Feyerabend's *Against Method*, which adopts such a stance, develops it by means of a sustained critique of Lakatos's programme. The position is often described as "irrationalist" but, despite the odd incautious remark, this appears only to be accurate given a conception of rationality which is subject to fairly stringent constraints, analogous to those of the geometric model. Feyerabend rejects such conceptions, speaking highly of a form of "*dialectical thinking . . .* that 'dissolves into nothing the detailed determinations of the understanding', formal logic included" (27; the embedded quotation, of course, is from Hegel). He appears to presuppose very general and flexible canons of rationality which apply indifferently in scientific as well as ordinary contexts, such that "rational theory acceptance . . . is theory acceptance carried through with deliberation, as a result of 'clear thought and experience'" (Lugg, 760).

[21] A useful model for analysing the possibilities is developed in Barker's 'Must Every Inference be either Deductive or Inductive?'. While expressing certain reservations with Barker's model, Haack (2) has more recently argued that "deduction is no less in need of justification than induction" (see also Haack (3)).

In their search for patterns of reasoning which are neither deductive nor inductive, some philosophers have continued to be attracted by scientific methodology. Shepherd, for example, has attempted to revive Peirce's theory of "abduction" not merely in the philosophy of science but as an appropriate guideline for philosophical reasoning (see also Achinstein and Fann). Peirce presents abduction schematically as follows: "The surprising fact, C, is observed; But if A were true, C would be a matter of course. Hence, there is reason to suspect that A is true"; he traces this pattern of argument to one discussed in Aristotle's *Prior Analytics* ((1), B, 69a). According to Peirce, "Deduction proves that something *must* be; Induction shows that something *actually is* operative; Abduction merely suggests that something *may be*" (Peirce, v. paras. 189, 144 and 171).

inbuilt requirement that prior probabilities be determined (Cohen (3), 92–115, 277–81). But although this notion of convergence has important parallels with Ayer's notion of "discrediting" a philosophical thesis where, too, prior probabilities are hardly calculable, Cohen's proposed alternative axiomatization is ill-suited to the wider philosophical arena; it is an essential requirement of the system that the items of evidence said to "converge" be strongly independent, but this cannot be assumed in the "appraisal of conceptual systems".

Ayer spoke of attempting to persuade a philosophical opponent by making his "interpretations appear so strained" that their assumptions become discredited. There are close analogies here with the procedure advocated by Wisdom, in discussing earlier work of Ayer, for when an opponent's "attitude must be altered by *rational* persuasion":

This is done by drawing attention rhetorically to the features of what we are talking about, insisting upon how different it is from this, how like to that, passing insensibly from the purely factual through the semi-factual, semi-critical, to the critical predicate at issue. Only this mixture is critical proof and the name of it is rhetoric ((1), 246).

Such "case-by-case" procedure has its place in the law courts, but its ambit is much wider and the general term 'rhetoric', so long as the persuasion aimed at is qualified by the epithet 'rational', is not inappropriate. The problem, clearly, is to justify the epithet, and some philosophers have attempted a reworking of the old rhetorical tradition in order to develop a model of argumentation for use when the standard deductive and inductive models break down.

Professor Perelman, for example,[22] maintains that here we can and must take account of "psychological and social conditions", which caused such problems for Kuhn, for "all argumentation aims at gaining the adherence of minds" (14), but this can be done without giving up the title to rationality since "rational argument is

---

[22] More recently, Professor Körner has also defended "metaphysical rhetoric": "The arguments of those philosophers who do not claim to be in possession of some absolutely cogent method can be described as honest rhetoric, i.e., attempts at arguing in favour of supreme principles which they themselves accept, by adducing reasons which they themselves find acceptable" (231; see also 180 and 191–3). Socratic arguments are adduced as exemplifying one type of this "nonsophistic" rhetoric. The discussion is, however, admitted to be "very brief and incomplete", and both analysis and defence remain undeveloped.

simply a particular instance of argumentation *ad hominem*" (507). Some of the teeth of this claim are drawn when we find that the instance in question is that of "argument that is claimed to be valid for all reasonable beings, that is, *ad humanitatem*" (110). But this position has its own built-in instability, for while philosophers seek the "agreement of the universal audience" (31) this universality is "imagined" rather than real; "everyone constitutes the universal audience from what he knows of his fellow men", and "if argumentation addressed to the universal audience and calculated to convince does not convince everybody, one can always resort to *disqualifying the recalcitrant*" (33)—but such disqualifications turn the arbiter of the rational ideal from a "universal" to an "élite" audience, and the problem of rationality is only pushed back one stage to that of establishing the criteria for admission into the élite class of "reasonable beings". Perelman's own leading criterion seems to be adherence to the "rule of justice" which requires "giving identical treatment to beings or situations of the same kind" (218), thus the strength of an argument is to be assessed on the principle, "that which was capable of convincing in a specific situation will appear to be convincing in a similar or analogous situation" (464). Such a move appears to bring us back to Wisdom's "case-by-case" procedure.

Geometry, science, law, rhetoric; the remaining extra-philosophical area to which philosophers have influentially looked for models of rationality is that of hermeneutics, broadly conceived. Mitchell (1) and (2) points out that the humanities generally, not just philosophy, frequently lack procedures which satisfy Cartesian ideals of rigour for conclusively establishing or refuting theses and interpretations; nevertheless, their procedures are often far from being irrational. It does not follow in the interpretation of a text, for example, that because a number of alternative explanations are logically possible and none are decisively refuted by empirical evidence, that all are equally good; sound judgement in a scholar consists precisely in the trained capacity to adjudicate in such controversial issues. If such judgement is possible here, why not in philosophy? He goes on to consider the ways a "cumulative case" ((2) ch. 3) may be built up in critical exegesis and historical controversy in manners reminiscent of Cohen's "convergence", but without the requirement of evidential independence on which the latter insists; it is urged that such cases provide a model for metaphysical argument. But even if we allow the acceptability of such patterns of argument in their own fields, the strength of the analogies with philosophical reasoning cannot be taken for granted. Cumulative cases in literary criticism and in history operate within frameworks provided by the disciplines in question in terms of which their canons of strength and weakness can be discussed and defended; it has to be shown that such discussion and defence also apply outside those contexts in the philosophical "appraisal of conceptual systems".

The analogy with hermeneutics can, however, be seen another way. The status of interpretations even within the more restricted fields is itself a matter of dispute, and if one is more impressed by the difficulties here than is Mitchell one may be led to see philosophy's position among the humanities as undermining its traditional claims to objectivity. Professor Rorty draws attention to the opposition between

the inconclusive comparison and contrast of vocabularies . . . characteristic of the literary culture, and rigorous argumentation—the procedure characteristic of mathematics. . . . Rigorous argumentation issues in agreement in propositions. The really exasperating thing about literary intellectuals, from the point of view of those inclined to science or to [traditional] Philosophy, is their inability to engage in such argumentation—to agree on what would count as resolving disputes, on the criteria to which all sides must appeal (Rorty (2), xli).

Paradigmatic for literary culture, it is suggested, is hermeneutics, the practice of interpretation, which is itself locked into

the "hermeneutic circle"—the fact that we cannot understand the parts of a strange culture, practice, theory, language, or whatever, unless we know something about how the whole thing works, whereas we cannot get a grasp on how the whole works until we have some understanding of its parts. This notion of interpretation suggests that coming to understand is more like getting acquainted with a person than like following a demonstration. In both cases we play back and forth between guesses about how to characterize particular statements or other events, and guesses about the point of the whole situation, until gradually we feel at ease with what was hitherto strange ((1), 319).

In such a practice, he suggests, "the acquisition of truth dwindles in importance" ((1), 365), and to the extent that the goal of "objective truth" is here legitimate, it is in the sense of "the best idea we currently have about how to explain what is going on" ((1), 385), rather than of propositions "representing things as they really are" ((1), 334). It is in these hermeneutic terms, he proposes, that we should henceforth see and practise philosophy; "systematic philosophy" of the Cartesian type should give way to hermeneutic or "edifying" philosophy.

This, however, is presented as a proposal rather than the conclusion of an argument, for

> There is no way, as far as I can see, in which to *argue* the issue. . . . There is no "normal" philosophical discourse which provides common commensurating ground. . . . If there is no such common ground, all we can do is to show how the other side looks from our own point of view. That is, all we can do is be hermeneutic about the opposition—trying to show how the odd or paradoxical or offensive things they say hang together with the rest of what they want to say, and how what they say looks when put in our own alternative idiom ((1), 364–5).

One is reminded of Ayer's claim, 'our only hope . . . is to make the interpretations appear so strained that the assumptions on which they rest become discredited' (Ayer, 27). But the claim that such a procedure does not count as argument seems to depend on the assumption that the only procedure worth the name is "rigorous argumentation—the procedure characteristic of mathematics", needing a foundation or "ground" for its deductive chains. Although Rorty is critical of the notion that there is "no middle ground between matters of taste and matters capable of being settled by a previously statable algorithm" ((1), 336–8), he suggests that without such an algorithm our only criterion of truth is "agreement"—a position reminiscent of Perelman, though without the confidence in a "universal" or even "élite" audience—and appears to regard traditional philosophy with its concepts as so wedded to the algorithmic or geometric ideal that in falling back on such a criterion he is giving up the classic notion of "argument".

Such a contention is itself open to challenge on two, interconnected, counts. First, it is by no means clear that the elements of circularity endemic in hermeneutics preclude decisive confirmation or disconfirmation of an interpretation; many of the attempts to show otherwise trade "reasonable assurance for total skepticism out of a misguided desire for certainty where it is not to be had" (Juhl, 265; see the whole of Professor Juhl's Appendix for an elegant critique of one such attempt). Second, efforts to find "reasonable assurance" rather than Cartesian certainty are to be found within the very philosophical tradition that Professor Rorty criticizes. Philosophers have repeatedly sought a middle ground between "system" and "taste" in opposition to the Cartesian passion to geometrize. Rorty's proposal that, rather than incorporate hermeneutics into philosophy in the style of Mitchell, we should allow a sceptical hermeneutics to swallow philosophy, testifies to the dominance the geometric model has in his reading of the post-Cartesian tradition, but may be premature.

The hold of this model is further illustrated by another recent discussion which, without invoking hermeneutics, also downgrades philosophy's aspiration to some form of objectivity. Professor Unger argues that often we are faced with "philosophical relativity"; in such instances,

the answer one prefers for a certain philosophical problem will depend upon what assumptions one has adopted in relation to that problem. And, irrespective of the problem in question, assumptions crucial to one's answer will always be somewhat arbitrary, not determined by objective facts. . . . One position on a philosophical problem is to be preferred only *relative to* assumptions involved in arriving at its answer to the problem; . . . there is nothing to determine the choice between the diverse assumptions and, hence, between the opposed positions (Unger, 5).

Here the geometric model appears to be alive and well, but with an anti-Rylean twist; philosophy has sometimes no option but to take its start from postulates or assumptions, and therefore there are indeed "alternative philosophical doctrines as there are alternative geometries". The claim that choice between such doctrines is "arbitrary" is itself a philosophical thesis, that of "Philosophical Relativity"—the end of the Cartesian road.

6. An Alternative Tradition

The dominance of the geometric model in philosophy appears to have contributed to the recurrent tendency to look outside philosophical practice for alternative patterns of sound reasoning. If the philosopher's conception of "argument" requires Rorty's "rigorous" deductive chains anchored to a "common commensurating ground", but the disposition to geometrize leads at best to the arbitrary assumptions of philosophical relativity, it is reasonable to explore the possibility that such disciplines as science, the law, rhetoric, or hermeneutics may be in a position to enrich that conception. Indeed, despite the recurring difficulty of showing the applicability to philosophy of inferential models developed in other contexts, some of these explorations have borne valuable fruit.

But while the geometric model has been dominant it has not been all-pervasive. Although a number of philosophers have drawn, usually briefly and somewhat schematically, on examples of contemporary philosophical practice in their reflections on method, there has been very little careful exploration for such purposes of those elements in the philosophical tradition which have remained undazzled by the geometric glare. Yet it is precisely here that we might expect to find alternative conceptions of rationality, not subject to the limitations of the more restricted disciplines. There turns out to be a family resemblance between several of these alternatives, to which it is appropriate to apply Pascal's term—'finesse'.

2
Classical Models of Rationality: Plato, Aristotle, and Cicero

Long before the Cartesian revolution, and the categories it has bequeathed to us, Classical writers engaged in controversies with contemporaries about the proper conduct of discussion, and about the relative merits of different types of verbal persuasion. It will prove useful to sketch models of rational argument developed by three such authors, which can be drawn on in subsequent chapters.

1. Plato's *Phaedrus*

Plato is best remembered in this context for his criticisms of the Sophists in so far as they were concerned with the teaching of rhetoric, with giving men skill in speaking so that they might make the impact they wished on public audiences. Different Sophists held differing views about the nature and teaching of rhetoric, as Plato was well aware, and Plato's own views on the matter underwent a number of changes. Thus I shall not attempt any consolidated account of these disputes; instead, I shall outline here only the most famous of Plato's discussions, that in the *Phaedrus*, with occasional reference to his earlier treatment of the topic in the *Gorgias*. The significantly different model of rational argument discussed and exemplified in the *Phaedo* will be the subject of the next chapter.

One important difference between the *Gorgias* and the *Phaedrus* turns on a shift in Plato's understanding of the nature of rhetoric. In the *Gorgias* he argues that it is not an art (τέχνη) depending on a coherent set of principles, but merely a practical skill which, because it has no integral concern with truth, is extremely danger-ous. At one point he seems to concede the possibility of a different, more "noble", type of rhetoric, striving "to say what is best"; but, we are imediately told, "this is a rhetoric you never yet saw" (Plato (8), *Gorgias*, 503a–b). In this assessment he appears to take the practice of its practitioners as providing sufficient material for understanding the only type of rhetoric which need be seriously considered, and on this basis compares it unfavourably with philosophy. There is, indeed, independent evidence that Gorgias himself made no attempt at a systematic presentation of his subject, and also held that the orator's concern was with pleasing and persuading his audience, not with the truth of what he was saying.[1]

In the *Phaedrus* the centre of attention has shifted. Rhetoric of the traditional sort is still attacked, but now it is contrasted not so much with philosophy as with the "noble" rhetoric of the *Gorgias*, which is expounded and defended. The latter is an art based on clear principles, among which is a fundamental concern with truth, and it is not so much a rival as a handmaid to philosophy. In part this change of perspective appears to reflect changes in the rhetorical tradition among the Sophists themselves, and in particular the rise of Isocrates, whose school of rhetoric was the most famous rival to Plato's own Academy. Whereas other teachers of rhetoric are treated critically in the dialogue, Isocrates is shown great respect, and in discussing the "noble" rhetoric Plato sometimes seems to echo Isocrates' own terminology. In the *Phaedrus* Plato seems to have felt the need to clarify his attitude to rhetoric now that it could no longer be dismissed as intellectually negligible.

Originally a pupil of Gorgias, Isocrates came to object to the notion that rhetoric was concerned merely with persuasion, not with truth or justice, and in his *Against the Sophists* and *Antidosis* he set out to criticize his predecessors and develop his own principles. He preferred to drop the term 'rhetoric' (no doubt because of its associations) as a description of his own concerns, and preferred instead 'philosophy' and 'the discipline of speech' (ἡ τῶν λόγων παιδεία) (e.g. *Antidosis*, 175 and 180); of this discipline he writes that "the power to speak well is taken as the surest index of a sound understanding, and discourse which is true and lawful and just is the outward image of a good and faithful soul" (*Antidosis*, 255; quoted from *Nicocles*, 7).[2] At the end of his life he takes the opportunity of a letter to the youthful Alexander the Great to compare Aristotle's teaching of "eristic" unfavourably with the "discipline of speech" for which he makes great claims:

---

[1] There is a useful summary of the literature in Kennedy (1), ch. 3. See also Dixon, ch. 2.

[2] All extended quotations from Isocrates are taken from the Loeb translation.

By means of this study you will come to know how at the present time to form reasonably sound opinions about the future, how not ineptly to instruct your subject peoples what each should do, how to form correct judgments about the right and the just and their opposites and, besides, to reward and chastise each class as it deserves (*To Alexander*, 4).

This ideal had great influence on Cicero and, especially through him, on much subsequent thought. But for Plato and Aristotle, Isocrates' contemporaries and rivals, the fundamental need was to make certain crucial distinctions within this general notion of "speaking well".

For Plato the fundamental distinction is between concern for truth and concern for persuasion. If our concern is primarily with persuasion, then what matters is what our audience can be led to believe rather than what is true; thus we are liable to presuppose the assumptions of our hearers in what we say, rather than accepting as premisses only those assumptions which can be shown to be true. This is improper and unworthy of a philosopher. There is, however, a more noble "art of speech" (τέχνη λόγων),[3] where concern for truth takes precedence over concern for persuasive success; this may be an impractical idea, but "provided one's aim is honourable, so is any ill success which may ensue" (274b).[4]

In introducing this notion in the *Phaedrus* Socrates[5] considers how it might be possible to reply to his criticisms:

Have we been too scurrilous in our abuse of the art of speech? [τὴν τῶν λόγων τέχνην] Might it not retort: Why do you extraordinary people talk such nonsense? I never insist on ignorance of the truth on the part of one ·

---

[3] As he terms it, for example, at the close of his discussion at 272b. He also calls it a τέχνη ῥητορική (271a), translated by Hackforth (1) as 'scientific rhetoric'. In each case the term τέχνη indicates that we are concerned with a discipline founded on a coherent set of principles.

[4] Jowett's rendering. Although rather free, it brings out the sense more clearly than Hackforth's more literal translation which requires a footnote to clarify it. All subsequent translations from the *Phaedrus* are taken from Hackforth (1) unless otherwise stated.

[5] My citations from the *Phaedrus* are taken from the second part of the dialogue, where it seems clear that "Socrates" is acting as the mouthpiece for Plato's own views. This second part is given over to a sustained discussion and exposition of the nature of rhetoric drawing on examples provided in the dramatically more complex first part. A far more sophisticated procedure than that employed here is required for the interpretation of dialogues, or parts of dialogues, where the dramatic element is more prominent than in this second part of the *Phaedrus*—as will become clear when we turn, in the next chapter, to the *Phaedo*.

who would learn to speak; on the contrary, if my advice goes for anything, it is that he should only resort to me after he has come into the possession of truth; what I do however pride myself on is that without my aid knowledge of what is true will get a man no nearer to mastering the art of persuasion (260d).

Socrates objects that this makes rhetoric an independent discipline, with only an extrinsic connection with truth; but it can only attain to the status of an "art" (τέχνη) if its connection with truth is intrinsic and it is thus built on philosophical foundations. At the close to the dialogue it is said of "composers of discourses" that

if any one of them has done his work with a knowledge of the truth, [and] can defend his statements when challenged, . . . he ought not to be designated by a name drawn from those writings [e.g. 'orator'], but by one that indicated his serious pursuit. . . . To call him wise [σοφόν], Phaedrus, would, I think, be going too far: the epithet is proper only to a god; a name that would fit him better, and have more seemliness, would be 'lover of wisdom' [φιλόσοφον], or something similar (278c–d).

Socrates goes on to suggest that the mind of Isocrates "contains an innate tincture of philosophy" (279a).

The major reason given for thinking that rhetoric must be internally related to truth is that it essentially involves disputation, and success in disputation requires an understanding of how the various items at issue resemble and differ from one another; one can only guide people successfully (whether towards or away from the truth), and one can only "expose the corresponding attempts of others" (261e), if one understands the facts of the matter oneself. 'It would seem to follow, my friend, that the art of speech displayed by one who has gone chasing after beliefs, instead of knowing the truth, will be a comical sort of art, in fact no art at all' (262c). If the speaker is concerned to lead his hearers to the truth, he will construct his speech so that it makes clear his understanding of the matter, offering a preliminary definition or description of his topic, and then breaking it down systematically into its different parts in accordance with his knowledge of how they relate to each other; clarity and consistency may thereby be given to the entire discourse. If the speaker is concerned to mislead his audience he should still pattern his speech after this model, but can adopt a misleading definition as a starting point; Socrates provides an example of such a procedure. If he does not adopt some such coherent structure, it is relatively easy for an opponent to expose inconsistencies and lack of cogency in what he says; once again, an example is given.

Apart from the initial definition or description of the topic, the crucial element is the ordering of the subject matter; 'The second principle is that of division into species according to the natural formation, where the joint is, not breaking any part as a bad carver might' (Jowett, iii. 265e). Socrates goes on to elaborate on this "natural formation":

I am myself a lover of these divisions and collections, that I may gain the power to speak and to think; and whenever I deem another man able to discern an objective unity and plurality, I follow "in his footsteps where he leadeth as a god". Furthermore, . . . it is those that have this ability whom for the present I call dialecticians (266b).

Since the initial definition which should represent the starting point of a speech is the result of a process of "collection"—"we bring a dispersed plurality under a single form" (265d)—both the principles laid down for ordering a speech are thus firmly grounded in "dialectic".

'Dialectic' is the term most frequently used by Plato to indicate the ideal philosophical method; as his conception of that method changed so did his use of the word, and the exploration of its shifts of meaning throughout Plato's work leads into a notorious exegetical maze.[6] However, certain features of its use are clear enough. In the so-called "middle" dialogues (especially the *Meno*, *Phaedo*, and *Republic*) "dialectic" is associated with the method of "hypothesis" —a method which itself is conceived differently in the different dialogues; but in the later dialogues (especially the *Phaedrus*, *Philebus*, *Sophist*, and *Statesman*) the method of "division" (with its associated notion of "collection") takes the place of "hypothesis".

In the *Phaedrus* itself we are given further clues. In a passage which can be read as enlarging on dialectic's concern with definition and analysis, it is suggested that in investigating the nature of anything we should develop our analysis with an eye to the causal relations it stands in with regard to other possible objects of enquiry (270d). We are also informed that dialectic aims at knowledge of the

[6] The classic treatment, despite its self-imposed limitations, is still Richard Robinson's *Plato's Earlier Dialectic*. See also Julius Stenzel, *Plato's Method of Dialectic*, I. M. Crombie, *An Examination of Plato's Doctrines*, ii. 5. and Michel Meyer, 'Dialectic and Questioning: Socrates and Plato'.

truth rather than opinion about probabilities (273), a feature which it shares with the earlier account of dialectic as expressed in the *Republic*. Further, we are told that dialectic is properly to be carried on not in writing but orally in the context of a dialogue where the "words can defend both themselves and him who planted them" (276e), and this emphasis on the importance of a context where question and answer are possible is one of the few unchanging elements in Plato's discussion of dialectic from the *Meno* to the *Philebus*; the point seems to be that in dialogue any conjecture is immediately laid open to criticism, but in set speeches (or written expositions) there is too much room to manœuvre away from pertinent criticism, and one may be persuaded without fully understanding (275d–e).[7]

Socrates defines 'the art of rhetoric' as 'a kind of influencing of the mind by means of words' both in private and in public gatherings (261a); it cannot, therefore, wholly fulfil the requirements of dialectic—the set speech has to take the place of question and answer, at least in public gatherings. Nevertheless, so far as is practicable it should allow itself to be guided by dialectic, which provides the starting-point of a speech and indicates the main principles appropriate to its ordering. Rhetoric is, or at least could be, a coherent subject; but it cannot be, as Isocrates would have it, an independent subject.

Dialectical principles provide no guidance, however, when the orator comes to consider his audience. Once dialectic has discovered the truth and put the subject matter of a speech in order, further rhetorical considerations may be invoked to discover which style is best fitted to what audience and how the speech is to be delivered.

Since the function of oratory is in fact to influence men's souls, the intending orator must know what types of soul there are. Now these are of a determinate number, and their variety results in a variety of individuals. To the types of soul thus discriminated there correspond a determinate number of types of discourse. Hence a certain type of hearer will be easy to persuade by a certain type of speech . . . , while another type will be hard to persuade. All this the orator must fully understand . . . ; when, further, he can, on catching sight of so-and-so, tell himself "That is the man, that

---

[7] See also Socrates' defence of the question and answer method in the *Gorgias* (487e), and his criticism of Protagoras' long speeches in the *Protagoras* (329a–b and 334cff.)

character now actually before me is the one I heard about in school, and in order to persuade him of so-and-so I have to apply these arguments in *this* fashion"; and when, on top of all this, he has further grasped the right occasions for speaking and keeping quiet, and has come to recognise the right and wrong time for Brachology, the Pathetic Passage, the Exacerbation and all the rest of his accomplishments, then and not till then has he well and truly achieved his art (271c–272a).

At the end of the dialogue Phaedrus asks for a summary, and in reply Socrates brings all these themes of truth, definition, analysis, psychological insight, and types of speech together:

First, you must know the truth about the subject that you speak or write about: that is to say, you must be able to isolate it in definition, and having so defined it you must next understand how to divide it into kinds, until you reach the limit of division; secondly, you must have a corresponding discernment of the nature of the soul, discover the type of speech appropriate to each nature, and order and arrange your discourse accordingly, addressing a variegated soul in a variegated style that ranges over the whole gamut of tones, and a simple soul in a simple style. All this must be done if you are to become competent, within human limits, as a scientific practitioner of speech, whether you propose to expound or to persuade. Such is the clear purport of all our foregoing discussion (277b–c).

The ideal rhetoric, therefore, has two elements: dialectical and psychological. The dialectician, we are told, must "select a soul of the right type" (276e) to debate with, but beyond that has no need of psychological skills; the orator, however, has to appeal to souls of every type. Thus where he is not trying to learn the truth in the context of dialectical question and answer, but rather to teach or persuade by means of speech or written word, he often needs to resort to devices that are not dialectical but are rather grounded in an understanding of the type of audience he is addressing and the techniques likely to appeal to it.[8]

---

[8] Such psychological knowledge is, of course, ultimately to be discovered by dialectic (269e–271b). There is a certain lack of clarity about how these two elements, the dialectical and the psychological, are to be harnessed together. Socrates frequently stresses the ways in which dialectical principles should give ordering to a discourse, but in the passage just quoted the psychological principles are said to "order and arrange" the properly constituted speech. Elsewhere Plato seems to run together principles of ordering that today would normally be described as "philosophical" and "literary" respectively (see 264a–d together with Hackforth's note on the passage); this fact will become particularly significant when we come to consider his *Phaedo.*

Here we have a picture of the sort of discourse which is appropriate both to persuasion and to a philosophical concern with truth which resembles in several ways the geometrical accounts discussed in the first chapter. In so far as there is a concern for truth, both its discovery and the primary ordering of its presentation are the concern of a method which has no concern with persuasion but only with such matters as definition, analysis, and conclusive proof that can give knowledge. In Pascal's terms, persuasion by means of the heart is essentially subordinate, and persuasion through the mind is the province of demonstrative argument. Professor Ryle's account is even closer to this Platonic model. His emphasis on the role of the *reductio ad absurdum* in philosophical arguments is closer to Plato's ideal of dialectic by question and answer[9] than is an insistence on axioms *more geometrico*. Ryle's thesis that persuasive force is a function of logical cogency—'arguments are effective as weapons only if they are logically cogent' ((2), 196)—has much in common with Plato's thesis that the ideal rhetoric should be structured on dialectically sound principles.[10] And the way he separates "rigorous" philosophical arguments from merely "conciliatory" ones in *The Concept of Mind* has Platonic associations: the "rigorous" arguments are dialectical, being concerned to demonstrate the truth of the overall thesis, and they determine the underlying structure of his book; the others are subordinate, put in on the rhetorical principle that one should take account of the nature of one's audience.

The parallels, however, should not be pressed too far. Both in Ryle and in more severely Cartesian writers the ideal of deduction provides the key to distinguishing "rigorous" philosophical arguments from others. Plato's requirements for dialectic, on the other hand, are not concerned merely with the form of the arguments. He insists that the ideal rhetoric should be structured on dialectically sound principles, and makes Socrates remark that dialectic gives

---

[9] If we supplement our understanding of the question and answer method of dialectical reasoning with an examination of it in contemporary and earlier dialogues, we find a favourite Platonic procedure being the criticism of proposed definitions by deriving absurd consequences from them. There are traces of this approach in the *Phaedrus* itself, though it is not so prominent here as usual.

[10] It is also reminiscent of Isocrates' characterization of the "art of discourse" as providing the best means whereby "we both contend against others on matters which are open to dispute and seek light for ourselves on things which are unknown" (*Antidosis*, 256).

him the power not only to think but also to speak (266b); but his reason is not that an argument with certain formal or formalizable properties is universally valid while any argument which lacks them is inherently dubious. His reason is rather that a discourse which is not dialectically informed is liable to mislead both its author and its audience, and can be demolished by an opponent—arguments are not "effective as weapons" unless they are dialectically sound; dialectic can give the necessary security because it takes place in a question and answer context where every argument is subjected to the most stringent criticism possible, and only those which survive this scrutiny are accepted. Thus if exposition is properly organized room can be made for "conciliatory" procedures which are based on psychology rather than dialectic; so long as they are merely used to render more vivid and comprehensible truths which the underlying structure of the speech is presenting, the fact that they are open to challenge does not matter; the dialectical arguments are the ones by which the truth of the whole stands or falls and these, by definition, are the ones that can stand up to criticism.

In his different dialogues, Plato made varied recommendations about how such dialectical arguments should be structured, what sort of criticism was involved, and how to assess an argument's success in meeting it. But what is constant through them all is the insistence on the question and answer context, and any formal requirements which may be developed are firmly grounded in this context. It would seem that for Plato the acceptability of a pattern of argument as dialectically sound depends on its success in weathering criticism in philosophical debate; for the Cartesian tradition, on the other hand, an argument is only acceptable in philosophical debate if it conforms to, or can be accurately represented in terms of, a particular—geometric—pattern.[11]

In this dispute Aristotle, despite certain reservations, appears to be on Plato's side.

[11] Cartesian deduction, "the pure illation of one thing from another" (Descartes (1), i. 3) is not formal in the Leibnizian sense, as we saw in ch. 1. It is, however, representable *more geometrico* in the form of successive self-evident steps, and the operation of *intuitus* does not require the Platonic question and answer context.

2. Aristotle

It is notoriously difficult to explore Aristotle's views on fundamental philosophical issues. Not only did they undergo radical changes as his thought developed, but these differing views can be found side by side in the same works. The texts which have come down to us were not revised by Aristotle for publication, but are mainly in the form of lecture notes edited after his death.[12] Thus materials from different periods are often found together in the same work, and the unravelling of the various strands represents a scholarly exercise of immense labour and subtlety; this is not the place to embark on it.

Fortunately, there are certain relevant issues about which we can be fairly confident. The bulk of the *Topics* is usually taken to be earlier than either of the *Analytics*,[13] and it is probable that most of the *Metaphysics* is later.[14] While the text of the *Rhetoric* probably contains matter from different dates,[15] the later material seems to have been prepared after drafts of both books of the *Analytics* had been written but before most of the *Metaphysics*; this material also indicates that Aristotle still endorsed much of the *Topics* even though he had now developed his *Analytics*.[16] There thus appears to have been a period during which Aristotle was prepared to endorse much of the content of the *Topics*, *Analytics*, and *Rhetoric* at one and the same time; so there is a case for attempting to construct a

[12] Only fragments of Aristotle's published dialogues, famous in antiquity, are now extant. In form they appear to have been at least as much "Ciceronian" as "Platonic", and Cicero himself appears sometimes to have modelled his own dialogues on them (cf. Cicero (11), *Ad Atticus*, xiii. 21).

[13] Gilbert Ryle, in discussing the logical enquiries of the time, remarks on "the route on which in his *Topics* lectures Aristotle is already toddling, and in his *Analytics* will before long be marching" ('Dialectic in the Academy', Bambrough (1) 65.) Evans has recently challenged the early dating of the *Topics* in his *Aristotle's Concept of Dialectic*, arguing for the unity of Aristotle's thought.

[14] This is not such a truism as the early date of most of the *Topics* but see, for example, Owen (3).

[15] This is the generally accepted view. For a recent attack on it, and defence of the unity of the *Rhetoric*, see Grimaldi.

[16] The *Rhetoric* contains several explicit references to the *Topics* and *Analytics* but none to the *Metaphysics*; the latter references sometimes seem to refer to the *Prior* and sometimes to the *Posterior Analytics*. At A. 1356b, which is generally regarded as one of the later passages, we are referred to the *Analytics* for further discussion of certain problems, and to the *Topics* for discussion of others. See also Kapp's 'Syllogistic' and Weil's 'The Place of Logic in Aristotle's Thought'.

coherent position from these three works together, with only occasional reference to the later, and sometimes incompatible, doctrines of the *Metaphysics*.

If we do this we find that in place of Plato's dichotomy between dialectic and rhetoric we are presented with a threefold distinction between demonstration (or "analytics"), dialectic, and rhetoric; the two books of the *Analytics* being primarily concerned with demonstration and the *Topics* with dialectic. Now Aristotle's conception of demonstration is that of axiomatized deductive reasoning after the model of geometry, and in the *Posterior Analytics* he argues that this is the logical form which the sciences should exhibit.[17] Scientific knowledge is properly represented in a deductive chain which starts from first principles (ἀρχαί) which are not themselves demonstrable; these are divided into common axioms, which are common to more than one science and some of which are presupposed by all forms of knowledge whatsoever (e.g. the law of non-contradiction), and theses, which belong only to a particular science; these latter may either be definitions or else "hypotheses" which posit the existence of the genus whose essential attributes are to be proved in the demonstration (e.g. in arithmetic we assume the existence of the unit). (See especially *Posterior Analytics*, A. 2 and 10.) There are certain further constraints specified about the ways in which these first principles support the conclusions of the chains of inference, but so long as these constraints are observed any body of knowledge which can be presented in this way is a science; astronomy, we are told, "proceeds in the same way", and theology too is held to be a science.[18]

But although Aristotle insists on the geometrical method as being of crucial importance, he differs from the Cartesians in his treatment of our knowledge of first principles. These cannot merely consist of definitions and analytic truths, for if the science under consideration is to relate to the world they must include existential

---

[17] Aristotelian demonstration is closer to Descartes's synthetic method of proof than to the analytic. It is not presented as a theory of scientific research, as has often been believed, but is rather an account of how scientific knowledge, once acquired, should be organized and made intelligible. See Barnes, 'Aristotle's Theory of Demonstration', and also the notes to his translation of the *Posterior Analytics*.

[18] For astronomy see *Posterior Analytics*, A. 76b. Theology is treated as one of the three theoretical sciences (the others being mathematics and physics) in *Metaphysics*, E; for a good discussion of the relation between the earlier works and the *Metaphysics*, see Owen (3).

"hypotheses"; yet they cannot themselves be demonstrated for the various sciences are autonomous, not deducible from some master science.[19] Aristotle does not resort to doubtful appeals to "self-evidence",[20] which is the only possibility left given the Cartesian doctrine that demonstrative reasoning is the only type permissible in "scaling the heights of human knowledge", but instead turns to a different pattern of reasoning—the dialectical.

Dialectic is most fully discussed in the *Topics*, which starts by distinguishing between demonstrative and dialectical reasoning:

> Reasoning is an argument in which, certain things being laid down, something other than these necessarily comes about through them. (a) It is a 'demonstration', when the premises from which the reasoning starts are true and primary, or are such that our knowledge of them has originally come through premises which are primary and true: (b) reasoning, on the other hand, is 'dialectical', if it reasons from opinions which are generally accepted. . . . Those opinions are 'generally accepted' which are accepted by every one or by the majority or by the philosophers [τοῖς σοφοῖς]—i.e. by all, or by the majority, or by the most notable and illustrious of them (*Topics*, A. 100a–b).[21]

This is not put forward as a definition but merely as a preliminary means of recognizing the distinction; whereas demonstration starts from true first principles, dialectic takes its starting-point from the opinions of the many or the wise, reputable opinions which may nevertheless be false for which Aristotle uses the technical term ἔνδοξα (often rather loosely translated 'probable').[22] In both cases we are concerned with a species of what is here translated 'reasoning', for which the Greek word is συλλογισμός, which in the *Prior*

---

[19] The conception of a master science we find in the *Metaphysics* is a later development (cf. Owen (1) and (3)). But even if we accept the idea of a master science we are still left with the problem of our knowledge of *its* first principles; in the *Metaphysics* Aristotle tries to establish them by means of dialectical argument.

[20] Traditionally *Posterior Analytics*, B. 19, has been taken as advocating two apparently inconsistent means of gaining knowledge of first principles; one being induction, the other "intuition" or "self-evidence". That this is a misreading of the text, and the alleged appeal to "intuition" a mirage, has been convincingly argued by Barnes in his notes to this chapter in his translation of the work; see also Kosman, Lesher, and Burnyeat.

[21] All extended quotations from Aristotle are taken from the Oxford translation, ed. Sir David Ross.

[22] These ἔνδοξα from a subclass within the more general category of φαινόμενα or "appearances". Sometimes it is, more generally, the φαινόμενα which are taken to provide the starting points for dialectic. See Owen (2) and Nussbaum.

Analytics becomes a technical term for syllogistic reasoning; although the theory of the syllogism had probably not been developed at the time this part of the *Topics* was written, "reasoning" already possesses syllogism's essential feature whereby the conclusion follows necessarily from the premises.

But we are soon told that there is a species of dialectical argument other than dialectical "reasoning" (so understood), and this is induction (ἐπαγωγή: literally 'leading on'):

Induction is a passage from individuals to universals, e.g. the argument that supposing the skilled pilot is the most effective, and likewise the skilled charioteer, then in general the skilled man is the best at his particualr task. Induction is the more convincing and clear: it is more readily learnt by the use of the senses, and is applicable generally to the mass of men, though Reasoning is more forcible and effective against contradictious people (*Topics*, A. 105a).

In the *Topics* these are the only two species of dialectical argument, and that this remained Aristotle's view is shown by the *Rhetoric* (A. 1356b) where we are told that "every one who proves anything at all is bound to use either syllogisms or inductions", and we are referred both to the *Analytics* and to the *Topics*.

The study of dialectical argument is held to have three main uses: as intellectual training (a justification Descartes conceded to it), to enable us to argue with people we meet, and in the sciences. On the last use Aristotle writes:

For the study of the philosophical sciences it is useful, because the ability to raise searching difficulties on both sides of a subject will make us detect more easily the truth and error about the several points that arise. It has a further use in relation to the ultimate bases of the principles used in the several sciences. For it is impossible to discuss them at all from the principles proper to the particular science in hand, seeing that the principles are the *prius* of everything else: it is through the opinions generally held on the particular points that these have to be discussed, and this task belongs properly, or most appropriately, to dialectic: for dialectic is a process of criticism wherein lies the path to the principles of all inquiries (*Topics*, A. 101a–b).

Thus dialectic is appropriate in the sciences at just the point where demonstration breaks down.

Dialectical arguments, then, must in form be either syllogistic or inductive, for these are the only patterns of argument possible in attempting to prove anything, but their form does not guarantee the truth of the conclusions reached. If syllogistic, their premisses are only ἔνδοξα, and if inductive the only form of induction which guarantees the truth of the conclusion given the truth of the premisses, perfect induction, is not envisaged in the example given; further, induction is specifically contrasted with 'reasoning', defined as that form of argument whose conclusion necessarily follows from its premisses.[23] Nevertheless, they are regarded as capable of establishing the truth of first principles, on which all science depends. Part of the explanation lies in the fact that dialectical arguments are not wholly to be appraised by purely formal or formalizable criteria, and here Aristotle is closer to Plato than to Descartes.

As it is discussed in the *Topics*, dialectic takes place in the context of the sort of philosophical discussion we find in many of Plato's Socratic dialogues, and the whole battery of methods and principles which the book expounds in detail presupposes a context of question and answer between two people who are co-operating in a genuine attempt to arrive at the truth. Dialectic is distinguished from "eristic" or contentious argument where no such co-operative aim is involved, with the result that, as Professor Owen puts it, "eristic employs methods and materials to which dialectic must not stoop" (Owen (4), 107; see also, for example, *Topics*, A. ch. 1 and 11.) The *Topics* attempts to systematize the ways in which dialectical argument goes on so that its practitioners may become more effective in their co-operative search for the truth through the systematic examination of received opinions, conducted in a question and answer manner.[24] When we in this way attempt to commend to our partner a new view of an issue, perhaps by reinterpreting or reassessing the various relevant ἔνδοξα, we are seeking to give evidence of that view's "superior ability to integrate and organise features of our lived experience of the world" (Nussbaum,

---

[23] In *Prior Analytics*, B, ch. 23, Aristotle argues that perfect induction is itself a form of syllogistic reasoning.

[24] Evans remarks that for both Plato and Aristotle "the problem from which they start is: To what extent can intellectual advance be achieved by the method of question and answer?" (8). For the dialectical practices which it is the concern of *Topics* to codify, see Gilbert Ryle's 'Dialectic in the Academy', and his *Plato's Progress*, ch. 4; see also Paul Moraux, 'La Joute dialectique d'après le huitième livre des *Topiques*'. The disputations which played such an important role in the mediaeval universities were conducted (in part) on the principles developed in the *Topics*.

292). And in such an endeavour, for Aristotle as for Plato, the question and answer framework is crucial, for it helps to ensure that any doubtful move is subjected to criticism.

As the Aristotelian texts we possess are lecture notes rather than dialogues, we should not expect to find this ideal fully exemplified in them. Nevertheless, Aristotle sometimes contrives to relate his discussions of first principles to a speaker/hearer context. For example, he defends the "common axiom" of non-contradiction by arguing that anyone who would oppose it can be reduced to talking nonsense, "if our opponent will only say something"; a positive proof is in principle impossible, but a negative proof is possible against any antagonist—only the framework of debate makes the proof possible (*Metaphysics*, Γ. 1006a).[25] More often, however, the connections his dialectical discussions have with the context of live debate is more factitious. In the *Metaphysics*, *Physics*, and *Nicomachean Ethics* he starts exploring his subject by surveying the opinions of previous thinkers as well as generally current beliefs, and in examining their inconsistencies and other inadequacies he attempts to bring out some underlying principles on which, despite appearances, they are in real agreement, or which will solve the problems they raise. He argues both deductively and inductively from these ἔνδοξα, some of which he modifies or rejects in the course of the argument though he prefers not to upset too many of them, and when forced to choose has a tendency to prefer the opinions of "the many" (especially as enshrined in common linguistic usage) to those of "the wise"; his conclusions, unlike his starting-points, are not ἔνδοξα, but they are designed to be compatible with as wide a range of defensible ones as is possible and relevant.[26] This procedure is sometimes represented as involving a debate with dead

[25] The limitation of the negative proof of the principle of non-contradiction to a debating framework affects, of course, the status of the proof. Aristotle "does not say that this basic principle is true apart from the 'appearances' and from human conceptual schemes, true of the way the world is *behind* or *beyond* the categories of our thought and discourse . . . It is, for us, the starting-point of all discourse, and to get outside it would be to cease to think and to speak. . . . And if the opponent does choose to isolate himself from discourse, even the limited elenctic demonstration will not succeed . . . We cannot satisfy the sceptic's demand for external purity; we can ask him to accept our fellowship. But perhaps, if he is a sceptic bent on securing his equanimity against the risks attendant on community and human involvement, he will welcome that. We cannot, in any harder sense, show him that he is *wrong*" (Nussbaum, 285–6).

[26] For references and fuller discussion see Lee, 'Geometrical Method and Aristotle's Account of First Principles', and Owen (2) and (4).

thinkers, questioning their opinions and considering what answer they could make; thus Aristotle opens his summing up of an early phase of his discussion of causation in the *Metaphysics* with the words "From what has been said, then, and from the wise men who have sat in council with us, we have got thus much" (A. 987a); a conceit which betrays his (possibly earlier[27] but still lingering) conviction that dialectical argument should properly take place in the context of genuine debate.

There are other passages in Aristotle, even in works prior to the *Metaphysics*, where not only the practice but also the theory of approach to first principles diverges from the account given above. Thus in the *Nicomachean Ethics* we are told that "Of first principles we see some by induction, some by perception, some by a certain habituation [ἐθισμός], and others too in other ways" (i, 1098b), a remarkably relaxed account with no hint of the thesis that the proper route is via dialectical argument which may only be either deductive or inductive. On the other hand, in the notoriously obscure final chapter of the *Posterior Analytics* Aristotle argues that approach to first principles can only be made via induction, though since 'induction' here sometimes seems to mean no more than 'any cognitive progress from the less to the more general' (Barnes (1), notes to B. 19. 100b) the claim is less restrictive than it is sometimes taken to be; of this account Sir David Ross remarks that

The statement that the first principles of science are approached by way of dialectic is nowhere brought into relation with the other statement that they are approached by induction; but we must remember that induction is one of the two modes of argument proper to dialectic (Ross (1), 57).

Although much scholarly energy has gone into attempting to reconcile these various accounts, they may well represent independent approaches to the problem of knowledge of first principles which should not be subjected to "harmonisation".[28] In any case, it is the account which invokes dialectic as developed in the *Topics* which is most extensively worked out and, as we have seen, it is often reflected in Aristotle's philosophical practice; this account will bear further investigation.

[27] Though this discussion is probably from one of the earliest parts of the *Metaphysics* to be written.
[28] Barnes, (1), 259, suggests that the final chapter, B. 19, "began life as an independent essay on the subject, and was at some later stage tacked on to the discussions of B 1–18". If so, then its date is very uncertain.

More light is shed on the nature of dialectic by the *Rhetoric*. In the *Gorgias* Plato had dismissed rhetoric as "the counterpart [ἀντίστροφος] in the soul of what cookery is to the body" (Plato (1), *Gorgias*, 465e); Aristotle opens his study of the subject with a more favourable comparison, but using the same word: "Rhetoric is the counterpart of Dialectic". Taken strictly, the word indicates an exact correspondence of details,[29] and although Aristotle does not hold that dialectic and rhetoric are as closely related as that, he goes on to mark out some important correspondences.

Both alike are concerned with such things as come, more or less, within the general ken of all men and belong to no definite science. . . . Neither rhetoric nor dialectic is the scientific study of any one separate subject: both are faculties for providing arguments. . . . With regard to the persuasion achieved by proof or apparent proof: just as in dialectic there is induction on the one hand and syllogism or apparent syllogism on the other, so it is in rhetoric. The example is an induction, the enthymeme is a syllogism, and the apparent enthymeme is an apparent syllogism. I call the enthymeme a rhetorical syllogism, and the example a rhetorical induction (A. 1354a and 1356b).

But there are features of rhetoric which find no counterpart in dialectic. 'Rhetoric' is defined as 'the faculty of observing in any given case the available means of persuasion' (A. 1355b), and

Of the modes of persuasion furnished by the spoken word there are three kinds. The first kind depends on the personal character of the speaker; the second on putting the audience in a certain frame of mind; the third on the proof, or apparent proof, provided by the words of the speech itself. . . . The man who is to be in command of them must, it is clear, be able (1) to reason logically, (2) to understand human character and goodness in their various forms, and (3) to understand the emotions (A. 1356a).

Only the concern with proof is required in dialectic and this, thinks Aristotle, has misled some theorists, for the other "modes of persuasion" relate to ethics and political science and this has led some rhetoricians to masquerade as political experts (perhaps an allusion to Isocrates and his school is intended here); but it is the

---

[29] ἀντίστροφος is a term borrowed from the manoeuvres of the chorus in reciting choral odes, where the ἀντιστροφή or counter-movement exactly corresponds to the original manœuvre in the opposite direction. By extension it came to be used to refer to a set of verses, exactly parallel to those of the στροφή. In the *Prior Analytics* ἀντιστρέφειν is used to indicate that terms or propositions are convertible. See Cope, i. 1–4.

concern to reason logically which has priority, and thus rhetoric is not a branch of political science but rather "a branch [μόριον] of dialectic and similar to it, as we said at the outset" (A. 1356a). In all this, of course, there are clear parallels with the art of rhetoric as it is developed in the *Phaedrus*.

The reason for rhetoric's failure to be an exact counterpart of dialectic appears to lie in the nature of the audience presupposed.

The theory of rhetoric is concerned not with what seems probable to a given individual like Socrates or Hippias, but with what seems probable to men of a given type; and this is true of dialectic also. Dialectic does not construct its syllogisms out of any haphazard materials, such as the fancies of crazy people, but out of materials that call for discussion; and rhetoric, too, draws on the regular subjects of debate. The duty of rhetoric is to deal with such matters as we deliberate upon without arts and systems to guide us, in the hearing of persons who cannot take in at a glance a complicated argument, or follow a long chain of reasoning . . . , for we assume an audience of untrained thinkers (A. 1356b–1357a).

Rhetoric, it would appear, is conceived of as dealing with the principles of persuading popular audiences (in the limiting case an audience of one (B. 1391b)), whereas dialectic is concerned with the principles which govern the discussions of trained thinkers. Ideally, as we have seen, these trained thinkers should carry on their discussions by question and answer, but as Aristotle in his practice frequently sets aside this requirement it cannot serve as a sure distinguishing mark between dialectic and rhetoric. Both disciplines are concerned with persuasion, but whereas dialectic is concerned with persuasion among trained thinkers who are engaged in a serious attempt to arrive at the truth, rhetoric is concerned with persuading untrained thinkers by means of popular addresses. The nature of the rhetorician's audience brings non-dialectical consider-ations into play, for there will be emotional and moral resistances to be overcome as well as intellectual ones; emotional and ethical means of persuasion are completely ignored in the *Topics*. In rather similar fashion to that in which Plato allots psychological persua-sions to the sphere of rhetoric, merely demanding of the dialectician that he "select a soul of the right type" (*Phaedrus*, 276e), so Aristotle leaves emotional and moral persuasions to the rhetor-ician, advising that the dialectician should find a partner who is a trained thinker and who is prepared to participate in a co-operative enquiry.

But the parallel with Plato should not be pressed too far. In the *Phaedrus* dialectic provides the arguments, starting-points, and principles of arrangement for the orator, while rhetoric merely concerns itself with rendering these arguments palatable to his audiences and decorating his speeches through various stylistic techniques. For Aristotle, on the other hand, dialectic and rhetoric are "counterparts", relatively independent disciplines, and rhetoric has its own distinctive concern with the "mode of persuasion" provided by logical argument without constantly referring back to dialectic. Rhetoric, on this view, is a complete art of composition, and in its own right provides instruction in the discovery of arguments, their arrangement, style, and delivery. Dialectic is a similar art; the difference of context and audience envisaged determines the difference in type and manner of argument involved, as well as rendering style and delivery irrelevant. The connections are so close that, a generation after Aristotle and influenced by him, Zeno of Citium (the founder of the Stoic school) suggested that the relation of dialectic to rhetoric should be likened to that of the closed fist to the open hand; the tight discourses of the dialectician are seen as possessing a whole range of structural similarities to the more open discourses of the orator and populariser. This analogy was taken up by Cicero and Quintilian, becoming a cliché in the later Middle Ages and the Renaissance among those who found themselves in broad agreement with Aristotle rather than Plato.[30]

But on this analysis the relations between dialectic and rhetoric are too close for comfort; if both disciplines are primarily concerned with techniques of argument upon the same range of topics, the proposed means of separating them looks extremely weak. While many works can no doubt be classified into one or other of the two categories by the criterion (Plato's *Parmenides* and Demosthenes' *Philippics* for example), many others—such as those discussed in the body of this book—can plausibly be claimed by both disciplines. Thus it is worth considering the type of intellectual rigour attributed to rhetorical argument; if rhetoric has its own canons for distinguishing between good and bad arguments, they may be

---

[30] See, for example, Cicero (7), *De Finibus*, ii. 6, where he explicitly relates Zeno's analogy to Aristotle's analysis. Quintilian used the analogy to characterize dialectic as "really a concise form of oratory" (*Institutio Oratoria*, ii. xx. 7 and ii. xxi. 13). There is a useful survey of the literature in Howell (1) and (2).

appropriate in assessing works which seem to be at once dialectical and rhetorical.

Corresponding to syllogism and induction in dialectic, rhetoric employs the enthymeme and the example. The modern definition of the enthymeme as a deductive argument lacking a premiss—the result, in part, of the lingering influence of the *Port-Royal Logic* and behind this of Boethius and even Theophrastus—is not Aristotelian. In the *Prior Analytics* the 'enthymeme' is defined as 'a syllogism starting from probabilities [ἐξ εἰκότων] or signs' (B. 70a), and in the *Rhetoric* we are told that "enthymemes based upon probabilities are those which argue from what is, or is supposed to be, usually true" (B. 1402b).[31] The appropriate sense of 'probability' is further glossed as indicating "a generally approved [ἔνδοξος] proposition; what men know to happen or not to happen, to be or not to be, for the most part thus and thus, . . . e.g. 'the envious hate', 'the beloved show affection'" (*Prior Analytics*, B. 70a). Thus, like the dialectical syllogism, the rhetorical syllogism from probabilities takes its start from ἔνδοξα, but in this case they should only be "usually true"; that is, they should be understood as being almost, but not quite, universal. We are also told that such a "probability" "bears the same relation to that in respect of which it is probable as the universal bears to the particular" (*Rhetoric*, A. 1357a–b). Thus the conclusion of an enthymeme of this type should itself be concerned with particular cases; the conclusion, perhaps, that since Thersites has an envious disposition he also hates. The enthymeme from probabilities, therefore, moves from a widely approved general proposition which is usually true to a particular conclusion which it renders probable.

The other type of enthymeme starts from signs; we are told that

A sign means a demonstrative proposition necessary or generally approved [ἔνδοξος]: for anything such that when it is another thing is, or when it has come into being the other has come into being before or after, is a sign of the other's being or having come into being (*Prior Analytics*, B. 70a).

---

[31] Aristotle remarks that an enthymeme may "often" fit the *Port-Royal Logic* requirements (*Rhetoric*, A. 1357a), but these requirements are not part of the definition.

The main Aristotelian discussions of the enthymeme are in *Prior Analytics*, B. 27, and *Rhetoric*, A. 1–2 and B. 20–5. There are useful recent discussions in Madden, Miller and Bee, and Raphael.

A sign is "necessary" if the argument involving it can be turned into a valid first-figure syllogism because the sign and the thing signified always go together (e.g. 'if a woman has milk she has given birth': see *Rhetoric*, A. 1357b). If the sign is not necessary it is ἔνδοξον, but can only figure in syllogisms that are formally invalid because sign and thing signified only usually go together (e.g. 'The fact that he breathes fast is a sign that he has a fever': *Rhetoric*, A. 1357b). Both these examples exemplify cases where the sign "bears to the proposition it supports the relation of universal to particular", but it is also possible for a sign to work in the converse direction, as in "The fact that Socrates was wise and just is a sign that the wise are just" (*Rhetoric*, A, 1357b).

Enthymemes, therefore, typically move from generalizations which are usually true, whether or not the generalizations involve reference to signs, to particular conclusions which are only rendered plausible, not certain, by the argument. To this there are two exceptions possible if the argument involves reference to signs; it may move from particular instance to generalization, and it may be a fully valid deductive argument. It is important, however, that this latter can only happen where "signs" are involved, for in Aristotle "signs" are distinct from causes; signs only give one a reason for believing a thing to exist or to have certain properties (in this case a conclusive reason), but causes explain why it is as it is. Thus enthymemes of this sort, even if fully valid syllogisms, cannot function as part of a demonstration in a properly constituted science; they do not conform to essential constraints by means of which the first principles support the conclusions of the chains of inference.[32] The value of the enthymeme is dependent on the unscientific knowledge of the hearers, on what rules of thumb they have discovered to be usually or even always reliable; it does not turn on what must be the case as a matter of scientific necessity.

The enthymeme, we are told, is the rhetorical counterpart to the syllogism; similarly, the example [τὸ παράδειγμα] is supposed to correspond to induction. In the *Topics* induction is defined as "a passage from individuals to universals" (A. 105a; see also *Prior Analytics*, B. 23); in the *Rhetoric* argument by example is characterized as "reasoning from particular to particular" (A. 1357b; see also

---

[32] See Madden. The fact that enthymemes cannot function in demonstration does not prevent their being useful in discussions within the sciences; see *Rhetoric*, A. 1358a.

Prior Analytics, B. 24) where each particular is seen as exemplifying some (unstated) general principle (e.g. 'When Dionysius asked for a bodyguard he was aiming at tyranny, because Peisistratus and Theagenes seized power after they had gained bodyguards'[33]). As this form of argument operates by treating a feature of the example or examples as a sign of the general principle, it can also be regarded as one more form of enthymeme from signs—one which moves from particular to particular via an unstated generalization. The parallel with induction derives from the way it implicitly moves from particular example to general principle before applying the generalization so achieved to a further instance; unlike normal induction, its starting-point may be a single particular instance.[34]

On Aristotelian principles, therefore, some rhetorical arguments can furnish a "complete proof" (*Rhetoric*, A. 1357b) through being grounded on necessary signs; where they do this, however, they do not also provide scientific understanding, and their value for the orator depends on the knowledge of his "untrained" listeners. Where they do not do this, their conclusions are rendered persuasive by relying on reputable opinions acceptable to the audience to the effect that certain features of experience generally go together, or by reference to examples. Thus both in rhetoric and in dialectic considerable reliance is placed on the nature of the audience. In rhetoric as well as dialectic it is possible for the premisses to necessitate their conclusions, but where this does not happen—and where the premisses are no more than plausible—it is the context of trained debate that renders the dialectical arguments more reliable; rhetorical argument is like dialectical in taking account of the audience, and the inadequacies of that audience are what remove the orator from the dialectical arena.

Nevertheless, rationality is still possible in rhetoric, despite its audience and the use of psychological and ethical "modes of persuasion" this may necessitate, so long as the "mode" of logical argument remains dominant. This is not surprising, for the distinction between dialectic and rhetoric appears to be one of degree, turning on the level of expertise and type of motivation possessed by

[33] Raphael, 160; derived from the discussion at *Rhetoric*, A. 1357b.
[34] Raphael, 160–1, argues that all enthymemes save those from necessary signs can also be classified as arguments by example; they can all, accordingly, be classified as examples of induction. She concludes that Aristotle's classification of enthymeme and example as the rhetorical counterparts of syllogism and induction is therefore misleading.

those involved; reflection on the nature of actual philosophical debate,[35] as opposed to Aristotle's idealization of it and its practitioners, suggests that there is scope for rhetorical procedures which find no counterpart in the *Topics* to play their part in it. Thus we find Professor Ryle's "persuasions of conciliatory kinds", and the various strategies developed in the texts we shall be examining.

Perhaps it is a mark of realism in Aristotle's account that it separates rhetorical and dialectical skill far less sharply than does Plato.

3. Cicero

In Plato rhetoric, even at its best, is no more than a handmaid to dialectic; in Aristotle it is its "counterpart"; but in Cicero rhetoric and dialectic come near to being identified, and the wheel returns full circle to the Isocratean ideal of "speaking well".

> Whereas the persons engaged in handling and pursuing and teaching the subjects that we are now investigating were designated by a single title, the whole study and practice of the liberal sciences being entitled philosophy, Socrates robbed them of this general designation, and in his discussions separated the science of wise thinking from that of elegant speaking, though in reality they are closely linked together. . . . This is the source from which has sprung the undoubtedly absurd and unprofitable and reprehensible severance between the tongue and the brain, leading to our having one set of professors to teach us to think and another to teach us to speak (*De Oratore*, III. xvi. 60–I).[36]

Gorgias and Isocrates are particularly singled out as professors of that ancient "twofold wisdom" Cicero is concerned to recapture (ibid. 59).[37] It is fully in accord with this aim that in his *Topics*, a title

---

[35] Such as that we find, for example, in St Augustine. Admitting that in theory "truth cannot be better pursued than by question and answer", he makes "Reason" remark that "on the other hand hardly any one can be found who is not ashamed to be defeated in an argument, with the result that it almost always happens that a subject for discussion which is well begun is driven out of mind by the unruly noise of self-opinion, accompanied also by wounded feelings which are usually concealed but at times evident" (Augustine (1), I, *Soliloquies*, II. vii. 14).

[36] All extended quotations from Cicero are taken from the Loeb translations. The citations from those parts of *De Oratore* which are in dialogue form are taken from the speeches of Crassus, who acts as Cicero's mouthpiece here.

[37] On Cicero's relation to Isocrates, see Smethurst.

Cicero deliberately borrowed from Aristotle's work on dialectic, he explores types of argument found in both Aristotle's *Topics* and his *Rhetoric* without distinguishing between them.

But to be "closely linked together" is not to be indistinguishable, and Cicero did not simply ignore the distinctions that had been drawn by Socrates, Plato, Aristotle, and their successors. He admits that there can be a distinction on occasion between that "system of philosophy" which "is the truest" and that "which is the most fully akin to the orator" (*De Oratore*, III. xvii. 64), and the reason appears to be an Aristotelian one:

Whereas in all other arts that is most excellent which is farthest removed from the understanding and mental capacity of the untrained, in oratory the very cardinal sin is to depart from the language of everyday life, and the usage approved by the sense of the community (*De Oratore*, I. iii. 12).

Moreover, Aristotelian authority is invoked for one of his two main reasons for wishing to bring the two arts together again:

Just as Aristotle, a man of supreme genius, knowledge and fertility of speech, under the stimulus of the fame of the rhetorician Isocrates, began like him to teach the young to speak and combine wisdom with eloquence, similarly it is my design not to lay aside my early devotion to the art of expression but to employ it in this grander and more fruitful art: for it has ever been my conviction that philosophy in its finished form enjoys the power of treating the greatest problems with adequate fulness and in an attractive style (*Tusculan Disputations*, I. iv. 7).

For "wisdom" and "eloquence" to stand in these mutually profitable but somewhat external relations to each other it is clearly necessary that it be possible for the two to be conceived separately, whether or not they are "combined".

To this thesis, that the two arts are separable but each can benefit the other, Cicero was committed throughout his life. It is the starting-point of his youthful *De Inventione* and again of the second book of his late *De Natura Deorum*. Indeed, although there is some maturing of style and shift of emphasis between the *De Inventione*[38] and the later works, there is remarkable continuity between them, and among Cicero's later works there is no evidence, such as we find in both Plato and Aristotle, of alterations in beliefs and perspectives

---

[38] In the *De Oratore* (Cicero (3), I. ii. 5) he describes the *De Inventione* as "unfinished and crude essays, which slipped out of the notebooks of my boyhood, or rather of my youth".

as his thinking developed;[39] inconsistencies are as likely to be found within the same work, or between works written during the same period, as between works prepared at different times. The reason, no doubt, is that Cicero was not a creative and original thinker. The recently fashionable picture of Cicero as a philosophical innocent, merely copying, popularizing, and frequently misunderstanding the work of his intellectual betters, is now widely recognized to be little more than an unfair caricature.[40] Nevertheless the fact remains that his fundamental intellectual convictions in rhetoric and philosophy, particularly in the latter, were formed early under the influence of leading representatives of the various schools; however much he exercised a certain independent "discretion" in "criticising" these schools and providing his own "arrangement" of their doctrines (*De Officiis*, I. ii. 6 and *De Finibus*, I. ii. 6), they together provided him with his intellectual framework and methodological presuppositions. Many of Cicero's leading themes and doctrines are thus highly derivative, but since our knowledge of their earlier history is often fragmentary, it is convenient for our purposes to consider them in the context of Cicero's thought.

Cicero acknowledges, indeed, an important part of his intellectual indebtedness with regard to his second main reason for wishing to "combine wisdom with eloquence".[41] This reason turns on his conviction that while from some points of view philosophy and rhetoric can be considered separately, from others they are inextricably connected; for philosophical argument at its best uses rhetorical skills. This is clearly apparent as early as the criticisms of rhetoric

---

[39] Cf. Meador, 11: 'There seems no reason to suppose one may not take the philosophical premises set forth in 44 B.C. as having existed in Cicero's mind a decade earlier when he published *De Oratore*. In general his intellectual positions during the two, separated, periods of intensive writing seem remarkably consistent on both philosophical and rhetorical matters.'

[40] The urbane self-depreciation of one of Cicero's letters to his publisher (Cicero (11), *Ad Atticus*, xii. 52) which has so bedevilled literal-minded scholars should be set against the references given in the text, as well as his whole practice as an interpreter and translator. For recent recognition of this fact see, for example, Hunt, Douglas (1) and (2), De Lacy's article on Cicero in Edwards, Simon's contribution to the article on Cicero in Hammond and Scullard, Meador, Ross's 'Introduction' to McGregor's translation of the *De Natura Deorum*, and the first chapter of Grassi.

[41] I should do the same. Much more scholarly attention has been paid to Cicero's first reason than to his second, but recently Buckley has discussed his second one in a brilliant pioneering article 'Philosophic Method in Cicero'; its influence on my thinking about this aspect of Cicero is considerable.

made in Plato's *Gorgias*; speaking of those who decry rhetoric, Crassus (Cicero's mouthpiece in the *De Oratore*) remarks,

> But I was neither in agreement with these men, nor with the author and originator of such discussions, who spoke with far more weight and eloquence than all of them—I mean Plato—whose *Gorgias* I read with close attention . . . , and what impressed me most deeply about Plato in that book was, that it was when making fun of orators that he himself seemed to me to be the consummate orator (*De Oratore*, I. xi. 47).

Philosophy's commitment to rhetorical skills turns on a fundamental point of philosophical methodology, which Cicero learnt from the New Academy and traced back to Socrates.

In discussing this methodology, Cicero once again turns to the dispute with Gorgias:

> Socrates made fun of the aforesaid Gorgias and the rest of the Sophists also, as we can learn from Plato. His own way was to question his interlocutors, and by a process of cross-examination to elicit their opinions, so that he might express his own views by way of rejoinder to their answers. This practice was abandoned by his successors, but was afterwards revived by Arcesilas (*De Finibus*, II. i. 2).

In the *Tusculan Disputations* Cicero discusses his own procedure in that work, and goes on "This, as you know, is the old Socratic method of arguing against your adversary's position; for Socrates thought that in this way the probable truth was most readily discovered" (*Tusculan Disputations*, I. iv. 8). Arcesilas, in founding the New Academy, reinstated the method but without aiming at probable truth, for "he said, no one must make any positive statement or affirmation or give the approval of his assent to any proposition" (*Academica* I. xii. 45). It was left to his great successor Carneades to reinstate the full Socratic doctrine as Cicero conceived it and which he attempted to follow; among the "many warring philosophic sects" which have been produced by Socrates' "many-sided method of discussion" and breadth of interest,

> I have chosen particularly to follow that one which I think agreeable to the practice of Socrates, in trying to conceal my own private opinion, to relieve others from deception and in every discussion to look for the most probable solution; and as this was the custom observed by Carneades with all the resources of a keen intelligence, I have endeavoured on many other

occasions as well as recently in the Tusculan villa to conform to the same fashion in our discussions (*Tusculan Disputations*, v. iv. 10–11).[42]

This procedure, however, is held not only to be Socratic but also Aristotelian, and Aristotle is credited with first exploiting its connections with rhetoric:

These considerations always led me to prefer the rule of the Peripatetics and the Academy of discussing both sides of every question, not only for the reason that in no other way did I think it possible for the probable truth to be discovered in each particular problem, but also because I found it gave the best practice in oratory. Aristotle first employed this method (*Tusculan Disputations*, ii. iii. 9).

Aristotle's example is then contrasted with that of Philo of Larissa who "made a practice of teaching the rules of the rhetoricians at one time, and those of the philosophers at another"; although a pupil and, in some respects, a disciple of Philo, Cicero was far from being a mere slavish follower.

The consequences of these considerations for his own practice are perhaps most pithily expressed in the *Academica*;

It is our habit to put forward our views in conflict with all schools; . . . the sole object of our discussions is by arguing on both sides to draw out and give shape to some result that may be either true or the nearest possible approximation to the truth (*Academica*, ii. iii. 7).

The scepticism of Arcesilas taught Cicero to distrust the claims to certainty made by the dogmatic schools, but he agreed with Carneades that it was possible to show that some theses were more probable than others by means of a systematic cross-questioning of each side of every disputed question; the best way of doing this was to encourage representatives of all the schools to debate the matter together, either in reality or else, if in a written work, in a literary form which enabled each point of view to be systematically developed and opened to cross-examination.[43] Thus as J. M. Ross puts it, with only slight exaggeration, "for Cicero the dialogue was

---

[42] See also, for example, *De Oratore*, iii. xvii. 67–8, *De Natura Deorum*, i. v. 11, and *Tusculan Disputations*, i. ix. 17; ii. ii. 5; iv. xxi. 47.

[43] Where he himself was out of sympathy with the doctrines of a school, such as those of the Epicureans, or otherwise felt the need to make a conscious effort to be fair and accurate in representing its views, he frequently had recourse to quoting from current handbooks prepared by members of the school in question.

not merely a literary convenience: it was a philosophical necessity".[44]

For Plato philosophical argument can lead to certain knowledge; for Aristotle the first principles which dialectic establishes can be sufficiently certain to act as the foundation of scientific demonstration; but the epistemology Cicero inherited from Carneades allows us to reach no more than probability, thus putting the results of dialectical discussions on the same level as those achieved, on Aristotle's account, by good rhetorical argument. As such dialectical discussions provide "the best practice in oratory", the only fundamental differences between dialectician and orator lies in the latter's need to employ everyday language and common assumptions in his practice. Only the nature of his audience distinguishes the one from the other, and the relativity of this distinction—implicit in Aristotle—is exploited by Cicero; his *Topics*, as we have seen, ·includes material from Aristotle's *Rhetoric*, and he invokes Aristotle's authority for "joining rhetoric with philosophy" (*De Divinatione*, II. i. 4).[45]

But Cicero's account of the proper philosophical method turns not only on epistemology but also on a theory of language concerning the interdependence of *res* and *verbum*; in the *De Oratore* Cicero represents Crassus as learning of this interdependence between the content of his speeches and the words which he used in the course of his training as an orator; as a youth he had, as part of his daily exercises, begun to

set myself some poetry, the most impressive to be found, or to read as much of some speech as I could keep in my memory, and then to declaim upon the actual subject-matter of my reading, choosing as far as possible different words. But later I noticed this defect in my method, that those words which best befitted each subject . . . had already been seized upon. . . . Thus I saw that to employ the same expressions profited me nothing, while to employ others was a positive hindrance, in that I was forming the habit of using the less appropriate. Afterwards I resolved . . . to translate freely Greek speeches of the most eminent orators. The result of reading these was that, in rendering into Latin what I had read in Greek, I not only found myself using the best words—and yet quite familiar ones—but also coining by analogy certain words such as would be new to our people, provided only they were appropriate (*De Oratore*, I. xxxiv. 154–5).

---

[44] In his 'Introduction' to McGregor's translation of the *De Natura Deorum*, 26.
[45] See also *De Oratore*, III. xix. 69–73; *Brutus*, vi. 23; *De Finibus*, v. iv. 10.

In his translations of the Greek works Cicero himself became the founder of Latin philosophical terminology, thus, being an orator himself, he was no doubt drawing on his own experience in putting these remarks into the mouth of his spokesman, and he applied it in his own philosophical works.[46] Paraphrasing the opinions of a philosophical opponent in your own words is likely to distort them; if he has expressed himself carefully his words will take their sense from the whole context and interconnected vocabulary of his school, and be the best possible in that framework; to put them in your own words may be useful, but only if it is seen as an exercise in translation, with full acknowledgement of the shift in nuance and presupposition this involves.

Thus his typical practice is to "lay before my readers the doctrines of the various schools" (*De Nature Deorum*, I. vi. 13) and allow each to speak for itself. In the philosophical dialogues we find the various doctrines of one school first developed at length by a member of the school, and then submitted—at comparable length—to criticism by a representative of another; the aim is to bring the various perspectives into relation to each other and so reveal the strengths and weaknesses of each. As Fr Buckley describes the procedure,

Philosophizing lies precisely in this ongoing conversation, the clash of statements and judgments, and the value of the method converges precisely in this discrimination of perspectives and the differentiation of frames of reference. As one cannot think outside of such a reference, the philosophic dialogues attempt to examine the varying products of the divergent schools (Buckley, 'Philosophic Method in Cicero', 148).

In certain cases such a procedure may show that a clash is more apparent than real, that—at least from an Academic perspective —"the doctrines of the Stoics, though differing in form of expression, agree in substance with those of the Peripatetics" (*De Natura Deorum*, I. vii. 16; cf. *Academica*, I. iv. 17). Here Cicero's doctrine of the correlative significance of *res* and *verba* is important; if the schools are saying much the same thing in different terms, then what are effectively different languages must be involved. If so, we need a method which,

will allow for their peculiar coordinate systems to be introduced, for the ambiguous terms common to all will only achieve determined significance

---

[46] Though Cicero is far from consistent in holding to Crassus' thesis.

and translations by reference to their own systems. Ciceronian method becomes an attempt to discover what is the case by taking such statements and locating through debate the senses in which they can be asserted and denied. . . . This allows the controversy both to discover that the different philosophers are stating the same truth in different ways and to judge probabilities by setting one doctrine against its real opponent (Buckley, 148–9).

The assessment of such probabilities, Cicero holds, properly lies with the reader; thus he himself is frequently concerned to "conceal my own private opinion" (*Tusculan Disputations*, v. iv. 11) for fear that it will have undue weight with the reader;

Those however who seek to learn my personal opinion on the various questions show an unreasonable degree of curiosity. In discussion it is not so much weight of authority as force of argument that should be demanded. Indeed the authority of those who profess to teach is often a positive hindrance to those who desire to learn; they cease to employ their own judgement, and take what they perceive to be the verdict of their chosen master as settling the question (*De Natura Deorum*, I. v. 10).

This reticence, however, is exercised with some subtlety. Cicero himself was known as an adherent of the New Academy, and in the same work in which he objects to enquiries into his personal opinions, indeed in the following sentence, he acknowledges his "allegiance" to "that system". But as the work proceeds, and from other works,[47] it becomes clear that his primary allegiance is to the philosophical method favoured by that school understood as a means of assessing probabilities, rather than to that school's actual assessment of particular probabilities. On ethical matters, indeed, he often shows himself drawn to Stoic doctrines,[48] and on theological issues—as expressed in *De Natura Deorum*—he displays a studied ambiguity. Here the Academic representative, Cotta, is given the last long speech, which consists of a detailed criticism of Stoic theology, and he is similarly given the last word in criticizing the Epicurean doctrines; as elsewhere Cicero expresses himself impressed by the "Socratic schools" in giving both sides of the

---

[47] Particularly from the *Academica*, to which Cicero explicitly refers in acknowledging this "allegiance" (*De Natura Deorum*, I. v. 11). See also *Tusculan Disputations*, II. ii. 5, and IV, xxi. 47; and *De Divinatione*, II. lxxii. 150.

[48] Especially in *De Officiis* and *Paradoxa Stoicorum*; see also *De Oratore*, III. xviii, and *De Finibus*, v. xxviii. There are interesting discussions of Cicero's "Stoicism" in ethics in Douglas (2), and in ch. 1, 'The Ciceronian Model', of Seigel.

question but ending with the side they prefer (*Ad Atticus*, II, iii), it might seem that he, a fellow Academic with Cotta, is endorsing Cotta's arguments. But on the other hand he represents himself in the dialogue as explicitly rejecting the charge that he is Cotta's ally and as insisting that he has come "as a listener, and an impartial and unprejudiced listener too, under no sort of bond or obligation willy nilly to uphold some fixed opinion" (*De Natura Deorum*, I. vii. 17); at the close of the dialogue—in which 'Cicero' has indeed been a "listener" rather than a participant—he gives his vote not to Cotta but to the Stoic: 'Here the conversation ended, and we parted, Velleius thinking Cotta's discourse to be the truer, while I felt that that of Balbus approximated more nearly to a semblance of the truth' (*De Natura Deorum*, III. xl. 95). In *De Divinatione* Cicero represents his brother as being puzzled by the relation between Cicero's own opinions and those of Cotta in the *De Natura Deorum*,[49] and the controversy which has surrounded the attempts to identify Cicero's theological beliefs ever since[50] shows the success with which he has countered such "an unreasonable degree of curiosity". Whatever his "own private opinion", the way 'Cicero' sides with Balbus in the dialogue helps to redress its balance, which is otherwise weighted firmly in favour of Cotta, and to display the fundamental Academic principle that we are, at best, faced only with probabilities. As A. S. Pease puts it,

The puzzling last sentence . . . indicates that the dialogue is intended to exemplify Academic methods of inquiry rather than Academic dogma, and to illustrate the freedom of the Academy from dogmatic bonds and the possibility of using such individual liberty for the acceptance of any working principle.[51]

Not all Cicero's works show the same reticence, or exemplify so fully his methodological concerns. A variety of uses of the flexible dialogue form are explored, and his letters show that in such explorations he is often consciously experimenting with the genre;[52]

---

[49] *De Divinatione*, I. v. 8–9. Cicero purports to express his own opinions on the matter at the close of the work (II. lxii. 148–9).

[50] To which we shall return in ch. 6.

[51] In his edition of the *De Natura Deorum*, I. 9. See also his 'The Conclusion of Cicero's *De Natural Deorum*'.

[52] See, for example, *Ad Atticus*, XIII. xix. For an ironic comment on such experiments, see *De Legibus*, III. xi. 26.

even in works like the *De Natura Deorum* he starts with a preface where he discusses his practice and its historical antecedents in his own voice. Thus we have both comparatively unambiguous statements about how philosophy should be carried on through "controversy", and exemplifications of such controversy in which it is sometimes dangerous to identify Cicero's opinions too simply with any single one of the participants.[53] From these discussions Cicero's somewhat eclectic, but interesting and influential, conception of philosophic method emerges. Philosophy should properly be carried on by means of cross-examination with an eye to revealing the probable; this will only be adequately done if each position is expounded at length so that each school's opinion on a particular matter can be seen in its larger context, and its conceptual framework seen in relation to those of its rivals; as demonstrative certainty is impossible here, the persuasive force of such controversy in revealing what is most plausible has much in common with that of the best rhetoric; the philosopher, therefore, should be "versed in rhetoric", and the orator in the Academic "system of philosophy" (*De Natura Deorum*, II. i. 1).

There are remarkable similarities here with some of the more recent approaches to the problem of appraising rival "conceptual systems" discussed in Chapter 1. Sir Alfred Ayer, it will be remembered, holds that so far as a rival thesis is an integral part of a consistent system "Our only hope . . . is to make the interpretations appear so strained that the assumptions on which they rest become discredited" (Ayer, 127): an approach reminiscent of Cicero's concern to reveal the probable through controversy. Professor Wisdom comes even closer to recommending Ciceronian controversy, with "each presenting and representing the features . . . favouring his hypothesis, that is, fitting his model for describing the accepted fact" (Wisdom (1), 159); while Dr Waismann lays particular stress on the persuasiveness of examples in philosophy, although on Aristotle's analysis argument by example is a feature of rhetoric rather than of dialectic. No doubt none of these writers would agree with all aspects of Cicero's approach to philosophical method, and few contemporary philosophers would be happy to advocate a

---

[53] In works like *De Oratore*, however, which make no attempt to exemplify Cicero's philosophical method, he uses one of the participants in the dialogue as a spokesman for his own opinions.

return to Isocratean traditions; nevertheless, the obvious parallels in Cicero's thought with contemporary discussions suggest that it has a significance beyond that of a mere historical curiosity.

4. Post-Classical Hubris

Both Plato and Aristotle thought philosophical argument could lead to knowledge. For Plato this led him sharply to differentiate dialectic from the rhetoric of the Sophists; only dialectical argument was acceptable in philosophy, and its power in the search for knowledge derived not only from its form but also from the fact that it was embedded in the context of live philosophical cross-questioning. For Aristotle, too, this was an important element in dialectical argument, enabling one to move from ἔνδοξα to first principles, and hence to scientific knowledge. Cicero, on the other hand, held that philosophical argument could at best lead only to probabilities, and that these were best brought out by his favoured means of cross-questioning between representatives of differing schools; formal considerations play a significantly less crucial role than they do in either Plato or Aristotle, with the result that dialectic and rhetoric are once more "joined together".

Common to all these approaches is an implicit denial that formal or formalizable considerations, or such patterns as the geometric, are sufficient by themselves for "scaling the heights of human knowledge", or even—so far as Cicero was concerned—for properly assessing probabilities. Descartes was content to philosophize alone beside his stove, putting out of his mind all received opinions save those which he clearly and distinctly perceived to be true; for the authors we have been considering this would have been sufficient of itself to call his result into question—in their view philosophy is a co-operative endeavour which develops by systematic cross-questioning of received opinions.

The Cartesian practice of philosophizing as nearly as possible in a vacuum had great influence, and was elevated into an ideal by John Stuart Mill for whom "logic" and "rhetoric" were accordingly sharply separated:[54]

[54] An analogous distinction between conviction and persuasion leads Kant, too, to exclude rhetoric from the field of philosophical reasoning: "The holding of a thing to be true is an occurrence in our understanding which, though it may rest on objective grounds, also requires subjective causes in the mind of the individual who makes the judgment. If the judgment is valid for everyone, provided only he is in

The sole object of Logic is the guidance of one's own thoughts: the communication of those thoughts to others falls under the consideration of Rhetoric, in the large sense in which that art was conceived by the ancients; or of the still more extensive art of Education. Logic takes cognizance of our intellectual operations, only as they conduce to our own knowledge, and to our command over that knowledge for our own uses. If there were but one rational being in the universe, that being might be a perfect logician; and the science and art of logic would be the same for that one person as for the whole human race (Mill, 'Introduction', s.3).

It may be this ideal which is at the root of our contemporary problems in philosophical methodology, as discussed in the first chapter. Whether this is so or not, we should not presuppose it in attempting to understand the works to be discussed in the following

---

possession of reason, its ground is objectively sufficient, and the holding of it to be true is entitled *conviction*. If it has its ground only in the special character of the subject, it is entitled *persuasion*. Persuasion is a mere illusion, because the ground of the judgment, which lies solely in the subject, is regarded as objective. Such a judgment has only private validity, and the holding of it to be true does not allow of being communicated. But truth depends upon agreement with the object, and in respect of it the judgments of each and every understanding must therefore be in agreement with each other. . . . The touchstone whereby we decide whether our holding a thing to be true is conviction or mere persuasion is therefore external, namely, the possibility of communicating it and of finding it to be valid for all human reason" ((1) *Critique of Pure Reason*, 'The Canon of Pure Reason', A820/B848). The rhetorician, it would appear, appeals to the distinctive features of a particular audience, whereas the true philosopher "appeals to the reason which all audiences possess by virtue of being human audiences" (Holley, 277); thus the account is closer to Mill's than the apparent reversal of the notions of privacy and communication would superficially suggest. The strength of the hold of crucial aspects of the Cartesian methodological tradition on Kant's thinking is revealed by his taking of the fact of disagreement as a sign of the breakdown of reason and use of this sign as a touchstone for acceptable philosophical reasoning. The "illusory" character of persuasion leads Kant to a critique of rhetoric as far-reaching as that of the *Gorgias*, without any Platonic concession to the possibility of the "more noble" rhetoric: "Rhetoric, so far as this is taken to mean the art of persuasion, . . . is a dialectic, which borrows from poetry only so much as is necessary to win over men's minds to the side of the speaker before they have weighed the matter, and to rob their verdict of its freedom. Hence it can be recommended neither for the bar nor the pulpit" ((2) *Critique of Aesthetic Judgment*, 'Analytic of the Sublime', s. 327). For Cicero, of course, we may come to an agreement through communicating our grounds for "holding a thing to be true" by means of a principled rhetoric which does not depend on the assumption that what is agreed meets the quasi-mathematical ideal of a Kantian "science" which may be found "to be valid for all human reason". See also ch. 1 n. 3.

chapters, few—if any—of which acknowledge it. In exploring these works the principles of Plato, Aristotle, and Cicero may prove at least as helpful as those of Descartes and of John Stuart Mill.

3

On Taking the *Phaedo* Seriously

There is a perennial danger besetting even the most learned scholar in exploring ancient texts that, in peering through the deep well of his own scholarship, he will discern something disturbingly akin to the reflection of his own face. The problem has been most thoroughly canvassed in the field of New Testament criticism, but the danger of reading one's presuppositions into the texts is a universal hazard, and the history of Platonic scholarship provides an object lesson in its Hydra-like qualities. Despite Plato's own methodological discussions, commentators regularly employ modern models of philosophy in discussing his works, models which allow little more than a decorative significance to the dialogue form with its exemplification of that question and answer context which we have seen to be fundamental to Platonic thinking about dialectic. This first case study will be concerned to argue that, if we are to understand and appraise Plato's *Phaedo* adequately, we must reject certain current assumptions about its nature which import the modern dichotomy between 'philosophy' and 'literature' into the enquiry.

1. Philosophy and Literature

The most recent English translation with commentary of the work[1] opens with the words "This book is designed for philosophical study

---

[1] Since the publication of Gallop, two further commentaries (without translation) have appeared. Bostock follows in an extreme form the standard "analytic" tradition; the work "concentrates entirely on the philosophical interest of the dialogue, and has nothing to say of its considerable literary merits and dramatic power" (v). Dorter, however, shares many of the concerns of this study; he is concerned with "the rigour of the organic structure" (46), brings out the way that "Plato's dramaturgy"—through judicious use of what I have termed the "frame" of the dialogue—emphasizes "the crucial importance of the threat of misology" (87), takes seriously the relation between philosophy and music (app.), and in general seeks to

footnote continued overleaf

of the *Phaedo*" (Gallop, v). It is admitted that "thought and action are interfused throughout in the manner typical of Plato's maturity as a philosopher-dramatist" (74), and occasional reference is made to the "dramatic setting" (226). Nevertheless, the notion of "interfusion" is not followed through in the body of the commentary, where it is assumed that "philosophical study" can be adequately carried out with only perfunctory reference to the "setting" to which the discussion is "matched", a conception of what counts as 'philosophical' more at home in the Clarendon Plato Series of which it is a part than in the thought of Plato himself.

Professor Gallop is in good company. He ably represents a tradition of exegesis upheld in the two other full-length commentaries on the *Phaedo* which have been published in English since the last war; of these, that of Dr Bluck is the more explicit about its assumptions:

There is sometimes a tendency to treat the *Phaedo* primarily as literature, and only secondarily as philosophy. But although this dialogue is, indeed, a masterpiece of dramatic literature, its author undoubtedly intended it to be first and foremost a work of philosophy. In presenting a magnificent portrait of Socrates, he was not only paying a personal tribute: the Socrates of the *Phaedo*, propounding what is often Platonic rather than genuinely Socratic thought, represents the type and explains the doctrine of the 'true philosopher' (Bluck, vii).

He goes on to argue that we should approach the work "primarily as philosophy", and follows his own advice in the body of the commentary. If we are forced to choose between these two approaches no

---

footnote 1 cont.

"synthesize" the "analytic" and "dramatic" methods of commentary (ix). Its central focus, however, is different from that of this study, being concerned with the type of immortality argued for rather than with Plato's conception of rational argument as such. Dorter argues for a sharp distinction between myth and argument, with the former operating as a "noble lie" and "deliberately obscuring" what the latter can sustain (81 and 68); both mythologizing and dramaturgy are seen as in tension with the argumentation, the former endorsing personal immortality, the latter undercutting it. His remarkable conclusion that the *Phaedo* "does not put forth a serious doctrine of personal immortality" (167) arises in part from a failure to examine carefully its conception of rational argument. On my account, myth, argument, and dramaturgy mutually support each other, and when Socrates at the close (115d) insists to Crito that his discourse about the land of the blest, to which he hopes shortly to depart, is not "idle talk, intended to console" he tells no lie, however "noble"; in this respect, at least, my own account is at once more orthodox and possesses the virtue of economy.

doubt Bluck (and Gallop) have chosen wisely;[2] but they nowhere consider whether the dichotomy is itself appropriate to the text in question, or whether treating it "as literature" may be a necessary element in treating it "as philosophy".[3]

Similar considerations apply to Professor Hackforth's commentary. Although it opens with the dictum "That the *Phaedo* is a work of supreme art, perhaps the greatest achievement in Greek prose literature, is something that needs no argument" (Hackforth (2), 3), the approach soon turns out to have a great deal in common with those of Gallop and Bluck, being centrally concerned with elucidating and assessing the arguments employed, examining the doctrines promulgated, and clarifying the obscurities of those passages commonly designated 'mythical'; discussion of aesthetic issues soon drops out of sight. The consequences of such an approach are most spectacularly apparent in his handling of the close of the dialogue. He divides the work into twenty-two sections, and for all save the last he provides both a commentary and a summary; but then we read, under the heading 'The Last Scene', "This final section needs neither summary nor comment" (187). Now Hackforth maintains in his 'Introduction' that

the fundamental purpose of the dialogue . . . [is] to extend and deepen, through the mouth of a consciously Platonised Socrates, the essential

---

[2] For an object lesson in the pitfalls of the other approach, see Reichenbach (ch. 2). In the course of his (strongly positivist) argument it is suggested, roughly, that we should treat several of Plato's dialogues as poetry because the arguments are so bad; "The poetic simile is not bothered by logic. . . . Plato's philosophy is the work of a philosopher turned poet."

[3] The working assumption of a great deal of Platonic commentary was summarized more than 50 years ago by Billings (95): "One of the most important features of Platonic style . . . is his playful blending of real arguments with mere literary devices for carrying out an illustrative imagery"; he maintains that it is important "to distinguish the literary machinery from the real argument" and describes Plato's blending of the two as a "puzzling confusion".

However, in a distinguished recent discussion of Plato's *Sophist*, Professor Rosen argues for a "dramatic" rather than "ontological" approach to the work, maintaining that "a comprehensive understanding of the "technical" passages, to the extent that such is possible at all, depends . . . upon grasping their function within the organic dialogue" (1; see also 12). He adds that "the ontological approach to the *Sophist*, of which the analytical version is in my opinion the most fruitful, errs in disregarding the dramatic context of the narrowly technical passages" (28). His supporting arguments imply that the appropriateness of the "dramatic" approach is a function of Plato's use of the dialogue form more generally. See also the argument of Hathaway (206), which also makes decisive use of the *Sophist*, to the effect that in Plato "the Dialogue as art and the Dialogue as philosophy are in essence one".

teaching of Socrates himself, namely that man's supreme concern is the 'tendance of his soul', or (in more modern language) the furthering of his insight into moral and spiritual values and the application of that insight in all his conduct (3).

Thus it appears that he regards his type of discussion as inappropriate to the last scene of a drama where the application of such insight to conduct is put to its final test in accordance with "the fundamental purpose of the dialogue". If the approach we favour is that of Hackforth, Bluck, and Gallop it would seem to follow that such dignified restraint about "The Last Scene" is entirely appropriate, but this is hardly to treat the dialogue on its own terms—it is rather to impose one's own terms, to look in it for those elements which fit one's own predispositions and set aside as irrelevant to the discussion other elements, even if they are seen as integral to the work's "fundamental purpose". The danger that such an approach may distort one's understanding of the text is apparent enough; if this counts as treating the dialogue "as philosophy", then there is at least a prima facie case for also invoking a traditional question of literary criticism and asking what sort of treatment this "work of supreme art" requires if regarded as an integrated whole.[4]

A glance at the historical context of the dialogue may help to reinforce this case. It was written in the afterglow of the great age of Greek tragedy, and has at least as much claim to be regarded as a drama as a philosophical treatise. The word φιλοσοφία existed by this time, but philosophy had not yet become firmly established as a clearly distinct form of writing; with the Sophists and others there had developed a kind of writing about "wisdom" which was neither "history" nor "poetry", but its separation from these other kinds was not absolute and this immature mode did not yet have separate canons of exact, rigorous, logically argued, and "non-poetic" style such as we have since learnt to associate with philosophy, largely from Plato's own explorations in his later dialogues and from the example of Aristotle. Again, the notion of 'literature', as distinct from 'poetry' or that 'service of the Muses' discussed by Socrates in the opening phase of the dialogue as being capable of including

---

[4] Hackforth does not in fact abide by his self-denying ordinance, but his only substantial comment here—on Socrates' last words—serves to reinforce the impression that he has little concern for the work's artistic unity; see below. Bluck and Gallop are only a little more forthcoming.

'philosophy', is also anachronistic.[5] Thus to ask whether the work is "primarily" literature or philosophy, and hence to be treated in accordance with the appropriate canons, is to insist on a dichotomy which may well be less than wholly appropriate.

Indeed, the attempt to find a distinctive form of writing extant in the period to which this dialogue may plausibly be assimilated proves singularly unrewarding. It is, of course, a "philosophical dialogue", but our knowledge of the conventions governing the genre at the time is almost wholly drawn from our attempts to make sense of extant examples, and is at best dubious and fragmentary. The fact that it belongs to this genre may encourage us to set the *Phaedo* alongside other apparently similar dialogues of earlier or contemporary date—particularly Platonic ones—but it provides us with few methodological tools and leaves us still asking of this (and similar) texts what sort of treatment it requires if we are to make sense of the whole of it, and not merely those selected parts which best fit our current predispositions. The question may have "new critical" associations, but it is neither anachronistic nor particularly new.[6]

In what follows I shall give rather more attention than is usual to this question. Any adequate reading of the dialogue must clearly take into account both historical scholarship and logical analysis, but it must also take account of structure, tone, and dramatic coherence. If we do this, paying more than lip-service to the claim that it is "a work of supreme art", we are led to an understanding of what is at stake in the *Phaedo* rather different from what is commonly assumed, and with significant implications for philosophy.

2. Philosophy as "Music"

Let us start by considering the dialogue's ostensible setting. This is provided by a conversation between Phaedo and Echecrates which

---

[5] Plato's famous opposition of philosophy to poetry in the *Republic* does not mark quite the same distinction. On the one hand, the conception of 'philosophy' involved will not bear the weight required here; on the other, it is possible to treat a work as 'literature' without thereby treating it as 'poetry' in Plato's sense of that term.

[6] Kennedy (2) (56) cites the critical method of the Neoplatonists of late antiquity who, drawing on the authority of the *Phaedrus* (264c), "insisted on approaching the Platonic dialogues and other major works of literature as absolutely consistent wholes"; he points out that "the idea was partially anticipated in the *Gorgias* (505d)".

serves as a "framing" device, to set up expectations, and—occasionally—to supply a commentary. At the outset it is used to indicate that Socrates is already dead, and his death provides the context of the whole discussion as well as its leading theme. The next move is to establish a context of reliability; Phaedo claims to be providing a firsthand report, other witnesses are named, and the convention is soon set up that he is to be taken as a trustworthy witness and raconteur; nothing is said later to undermine this first impression, a matter which will prove of some importance when we come to consider his later comments. The entire debate is then given a religious setting associated with Apollo—who is *inter alia* the god of "music", an association which is soon taken up—and we are afforded at least a hint that there is some tension between executing Socrates and honouring the god. Thereupon, in swift succession, Socrates is sketched in as being at once a "dear friend" and extraordinarily impressive, we are told that what took place was "one of our regular philosophical discussions", and the theme of the blending of pleasure and pain is adumbrated—which Socrates is shortly to employ as his opening gambit.

If we take this preliminary conversation as an overture to the whole and follow its leading themes through, we find that they interlock in important ways. The central issue is not just the abstract question of death, but the death of Socrates—and the person of Socrates is pivotal to the dialogue. In Bluck's words, he "represents the type and explains the doctrine of the 'true philosopher'", and if this is so then our understanding of the "doctrine" must be tempered by the manner in which Socrates exemplifies it. Let us consider how this operates.

The first extended exposition of what may reasonably be described as "doctrine" in the dialogue comes early on when Socrates expresses his confidence that it will be well with him after death, and defends this thesis by arguing that the body is harmful to man, it "befouls" us, "confusing, disturbing and alarming us" so that "we have no leisure for philosophy" (66b–d). He goes on

While we are alive we shall, it would seem, come nearest to knowledge if we have as little as possible to do with the body, if we limit our association therewith to absolute necessities, keeping ourselves pure and free from bodily infection until such time as God himself shall release us. And being thus made pure and rid of the body's follies we may expect to join the company of the purified, and have direct knowledge of all truth unobscured (67a–b).[7]

But the formidable austerity of the true philosopher in his search for knowledge sketched here needs to be taken in conjunction with Socrates' own capacity for friendship, humanity towards those who are not philosophers (116d), and penchant for using sensuous imagery to express the highest spiritual aspirations (110b–e). Indeed, the whole dramatic movement of the work needs to be taken into account; when Socrates first appears he is a somewhat austere figure, dismissing his wife and immediately embarking on a discussion of the nature of pleasure and pain, which before long has broadened out into the ascetic preaching just cited. Gradually, however, the portrait is filled out and the ascetic figure becomes more humane, so that there is no sense of shock when we find Socrates playing with Phaedo's hair and stroking his head at 89b. Socrates' fullness as a person is held in abeyance at the start, and then slowly develops until in the end we can both feel with Socrates' friends in their sadness and yet perceive its ultimate inappropriateness; the whole of life is a preparation for death, and for one who has prepared as Socrates has done death is no cause for sorrow. Similarly, the doctrine is filled out so that, once it is established that the philosopher must "have as little as possible to do with the body" and its senses, it is possible to allow that he may appropriately understand spiritual matters in terms of analogies drawn from the senses, however lush.

But apart from the negative, ascetic side of the life of the true philosopher, that he do his best to keep his soul uncorrupted by the body, there is also—and crucially—a positive element involved in the "tendance of the soul"; and here we find mutual reinforcement in the dialogue between the theory of how we should live as preparing for death, and the portrait of Socrates presented as the dying philosopher. In positive terms, the philosopher's soul "reaches out after reality" and "If then any part of reality is ever revealed to it, must it not be when it reasons? [ἐν τῷ λογίζεσθαι]" (65c): a question expecting (and receiving) the answer 'Yes'. The term λογίζεσθαι is unclear,[8] but the sorts of way in which

---

[7] I have given Hackforth's rendering of passages from the *Phaedo* except where otherwise stated.

[8] See Hackforth's note to the passage.

the philosopher's soul reaches out after reality through reasoning
are discussed extensively in the text, both in general terms (e.g.
89d–90a, 107b) and in terms of Socrates' own experience (96 ff.),
and these discussions are both illuminated and reinforced by the
presentation of Socrates' own practice in the dialogue, which
activity he himself comments on (e.g. 61e, 63b–c, 114d).

The importance to the work of this positive side of philosophy,
the attempt to attain knowledge of truth through reasoning, is
underlined by Phaedo's own comments. The purported eyewitness,
whom Echecrates asks to give "a reliable report" (58d) at the start,
and into whose mouth Plato puts Socrates' epitaph at the close—the
closest we come to an "authorial voice" in the dialogue—comments
twice on the discussion in conversation with Echecrates, and each
time the issue highlighted is the nature of rational enquiry.

The first, and most substantial, occasion on which the "frame"
thus intrudes into the "picture" occurs almost exactly halfway
through the text. Immediately after Simmias and Cebes have
delivered their criticisms of Socrates' position Phaedo observes

These remarks by Simmias and Cebes had a disquieting effect on all of us;
indeed we afterwards admitted to each other that, having been completely
convinced by the argument preceding, we now felt disturbed and reduced
to scepticism not only about what had already been asserted but as regards
future arguments as well. Were we perhaps quite incompetent to judge?
Did the problem, of its very nature, admit of no certain solution? (88c)

That we should take such disquiet seriously is indicated by the fact
that Echecrates now breaks his long silence to endorse and broaden
it, "What argument shall we ever rely on after this?", and anxiously
enquires whether Socrates was able to meet the challenge with
complete success.

Phaedo's first move is to re-establish confidence in Socrates the
man before recounting Socrates' attempt to re-establish confidence
in argument:

I would have you know, Echecrates, that though I have admired Socrates
on many occasions, I never found him more wonderful than at that
moment. That he should not be at a loss for a reply is perhaps not
surprising; but what I especially admired was, first, the pleasure, the
kindness, the respect with which he received those young man's observations, and secondly his swift perception of the effect upon us of their words
and the success with which he healed our distress, rallying the routed

battle-line and encouraging us to follow where he led in a re-examination of the question (88e–89a).

Immediately thereafter Phaedo reports how he was himself incorporated, for the first and only time, into the discussion when Socrates moves from playing with his hair to inviting him to share the burden of his defence:

> 'Well then,' said he 'call me in as your Iolaus, while the daylight lasts.'
> 'Yes, I will,' I replied, 'but it will be the other way round, Iolaus calling in Heracles' (89c).

With these preliminaries, which serve to provide the narrator's endorsement of Socrates' manner of "rallying the routed battle-line" and to emphasize the matter's importance, Phaedo recounts Socrates' counter-attack. He starts by warning against "The danger of coming to hate argument in general, even as some people come to hate mankind in general. Such 'misology' is the worst thing that can befall a man" (89d), and is liable to arise from having frequently put trust in arguments which one has later decided to be bad, because one lacks any method of telling good from bad ones.

> 'Then, Phaedo, wouldn't it be a lamentable event if there were in fact a true, solid argument capable of being discerned, and yet as the result of encountering the sort of arguments we were speaking of, which seemed true at one moment and false at the next, one were not to find the fault in oneself or one's own lack of address, but to find a welcome relief for one's distress in finally shifting the blame onto the arguments, and for the rest of one's life to persist in detesting and vilifying all discussion, and so be debarred from knowing the truth about reality.'
> 'Yes,' said I, 'most assuredly that would be lamentable.'
> 'Then let us before all things be on your guard against that: let us never entertain the idea that all arguments are probably unsound; let us rather believe that it is we ourselves who are not yet sound, but should manfully exert ourselves to become so; you, Phaedo, and you others out of regard for your remaining lifetime, I out of regard for death itself' (90c–e).

The importance of the issue, both intrinsically and in terms of what is requisite for the true philosopher in the tendance of his soul as preparation for death, could hardly be more clearly underlined; and as if the crucial point has now been made and endorsed Phaedo thereupon drops out of the conversation. This phase of the discussion closes with Socrates ironically reflecting on his own security with regard to this "danger" (the general discussion of true philosophy being seen in counterpoint to Socrates' own exemplification of the theory) and summing up:

'There then, Simmias and Cebes, is the prepared position from which I advance to the discussion; but if you will take my advice, you will pay heed not so much to Socrates, but rather to the truth; and if you think what I say is true, then accept my conclusions; if not, you must oppose me with every argument you can muster' (91b–c).

Only now is he ready to begin his detailed refutations of his critics, and to rebuild his own case.

Hackforth describes this whole passage as an "interlude" and the discussion of "misology" as a "digression" (Hackforth (2), 105 and 109), but the way the latter is presented, its endorsement by the narrator, its central position in the text, and the emphasis that is given to the importance of the issues raised, together suggest that it is rather more than this, possibly the crux of the entire dialogue; and this possibility is further supported by the other occasion on which Echecrates and Phaedo discuss the debate.

In his commentary on the discussion of "misology", Hackforth notes a parallel with the *Gorgias* and *Phaedrus* where sophistry and rhetoric are criticized by the Platonic 'Socrates':

The main ground of his condemnation . . . was their indifference to truth and knowledge, for which were substituted opinion and plausibility; but it was not always a case of deliberate falsification: often it was a negative defect, the lack of a *method*, an orderly procedure for attaining truth. In default of such method, for which Plato's word is 'dialectic', no λόγος could be assured of validity, and everyone was at the mercy of the plausible speaker, whose thesis, however, could be countered next day by one more plausible.

It is this lack of method, this absence of τέχνη four times referred to (89d5, e7, 90b7, d3), that is uppermost in Plato's mind in the present section; later in the dialogue he will let Socrates describe his own method of seeking truth (110).

The reference he gives for this later passage (99d ff.; the discussion of the so called "hypothetical method") turns out to be crucially relevant to Echecrates' and Phaedo's second intervention.

Socrates has been discussing his own intellectual development, and the impasse into which his original investigations had led him; he then tells, in a notoriously condensed passage, of his decision to change his approach and have recourse instead to "a second-best method to help my quest of τῆς αἰτίας" (99d).[9]

'I decided I must take refuge in propositions, and study the truth of things in them. . . . On each occasion I assume the proposition which I judge to be the soundest, and I put down as true whatever seems to me to be in agreement with this, whether the question is about αἰτίας or anything else; what does not seem to be in agreement I put down as false. But I should like to make my meaning clearer to you: I fancy you don't as yet understand.'
'Indeed no,' said Cebes, 'not very well' (99e–100a).

We may well sympathize with Cebes, and indeed it would appear that we are supposed to do so—for Socrates purports to explain his meaning by giving an example (which uses the existence of the forms as representing the proposition assumed), taking us through the argument so engendered and elaborating on the method advocated in the light of it, until the climax:

'What you say', replied Simmias and Cebes together, 'is perfectly true.'
Echecrates. Upon my word, Phaedo, they had good reason to say so. As I see it, Socrates made matters wonderfully clear even to a feeble intelligence.
Phaedo. Just so, Echecrates: that is what everyone there thought.
Echecrates. As do we who were not there, your present audience. But how did the conversation proceed?
Phaedo. It was like this, I think. When Socrates had gained their assent (102a–b).

Few of us like to think that our intelligence is less than feeble, thus this latter passage acts as a rhetorical device encouraging us to go along with a particularly difficult piece of argument by suggesting that to understand it is to see its validity; both of Socrates' critics are immediately convinced—it is the only time they speak in chorus in the dialogue. The reference to "we who were not there, your present audience" seems a particularly clear, even brazen, indication that the auditors (or readers) of the dialogue should involve themselves in this argument above all. But what is this argument? It is tempting to see the postulation of the forms as αἰτίαι as the crucial thesis to which we are being invited to assent,[10] and there is some

---

[9] I leave the Greek instead of using Hackforth's traditional translation of αἰτία ('cause') for reasons which will become clear later.
[10] Strictly, it is only the existence of the forms that is said to be "Hypothesised"; but as Gallop (179) urges, the thesis that the forms have an explanatory function is inseparable from that hypothesis "being integral to the Theory of Forms itself".

truth in the suggestion; this postulation is the one chosen to exemplify the method, is used to ground the final and "decisive" argument for immortality, and—as we know from other dialogues —plays a crucial role in Plato's thinking at this time. But it is not the whole truth, for this rhetorical passage clearly serves to counterbalance Cebes' initial lack of understanding of the method involved, and the chorus of assent is in direct response to Socrates' elaboration of the method in the light of the example; so it is not just the example but also the method which is here underlined and endorsed.

Thus Plato intrudes the "frame" of his dialogue to underwrite and emphasize the importance of argument, the need for a method of discriminating good from bad argument, and the method both proposed and used by Socrates. From this it would appear that the issue of the nature of true philosophy, as exemplified by Socrates the true philosopher and with particular relation to the nature of philosophic argument, is central to the work. And this supposition is at once endorsed and modified by considering another theme which is foreshadowed in the "overture": that of religion.

In the preliminary conversation we are told that after "the priest of Apollo has crowned the ship's stern" no public execution can take place until the ship has returned from Delos; Socrates is thus living, and the whole discussion taking place, under the aegis of a temporary reprieve provided out of respect for Apollo; already, for those who remember the *Apology*, a hint is here provided that there is more to this than immediately meets the eye. The god in question is Apollo Hyperboreus of Delos, but—as Burnet points out— "there would be no difficulty in identifying him with the Pythian Apollo who had given the famous oracle, and to whose service, as we know from the *Apology*, Socrates regarded himself as consecrated" (Burnet, note to 60d2). These cues are immediately taken up when Socrates explains his reasons for composing a hymn to Apollo: "my first work was in honour of the god whose feast was being kept" (61b) in order to discharge "a sacred obligation" laid upon him by a figure who constantly came to him in his dreams, and whose repeated injunction—"Socrates, be diligent and make music"—he had hitherto taken as encouraging him to continue with philosophy; again we have echoes of the *Apology*, where Socrates claims to have had the philosophical task he undertook in response to Apollo's oracle enjoined upon him "through oracles and dreams" (*Apology*, 33c). These echoes and hints are crystallized later in the *Phaedo* when at 85b Socrates associates Apollo with prophetic song and describes himself as "dedicated" to him. So the whole debate is only able to take place under the protection of the god who first put Socrates' feet on the path of philosophy, to whom Socrates regards himself as dedicated, who is the god of music, and who is explicitly associated with prophetic song. The discussion opens with an explanation of Socrates' attempt to "make music in the commonly accepted sense" in honour of that god, and an association is made between "making music" and doing philosophy. Hackforth purports to explain this by remarking that "we are still probably in the realm of historical fact" (Hackforth (2), 36), but if the matter is left there we are presented at the outset of this "work of supreme art" with an unassimilated historical gobbet. The antecedent improbability of this suggestion is strengthened when we remember that historical considerations need not rule out aesthetic ones and that the overall strategy of the work is to use the historical setting as a springboard rather than as a constraint.[11] Thus it is worth considering whether the relation between Socrates and Apollo is used to throw light either on Socrates' activity as recounted in the dialogue or on philosophizing more generally.

In seeking answers to these questions, we find that they interlock illuminatingly with what we have already learnt from Plato's use of his structural "framing" device. Let us start with Socrates' initial explanation of his "music-making". Here two crucial terms stand out, μουσική and μῦθος, both of which appear in the text for the first time. With regard to the former Hackforth's note is to the point:

μουσική must inevitably be translated by 'music'; in Greek it sometimes of course has that meaning, but it is often used to cover anything over which one of the Muses presided, so gaining the associations of 'humanism' or 'culture' . . . [It] is in essence the culture or tendance of the soul or spirit, . . . and 'philosophy' for Socrates meant just that. In fact, the interpretation which he put upon this dream, until in the last days he substituted a

---

[11] That the *Phaedo* should not be understood in terms of the constraints of historical recording is now generally recognized. For a particularly striking local example (among many) of use of the historical setting for theoretical purposes, see the use of the prison in which the discussion takes place as an image of the body in relation to the soul, noted by Gallop (76 and 226). See also my discussion of Socrates' last words, below.

different one, is precisely that which he conceived as his divine mission according to the *Apology*: 'God laid upon me, so I thought and believed, the duty of living a life of philosophy, examining both myself and others' (37–8).

So philosophy is conceived of by Socrates as an activity which can be aptly thought of as coming under the patronage of the Muses, and characterized by a term which includes the literal making of music as one of its central meanings; it is further indicated that a life dedicated to philosophy can properly be seen as an appropriate consequence of dedication to the god of music.

This association of philosophy with the making of music is elaborated later in the dialogue. Socrates has developed a battery of arguments in favour of the immortality of the soul, and concluded with a sustained flight of eloquence to the effect that we need have no fear of death. After a brief silence and hesitation Simmias indicates that neither he nor Cebes are fully convinced, but are reluctant to urge their points in view of Socrates' "sad situation".

At this Socrates smiled and proceeded: 'Dear me, Simmias. It looks as if I should have a hard task to convince the world in general that I don't consider my present situation a sad one, when I can't convince even you two, who are so afraid that I am in a more disagreeable plight now than I ever was before. And I fancy you must think me a poorer sort of prophet than the swans; for they, when they realise that they have to die, sing more, and sing more sweetly than they have ever sung before, rejoicing at the prospect of going into the presence of that god whose servants they are; . . . belonging as they do to Apollo, they are prophetic creatures who foresee the blessings in store for them in Hades, and therefore sing with greater delight on that last day than ever before. And as for me, I count myself a fellow-servant of the swans, dedicated to the same god, and favoured by my master with prophetic power equal to theirs; nor am I more sorrowful than they in departing this life. No; so far as that goes, you should say what you will and ask what you will, so long as the prison authorities of Athens permit you' (84d–85b).

Here we have Socrates' conduct on his last day—with special reference to the cut and thrust of philosophical debate—being compared at once to song and to prophecy, both under the patronage of that god to whom the very possibility of this last day's activity is owed. Philosophic argument, we remember, is for Socrates a sacred obligation, and (as we have seen) his first move after Simmias and Cebes have had their say is to warn against distrusting it; now it is suggested that there is a prophetic and a "musical" element in philosophical endeavour. We are reminded of the earlier occasion on which Simmias and Cebes have expressed doubts, when Socrates spoke of the persuasive power of arguments in terms of pronouncing "charms" to drive such doubts away; Socrates himself, indeed, was then characterized by Cebes as "an expert at such charms" (77e–78a). These associations and images are difficult to interpret, but they seem to hint at a conception of the philosophical activity which goes beyond mere argumentation,[12] and these hints are filled out if we consider the other critical term I mentioned as relevant in Socrates' explanation of his "musical" activities—the word μῦθος.

This term is first used in contrast to λόγος, in which case—as Burnet remarks—"the distinction is almost the same as ours between 'fiction' and 'fact'" (Burnet, note to 61b4). Socrates explains that

feeling that one who means to be a real maker of music should concern himself with fancy rather than fact, and that I myself had no gift for that sort of thing, I made my poems out of the first readily available material, something that I knew by heart, namely Aesop's fables (61b).

Twenty-eight lines later we find the word μυθολογεῖν, but this time in the context of that music-making which is philosophy. Here again Socrates claims to have gathered his material from elsewhere, and once more there is a contrast with that which is less "mythical":

A question then came from Cebes: 'How do you make that out, Socrates, that it is wicked to do violence to oneself, and yet that a philosopher will be ready to follow in the steps of the dying?'

'What, Cebes? Haven't you and Simmias been told about such matters in your studies with Philolaus?'

'Nothing definite, Socrates.'

'Well, of course I myself can only say what I have been told about it; however, I have no objection to repeating that; indeed I suppose it is highly suitable, now that I am on the point of passing to another place, that I should examine our ideas about it, and let fancy dwell upon our habitation yonder. What else should one do until the sun goes down?' (61d–e).

---

[12] While evidence from later dialogues about the interpretation of terms used in earlier ones needs to be used with considerable caution, the account of μουσική in the *Laws* (658–60) as producing "charms" which promote a harmony between "right reason" and the emotions is fully concordant with the interpretation offered in the text.

It is far from clear how seriously we are supposed to take the contrast between "examining ideas" and "mythologizing" ("letting fancy dwell"), partly because—as the dialogue proceeds—the two activities turn out to be very closely intertwined.[13] There is a temptation to divide the bulk of the work into two parts; the first being given over to philosophical argument (examining ideas) and the second to mythologizing; one is then faced with the task of explaining the relation between these two disparate parts. But this is to misconstrue the text, for the parts are more interdependent than this (fairly standard) interpretation would have us believe.

In the first place, stories about "our habitation yonder" are employed several times in this "first part" of the dialogue; the most obvious examples are at 69c–d, where the stories associated with "mystery rites" are invoked, and at 80d–82d, where the fate of the philosopher's soul is contrasted with that of others. In each case the "myth" is introduced as the culmination of a pattern of argument, although in the second instance it is immediately followed by an explanation (in response to a question by Cebes) of the way in which the story fits in with the arguments that have gone before.

Secondly, Socrates does not unambiguously term the whole of the story about the soul and its habitations in the "second part" mythical; he only claims to be introducing μῦθος when he enters upon his description of the "upper earth" (110b). However, there appears to be some flexibility in Socrates' use of the word, and once the story is done he remarks

'Now to affirm confidently that these things are as I have told them would not befit a man of good sense; yet seeing that the soul is found to be immortal, I think it is befitting to affirm that this or something like it is the

---

[13] As is noted by Gallop (78 and 228) who does not however, explore the implications of "argument and tale-telling being interwoven throughout". For a complete listing of Plato's use of μῦθος and its derivatives, see Zaslavsky (app. 1). In his analysis of this material, Zaslavsky limits the Platonic use of this term to indicate "a synoptic genetic account" (96); on his account, several of the examples I discuss count as ἀκοαί or παραμυθίαι. However, his discussion, though valuable, is limited by failure to consider the use of such (listed) derivatives as μυθολογεῖν and to take account of several of the types of consideration presented in the text; further, the sharp distinction drawn between 'myths' and 'paramyths' such that all the latter are "lies" but the former need not be is grounded in an unimpressive reading (210–14) of the opening of bk. x of the *Laws*, and the crucial passage at *Gorgias* 523a is susceptible of other interpretations than the one offered in ch. 7. With respect to the *Phaedo*, Zaslavsky's analysis (132) of 60d–61b is ingenious rather than convincing and should be compared with that of Dorter (6–8).

truth about our souls and their habitations. I think too that we should do well in venturing—and a glorious venture it is—to believe it to be so. And we should treat such tales as spells to pronounce over ourselves, as in fact has been my own purpose all this while in telling my long story [τὸν μῦθον]' (114d).

Hackforth suggests that "my long story" covers the whole of the "second part" (Hackforth (2), 171–5), and in view of the way this passage picks up Socrates' programmatic remark at its start—"now that we have found the soul to be immortal" (107c)—this seems plausible. But associations are also being made with the arguments of the "first part", for the word Hackforth here translates as "spells" is the same that he translates as "charms" at 77e where, as we have seen, the persuasive power of arguments is spoken of in terms of pronouncing charms.

Now clearly there is some difference between pronouncing charms by means of argument and doing so by mythologizing, and Socrates provides a clue to his understanding of the difference early on when he says

'But as it is, rest assured that I will expect to join the company of good men, though that indeed I will not affirm with full certainty; but that I shall come to be with gods that are the best of masters, yes: you may rest assured that, if there is one thing that I will affirm in such a matter, it is that' (63b–c).

Exactly what Socrates means by being "with gods that are the best of masters" is far from clear, but the main point is that his soul will both exist and be benefited after death. It is of this that he is fully convinced, though how this will occur is less certain. Now the "arguments" in the dialogue are concerned to show that the soul is immortal and that this immortality is desirable for the true philosopher, but the "mythologizing" is concerned with the manner of the soul's existence after death, of which the best that we can say is "that this or something like it is the truth".

But it does not follow from this that we are faced with a simple contrast between imaginative conjecture and "scientific proof".[14] On the one hand there are controls on the conjectures, both rational in that they arise out of and have to be justified in terms of the argumentation (cf. especially 82dff.), and religious in that they are

[14]   Burnet's term (see his notes to 61e2, 110b1 and 114d1) echoed by Hackforth (2) in the note to 70b.

not drawn out of the philosopher's imagination (for a true philosopher such as Socrates has "no gift for that sort of thing") but
grounded in the authority of religious "revelation". On the other
hand the status of argumentation is not seen as that of "scientific
proof"; not even the "hypothetical method" can provide that.

This latter point is most clearly brought out when the arguments
are at length abandoned for story-telling. In the course of the final
argument we have been introduced to the method of "hypothesis",
and shown how an argument constructed with its help may lead us to
the conclusion that "Beyond all doubt then, Cebes, soul is deathless
and imperishable, and our souls will in truth exist in Hades" (107a).
But this triumphant declaration is at once modified:

'I for my part, Socrates,' replied Cebes, 'cannot dispute that, nor can I
feel any doubt about our arguments. But if Simmias here or anyone else has
anything to say, it is desirable that he should not suppress it; any further
discussion of these matters that may be desired can hardly, I think, be put
off for a later occasion.'

'I can assure you', said Simmias, 'that I find it as impossible as you do to
feel any doubt arising from our arguments; nevertheless the great importance of the matter under discussion, together with a poor opinion of human
fallibility, forces me still to remain doubtful about our assertions.'

'You are quite right there, Simmias,' replied Socrates, 'and I would add
this: our original assumptions, acceptable as they are to you both, ought
nevertheless to be more precisely examined. If you have a thoroughgoing
inquiry into them, you will be following up the argument to the furthest
point accessible to man; and if that inquiry itself ends in certainty, you will
be at the end of your quest' (107a–b).

That Simmias' doubts are not to be dismissed as mere "misology" is
shown by the fact that they are commended by Socrates. "Examining our ideas" about these matters is in principle an open-ended
inquiry; for however well the method of hypothesis is followed, the
original starting-point can always be put in question. There is,
however, a terminus to argument which may properly be reached in
particular cases, and that is when—having followed up the argument "to the furthest point accessible to man"—one ends with
certainty; in the imagery of 77e, one has "charmed the bogy away".
Thus the final test of an argument is taken to be persuasiveness. Of
course, a necessary element in persuasiveness is argumentative
rigour and the power to demonstrate error in counter-arguments
—hence the attack on "misology" and the employment of

"method"; but when we have done all, ultimately the test is one of personal conviction.[15]

For the *Phaedo*, therefore, argumentation is essential to the philosophical activity, but it is not understood in such a way that it excludes the relevance of other means of "charming" doubts away —as if we were faced with an opposition between imaginative conjecture and "scientific proof". So Plato is writing wholly in consonance with his general views about the nature of philosophy, as expressed in the dialogue, in running together dramatic, mythical, and logical elements. And if the whole has a spellbinding power, that is—on Plato's premisses—as it should be.

So let us consider how the spell works.

3. The Weaving of a Rational Spell

I have suggested that the opening conversation can plausibly be taken as setting up a structure and adumbrating a number of themes which are developed as the dialogue proceeds. The structural "frame" is used to underline two of these themes—the nature of philosophic argument and Socrates' exemplary role as the dying philosopher—which interlock with yet another, the religious strand in the work which presents Socrates as the prophetic charmer and

---

[15] This passage alone is not decisive, since the word σαφές is almost as ambiguous as Hackforth's translation 'certainty'; but the reading offered is a reasonable construal of the text, and must ultimately stand or fall by the way it makes sense of the dialogue as a whole.

Socrates' endorsement of Simmias' doubts about "human fallibility" fits in both with his warning against mistrusting argument, "let us rather believe that it is we ourselves who are not yet sound" (90e), and with his insistence on the importance of purification and death—"if we are to have clear knowledge of anything, we must get rid of the body" (66d). Whether or not the Socrates of the *Phaedo* would have conceded that some philosophic arguments may amount to "scientific proof", he is clear that while in our incarnate state we can never have "clear knowledge" that they do so. In the *Republic* this position appears to have been modified, nevertheless the centrality of personal conviction in philosophy was to remain with Plato. See, for example, the famous passage on philosophical knowledge in the *Seventh Letter*: "Acquaintance with it must come rather after a long period of attendance on instruction in the subject itself and of close companionship, when, suddenly, like a blaze kindled by a leaping spark, it is generated in the soul and at once becomes self-sustaining" (341c–d) (tr. L. A. Post in Plato (1); whether or not authentic, the Letter appears to be reliable as a guide to Plato's philosophical thinking). The relevance of the imagery of 77e–78a is clearest on the interpretation of Verdenius (212): "After [Socrates'] death they will have to question one another, and thus charm away their fears."

the philosophic activity he exemplifies as involving not only argument according to method but also mythologizing; these latter two
elements being closely intertwined and brought together under the
figure of music.

The only component of this initial "overture" I have not yet
touched on is the theme of the blending of pleasure and pain, which
plays a minor but dual role. In the first place it introduces a certain
subtlety of tone into the dialogue, for Socrates' whole demeanour is
such that the pity "such as might naturally be expected at a scene of
mourning" (59a) is minimized in the face of his happiness and
Phaedo's conviction that "he had heaven's blessing"; nevertheless,
the situation was such that Phaedo did not "feel pleasure in the
prospect of one of our regular philosophical discussions, as in fact it
was". The resulting "strange sort of blend of pleasure and pain"
recurs several times in the work, and particularly at its close where
the uninitiated weep for Socrates but those, such as Phaedo, who
have learnt philosophy's true nature weep "not for him, no, but for
myself and my own misfortune in losing such a friend" (117c).[16]
Now that we have learnt from Socrates we can see that "philosophical discussion"—as Socrates understands and conducts it—is
after all appropriate; what else should they have done until the sun
went down? At this level, the tone reinforces the dialogue's concern
with the nature of true philosophy as exemplified by Socrates.

Secondly, this theme provides a linking device in that the blending of pleasure and pain serves as the subject-matter of Socrates'
opening remarks, though now it is physical pleasure and pain that is

---

[16] The tightrope that Plato is walking is instructive. At the outset of the dialogue
the two emotions Aristotle was to highlight as distinguishing marks of tragedy are set
aside—"it wasn't pity that visited me, . . . so fearlessly and nobly was he meeting his
end" (58e, Gallop)—thereby anticipating the critique of the tragic emotions provided in the *Republic*; indeed, Socrates himself mocks the tragic conventions (115a)
in the lead-in to the concluding death scene with an effective use of bathos.
Nevertheless, the philosophizing is not presented as detached from the emotionally
charged circumstances as if such matters could with integrity be wholly ignored; the
Socratic austerity is here tempered by Platonic realism. The philosopher may aspire
to be "rid of the body's follies", yet it is not by pretending that we have already joined
"the company of the purified" but rather through allowing our philosophizing to
transform our familiar human emotions into something "strange" that we can
prevent them from "confusing, disturbing and alarming us". As in the *Symposium*,
wisdom is to be achieved not through simple rejection of the non-rational aspects of
our sensibilities but through their sublimation—and the "literary" procedures
employed by Plato are apt for enacting this; *Republic* 604e can be profitably read as
ironic commentary.

meant—arising naturally out of the removal of Socrates' fetters.[17]
A concrete instance of pleasure and pain is thus provided, together
with some reflection on its nature, which provides a backcloth for
the doctrine Socrates is soon to preach of the need for the true
philosopher to overcome concern with such matters.

This doctrine is introduced as Socrates' response to the insistence
of Cebes that he defend his belief that "a philosopher will be ready
and willing to die" in the light of apparently countervailing considerations, and it is illuminating to consider how Plato sets up Socrates'
opening move in the debate that is to dominate the entire dialogue.

On hearing this Socrates seemed to me to be delighted with Cebes's
insistence; glancing at us he remarked, 'Cebes is for ever hunting up
arguments, you know: he is not exactly inclined to believe promptly
everything he is told.' At this Simmias put in a word: 'But in point of fact I
think, myself, there is something in what Cebes says this time: for why
should men who are truly wise want to run away from masters better than
themselves? Why should they lightly get rid of them? Moreover I fancy that
Cebes is pointing his argument at yourself, for taking so lightly your
separation from us and from the gods whom you yourself acknowledge as
your good rulers.'

'A just remark', he replied, 'I think what you both mean is that I ought to
defend myself on this charge as I would in a court of law.'

'Exactly', said Simmias.

'Come then, let me attempt a more convincing defence before you than I
made before the court' (62e–63b).

The debate is thus likened to a trial, where what is sought is to
"convince" in the face of counter-arguments and scepticism. But
those whom it is appropriate to convince are, in the first place,
Simmias and Cebes who have already begun to study philosophy
under Philolaus (61d), and secondly those of "us" who have sufficient philosophical aptitude to be able to follow what is going on;
the fact that Crito remains unconvinced at the end does not show
that the defence has failed.

For the defence to be convincing it must not be a walk-over; thus
neither Simmias nor Cebes are mere "yes-men". Simmias is the less
acute and is sometimes muddled, but it is through his very imprecision of thought that an element of scepticism is able to be left
lingering, when all the argumentation is over, to be endorsed by

---

[17] As Gallop (75–7) points out, we need not construe Socrates as denying that
pleasure and pain may blend, "only that they can 'arise' at the same time".

Socrates (107b). Cebes is the prime mover of the debate and intellectually much tougher; later on he is to provide the weightiest objection to Socrates' position, but already by the time the argument proper begins we have grown to see his as a critical mind, and Simmias as being prepared to stop and ask questions, so that when Cebes does not object to Simmias' agreement with Socrates' crucial definition of death as "the departure of soul from body" (64c) our instinct is to play along with it for the moment. When, at 69e–70a, Cebes queries this original definition he is acting as the critical reader's spokesman, and thus our confidence in him is increased. Hence we are gradually led into treating him as our critical touchstone and the rhetoric of the argument moves toward involving the reader in Cebes' ultimate acceptance of Socrates' arguments, so that to convince him—together with Simmias, Phaedo, and Echecrates—is to convince us; if we are still not quite convinced we can identify our unease with Simmias' lingering scepticism, and as the latter is endorsed by Socrates we are once again drawn into the Platonic web.[18]

[18] The complexity of Plato's use of the roles of Cebes and Simmias is greater than has usually been noticed. Cebes typically looks ahead, raises anticipatory objections, can finish an argument of Socrates for him (106d), and has a philosopher's delight on encountering a paradox (62a). Simmias doubts the Socratic postulates, is easily caught in traps he does not anticipate, insists on having arguments spelled out (73a), and laughs at rather than with philosophers (64a–b). These characteristics inform their dual assault on the Socratic arguments which opens at 85b: Simmias criticizes the presupposed definition of the soul, proposes a conception (consistent with his non-philosophical character) in which the body has priority over it, and is soon led into self-contradiction; Cebes analyses the results of the arguments so far deployed, presents a possibility not covered by them which presupposes the reverse priority to that advanced by Simmias, and forces Socrates to move the whole discussion to a more fundamental level. The impression given by this critique of the two poles of the Socratic argument is that of complete analysis, but although both starting-point and conclusion are attacked the intervening reasoning remains relatively unscrutinized. (A fuller analysis along these lines of the roles of Simmias and Cebes in the total economy of the dialogue has been carried out in an unpublished paper by one of my graduate students, Douglas Burnham.)

From a dramatic point of view Socrates plays the role of the protagonist and the triangular pattern reflects the tragic convention established by Sophocles. But Plato is concerned less to remain within the conventions than to show how philosophy can transform them; thus in this philosophical drama the ἀγών is presented as ultimately a form of dialectical collaboration in pursuit of a truth which transcends and is recognized as transcending all the actors, and philosophy's capacity to transform the tragic emotions enables the death scene to be enacted with perfect propriety "on stage". The strategy adopted by Socrates in response to Simmias' challenge to "persuade us of what you say" (63d) can profitably be compared with those developed in Greek tragedy (see, for example, Buxton); a detailed comparative analysis would, however, be beyond the scope of this book.

The spell is thus a strong one, and the only ways to break it are either to refuse to treat it seriously—in which case we identify ourselves with the imaginatively flat-footed and philosophically incompetent Crito—or else to out-Cebes Cebes and find detailed arguments against those of Socrates. But if we do the latter we are again playing Socrates' game; we can infer that Socrates would "be delighted with" our insistence and so find ourselves engaging in philosophy on his terms, whatever the outcome of the argument about the immortality of the soul.

The power of this persuasive structure may well make us uneasy. The "trial" cannot be genuine because it is wholly under Plato's control; it is he who manipulates his characters' agreements and disagreements and finally pronounces the verdict. In so far as we participate in it we find ourselves manipulated in our turn. But Plato was well aware of this, and elsewhere voiced such objections for us. Both in the *Phaedrus* (275–6) and in the *Seventh Letter* (341) he comments disparagingly on the attempt to philosophize in writing, holding that the cut and thrust of "living speech" is the only form of discourse "that goes together with knowledge".[19] What we are presented with in the *Phaedo* is an object lesson in philosophizing. We are shown a picture of Socrates engaging in philosophy and talking about it; no doubt the picture is intended to be instructive in a number of ways, but it is not suggested that we can gain knowledge through it. As we have seen, Socrates is clear that his interlocutors (and, by extension, we) need to follow up the argument "to the furthest point accessible to man" before there is the possibility that we may be at the end of our quest, and that quest has already been characterized as "the attainment of knowledge" (66e).

But if in the *Phaedo* we are presented with an object lesson in philosophizing, we are also given an object lesson in a certain kind of faith. These two elements harmonize because the faith is a faith in philosophy as a training for death and it is seen as needing to be supported by philosophical reasoning. Thus Socrates' first move after likening the debate to a trial—a contest in which philosophy itself, as Socrates conceives of it, will turn out to be at the bar—is to affirm his belief that it will be well with him after death.[20] He then

---

[19] See my discussion of the *Phaedrus* in ch. 2.

[20] Compare Hackforth ((2), 41): "Socrates begins his 'defence' against a new charge, of ungrounded confidence in face of death, before a jury of good friends, with a declaration of faith so strong that he can use the strong word διισχυρίζεσθαι of it."

develops a preliminary definition of 'death' and a preliminary sketch of philosophizing in order to show that "genuine philosophers" must "find themselves holding" this sort of belief (66b). He concludes this phase of the discussion by applying the argument to his own case and invoking mythology.

The main elements of the debate have now been assembled: the definition of 'death', the nature of philosophy and its relevance to that definition, the need for argument, and the invocation of myth. It is fully set in motion by Cebes, who questions Socrates' definition of 'death' as presupposing the continued existence of the soul after death. In response, Socrates starts by invoking the "ancient doctrine" that "the living originate from the dead" as providing a thesis which—if demonstrable—would afford "good evidence for what we have been saying". He then supports this thesis by arguing that whatever comes to be comes to be from its opposite, but 'living' and 'dead' are opposites, therefore whatever begins to be dead must previously have been alive and whatever begins to be alive must previously have been dead (70c–71e).

Here three points are worth noting. First, Socrates takes his starting-point from religious doctrine; religion is seen as providing plausible conjectures for philosophers to use as guidelines, but not as having probative force in itself; reason and faith thus continue to be intimately connected. Second, the argument employs a hypothesis but does not employ the "hypothetical method" to be advocated later, for it starts by attempting to establish the hypothesis rather than by considering all its consequences; thus it is not given the weight of the final argument even though, and this is the third point, it is a good deal better than has often been supposed. The argument appears to be valid and each premiss can be defended; its most obvious weakness to modern eyes is that in assimilating coming to be alive and coming to be dead to examples such as coming to be awake and coming to be asleep Plato is in danger of treating 'existence' as a predicate in a logically vicious fashion—but it is by no means obvious that the danger is unavoidable, and it is unlikely that such technical difficulties were clear to Plato.[21] Thus

[21] The argument has been brilliantly explored, and some of the standard objections to it dismantled, by Williams (4). Even Gallop (104) who is more dismissive of the argument admits that "it deserves more credit for ingenuity and subtlety than it is usually given". The correct interpretations of both this and the "final" argument are matters of considerable dispute.

there is reason to believe that he intended this argument to be taken seriously, even though he clearly did not regard it as probative.

The argument needs support, however, if it is indeed to show that "our souls do exist in Hades" (71e), for it in no way proves personal immortality nor that the soul as shown to pre-exist is the soul that is able to think and attain knowledge. For this a second argument is needed,[22] which is introduced by Cebes as pointing "the same way" (72e); once again it turns on a hypothesis—"that learning is really just recollection"—but this time introduced as standard Socratic doctrine and associated with the theory of forms. Again the first move is to defend the hypothesis, this time by setting out to "convince" Simmias of it. Socrates then explicitly puts the two arguments together (77c–d).

At this point Socrates remarks that "you have the complete proof", but that nevertheless Cebes and Simmias still "have a childish fear" that the soul may be blown to bits after death and need to be "charmed" out of that fear. Thus it is assumed that "completeness" is not the final test of an argument's adequacy, but rather the bringing of conviction. The charm takes the form of an argument to the effect that the soul is not the sort of thing that could be dispersed in this way because of its kinship with the forms.[23] The question then arises as to what happens to the discarnate soul if it is not dispersed, and Socrates once again recounts what "is alleged" about the afterlife—harmonizing the story with what has been argued about the soul's kinship with the forms—and concludes with exhortation to true philosophy in the light of what has been said (80c–84d).

Cebes and Simmias, however, are still unconvinced. Simmias is sceptical about the possibility of knowledge on such matters, thinks that one should adopt conclusions as probable only after "thorough-going enquiry", expresses an ambiguous attitude to "doctrine divinely revealed", and produces a counter-example. Cebes agrees that the soul's kinship with the forms makes it "stronger and longer-lasting than a body", but objects that we cannot know it is

[22] As Hackforth (2) (79–80) argues.
[23] This argument has also found its modern defenders. For example, Dorter (72–6) holds that it is at once "the most important" and "the most persuasive" of the arguments for immortality in the *Phaedo*. While this is hardly Plato's assessment of the matter, it indicates once again that even the subordinate parts of Socrates' spell deserve to be taken seriously.

strictly immortal unless it can be proved "that the soul is absolutely incapable of death or destruction" (85b–88b).

As we have seen, Plato underlines the significance of Socrates' response to this challenge by allowing Echecrates to break in upon the narrative. We are warned against allowing such reversals of argumentative fortune to lead to a distrust of argument, and it is indicated that what is needed is a method of distinguishing between good and bad arguments. Socrates then first considers the hypothesis that the soul may properly be considered in terms of Simmias' counter-example, and argues that its consequences are incompatible with another philosophic thesis which they both accept ("that learning is recollection" (92c)), with moral convictions they both hold by, and with common sense—this final consideration being supported by an appeal to the authority of Homer. Simmias agrees that his counter-example is discredited.

Cebes, however, is not so easily dealt with. In order to show that something is "absolutely incapable of death or destruction" we need to have a general account of how things come to be and cease to be, and this is just part of the wider issue of understanding what brings it about that things are as they are. I have used this clumsy phraseology rather than the more usual description of the issue as that of "the causes of things" because the sort of account that Socrates regards as necessary has to cover all sorts of different types of example, including mathematical ones, where no single English word will really serve. I shall therefore retain the Greek word αἰτία and thus avoid the differing associations of 'cause', 'explanation', or 'reason' in a context the point of which is to attempt to discover what sort of associations are the appropriate ones.

Socrates recounts his own early search for teleological αἰτίαι, and his disappointment when he discovered that the scientists could not show why things were as they were but only give ever more detailed descriptions of what was the case. Thus he had recourse "to a second-best method to help my quest of τῆς αἰτίας" (99d), and this turns out to be the "hypothetical method with its attendant example of the forms as the true αἰτίαι: 'that every form was a real existent, and that other things bore their names by virtue of participating in those forms' (102a–b). In its light Socrates argues that two answers can be given to the question: What is the αἰτία of an individual's having a given characteristic? The "safest" answer is that it has it in virtue of participating in that form which corresponds to that characteristic; that is, the individual may truly be described as possessing those elements which together make up the logical conditions for participation in the relevant form. Here the αἰτία in question is a logical one and its point is that it weaned Socrates away from looking for inappropriate physical ones. However, Socrates suggests that there is a further and less truistic αἰτία which we may discover: 'In some of these cases we find that it is not only the·form itself that is entitled to its own name for all time, but something else too which, though not being that form, yet always bears that form's character, whenever it exists' (103e). The point seems to be that there are inferential relations among the forms, such that if an individual participates in one form (e.g. fever) it may follow that it must also participate in another (e.g. sickness). Now many of these inferable forms fall into pairs of opposites (sickness/health; heat/cold; the odd/the even), so if we can infer participation in such a form we can also infer non-participation in its opposite (if you have a fever you cannot be healthy); the initial form cannot "admit" the opposite of the inferred form, and may be said to "bring" the inferred form to the individual (fever cannot "admit" health and "brings" sickness). Here we still have a set of logical relationships, but they are taken to have causal implications; these latter are grounded in the relationships between the forms, which are immutable "for all time".

Having established this general account of the αἰτίαι of things, Socrates is ready to address Cebes' objection directly: '"Then tell me, what must come to be present in a body for it to be alive?"' (105c). The answer he is given, 'soul', then enables him to argue that, since life is the opposite of death and soul brings life to the body, soul cannot "admit" death; thus there cannot be a dead soul. As these relationships stand "for all time" it follows that "the soul is absolutely incapable of death or destruction"; '"Beyond all doubt then, Cebes, soul is deathless and imperishable, and our souls will in truth exist in Hades"' (107a).[24]

Nevertheless, as we have seen, Simmias retains a certain scepticism—congruent with his general doubts about the possibility of knowledge in such cases, even though his specific argument has

---

[24] The interpretation favoured here of this difficult and controversial passage follows the general lines of that characterized by Gallop (203–5) as 'Version B'. See also the classic discussion in Vlastos (1).

been discredited—and Socrates urges that "our original assumptions, acceptable as they are to you both, ought nevertheless to be more precisely examined"; these original assumptions presumably incorporate the original "hypothesis" that led to the final conclusion, and the relevant procedure for this examination has already been sketched:

If anyone were to fasten upon the hypothesis itself, you would disregard him, and refuse to answer until you could consider the consequences of it, and see whether they agreed or disagreed with each other. But when the time came for you to establish the hypothesis itself, you would pursue the same method: you would assume some more ultimate hypothesis, the best you could find, and continue until you reached something satisfactory. But you wouldn't muddle matters as contentious people do, by simultaneously discussing premiss and consequences, that is if you wanted to discover a truth. . . . You, I fancy, if you are a philosopher, will do as I have said (101d–e).

Socrates seems to be maintaining that when in doubt we should embrace hypothetically the conjecture which seems most probable, then scrutinize it for inconsistencies both within itself and with our already accepted beliefs, and finally attempt to back it up by resting[25] it on a "more ultimate" hypothesis until we reach something both I and my opponent find convincing, keeping the processes separate. This latter insistence is difficult to interpret, but Mr Crombie's comments are plausible:

[25] I here follow the standard interpretation, but if Dorter's suggestion (131–4 and 218) that διδόναι λόγον should be rendered 'give an account of' rather than 'establish' is followed, we are presented with the attractive possibility that the "more ultimate" hypothesis may not only be one that supports the original one but may also be one that gives the reason for its inadequacy in those cases where it is found inconsistent—which would better fit a good deal of the practice of the Platonic Socrates and anticipate a crucial element in Aristotle's account of dialectic (see ch. 2). On Dorter's reading, of course, similar considerations to those presented in the text would be relevant to deciding whether the explanation given of the inadequacy of the original hypothesis is convincing.

On either account there is a concern to ensure consistency, and this is characteristic of Socratic practice as recorded by Plato. Here is the strength of the "analytic" approach to the Dialogues, which is highly appropriate to the unravelling of several of the *Phaedo*'s arguments; for the purposes of this study I have directed attention to those aspects of the Dialogue where this approach most markedly shows its limitations.

Plato's accounts of the hypothetical method have important analogies with those contemporary geometric practices of analysis and synthesis on which Descartes was later to draw, but with significant variations; see Meyer, and also ch. 1, n. 9.

The point that must be seen clearly is that a higher hypothesis, such as one would cite in defence of a lower hypothesis, may be as good grounds for an untenable as for a tenable lower hypothesis, and that this may be so even though the higher hypothesis is true. The reason for this, of course, is that the higher hypothesis does not entail, but merely supports, the lower. Therefore an eristic could easily confuse his opponent by first producing what seemed to be a clinching argument in defence of some view, and then showing the view to be untenable. Such practices could easily induce in their victims *misologia* or distrust of argument, a condition which Plato deplores in the *Phaedo* (89d) and which is, he says, incurred by putting excessive trust in an argument which subsequently turns out to be untrustworthy. Such excessive trust will be prevented if we first make sure that there is nothing against an opinion before we consider what there is to be said in its favour (Crombie, ii. 545).

So it would appear that Socrates is insisting that we should test any hypothesis by using a method which will enable us to discern the different logical relations in which other propositions may stand to it, together with its own logical status, and hence be steered clear of the danger of "misology"; "if you are a philosopher, you will do as I have said". Providing that we follow this method through in debate with a philosophically competent opponent, then the common conviction of certainty will indicate that we have "reached something satisfactory"; "if that inquiry itself ends in certainty, you will be at the end of your quest".

Repeating the pattern established earlier in the dialogue, once the argument is concluded—"now that we have found the soul to be immortal" (107c)—Socrates considers the upshot of their findings. The arguments have reinforced Socrates' initial declaration of faith to the effect that philosophy is a training for death and that the degree to which we train—attempting to become "as good and intelligent as possible"—will decisively affect our life hereafter. And, as before, he attempts to bring this out by recounting what "we are told" in story form about the next life.

Hackforth suggests that the aim of this "myth" is that of

reinforcing or supplementing philosophical argument by an appeal to the imagination, . . . to supplement the bare doctrine of immortality, which is all that Plato conceives susceptible of proof, by such an imaginative picture of the after-life of souls as will satisfy the ethical demand for discrimination between the righteous and the wicked (Hackforth, 171–2).

However, as we have seen, this contrast is too sharply drawn, for the notion of "proof" here involved is a distortion of what Socrates has been presenting. Hackforth introduces the notion in his note to 70b and the passage is worth considering in the present context. Socrates has laid out the main elements of the debate and concluded with an appeal to mythology; Cebes questions his initial definition of death, and before launching into his first main argument Socrates asks '"Would you like to διαμυθολογεῖν this particular point amongst ourselves, and see whether or not the thing is likely?"' Hackforth comments that

It is just scientific proof of immortality that our dialogue purports to give: it would therefore be inappropriate for Socrates to suggest their having a μυθολογία in the sense of an imaginative discourse, though indeed we do get a myth at the end, when the 'proof' has been achieved. I therefore think that here, as in the *Apology*, the word means simply 'discuss'.

Here we see Hackforth reading a dichotomy between "scientific proof" and "imaginative discourse" into the dialogue at a point where there is no evidence for it but rather the reverse.[26] Whereas our reading of the work has suggested that it does not purport so much to give "scientific proof" as to cast a rationally persuasive spell.

Integral to this enterprise is the telling of stories grounded in the authority of tradition, which are consonant with what the argument has shown, in order to provide us with imaginative pictures of how the theoretical conclusions might be instantiated; of such pictures we may say "this or something like it is the truth". In this last phase of Socrates' discourse, he reworks a number of time-honoured and more recent cosmological speculations, using them as the setting for a story which is, as we should expect, structured by reference to religious traditions.[27] The whole is clearly intended to be symbolic;

[26] Compare Gallop (228): "The argument from opposites that now follows contains a striking fusion of myth with logic, and the verb διαμυθολογεῖν may possibly be used with this in mind."

[27] The use of speculative science and religious traditions of which we are today largely ignorant together serve to make this myth somewhat alien to modern sensibility—with much less contemporary resonance than "Aristophanes'" tale of human loss in the *Symposium* or even the eschatological myth of the *Phaedrus*. So far as the religious background is concerned, our situation is analogous to that of a reader of The Revelation of St John the Divine with only sketchy acquaintance with the rest of the Bible, and virtually none with the intertestamental apocalyptic literature. In outline, the cosmology is designed to cut down our picture of the world of ordinary experience to its true significance.

so much so, indeed, that the splendour of the "true earth" is described in terms which, taken literally, would have no appeal to one who has risen above sensual pleasures.[28] At length the story is complete and the moral underlined; ' "But now, Simmias, having regard to all these matters of our tale, we must endeavour ourselves to have part in goodness and intelligence while this life is ours; for the prize is glorious, and great is our hope thereof" ' (114c). And so we move to the conclusion where the true philosopher goes to claim his prize.

Throughout the dialogue we have been conscious of the pressing relevance of the discussion; there has been constant interplay between the debate about soul in general and the revelation of Socrates' own soul, and also between the discussion of philosophizing and Socrates' own practice. Now he who has been preaching and practising the training for death does not falter when put to his final test. The restrained power of the writing in this "Last Scene" has often been noted, and the dramatic aptness of the passage is in outline obvious enough. But there are three points of detail which are worth bringing out in order to clarify Plato's intentions.

First, it may not be entirely accidental that when Socrates prays to the gods "for a happy journey" to the next world (117c), the word he uses can also mean 'lucky'; perhaps 'fortunate journey' would render the ambiguity of εὐτυχῆ better. Professor Jackson comments on this passage as follows:

By praying for luck Socrates implies that there were things about the migration of his soul which were outside of his control and in the control of the gods. . . . Socrates had developed the requisite skill for his journey, namely, philosophy; now as death comes he prays for good fortune . . . just as a skilled navigator prays for good weather before setting sail (Jackson, 18).

---

[28] Dorter goes so far as to "take the myth as representing what in our present embodied existence we make of ourselves for all time" (165), maintaining that "throughout the *Phaedo*, Socrates connects his conclusions with their analogues in popular religion; . . . however, one finds that the relation between Socrates' conclusions and the tenets of popular religion is one of metaphor, not identity" (77); see n. 1 above. Gallop (222) points out that "by contrasting our earth with 'the true earth' above, [the myth] symbolizes the distinctions between the sensible world and the world of Forms". Annas provides a most impressive, if condensed, analysis both of the role of myth in Plato's dialogues and of the *Phaedo* myth in particular; her whole article repays study.

If this interpretation is on the right lines, then there may be an echo here of the dialogue's teaching that mastery of method and related skills is necessary but not sufficient for the philosophic goal.

Second, Plato is highly selective in his account of the symptoms of hemlock poisoning. He focuses on the progressive numbness spreading from the feet up into the body, but omits similar effects in the arms, let alone the more distressing accompaniments of such a death. No doubt there are various reasons for this, but it is hard to avoid the impression that part of Plato's purpose is, as a recent study puts it,

> that of illustrating a major theme in the *Phaedo*: the liberation of the soul from the body. . . . For Plato sensation is an activity in which the *psyche* uses the body as its instrument. . . . The gradual loss of sensation, then, would be seen as the departure of the *psyche* from the body. The *psyche* begins its journey from the physically lowest region, the feet; in Plato's account, it was when the *psyche* had passed out of a bodily region that was 'low' and 'physical' in another sense, the groin, the area of sexual lust and generation, that Socrates uncovered his face to make his last ironic remark, that he owed a cock to Asclepius, since he had now recovered from the sickness of being alive. . . . The vivid and detailed picture of this death that Plato gives is not that of a man reproducing an actual event in every particular, but of an author selecting and embellishing those features which will illuminate, in visual form, the intelligible meaning of his argument (Gill, 27–8).

In casting his persuasive spell, Plato here as elsewhere "interfuses" thought and action.

Finally, Dr Gill's mention of Socrates' "last ironic remark" touches on a matter where contemporary scholarly dispute is particularly revealing. Socrates' last words as the poison takes hold are ' "Crito, we owe a cock to Asklepios; pray do not forget to pay the debt" ' (118a). Bluck (following Burnet) comments "The god of healing. A cock was the customary offering in gratitude for a cure. Socrates regards death as release from all human ills" (Bluck, 143). Gill characterizes this as "the usual interpretation". But usual or not it is dismissed by both Hackforth and Gallop. The former invokes Teutonic authority:

> Wilamowitz (*Platon* II, pp. 57f) rightly rejects the idea that the offering to Asklepios is for his healing Socrates of the sickness of human life: 'das Leben ist keine Krankheit, und Asklepios heilt kein Übel der Seele.' ['Life is no sickness, and Asklepios heals no ill of the soul.'] I have little doubt that

these were in fact the last words of Socrates, and that they mean just what they say; but it is of course idle to speculate about the occasion for the vow (Hackforth (2), 190).

Gallop concurs, adding that "The idea that life is a sickness, . . . is nowhere espoused by Socrates, and is hardly compatible with 90e2–91a1. It is simpler to take the words as referring to an actual debt, incurred in some connection unknown" (Gallop, 225). The cited passage is the close of Socrates' consideration of "misology", where he urges Phaedo that they should admit that it is they themselves, rather than arguments as such, that are not yet sound, "but must strive manfully to become sound—you and the others for the sake of your whole future life, but I because of death itself" (Gallop's translation). The thought, presumably, is that "your whole future life" cannot be a worthwhile cause if life itself is but a disease.

But it is hardly a conclusive one. The purpose of the philosophical activity, with its respect for argument, which is being urged is, as we have seen, training for death; and the "soundness" to which we should aspire is one which we may only fully attain when we have been "made pure and rid of the body's follies" (67a). The value of life, it would appear, is subordinate to that of death, and how one conducts one's life is important for its effect upon one's immortal soul; as Socrates puts it, while we are alive we should "have as little as possible to do with the body, . . . keeping ourselves pure and free from bodily infection". The stress in the passage cited by Gallop lies not so much on "future life" as on "death itself"; its relation to the "usual interpretation" of Socrates' last words is hardly one of sheer incompatibility.

So more general considerations are in place. Now certainly Socrates nowhere explicitly describes life as a sickness, and there would be problems in trying to reconcile such a doctrine—taken literally—with many elements of Plato's teaching. Again, the Hackforth-Gallop conjecture is also plausible, for Plato may well have felt it incumbent upon him to report Socrates' last words, and if so we shall probably never know what prompted them. Nevertheless, this does not so much solve problems as pose them, for on their interpretation we are at the close of "a work of supreme art" presented with an unassimilated piece of historical fact about whose significance it is idle to speculate, and the "interfusion" of thought and action, "typical of Plato's maturity as a philosopher-dramatist", which has continued (as we have seen) right up to the last moment, is suddenly abandoned. But this alleged loss of artistic control, antecedently so implausible, is not properly made out.

Apart from the fact that Plato elsewhere marries aesthetic and historical criteria with great success, a principle of artistic balance appears to be operating on the passage. As the discussion opens, Socrates speaks of "discharging a sacred obligation" in honor of Apollo (60e) and indicates that the relevance of philosophy and the philosophic life to this obligation is ambiguous; in his last words, Socrates speaks of discharging a religious obligation to another god; there thus seems some reason to expect that here too the relevance of philosophy and the philosophic life will stand in an ambiguous relation to the obligation, though no doubt with its own distinctive twist.[29] And this expectation finds support, for the main themes of the dialogue are concerned with life and death in the context of what is good or ill for man, and in particular for Socrates who is now passing from life to death; death is seen in terms of escape from the prison-house of the body, which is harmful to man—"befouling", "infecting", and "tainting" him so that he has "no leisure for philosophy" (66b–67b and 83d). It is true that this is not explicitly to describe life as a sickness, but it involves no great imaginative leap from this standpoint to interpret death in terms of healing and see Socrates' last words as making the connection. This is not to say that the connection was Asklepian doctrine, nor to see the dialogue as a polemic against the Asklepians, but rather to suggest that what Socrates has "been maintaining this long while" about philosophy and the philosophic life has given grounds for understanding his death in such a way that it calls for "the customary offering" to the god of healing, even if such an understanding transcends the doctrines normally associated with the god.

Taken in this way, the passage fits into place in the conclusion of the dialogue, and we can also see the irony implicit in the request's being made to Crito. On one level he is the old friend who has the responsibility of carrying out last rites and last wishes, but on another he is the one for whom it has just been established that all

[29] The twist is prepared for at 117b when Socrates takes the cup of poison with the words "What do you say to using the drink as a libation? Or is that not allowed?". Professor Friedlander's comment ((3), 61) is apt: "To offer poison to the gods? That would be a sacrilege but for the fact that the poison here is something good, a healing power."

the connections that Socrates has been making are "idle talk", and
hence the least likely to take the point; a fact attested by his literal
minded reply, " 'It shall be done', said Crito. 'Is there anything else
you can think of?' ". Crito and Wilamowitz, one feels, would have
got along famously.

On this reading we are faced with no loss of control at the close of
the dialogue, but rather with a masterly interweaving of artistic and
(probably) historical strands. Socrates' last words are at once ironic,
religious, and philosophical, asserting no doctrine (which might
then clash with other doctrines to which Plato was committed) but
embodying a final imaginative flash of whose implications, had he
been confronted with them, he might well and consistently have
replied "this or something like it is the truth" (114d).[30] The "usual",
and traditional, interpretation of Socrates' last words fits this
account perfectly, and the rejection of this tradition on curiously
slight evidence by several recent commentators in pursuit of some
such ideal as "simplicity" throws a lurid light on their hermeneutic
principles. On the sounder account, he who has been all his life
training for death dies ironically expressing a final philosophical
insight into his own condition, consonant with but going beyond
where the argument has led. Thus with no abrupt break (such as is
forced on us by the Hackforth-Gallop reading) we are led directly to
the epitaph: 'And that, Echecrates, was the end of our friend, the
finest man—so we should say—of all whom we came to know in his
generation; the wisest too, and the most righteous.' The spell, it
may be said, is complete.

4. External Considerations

Elements in this analysis of the *Phaedo* are uncontroversial. Few
would deny that it is concerned to teach that man's supreme concern
is the "tendance of his soul", that this tendance is philosophical, and
that it involves—as a negative constituent—the attempt to set aside
the concerns of the body. However, I have also argued that it is
concerned to present a positive picture of the philosophical activity
as involving argument which—though according to method—is not

[30] It is sometimes plausibly suggested that Plato had propagandist motives in
portraying Socrates on his deathbed as no atheist; this may well be so, but it in no way
invalidates the suggested reading—rather it indicates yet one more strand Plato is
weaving into his persuasive spell.

probative; its aim is rational persuasiveness,[31] but ultimately the only test of this is the actual persuasion of those who are fitted to judge and have argued rationally, following the types of procedures discussed and exemplified in the dialogue. In this "art of persuasion" rational argument may be transcended but must never be ignored; without it persuasive spells are objectionable, "before all things" we must be on our guard against misology.

If we now look outside the text, there are two considerations which may be thought relevant to assessing the plausibility of this reading: the extent to which it fits in with what we know about Socrates and Plato, and the inherent plausibility of the work's teaching (for Plato would hardly have defended an obviously absurd thesis). On the first head there are, as we should expect, several discrepancies with the doctrine of the later *Phaedrus*, but there is also an obvious continuity. In terms of this doctrine, as outlined in Chapter 2, the *Phaedo* counts as a form of "ideal" or "noble" rhetoric, guided by dialectic but going beyond it in order to persuade the reader of the nature and value of the philosophic enterprise.[32] A thoroughly self-reflexive work, it makes no claims to finality on its own account, but invites the reader to "follow up the argument" in the context of the sort of critical cross-questioning in accordance with method that Socrates, Simmias, and Cebes have been shown as displaying. The account of dialectical method has, of course, changed by the time of the *Phaedrus*, as have the claims made for the status of its conclusions—claims which enable a sharper discrimination to be made between the approved form of rhetoric and dialectic proper than is available to the *Phaedo*; but these changes are of a piece with what we know of Plato's intellectual evolution. On the Socrates of Plato's early dialogues, Professor Vlastos has argued that

When he renounces "knowledge" he is telling us that the question of the truth of anything *he* believes can always be sensibly re-opened; that any conviction he has stands ready to be re-examined in the company of any sincere person who will raise the question and join him in the investigation (Vlastos (2), 10).

[31] Gallop (155) sees part of this; Socrates' "concern to convince himself is genuine. It is a mark of the true philosopher, and shows continually in what he says."

[32] Being written, of course, it has less scope for being guided by psychological considerations about the intended audience than an oral discourse. Nevertheless, as we have seen, many of Plato's principles of ordering have considerable impact even today (compare ch. 2, n. 8).

The case is grounded in a wide range of the early dialogues, and is very plausible. It does *not* draw on the *Republic*, and it seems likely that overmuch reading of this later work into the *Phaedo* has led to the widespread wish to read the latter as purporting to give "scientific proof", rather than as a final testament to the conception of philosophy adumbrated in the earlier dialogues—which are probably closer in spirit to the historical Socrates with whose death it is concerned.[33] At all events, Vlastos's interpretation of the earlier doctrine is fully consistent with the teaching I have attributed to Socrates in the *Phaedo*.

On the issue of inherent plausibility, it is worth remembering that Aristotle appears to have held a similar doctrine. If "dialectic is a process of criticism wherein lies the path to the principles of all enquiries" (Aristotle (1), i. 101b3), then in Plato's terms it would seem to be relevant when we are concerned "to establish the hypothesis itself", at least if a fair example of such a hypothesis is the theory of forms conceived of as the fundamental principle of all enquiry into αἰτίαι. Now we saw in Chapter 2 that for Aristotle dialectic, like rhetoric, is concerned with "what seems probable". Both disciplines may take their start from premisses that are no more than plausible, and the two are parallel "with regard to the persuasion achieved"; the main difference being that rhetoric deals with the principles of persuading popular audiences, and dialectic with persuading trained thinkers. In each case we aim at the nearest approach to truth possible under the circumstances. In Aristotle, as in the *Phaedo*, debates about fundamentals cannot be resolved by "scientific proof" (or Aristotle's "demonstration") but rather by arguments the final test of which is their persuasive success in competent philosophical debate.

The argument of my first chapter has shown how difficult it is to find a satisfactory alternative to this conclusion. Descartes, of course, thought he had found it with the deductive model of philosophical reasoning advocated in the *Regulae*; the snag lies in

---

[33] Tait (113–14) rightly objects to attempts to read the *Republic* into the *Phaedo*'s account of hypothetical method: "A passage in any dialogue should be interpreted in the first instance within the context of that dialogue, not in the light of a later one. . . . To believe in the 'Unity of Plato's Thought' is not to deny its development." His claim that when the "something satisfactory" aimed at by the method has been achieved, then "truth will have been reached adequate to the subject of investigation as thus far comprehended" has obvious affinities with my own account.

the starting-point of the deductions, as Aristotle had long ago seen. Thus we find philosophers like Waismann coming close to that "misology" which arises from despairing of argument: 'Philosophic arguments are not deductive; therefore they are not rigorous; and therefore they don't prove anything' (Waismann, 471). The concern of philosophy is not with proofs and rigour, but rather with aiding our understanding by means of examples.

The Socrates of the *Phaedo* would certainly have sternly rebuked any traces of misology implicit in such abandoning of philosophy's claims to "rigour", but he would have endorsed the importance of aiding our understanding by means of examples. He might have suggested that too sharp a wedge was being driven between rigorous argument and the use of examples—to which he would, no doubt, have added "stories"—as smacking too much of the dichotomy between "scientific proof" and "imaginative discourse" which we have seen Hackforth so anxious to foist upon him. We have seen how he might have attempted to sustain his case. In short, the teaching about philosophical method I have discerned in the *Phaedo* is by no means irrelevant to current philosophical discussion. Regardless of the final success of the arguments for immortality it contains, if we interpret the dialogue on its own terms we find that it is worth taking seriously.

4

Job versus His Comforters:
Rival Paradigms of "Wisdom"

1. On Approaching the Book of Job

The Biblical Book of Job is the most elusive of all the texts we are to consider. The standard categories of philosophical and literary analysis here seem to be at their least appropriate, and the attempts by scholars to explore its form and content have proved notoriously inconclusive. More than eighty years ago MacDonald drew sceptical conclusions from these difficulties:

No two exegetes have yet agreed as to what the writer intended to teach. May we not cut the knot and say that he did not intend to teach anything? He followed the instincts of his being and created in language. . . . The poet of Job created, but that which he created is strangely amorphous to us. We cannot place it in any of our divisions of literature; it is not drama, nor lyric, nor epic; it is not novel, nor essay, nor romance (MacDonald, 70–1).

Fifty years later we find Pfeiffer sounding a similar note:

We should not impose the straitjacket of our Aristotelian logic and consistency on an ancient Oriental poet of great imagination and insight, and expect that his work should fit within one of our categories as purely lyric, epic, dramatic or didactic. The Book of Job which left the hands of the original author is not necessarily in harmony with the literary standards demanded of it by modern critics (Pfeiffer, 674).

But although the work is highly enigmatic it is not unintelligible, and repays serious study. Even MacDonald admitted that poetry "may, even must, teach", and for two millennia men have found that in wrestling with it they have learned much.[1]

---

[1] MacDonald's comments may be instructively compared with those of Gray: 'It would no doubt be as inadequate a description of Job, as, for example, of *Paradise Lost*, to call it merely a didactic poem; it would be even further from the truth to regard it as a purely objective dramatic poem in which the author maintained an interested but quite impartial attitude towards the various characters which are introduced and the various points of view which are expressed by them' (Driver and Gray, li). For an authoritative survey of modern Job scholarship, see Barr.

At the heart of the book is the dialogue between Job and his friends about the explanation and significance of his misfortunes; Job is convinced that he has committed no sins such as would justify his sufferings in terms of punishment, and thus the issue is broadened to include the general question of why God permits the innocent to suffer. The Book of Job faces us in an acute form with the so-called "problem of evil", an issue of perennial philosophical and theological concern, and explores it in a way which readers have found rewarding over the centuries. But when we attempt to assess its explorations, we are told that the canons of "Aristotelian logic" are inadequate or inappropriate, and its methods of procedure are certainly far removed from those of a philosophical or theological demonstration *more geometrico*.

In the light of previous discussion this should come as no surprise. The nature of God, with particular reference to his justice in relation to men, represents one of the "fundamental principles" of the "science" of theology, and thus even on Aristotle's own showing we should not look for demonstrative methods here. But when we investigate the book's actual procedures we find such great difficulty in characterizing them that some have been led to doubt whether they should be seen as being "intended to teach" or persuade at all; to use another Aristotelian classification, in so far as rhetoric is essentially concerned with persuasion, is there any rhetoric to explore?[2]

Detailed examination suggests that the situation is not so desperate as many have supposed, for many of the apparently insoluble disputes that have divided the scholars have been of those scholars' own making. Job is notorious as a text into which commentators have read their own preconceptions:

With some notable exceptions, Jewish interpreters in the premodern period Judaized Job and Christian expositors Christianized him. . . . Even in the modern period and in some contemporary writing the interpreter's intellectual preoccupation still tends to determine his reading of the book and causes an adaptation of Job to his own thinking or needs. The rationalist, the idealist, the psychologist, the existentialist—each is tempted to appropriate the book of Job as documentation of his own interest (Glatzer (2), 11–12).

---

[2] Appeals to "intention" are more than usually barren, for there is even less agreement about the nature of the work's authorship than there is about its own character.

But eisegesis goes further than this; insistence that the work is "poetry" and hence to be seen neither as "teaching" nor as wrestling with serious intellectual problems trades on anachronously conceived alternatives in a way similar to that in which we saw philosophers attempting to claim the *Phaedo* for logic at the expense of drama. We should explore Job in the light of categories more nearly contemporary with it if we wish to understand the text.

2. Textual Integrity

> Where understanding fails, says Goethe, there immediately comes a word to take its place. In this case the word is 'text'.
>
> (Cioffi, 101)

Cioffi's trenchant criticism is pertinent here, for what is to be counted as the text of Job remains a much disputed question. The classical Hebrew Massoretic text provides us, of course, with our starting-point; it has clearly suffered from various corruptions —and other ancient versions cast light on some of these—but in general it provides us with the text as it stood when the Hebrew canon was closed. However, there are signs that by then there had already been both interpolation and disturbance on a large scale; how clear these signs are and how the text should be rectified are matters of keen dispute. This is not the place to enter these controversies in detail but, as Irwin points out, "more than in any other book of the O.T. an understanding of Job is dependent upon its analysis" (391) and some notice must be taken of the textual problems in any serious attempt to engage with it.

The work as we have it falls into five distinct parts; two in prose, the other three largely in poetry. The prose sections represent a prologue and epilogue; the former introduces Job as a man of outstanding integrity, and we are told how God permits him to be afflicted by a series of disasters in order to test whether his virtue is truly disinterested. Although he has no knowledge of the divine plan, and despite his wife's prompting—"Do you still hold fast your integrity? Curse God, and die." (2: 9)[3]—Job bears all with patience and does not turn against God; three friends hear of his plight and

---

[3] For present purposes the notorious corruption of this verse by a pious scribe can be ignored. Except where otherwise indicated, the Biblical text used in this chapter is from The Revised Standard Version, copyright 1946, 1952, 1971 by the Division of Christian Education of the National Council of the Churches of Christ in the USA, and is used by permission.

come to comfort him. In the epilogue God criticizes these friends
—"for you have not spoken of me what is right, as my servant Job
has." (42: 7)—and "restores" Job's fortunes. These sections read
like a finely worked version of an old folk-tale, and there is
independent evidence both that a folk-tale with this general plot was
current at the time, and that among the Jews it was associated with
one 'Job', who was remembered particularly for his patience.

All this leads us to expect the main body of the work to represent
a confrontation between Job and his friends, with Job counselling
patience and the friends taking the part of his wife. When we look at
the poetic sections, however, these expectations are confounded.
Job appears as a rebel; he does not curse God, but he curses the day
of his birth and angrily attacks God for his injustice. In the first of
the three poetic sections Job is seen in confrontation with his three
friends, who counsel repentance and submission; in the second a
new figure is introduced, a young man who criticizes the friends for
not convincing Job, and calls on Job once again to repent and
submit; in the third God himself challenges Job, ironically displays
the latter's lack of wisdom and power, and finally brings him to
repentance and submission.

The discrepancies between the poetical and prose sections have
led many to attribute them to different hands.[4] Stevenson holds that
reading the poetic sections in the light of the "folk-story" has done
immense harm to their proper interpretation and lays it down as a
"fundamental principle that in the first place the poem should be
studied by itself apart" (v). More recently, I. A. Richards has
argued that the Job of the main body of the work could not possibly
be represented by God as having "spoken of me what is right" on
"any sane interpretation"; he lays stress on the prevalence of the
proper name 'Jahveh' throughout the prose sections, in contrast to
the others where 'El', 'Eloah', and 'Shaddai' are preferred, and
concludes that "Jahveh's values are too unlike Shaddai's to permit
continuity" (73).

Scholarly opinion, however, is divided on the issue. Ever since
the classic Driver and Gray commentary was issued in 1921 exegetes
have had to reckon with its detailed arguments to the effect that

---

[4] As Charles Williams remarked, "it is thought that the author of most of the book
would be ashamed of the author of the last chapter, who provided Job with a happy
ending, much as Shakespeare provided reckless marriages—the official equivalent
of a happy ending—in so many of his last acts" (Williams (2), 29).

prologue and epilogue are from the same hand as wrote the main body of the work and integral to it. The most substantial recent commentary in English, that of Professor Rowley, endorses the same position. In terms of detailed scholarship the evidence does not appear to be decisive either way; as Irwin puts it, "the interrelations of the parts are a matter of opinion: scholarly, well-considered and keenly debated opinion, but still opinion" (391).

Once we start breaking the book into fragments the text loses much of its elusive challenge. Depending on the fragments we resolve it into, the Book of Job can be made to fit all sorts of preferred interpretations. Stevenson sees the main body of the work as endorsing the position of Job's comforters; for Richards, folk-tale and poem are concerned with two different conceptions of divinity, and much of the interest of the work turns on assessing their relative degrees of inadequacy. But these are comparatively conservative critics who keep the bulk of the structure as we know it. Irwin not only attributes each of the five parts to a different hand, but further subdivides most of them between further authors; of the forty-two chapters of the book he regards only Chapters 3 to 27 as "original" and being (with various corruptions and substantial interpolations) by a single hand. Despite his warnings against eisegesis it hardly comes as a surprise to find that a Biblical text cut down to fit the presuppositions of a Christian theologian turns out to have a Christian message, which Irwin summarizes with a passage from St Paul.

Throughout the centuries, however, the book has been read as a single composition. Although it is possible to trace the theory of separate authorship as far back as the seventeenth century, the Job which may be regarded as having "stood the test of time"—as men have grappled with the mystery of evil in the light of it—has been the work of its final editor, and Stevenson's "fundamental principle" has played no part. For our purposes this fact is decisive. Only if it proves impossible to find "any sane interpretation" of the text as it stands will we need to fall back on the theory of lack of unity, whatever the historical facts concerning its origin of composition may be. It is when we attempt to consider the book as it stands, only questioning its integrity when the plain sense of the text clearly demands it and scholarly opinion is decisive, that we begin to understand why it has been found so rewarding. Its very complexity, which precludes the abstraction from it of any simple "message", provides an essential element of its power.

Given these considerations, there are three places remaining where textual problems intrude in a serious way; two of them occur in the first of the poetical sections, the other is concerned with the status of the second. The opening poetical cycle begins with Job cursing the day of his birth and ends with him pronouncing a solemn oath of innocence. In between the three friends speak in turn, and after each speech Job replies. This happens twice, but thereafter although the first friend speaks at ordinary length and is replied to by Job, the second friend is provided with a speech only one sixth as long and the third friend disappears altogether. The collapse of this third and final cycle of speeches could be seen as a dramatic device to show that the friends are giving up, but there is no sign of this in what they say and—more importantly—whole sections of the remaining speeches of Job (which are broken up in ways we have not seen before) put into his mouth views of the friends which he elsewhere violently repudiates. Past translators have sometimes inserted a "You say that" before such troublesome passages, and commentators suggested that we should read such passages ironically. But the overwhelming opinion of scholars throughout this century has been that here we have the result of damage to a manuscript; that originally there was a complete third cycle of speeches; and that the offending passages helped to complete the truncated speech of the second friend and provide one for the third. There is less agreement about how exactly these speeches should be apportioned; for this reason, as also because readers in past centuries have made little of such chaotic material, we should do well to place comparatively little weight on the latter part of the supposed third cycle of speeches.

Immediately after this chaotic part of the text, and before Job's final soliloquy, there appears a self-contained poem concerning "Wisdom". Standing where it does it sits uneasily in the mouth of Job—undercutting his final speech and both the following sections —and hardly better in the mouth of one of the friends.[5] It would

[5] The immediately preceding section is one which appears to belong to one of the friends, probably Zophar—the third speaker in the earlier cycles; it paints a black picture of the fate of the wicked. Zophar has elsewhere stressed man's inability to know the divine wisdom, the theme of most of the present poem, which might therefore with some reason be attributed to him; if it is so interpreted it must be read in terms of his other utterances. In tone, however, it does not read like an utterance of Zophar, who is otherwise represented as hasty, coarse, and bitter, far removed from the serenity of the poem. Such considerations, together with more linguistic ones, have led most scholars to treat this section as an independent poem.

certainly fit were it to stand as Job's meditation at the close of the work, but taken in its place it is probably best read as an independent reflection on the debate, not tied to any of the antagonists, in a manner similar to that of a chorus in Greek tragedy.[6] Scholars are generally agreed in taking it as an independent composition interpolated into the text, though many believe it is by the same author.[7]

Our remaining textual problem concerns the second poetical section. It introduces a new character, Elihu, of whom no hint has appeared so far, who makes four speeches in a style quite unlike any others in the book—to none of which anyone replies—and then disappears. When God issues his judgement on the debate in the epilogue he refers to Job and the three friends but makes no mention of Elihu, who is referred to nowhere else. Not only could the whole section be omitted without requiring any changes elsewhere, but the dramatic structure of the whole would be considerably tautened; at the close of the immediately preceding oath of innocence Job challenges the Almighty to answer him, and the immediately following section opens with the Almighty's reply. It has long been realized that there is something peculiar about the status of Elihu, and Ibn Ezra's suggestion that he should be seen as a transitional figure—preparing the way for the conversion of Job by arguments which were perfected in the speeches of the Lord—was further developed by Maimonides, thus gaining considerable influence throughout the Middle Ages and beyond.[8] The suggestion can, of course, be interpreted in a number of ways, but in its traditional form its main difficulty lies in the content of the speeches themselves, which endorse the position of the three friends at the precise point—Job's sinfulness—where we are assured from the very first verse of the whole book that they are wrong and where it appears that God condemns their words in the epilogue; Elihu's arguments represent not so much a transition as an attempt to expound more convincingly the basic position of the friends.

[6] Such a suggestion is not new. The comparison was developed much further than this by H. M. Kallen in *The Book of Job as Greek Tragedy*. In more restrained form it has been revived by Junker and Terrien.

[7] Its position at the end of the disordered section of the manuscript may provide a clue to how the writer's poem came to be intruded into another of his own works if this hypothesis is accepted.

[8] Maimonides, *The Guide of the Perplexed*, iii. 22–3. See also Glatzer, 'The Book of Job and Its Interpreters'.

There is wide agreement among modern scholars that the whole section is the work of a later hand[9] (or, more probably, several later hands). It shows detailed knowledge of much of the rest of the book, being highly critical of both Job and his friends, and is thus generally thought to be a critical commentary on the whole book by authors who were dissatisfied with the work as it stood, and were concerned to make it more acceptable to orthodoxy. Although for present purposes we cannot merely drop this section as inauthentic (for most readers have treated it as integral to the whole), we should not ignore these scholarly findings. For if correct, the section should provide us with important clues about the teaching of the rest of the book as it was understood by near contemporaries.

3. Context and Genre

So let us consider the Book of Job, so far as is possible, in terms of its contemporary categories. The work is notoriously difficult to date, but it is most generally held that it reached more or less its present shape sometime in the fifth century BC, with the Elihu section being added a little later. If one looks for parallels and possible models for the work it soon becomes clear that it should be seen as a contribution to the cosmopolitan "Wisdom" literature of the time; its theme and dialogue form are closely paralleled by earlier writings in the tradition, and there are clear allusions to works of Wisdom literature that have come down to us independently. The "Wise" of Israel constituted a distinctive educated class which had its counterparts both in Egypt and in the eastern countries, and whose members were frequently called upon to serve as counsellors to the rulers. In its literature the Wisdom movement shows itself to possess a somewhat "rationalist" temper, and to be centrally concerned with the nature and destiny of man in the light of observation both of the natural order and of the way men live. God's nature, and his relations with men, tend to be treated in the context of an attempt to understand the human predicament, a treatment rather different from that favoured by the literature of the religious cults.

Yet although there are earlier Wisdom works from both Egypt

---

[9] A few scholars have argued that the section was added by the author of the rest of the poem himself at a later date, when his thinking about these matters had changed. See, for example, Snaith, *The Book of Job: Its Origin and Purpose*, ch. 8.

and Babylon which are not only concerned with the apparent indifference of the Gods to the sufferings of good men, but also written in dialogue form, the Book of Job does not appear to be modelled directly on any of them.[10] Such Wisdom writings rather provide evidence of a broad milieu of thought and opinion, throwing light on the context of the debate to which the book contributes and preventing us from treating it in exclusively Jewish terms. As Stevenson argues,

When Elihu addresses Job's three friends as "wise men" (xxxiv 2), the title is to be understood in its specialised sense. In the poem of Job the disputants frequently measure the strength of their opponents' argument by referring to an assumed standard of Wisdom. This suggests that they dispute as Wise men or Sages. All the four human characters in the poem are foreigners. Eliphaz the Temanite came from Teman, in Edom, which seems to have had a special reputation for Wisdom (Jer. xlix 7). The poet's work must not be judged as if it had issued from a merely Hebrew environment (76).

Nevertheless the Hebrew environment cannot be ignored. There are a number of Wisdom books in the Old Testament and Apocrypha, and Job has significant relations with all of them (see Crenshaw). In Proverbs and Ecclesiasticus we find the conviction that God visibly rewards virtue and punishes wickedness given considerable prominence—a doctrine which lies at the heart of the position of Job's three friends; and the further suggestion of these books that sometimes God uses calamity educationally, as a means of correction, is accepted by them and developed by Elihu. In Ecclesiastes we find these convictions rejected; the evidence of history shows that the moral law is not upheld—a thesis Job is concerned to defend against his friends. The Wisdom of Solomon rejects this scepticism by appealing to a life hereafter—a notion which Job considers inconclusively several times—and concludes by illustrating the role of the divine Wisdom in history. The dating of all these works provides problems, but it seems likely that most of Proverbs was written before most of Job, and the others after.

But if the intellectual concerns of Job are those of the Wisdom movement, for much of the book they are explored through the

---

[10] Guillaume has suggested that it is rather modelled on poetic contests at Arabic fairs, and that hence the appropriate canons for interpretation are those of ancient Arabic literary criticism rather than those of the Wisdom movement. The proposal has so far found little favour.

medium of Hebrew poetry, and in the Hebrew canon Job is associated not so much with the other Wisdom literature as with the poetical books. Hebrew poetry depends very little on rhyme or metre but rather on parallelism and rhythm (which renders it unusually open to translation), these providing a remarkably flexible framework within which there is room for wide variety, and Job ranges widely within it. A number of "cultic" forms are embedded in the work—lament, hymn, confession, prayer, oath, and theophany—but this does not show that it arose out of the national cult, which would put in doubt its status as a Wisdom document; as Rylaarsdam maintains, "Job shows a pioneer effort, and a very able one, on the part of a thinker and poet in the wisdom movement to adopt cultic literary forms for his own purpose" (389).[11] Nor does the book confine itself to cultic forms. Apart from the use of dialogue we find Job's initial curse (which seems to use magical formulae), the language of the law courts, descriptions of the happiness of the righteous and ruin of the wicked—and vice versa where Job parodies these well-known forms—vignettes of nature, the supernatural and the afterlife, and even the occasional proverb (see Pfeiffer, 684–9).

When, however, one steps back and attempts to find suitable categories to describe the work as a whole it is difficult to find a route between the inappropriate and the vacuous. Kraeling's suggestion (238) that the book is a combination of character dialogue (predominating in the first half) and philosophical dialogue (predominating in the second) is as helpful as any, though the prologue and epilogue only fit uneasily into this scheme and the term 'dialogue' has to be treated with some caution.[12] Other suggestions have included "A poem with dramatic movement and essentially didactic tendency",[13] "A dramatic poem framed in an epic story" (Moulton, 1034), an "epic of the inner life" (Genung, 20–6), and "An epopee

---

[11] The significance of this incorporation of cultic forms into a Wisdom book will appear later; see n. 56.

[12] Cf. Driver and Gray, xxiv: 'It is barely possible, though not probable, . . . that the author of Job wrote later than Plato; yet between the dialogue of Job, consisting exclusively of long set speeches in poetical form, and the prose dialogues of Plato, with their closely knit analytical argument carried on by means of much quickly responsive conversation, the difference is so great that the probability that the Hebrew writer was influenced by those Greek literary models is so slight as to be negligible.'

[13] Delitzsch, *Das Buch Hiob*, 15; cited from Pfeiffer, 684.

of mankind, a theodicy of God".[14] All this lends support to Irwin's (somewhat florid) insistence that

No engrossment in formal features may obscure the basic reality that the concern of the authors of the book far transcended limits and guides of rules for writing, which instead they used only as tools for their high purpose. The essential matter in a study of the Book of Job is the thought and its movement, therein presented (392).

To an examination of these we must now turn.

4. The Commentary of Elihu

It is worth starting with the intervention of Elihu. We have seen that modern scholarship renders it reasonable to regard this section as an early commentary on the rest of the book by other members of the Wisdom movement, and in the book as we have it Elihu insists that he is "perfect in knowledge" (36: 4)—a phrase he elsewhere applies to God (37: 16)—without being anywhere criticized. Thus it would appear that Elihu's understanding of the nature of the debate is especially privileged. Let us consider it.

Elihu opens by criticizing the discussion so far:

> I am young in years,
>   and you are aged;
> therefore I was timid and afraid
>   to declare my knowledge to you.
> I said, 'Let days speak,
>   and many years teach wisdom.'
> But it is the spirit in a man,
>   the breath of the Almighty, that makes him understand.
> It is not the old that are wise,
>   nor the aged that understand what is right.
> Therefore I say, 'Listen to me;
>   let me also declare my knowledge.'
>
> Behold, I waited for your words,
>   I listened for your wise sayings,
>   while you searched out what to say.
> I gave you my attention,

---

[14] Herder, *Vom Geist der Ebräischen Poesie*, i. 148. Cited from Pfeiffer, 684.

> and, behold, there was none that confuted Job,
> or that answered his words, among you.
>
> (32:6–12)[15]

After further criticisms of the supposed wisdom of the friends, he turns on Job himself concluding his first speech with the words:

> 'Give heed, O Job, listen to me;
>   be silent, and I will speak.
> If you have anything to say, answer me;
>   speak, for I desire to justify you.
> If not, listen to me;
>   be silent, and I will teach you wisdom.'   (33: 31–3)

It is clear that for Elihu "Wisdom" is the key to the debate, to be understood in terms of the concepts of "Knowledge" and "Understanding".[16] This insistence continues throughout his speeches, whether or not they are from the same hand.

Thus the second speech opens by invoking "you wise men, . . . you who know" (34: 2) and concludes by charging Job with lack of knowledge. The third ends similarly and the final speech opens with Elihu setting out to bring to Job the knowledge that he lacks:

> 'Bear with me a little, and I will show you,
>   for I have yet something to say on God's behalf.
> I will fetch my knowledge from afar,
>   and ascribe righteousness to my Maker.
> For truly my words are not false;
>   one who is perfect in knowledge is with you.'   (36: 2–4)

The disobedient, we are told, "die without knowledge" (36: 12), whereas God is "perfect in knowledge" whose works men cannot "understand" (36: 29), "comprehend" (37: 5) or "know" (37: 15), for "'Behold, God is great, and we know him not;│the number of his years is unsearchable,'" (36: 26). With biting sarcasm he repudiates the possibility of Job, or any man, having knowledge sufficient to challenge God (37: 18–20), and his final words ram the point home:

---

[15] דֵּעַ translated by RSV as 'opinion' in vv. 6 and 10 should be more literally rendered 'knowledge', as is recognized by NEB, hence the departure from RSV in the text.

[16] Consequently Maimonides interpreted the whole book in these terms, drawing on a tradition running back through Ibn Ezra to earlier Jewish commentators.

'The Almighty—we cannot find him;
    he is great in power and justice,
    and abundant righteousness he will not violate.
Therefore men fear him;
    he does not regard any who are wise in their own conceit.'

(37: 23–4)

The last line is difficult, for the Hebrew has "the wise of heart"; the sense seems to be that God is so high above men that even the wisest are beneath his notice (Rowley (2), 308).

Elihu, of course, has a great deal more to say than this in diagnosis of Job's situation and in exposition of the ways of God with men—so much indeed that he occasionally seems to come close to overstepping the bounds of his official scepticism about the limits of human knowledge—nevertheless, all this other teaching is set in the context of his understanding of the nature of the issues at stake. On this account, both Job and his three friends have shown themselves deficient in Wisdom; Job because he lacks the knowledge he claims to possess (34: 9), and the friends because they have been unable to demonstrate this to him; the knowledge Job claims is impossible for men, and it is a mark of true Wisdom to recognize this.

When we begin to examine the rest of the book with Elihu's diagnosis in mind, we find that it is pertinent, and the concept of "Wisdom" crucial. Elihu shows detailed knowledge of the debate, constantly quoting, echoing, criticizing, and parodying what has been said—and his opening words are no exception. His insistence that it is not so much the age of the friends as the spirit of God which gives wisdom clearly echoes Job's criticism:

'Does not a man's mind test what he is told,
    as the palate tastes food for itself?
. Wisdom, you argue, lies with aged men,
    a long life means intelligence?
Nay, wisdom and authority belong to God;
    strength and knowledge are his own.'   (12: 11–13)[17]

The friends, on the other hand, put considerable weight on the accumulated weight of tradition and Eliphaz—their leader and (probably) senior—certainly appears to associate wisdom with age:

---

[17] Moffatt's translation, supported in essentials by Driver and Gray and many other scholars; also by RV margin.

'Are you the first man that was born?
  Or were you brought forth before the hills?
Have you listened in the council of God?
  And do you limit wisdom to yourself?
What do you know that we do not know?
  What do you understand that is not clear to us?
Both the grey-haired and the aged are among us,
  older than your father.'

(15: 7–10)

Lack of Wisdom, indeed, is central to the charges that Job and his friends hurl at each other. As none of them have "listened in the council of God" they are, no doubt, all of them deficient to some degree; the reader, on the other hand, has—through the prologue—been given the knowledge they lack and thus put in a position to assess such deficiencies. So let us turn to the prologue.

5. The "Council of God"

There was a man in the land of Uz, whose name was Job; and that man was blameless and upright, one who feared God, and turned away from evil.

(Job, 1: 1)

The opening verse declares that Job is "blameless" and "upright" —the words used indicate integrity and straightforwardness— reverencing God and avoiding evil; thus from the outset we are assured that Job's ills cannot derive from inadequacy on any of these counts. In the heavenly council God endorses this judgement, using the same formula, and declares that in these respects "there is none like him on the earth" (1: 8 and 2: 3). The Satan, however, casts doubt on his integrity:

'Does Job fear God for naught? Hast thou not put a hedge about him and his house and all that he has, on every side? Thou hast blessed the work of his hands, and his possessions have increased in the land. But put forth thy hand now, and touch all that he has, and he will curse thee to thy face' (1: 9–11).

God permits the test to be made. All Job's possessions are stripped from him and his children are killed, but Job passes the test:

Then Job arose, and rent his robe, and shaved his head, and fell upon the ground, and worshipped. And he said, 'Naked I came from my mother's womb, and naked shall I return; the Lord gave, and the Lord has taken away; blessed be the name of the Lord.' In all this Job did not sin or charge God with wrong (1: 20–2).

The test is now made more stringent; he is afflicted with "loathsome sores" and sits on a dunghill outside the town—probably ejected as a leper—scraping himself with a potsherd; but still he confutes the Satan's claim:

Then his wife said to him, 'Do you still hold fast your integrity? Curse God, and die.' But he said to her, 'You speak as one of the foolish women would speak. Shall we receive good at the hand of God, and shall we not receive evil?' In all this Job did not sin with his lips (2: 9–10).

Job maintains that to speak as the Satan had predicted would display lack of wisdom, and we are emphatically told that the prediction remained unfulfilled.

Having "listened in the council of God" we are in a better position than Job and his friends to understand the situation. In the first place, Job is not being punished for any sin—so any suggestions to the contrary, and any doctrine that all suffering must be due to sin, are false—displaying lack of "knowledge". In the second place, God is represented as being much concerned with human behaviour —it is, indeed, Job's very integrity that leads God to permit his trials—so any doctrine of God's transcendence which leads to the conclusion that human affairs are of no concern to him is again defective.

The third point is more difficult; it concerns the validity or otherwise of the charges that Job is soon to make against God, that the latter is acting unjustly in persecuting him. Some have found no problem here; thus Moulton sees the whole matter in terms of a scientific experiment and holds that,

so vast is the disproportion between the suffering of the individual and the question of the possibility of earthly perfection, that Job himself, could he have assisted at that session of heaven's court, would have gladly assented to the test of the Adversary (1484).

On the evidence of the prologue this may well be plausible, but Job was neither consulted nor informed, nor was he the only one involved; his wife, it seems, might well have felt differently, and his children and servants are left out of consideration altogether.

Gilbert Murray's revulsion is at least equally defensible; he describes the Satan's proposal as "atrocious" and goes on "it is like torturing your faithful dog to see if you can make him bite you" (93).

As it stands, the prologue gives some support to the claim that God is unjust, but it does not stand alone and the epilogue shows God making a form of restitution: "And the Lord blessed the latter days of Job more than his beginning" (42: 12). However inadequate we may regard such a gesture as being (his children, for example, are not restored to life), its existence is significant; taken as a whole, the book clearly sees God not merely as being concerned with human justice, but as being himself just. Such considerations may, of course, lead one to a radical critique of the morality of the book itself,[18] but they need not do so—since the more objectionable elements in this "atrocious" tale act more as stage machinery than as integral parts of the main body of the work. The major point of this part of the machinery is to tell us that Job's sufferings are within the providence of God and yet are not to be understood in terms of punishment for past sin; if the author has difficulty in imagining morally acceptable alternatives to the theory of divine punishment, part of the message of the work is that God's counsel is "too wonderful" for man (42: 3) and this very difficulty serves to reinforce the message.

However there remains, fourthly and finally, the indication that the perennial question of the disinterestedness of virtue is here at issue. None of the earthly antagonists have any knowledge of the divine plan, and the debate unfolds without reference to its details, but it is noteworthy that whereas Job starts in agreement with his friends that virtue ought to be rewarded he is led to the conclusion that such doctrines must be abandoned: '"Therefore I have uttered what I did not understand, things too wonderful for me, which I did not know"' (42: 3). The author (or editor) who set the poetic sections of Job within the context of the old prose folk-story was thus not blindly juxtaposing incompatibles,[19] he was pointing up what was in any case implicit in the poem.

---

[18] Such critiques, very different in character, have been mounted by, for example, Jung ('Answer to Job'), Weiss, and Richards.

[19] Compare T. S. Eliot's dictum that a transition between poetry and prose in a play is "justifiable when the author . . . wishes to transport the audience violently from one plane of reality to another" (13–14).

6. Static versus Dynamic Models of "Wisdom"

The prologue ends with Job's three friends, Eliphaz, Bildad, and Zophar, coming to comfort him:

And they sat with him on the ground seven days and seven nights, and no one spoke a word to him, for they saw that his suffering was very great.
 After this Job opened his mouth and cursed the day of his birth (2: 13–3: 1).

Although in ignorance of any reason for his suffering, Job curses not God (as the Satan had predicted) but the day of his birth; he does not repent his integrity nor—so far—complain of injustice, but rather wishes he had been born dead and wonders why life is given to those who are in misery and long for death;

> 'For the thing that I fear comes upon me,
>   and what I dread befalls me.
> I was not at ease nor quiet;
>   I had no rest, but trouble came.'   (3: 25–6)[20]

Eliphaz responds to Job's opening cry of desolation with dignity and consideration. He speaks as one of the Wise recalling another to the wisdom that he in the past himself taught, but in his present plight seems to have forgotten; he delicately hints that suffering shows the afflicted to be a sinner, though in so far as the sinner has in general lived a life of integrity he has ground for hope (4: 1–8). From this proverbial wisdom he turns to recounting a numinous vision in which a supernatural visitor revealed to him that the distance between creator and creature is such that before God all men are imperfect, both in righteousness and in wisdom (4: 12–21). Eliphaz draws the appropriate conclusions; if suffering is the concomitant of sin and all men are sinful, then suffering is inevitably part of the structure of human life; Job should not give way to foolish resentment, for "vexation kills the fool", but rather follow the path of wisdom and submit to God's discipline of suffering:

> 'Behold, happy is the man whom God reproves;
>   therefore despise not the chastening of the Almighty.
> For he wounds, but he binds up;
>   He smites, but his hands heal.'

(5: 17–18)

[20] Using Irwin's translation of v. 26 for the linguistic reason there given (393).

If he does so, then the rest of his life may yet be crowned with happiness and prosperity in a ripe old age; '"Lo, this we have searched out; it is true.│Hear, and know it for your good"' (5: 27).

This first speech of Eliphaz contains in embryo the main lines of the case which he and his two companions are to develop, but to Job such words in the mouths of his friends sound like betrayal—for he is certain that no sin of his warrants the suffering that God has brought upon him. His speech in response develops according to a pattern which becomes characteristic of his contributions from now on,[21] a pattern within which the original thoughts are elaborated and modified; it is, therefore, worth outlining its development.

Job opens with a direct response to his counsellor; he admits the charge of vexation but pleads extenuation, "'For the arrows of the Almighty are in me;│my spirit drinks their poison;│the terrors of God are arrayed against me'"(6: 4). Turning to God he pleads for death; his confidence in his innocence would console his death agony, but all his other resources are exhausted, even his friends who, in betraying him, have incurred God's displeasure, for "'He who withholds kindness from a friend,│forsakes the fear of the Almighty'"(6: 14), and he appeals to them for a fair hearing. Presenting human life as a time of hard service, he draws on his own condition to illustrate the point and reminds them that man's only chance of happiness is in the here and now; from death there is no returning (7: 1–10). This meditation on his own suffering and man's miserable lot leads him to turn again to God, not now so much in appeal as in accusation. God's action in tormenting him, pursuing him even in his sleep with terrifying dreams, is sadistic; God is deploying all his forces against him as if he were the primeval monster of chaos. He parodies the orthodox wisdom as expressed in the eighth psalm; the latter speaks of God visiting man in order to "crown him with glory and honour", but in fact malevolence motivates the "watcher of men" (7: 17–20). If man is so insignificant, why is God taking so much trouble to hound him? Yet the belief in a God of justice is not completely lost, and the mood of the speech alters once again in the final lines where he pictures the scene when God, realizing his mistake, will want to admit it to Job—but it

---

[21] At least for the first half of this section; towards the end of the second cycle variations in the pattern develop as if to highlight aspects of the changing nature of the debate; the disorder of the third cycle makes generalizations here hazardous.

will be too late: " 'For now I shall lie in the earth; | thou wilt seek me, but I shall not be' " (7: 21).

Alternation of mood, indeed, is characteristic of Job's speeches. They usually begin by responding to the friends—at first tractably but later with increasing impatience—and reminding them of his sufferings and God's ways with him; there follows an exposition of his hope—sometimes pleading with God, sometimes lamenting the uselessness of such pleas—set against the background of the finality of death; they tend to conclude with a return to the theme of God's persecution of him. In this first response to his friends his hope is primarily of death, but the bare hint of a longing for vindication we find in its closing lines becomes more prominent as the speeches proceed, as also does the tension between two conceptions of God. Here the contrast is between the God who unjustly persecutes and the God who demands kindness of friends and will eventually wish to vindicate him, and this contrast becomes ever more marked. As Rowley puts it, "Two views of God are struggling in his mind, and he appeals to the God of one view against the God of the other" ((2), 83).

Job's speeches, then, do not progress in a logically straightforward sequence.[22] We can speak of Eliphaz drawing "the appropriate conclusions", and the other speeches of the friends similarly display a deductive, quasi-geometric, structure; they are expounding and applying the conventional wisdom, thus the traditional methods of exposition from first principles are apt for their purpose. Job, however, is doing something very different, in reacting against the teaching of his friends he has no settled doctrine to put in its place, thus the words put into his mouth approximate to what has been called (in perhaps a somewhat *simpliste* manner) a "poetry of search"—alternating between hope and despair in a "pendulum figure" (Moulton, 1487)—conrasting with the friends' more settled "poetry of statement" (Sayers, ch. 1). By representing Job not as starting with theory but rather as faced by a (sharply imagined) situation, and as developing in reaction against orthodox theories about it, the author has encouraged generations of readers to identify themselves with him. But Job's appeal is more subtle than this alone would indicate, for he represents with remarkable accuracy a widespread and distinctive psychological

---

[22] Cf. Irwin, 394: 'The thought advances, not by logical process but through deep emotion.'

process,[23] and perhaps also type, which—despite the historico-cultural gap with its attendant dangers of anachronism—contemporary psychiatrists have not only recognized but found paradigmatic.

In the present state of psychiatry, of course, the interpretation and assessment of such claims is a matter of some delicacy—with each writer analysing the phenomena in terms of his preferred theoretical apparatus. What matters for present purposes, however, is the apparent overlap between contemporary experience and that with which we are presented in the Book of Job, testifying to its perennial significance. Two examples will suffice to indicate the form of experience at issue. Dr Kahn argues that

The story of Job is one of maturation to levels which could only be attained after intense inner suffering. . . . From a purely psychiatric point of view, it is possible to find in the Book of Job a sensitive and detailed account of the onset, course, and treatment of a mental disorder in which the most prominent feature is depression. There is an additional element: when the illness is resolved in the final chapters, a further stage is achieved—Job reaches a more mature level than that at which he had begun in his premorbid state. The vehicle by which his maturation is accomplished is, in fact, the very suffering which he undergoes (11–12).

Although his exposition of the "illness" is in terms of Job's supposedly premorbid "obsessional personality" (17), the apparent narrowness of this interpretation's range of focus is partially offset by the claim that it is "possible to trace within each normal individual something of any experience which is characteristic of different psychotic conditions" (xiii). Thus it is maintained that the story of Job "has become a paradigm of the effects of disaster on the personality of an individual" (25).[24]

[23] Cf. Strahan, 101: 'The poet displays a wonderful insight into the psychology of moods, making Job's fear of God and his longing for Him, his contempt of life and his yearning for it, alternate throughout the whole book with a perfect fitness.'

[24] It is only to be expected that Dr Kahn's overall interpretation should be profoundly influenced by his preconceptions. These become intrusive, however, when they lead him to modify the text. While relying on certain parts of the prologue, he has no use for those sections which concern "the council of God", but rather declares his intention to "alter this framework by giving a naturalistic explanation of Job's experiences" (51). He thereby frees himself to interpret Job's maturation as involving the recognition that "his previous perfect and upright image must have concealed imperfections. . . . His integrity was previously maintained only by ignoring the existence of qualities which were considered bad" (147). This, of course, aligns him with the friends whose approach is condemned in the epilogue (42: 7) and evades the central challenge of the book, which concerns suffering which is not the consequence of any previous fault. Dr Lake's more sensitive reading is allied to his greater theological sophistication.

Analogously Dr Lake, the founder of the Clinical Theology Movement, argues that the work presents us with a pattern of response to affliction characteristic of a common psychological type, a pattern which remains recognizable when sufficiently extreme to count as a mental disorder; "the condition has a long ancestry. The custom of naming diseases after the man who gave the first classical description of it could have led to the term 'Job's disease'" (558). The capacious confines of Jung's "Introverted Personality Type" are seen as providing an approximate specification of the psychological type prone to respond to affliction in ways which resonate with Job's experience, whether or not that response is such as to be properly classifiable as a disorder (572–5). Examples of those whose writings or recorded experiences indicate that they fall into this category, it is suggested, include St John of the Cross, Pascal, Dostoevsky, Nietzsche, and Simone Weil (581–99), to which list are added St Augustine together with William James (701) and, more tentatively and with discussion of the apparent paradox involved, Luther (885–7).

For Dr Lake, the opening of the first poetic section is characteristic of this pattern of response to catastrophe. Job does not curse the series of disasters but rather his birth and, having been born, his nurture. Further the dread and terror, the recurrent "pendulum figure" and the abrupt changes of mood and direction faithfully echo the pattern of thinking and feeling of one thus afflicted. But Job's thought also develops, and here too Lake traces a paradigmatic intensification:

As the book of Job's conversations proceeds it is less the mental terror that daunts him than a sense of the awfulness, in both senses, of God himself. . . . It is not the surrounding darkness that is his primary fear now. It is the character of God Himself, who can permit a man to undergo such abysmal darkness and not deliver him from it (582–3).

He sees the book's final standpoint as being that "the afflicted man will find that it is blessed to call evil evil, and, nevertheless, to endure it with God" (763), and identifies this as the classic pattern, for this personality type, of deliverance from affliction.

In terms of Pascal's dichotomy, therefore, Job appeals to the "heart" as well as the "mind". The "wisdom" it is exploring takes account of the more intellectual formulations of the friends, but goes beyond them; what is being sought is a form of wisdom that will not merely come to terms with Job's intellectual dilemma but also resolve the psychological conflict or, in more traditional terms, provide a spiritual solution. In so far as Job faithfully represents a widespread human condition (possibly the writer drew on his own experience, seen as being of wider significance), the adequacy of the book's "solution" should be assessed in terms of Job's development as it is represented in the book as well as its intellectual coherence considered independently. To see Job primarily as providing us with a series of proposed solutions to the problem of suffering, or the problem of disinterested virtue, solutions which can be adequately understood and assessed when abstracted from the ongoing movement of the book, is to oversimplify it. So let us return to this movement.

Job has appealed to the friends for a fair hearing, but this is not the spirit in which Bildad now enters the debate; angry at Job's rejection of the traditional wisdom, he introduces a note of personal animosity which becomes steadily more prominent as it proceeds. God does not "pervert justice"; the wisdom of the ages far surpasses any understanding of our own, and its clear testimony is " 'Behold, God will not reject a blameless man, | nor take the hand of evil-doers' " (8: 20).

In response Job takes up both Eliphaz's insistence that no man can be righteous before God and Bildad's notion of perverting justice. He begins by sarcastically purporting to agree with Eliphaz's doctrine; a man cannot be just before God, but this is because God overwhelms man with his power and refuses to appear with man at the bar of justice;

> 'If it is a contest of strength, behold him!
>   If it is a matter of justice, who can summon him?
> Though I am innocent, my own mouth would condemn
>   me;
>   though I am blameless, he would prove me perverse.'
>
> (9: 19–20)

Nevertheless, he will boldly proclaim his challenge to God's justice and calls on God to cease to torment him:

> 'There is no umpire between us,
>   who might lay his hand upon us both.
> Let him take his rod away from me,
>   and let not dread of him terrify me.'   (9: 33–4)

His speech closes with renewed complaint; all the care and love God
has lavished on him in the past have been motivated by malice—he
has been built up so that he may be humiliated; this may not be
Bildad's traditional wisdom, but "I know that this was thy purpose"
(10: 13).

Zophar now joins in; he appeals neither to mystical revelations
nor the tradition of the fathers, but relies on sheer assertion.
Apparently losing his temper, he roundly asserts that Job's punishment is less than he deserves; the latter may be unaware of his sins,
but God knows them and is chastising him in order to bring him to
repentance and amendment of life; if Job does not realize this, it is
because God's wisdom is so far beyond him:

> 'You say, "My life is pure,
>   I am clean in thy sight"?
> If God would only speak,
>   and open his lips against you,
>
> Unfolding all the mysteries of his wisdom,
>   the marvel of its methods,
> Then you would learn that God
>   does not remember all your guilt against you!
>
> Can you discover the deep things of God?
>   can you reach the Almighty's range of wisdom?
> Higher it is than heaven—how can you match it?
>   deeper than death—how can you measure it?'
>
> (11: 4-8)[25]

The first round of speeches is now complete; having heard from
all his would-be comforters,[26] Job turns on them—thereby clarifying the nature of the gulf between them. Ironically admitting their
claim to a monopoly of wisdom, he goes on to deny its reality:

> 'No doubt you are the people,
>   and wisdom will die with you.
> But I have understanding as well as you;
>   I am not inferior to you.
> Who does not know such things as these?' (12: 2-3)

[25] Using Moffatt's translation for the sake of clarity.
[26] Cf. Irwin, 396: 'In this first cycle of speeches, at least, they are not pale puppets,
but possess vivid personality. Eliphaz is polite and deferential, but brutal in his
pompous orthodoxy; Bildad is brusque and outspoken, but essentially kindly. On the
other hand, Zophar is hot-headed, loses his temper, and converts the argument into
the wrangle that it continues to the end.'

"These" turn out to be examples—including his own case—that all
is not well with the world; Bildad has appealed to the wisdom of the
fathers, Job appeals to the testimony of the whole animal creation
—maintaining that wisdom is not the prerogative of old men but of
God. He agrees with Zophar that God's wisdom and power utterly
transcend man's, but his examples are drawn from his destructive
and subversive acts in a passage that Stevenson (47) aptly terms a
"pseudo-panegyric of God's practices", the point being that God
exercises his power and wisdom unjustly. Job's understanding,
unlike that of his companions, is the fruit of his experience:

> 'Lo, my eye has seen all this,
>   my ear has heard and understood it.
> What you know, I also know;
>   I am not inferior to you.
> But I would speak to the Almighty,
>   and I desire to argue my case with God.
> As for you, you whitewash with lies;
>   worthless physicians are you all.
> Oh that you would keep silent,
>   and it would be your wisdom!
> Hear now my reasoning,
>   and listen to the pleadings of my lips.
> Will you speak falsely for God,
>   and speak deceitfully for him?
> Will you show partiality toward him,
>   will you plead the case for God?
> Will it be well with you when he searches you out?
>   Or can you deceive him, as one deceives a man?
> He will surely rebuke you
>   if in secret you show partiality.
> Will not his majesty terrify you,
>   and the dread of him fall upon you?
> Your maxims are proverbs of ashes,
>   your defences are defences of clay.'

(13: 1–12)

Stevenson lays stress on this speech as a turning point in the
dialogue:

According to the poet's conception Job and his comforters represent
opposing schools of Wisdom, that is of Philosophy. The division becomes
apparent during the first cyle of speeches and is openly acknowledged in the
second cycle, which commences with ch. 12. From this point onwards Job

condemns the friends for lack of "Wisdom", i.e. for want of a true understanding of the facts of life. . . . Because of this lack of Wisdom, their arguments, intended to bring comfort, cannot do so (43–4).

The "Wisdom" represented by the friends is primarily drawn from tradition and appears resistant to change; in their remaining speeches the friends show no development in their thinking, but rather a hardening of their position and a heightening of their accusations against Job. The latter, on the other hand, is still wrestling with his experience, and his thinking develops in increasing independence from the admonitions of the friends.

In this first speech of the second cycle he turns from attacking his companions to appealing to God; 'by a strange irony, Job's antagonism against his friends' misconstruction is leading him to appeal from them to the very God he had before pronounced inscrutable' (Moulton, 1487). The tension in his thinking about God has already been evident in his attack upon the friends—the God who unjustly persecutes nevertheless objects to false witness—and it increases as the speech proceeds. On the one hand, " 'Behold, he will slay me; I have no hope' " (13: 15) and on the other, " 'Behold, I have prepared my case; | I know that I shall be vindicated' " (13: 18). And when, according to the standard pattern, his speech concludes with meditation on his plight, the ambiguity remains. Indeed, an ambiguity of tone in the final section is characteristic of Job's speeches; in his reply to Eliphaz his concluding thought was that God would eventually wish to vindicate him; in his reply to Bildad he meditates on God's past love for him before declaring that it was all a cheat; so now he allows himself the wistful hope that God will call him back from death when his wrath is past (14: 13–15). Characteristically, the hope is expressed only to be dismissed; from death there is no returning.

The increasing opposition between Job and his friends has repercussions at more than one level. In terms of the Wisdom tradition, Job is represented as seeking a Wisdom other than the traditional —and Eliphaz sees this as subversive:

> 'Should a wise man answer with windy knowledge,
>   and fill himself with the east wind?
> Should he argue in unprofitable talk,
>   or in words with which he can do no good?
> But you are doing away with the fear of God,
>   and hindering meditation before God':

(15: 2–4)

Bildad is similarly critical and appears to point to Job as one "who knows not God" (18: 21). Job, on the other hand, is convinced that his knowledge is deeper than theirs, being grounded in his own experience; he does know God, but "those who know him never see his days" of dispensing justice (24: 1). Both their agreement and disagreement turn on this notion of justice; they are agreed that the demands of justice are such that, given the providence of a just God, men can suffer only as the result of sin; as Job is clearly suffering the friends conclude that he has sinned; but Job himself is conscious of his innocence, and thus his first response to the friends' reproaches is to accuse God of injustice. However, he cannot rest in this position, and as the debate proceeds we see him attempting to find a conception of God which will allow him to escape this conclusion; not having "listened in the council of God" he has yet to learn that it is their common assumption that needs to be abandoned; that the very presuppositions of the wise merely lead them to "darken counsel by words without knowledge" (38: 2).

In terms of the book's dramatic structure the development of Job's thought takes place by means of this tension, as he appeals to God against his would-be comforters:

> 'O earth, cover not my blood,
>   and let my cry find no resting place.
> Even now, behold, my witness is in heaven,
>   and he that vouches for me is on high.
> My friends scorn me;
>   my eye pours out tears to God,
> that he would maintain the right of a man with God,
>   like that of a man with his neighbour.'
>
> (16: 18–21)

If no one on earth will take up his case, his only recourse is to the very heaven which persecutes him but which he obscurely feels must ultimately be just; 'in his consciousness of innocence he scorns the friends who had failed him and turns from the God in whom they believed and the God he himself feels to be the source of his misery to the God who alone is worthy to be God' (Rowley (2) 150). From this hope he relapses into contemplation of his misery but, as we have come to expect in the concluding section of his speeches, the despair is not total:

'My eye has grown dim from grief,
    and all my members are like a shadow,
Upright men are appalled at this,
    and the innocent stirs himself up against the godless.
Yet the righteous holds to his way,
    and he that has clean hands grows stronger and stronger.
But you, come on again, all of you,
    and I shall not find a wise man among you.'

(17: 7–10)

Here we find the first recognition since the prologue that virtue can be disinterested; in the light of this new realization that virtue is its own reward, the friends are not wise at all—a new wisdom is beginning to supplant the old.

Only beginning, however; his subsequent speeches enlarge on the fact that there is no necessary causal connection between sin and suffering, either in his own case or in general (21 and 24: 1–17), but Job still feels this to be unjust and looks for vindication. In the immediately following speech this quest is once again developed in reaction against his friends' failure to support him:

'Have pity on me, have pity on me, O you my friends,
    for the hand of God has touched me!
Why do you, like God, pursue me?
    Why are you not satisfied with my flesh?
Oh that my words were written!
    Oh that they were inscribed in a book!
Oh that with an iron pen and lead
    they were graven in the rock for ever!
For I know that my Redeemer lives,
    and at the last he will stand upon the earth;
and after my skin has been thus destroyed,
    then without my flesh shall I see God,
whom I shall see on my side.
    and my eyes shall behold and not another.
My heart faints within me!'

(19: 21–7)

Remarkably, the speech does not swing back as usual to a meditation on present sufferings, but closes with a note of warning to his friends not to continue attacking him or God's judgment will smite them (the return to present misfortune is reserved to the opening of his following speech); this gives Job's affirmation unusual prominence. Unfortunately the text is notoriously corrupt; the most favoured interpretation is that Job's vindication "will come only when he is no more; but, even in death, Job will be conscious of it, and he will see God acting on his behalf" (Kissane, 120). What is clear is that Job's developing hope that in some way God will prove to be just, despite all appearances, is given especial prominence and associated with the deepest awe which causes his heart to "faint within" him.

The possibility that some third party or "redeemer" may play a role in this vindication takes further a thought which has been adumbrated before (the non-existent 'umpire' of 9: 33, the 'witness' of 16: 19); Christian commentators have naturally made much of it, but in the text as we have it such suggestions from now on drop away, and except for a suggestion made by Elihu the whole focus of the book begins to narrow on the direct relation between Job and God, without benefit of intermediary.[27] The thought of life after death as a significant possibility also drops out, as if the false alternatives provided by idle wishes are being winnowed out in Job's thinking until only two convictions remain—that God is in him persecuting the innocent, and that nevertheless God cannot be as utterly unjust as this suggests.

For reasons explained above, it is unwise to place great reliance on the later parts of the third cycle of speeches, but in its earlier sections both these convictions are further developed. On the one hand the cycle starts with a vivid picture of the prosperity of the wicked, whom God preserves even until death—when they have a magnificent funeral (21), and continues with equally vivid descriptions of the misery of those whom the wicked torment while "God pays no attention to their prayer" (24: 12); his own case is seen as a particular instance of a much more general pattern of injustice. But on the other, we find passages where Job is convinced that if God could be brought to listen to such prayers he would grant them for the sake of justice

> 'Oh, that I knew where I might find him,
>   that I might come even to his seat!

[27] Irwin argues that Elihu's use of the idea of an intermediary indicates that the original dialogue continued with this theme in sections now lost, a theme he interprets with reference to other Wisdom literature (see esp. 399 and 403–4). Such speculations do not affect the shape of the book as we now have it.

I would lay my case before him
  and fill my mouth with arguments.
I would learn what he would answer me,
  and understand what he would say to me.
Would he contend with me in the greatness of his power?
  No; he would give heed to me.
There an upright man could reason with him,
  and I should be acquitted for ever by my judge.

Behold, I go forward, but he is not there;
  and backward but I cannot perceive him;
on the left hand I seek him, but I cannot behold him;
  I turn to the right hand, but I cannot see him.
But he knows the way that I take;
  when he has tried me, I shall come forth as gold.'

                                    (23: 3-10)

The close of the above passage provides us with another fleeting
glimpse of a possibility sketched more fully in the prologue—that
his suffering should be seen in terms of testing—but as so often a
high point of exaltation is immediately succeeded by black
depression, and the glimpse fades from sight:

        'God has made my heart to faint;
          the Almighty has terrified me;
        for I am hemmed in by darkness,
          and thick darkness covers my face.'

                                    (23: 16-17)

The other hints at what we have read in the prologue during this
final cycle are more double-edged, and relate to the question of
disinterested virtue. Job complains that the wicked reject God
because it is not in their interests to do otherwise; he rejects their
conclusion but cannot fault their argument:

        'They say to God, "Depart from us!
          We do not desire the knowledge of thy ways.
        What is the Almighty, that we should serve him?
          And what profit do we get if we pray to him?"
        Behold, is not their prosperity in their hand?
          The counsel of the wicked is far from me.'

                                    (21: 14-16)

Eliphaz can only blandly reply that "Surely he that is wise is
profitable to himself" (22: 2) which begs the whole question and

provokes Job into giving further examples of the ruin of the innocent.

Eliphaz, indeed, is typical of the friends as they deliver their final speeches, in that he relies on sheer assertion to support an unchanged basic position; God rewards the innocent and chastises the wicked. Job's thinking, on the other hand, is far from static; although he feels it to be unjust that virtue should not be profitable, his nagging conviction that God will not ultimately turn out to be unjust is leading him both to an increased desire to confront God and an increased reliance on his own integrity—regardless of its profitability.[28] Thus in what appear to be his final words in the third cycle he declares,

> 'Far be it from me to say that you are right;
>   till I die I will not put away my integrity from me.
> I hold fast my righteousness, and will not let it go;
>   my heart does not reproach me for any of my days.'

$$(27: 5-6)$$

Glimpses of further possibilities have been vaguely discerned—as that the sufferings are a form of trial—but unless Job can confront God and "learn what he would answer me" they remain speculations. Thus as the debate between Job and the friends closes we find a meditation on the inadequacy of human reason as a vehicle for attaining the divine wisdom, with the suggestion that true wisdom lies not in the understanding at all, but in manner of life.[29]

The overall theme of this "chorus" or meditation is set out in its refrain: "But where shall wisdom be found? | And where is the place of understanding?" (28: 12) There is no known "way" to it, no "gold" can buy it; in short, man has no technique by means of which he may gain wisdom. Wisdom belongs to God alone, and when he created the world he linked it with holiness of life:

> God understands the way to it,
>   and he knows its place.
> For he looks to the ends of the earth,

---

[28] Cf. Kierkegaard's description of Job's dispute with his friends as "a purgatory in which the thought that he is nevertheless right becomes purified" (*Repitition*, 127).

[29] See above, s. 2. Some editors alter the whole sense of the passage by omitting the last verse—on very flimsy evidence. But the book has normally been read with the final verse intact and, as Rowley remarks, "it is a pity to rob the poem of its climax and turn it into the expression of unrelieved agnosticism", a procedure he rightly describes as "gratuitous" ((2), 234).

and sees everything under the heavens.
When he gave to the wind its weight,
    and meted out the waters by measure;
when he made a decree for the rain,
    and a way for the lightning of the thunder;
then he saw it and declared it;
    he established it and searched it out.
And he said to man,
    'Behold, the fear of the Lord, that is wisdom;
and to depart from evil is understanding.'

(28: 23-8)

The echo in this concluding declaration of the first verse of the whole book is arresting, for there we are told that Job "feared God, and turned away from evil". The implication would seem to be that already at the start he had all the wisdom that was possible to man,[30] and that the supposition—shared by both Job and his friends—that wisdom was bound up with theoretical knowledge concerning the profitability of virtue had led them vainly to pursue that which was accessible—if at all—only through the direct revelation of God. This declaration has long been seen as being of crucial significance. Snaith (70) goes so far as to describe it as "the nearest the author ever gets to a solution of his problem", and Kant regarded it as ultimately the only satisfactory solution; thus in the context of his discussion of the Book of Job he writes,

We have a concept of *technical wisdom* in the arrangement of the world which has led to a *physico-theology*. We get a conception of *moral wisdom* through our practical Reason. What we lack is an idea of how the unity between technical and moral wisdom is brought about. This could only be understood if we could penetrate the non-sensuous world and recognise its relation with the sensuous one. Every theodicy wants to be an interpretation of the world as an expression of God's intentions. But in this sense it is a closed book for us (*The Failure of All Philosophical Attempts Towards a Theodicy*, 234).

Job, however, is still insistent on opening the book. In a long final speech he now drops all pretensions to finding a solution for himself and calls on God to solve the riddle. First he lays out the facts of the case, his past happiness and present misery, and then solemnly

[30] Cf. Jeremiah 22: 16: 'He judged the cause of the poor and needy; then it was well. | Is not this to know me? says the Lord.'

swears his innocence; he goes through a catechism of evil deeds and thoughts far more stringent than any the friends have suggested and in the most solemn manner invokes his own doom if he be guilty.[31] Concluding[32] this solemn oath, as if before the bar of heaven, he calls on God to reply: '"Here is my signature! | let the Almighty answer me!"' (31: 35).

In the original text, it would appear, this bold demand is immediately and dramatically answered with the voice of God challenging Job out of a whirlwind. But in the work as we have it there follows the interposition of Elihu; both Job and his friends, this young man insists, have shown themselves to be lacking in wisdom, and thus it is left to him to teach them. By skilful use of allusions[33] he summarizes the main drift of the debate so far, and in his first speech welds together Eliphaz's teaching about suffering as God's discipline with Job's speculations about a mediator; God speaks to men through visions and through suffering in order to humble their pride—even at death's door God may send "an angel, a mediator" to bring home the lesson, "to declare to man what is right for him" (38: 23); if the sufferer repents he is saved from death, "accepted" by God, and led to praise God for his mercy, saying: '"I sinned, and perverted what was right, and it was not requited to me"' (33: 27).[34] Perhaps Elihu sees himself in this role as mediator,[35] but if so he does not achieve the response he looks for; Job has sworn his innocence and does not respond.

Elihu now appeals to the three friends, attempting to unite them

[31] This great 'Oath of Clearing' is probably based on the Negative Confession of the Egyptian *Book of the Dead*; see Stevenson, 76. It is intended to force God's hand; "Formal oaths of this nature involved the imposing of curses that were expected to strike anyone who lied under oath. If Job were innocent God's continued silence would clear his name and vindicate his integrity. If Job had sworn falsely God would be forced to intervene and impose the sanctions Job had designated" (Habel, 164).

[32] Assuming, as the text suggests and most scholars agree, that vv. 38–40 have been displaced and should come somewhere before v. 35.

[33] See, for example, the analysis in Irwin, 403.

[34] Cf. Irwin, 404: 'The sketch ends with the recovered invalid in an act of worship (apparently in the shrine), declaring his thanksgiving and confession. It merits comment that this is, as well, the ending of the so-called Babylonian Job, the poem known from its first line as "I will praise the Lord of Wisdom". . . . We have thus one more testimony to the familiarity of these writers with the literature of their time.'

[35] As suggested by Moulton, 1489–90; in the Old Testament, "angels" are normally messengers of God who may sometimes be human.

with all other men of wisdom in protest against Job, '"For he has said, 'It profits a man nothing, that he should take delight in God'"' (34: 9); in saying these things Job has both erred and revolted against God—who is supremely just as well as mighty. Elihu thus sees the issue of disinterested piety as crucial, but his contribution is weakened by the fact that his argument against Job begs the question in the same way as those of the friends had done— assuming that God is such that "according to the work of a man he will requite him" (34: 11). The friends, however, do not respond any more than Job had done, and Elihu turns on them both, drawing on themes from his previous two speeches; far from virtue profiting a man nothing, he is the only one it profits—God is too great to be affected by man; when it appears otherwise and men cry to God in vain for help, it is because they have not truly turned to him—which explains why God has been deaf to Job's appeals. In his fourth and final speech Elihu elaborates on what he has already said; God is just, destroying the wicked and saving those who see in their affliction God's discipline and thus repent their arrogance—Job should do likewise, for before God's wisdom and power man is as nothing; the speech concludes with a celebration of the inestimable wisdom and power of God as displayed in nature, and as a storm breaks from the north reaches its climax with the declaration that the Almighty is "great in power and justice" (37: 23).

Elihu, then, as well as seeing the debate in terms of Wisdom[36] takes the crux as being whether virtue is profitable—as was indicated in the prologue. He invokes all "men of understanding" in insisting that it is;[37] his reason is that only so can God's justice be preserved; against Job's objections he insists that God may make us aware through suffering (and sometimes a messenger) of sins we were unaware of—by adversity he "opens the ear" of the afflicted (36: 15)—and Job should therefore be prepared to acknowledge his ignorance before God's wisdom, learn of his sin and repent. As a comment by a later hand this is clearly highly critical of the book as a whole, implying that the situation set up in the prologue is not a

---

[36] See above, s. 4.
[37] Cf. Driver and Gray, pt. 1, 305: 'Elihu is attempting to harmonize certain obstinate facts with the eudaemonistic view of religion which he shares with the friends (cp. especially Eliphaz in c. 22) and with the Satan of the prologue; but which the author of the prologue repudiates, and from which in the dialogue he depicts Job emancipating himself.'

genuine possibility if God is just;[38] its positive doctrine is one which many have found of spiritual value and which is still widely endorsed.[39] But in terms of the book Elihu's teaching fails; it ranges him with the friends in insisting that the man of integrity does not serve God "for nought".[40]

In his concluding speech Elihu had indicated the signs of a gathering storm as he surveyed the wonders of nature. Now the storm breaks and the voice of God is heard:

> Then the Lord answered Job out of the whirlwind:
> 'Who is this that darkens counsel
>   by words without knowledge?
> Gird up your loins like a man,
>   I will question you, and you shall declare to me.'   (38: 1–3)

Job had demanded a reply to his questions; when it comes, the response is a similar demand. But the questions God asks are not concerned with Job's integrity or suffering; instead the whole context of the debate is enlarged.

God challenges Job's conception of God. In fighting for his own integrity Job has come perilously near denying such integrity of purpose to God. God's wisdom is beyond man's grasp, and the field of discourse must be enlarged and widened, for Job had come near trying to be as God, to have the knowledge of good and evil, that is, total knowledge (see Genesis 3). (Jones (1), 105; "perilously near" is an understatement.)

This key term 'knowledge' runs through the speeches of the Lord (Glatzer, 7); they take the form of questions addressed to Job, challenging his ability to know and act, and they are designed to

---

[38] It has also been seen as suggesting that any man who responded to his sufferings as self-righteously as Job does, thereby discloses the sin of pride in himself. (Cf., for example, Oesterley and Robinson, 177)

[39] It is noteworthy that in his *The Problem of Pain* C. S. Lewis presents a very similar case (see especially ch. 6, 'Human Pain'), and that in discussing it Austin Farrer ((4), 38) maintains that "it is difficult to deny that it is the distinctively Christian answer." More recently Dr McKay has made remarkably strong claims for the contemporary religious significance of the figure of Elihu.

[40] Cf. Rowley (1), 60,: 'In all this there is implied a penal as well as an educative purpose, and it is precisely here that its setting in the Book of Job exposes its insufficiency. That suffering may be effective in reclaiming to piety men who have forgotten God in prosperity is undoubtedly true. But the tacit assumption that suffering, educative as it may be, is evidence of some sin it is sent to purge away, ranges Elihu with the other friends of Job as one who does not believe suffering can be innocent suffering.'

show that he cannot have the knowledge on which judgement should rest, that it is wiser to bow humbly before God than to judge him; human wisdom cannot compass God.

In the text as we have it, there are two speeches from the whirlwind.[41] The theme of the first is Job's inability to understand or control either the physical or animal creation, and attention is particularly directed to those elements of it that have least to do with man. God's dealings with mankind are but a part of the outreach of the divine wisdom; the mystery of Job's suffering must be seen in a context wider than he can comprehend, and his conception of God accordingly revised. Under the pressure of this insistence Job confesses his inadequacy:

> 'Behold, I am of small account; what shall I answer thee?
> I lay my hand on my mouth.
> I have spoken once, and I will not answer;
> twice, but I will proceed no further.'

$$(40: 4-5);$$

this amounts to an apology for having spoken, and an admission that he cannot answer the Lord's questions, but it evidently does not go far enough for the voice renews its questioning: '"Will you even put me in the wrong? | Will you condemn me that you may be justified?"' (40: 8). Job is challenged to show his power, and in comparison God tells of his own in creating and taming Behemoth and Leviathan, primaeval chaos monsters of myth and travellers' tales.[42] Edgar

---

[41] It is generally thought that the second speech is by a later hand, and many would endorse McKenzie's comment that "If there is no literary difference between the first Yahweh speeches and speeches about Behemoth and Leviathan, then I do not see how literary differences can be detected anywhere" (471). It seems probable that it has been interpolated into what was originally a single response by Job to the divine challenge, and consequent adjustments made to the surrounding text.

[42] Both animals are clearly creatures of myth in other writings, and Leviathan is also seen as such when Job mentions him earlier in this work. On the other hand, their status here is highly obscure and many scholars discount the mythological associations; as Snaith puts it, "there is not enough of the myth and far too much of the actual creatures we know. There could so very easily have been so very much more of the myth" (43). It should also be noted that the detailed descriptions do not accurately fit any known animal, though various approximations can be made and incompatible identifications are confidently made by different scholars. It seems likely that the author had been much impressed by travellers' tales of marvellous creatures known in far places, and associated their powers and wonders with those of the fabled monsters of another age. Cf. Terrien, 229: 'The mind of classical antiquity did not distinguish rigorously between animals of myth and animals observed.'

Jones helpfully points up an important difference between the two
speeches:

In God's second speech we find the emphasis on the power of God rather
than his wisdom, so far beyond the range of man's understanding. Not only
does God ask, 'What can man understand about God's government of the
world' but also 'What could Job, if he were God, do?' . . . The essential
point is that beyond the phenomena of nature, a new cosmic dimension is
brought into the discussion. God has brought cosmos out of chaos—could
Job do it? That is, God challenges Job—'Could you create the world?
Could you be God? Can you, a creature, be the Creator?' (107–8)

Job's response this time is one of complete submission:

> 'I know that thou canst do all things,
>   and that no purpose of thine can be thwarted. . . .
> Therefore I have uttered what I did not understand,
>   things too wonderful for me, which I did not know. . . .
> I had heard of thee by the hearing of the ear,
>   but now my eye sees thee;
> therefore I despise myself,
>   and repent in dust and ashes.'

(42: 2–6)

7. The Role of the Theophany

The speeches of the Lord, together with Job's reply, represent the
climax of the entire book—but they are far from straightforward.
On the face of it they represent the defeat of Job and the victory of
his friends. Again and again Job has challenged God to answer him;
sometimes confident of vindication he nevertheless has at other
times feared that God would terrify him into submission—"Though
I am innocent my own mouth would condemn me" (9: 20)—and his
fears here appear to be borne out. On the other hand Zophar had
predicted that

> 'If God would only speak,
>   and open his lips against you,
> Unfolding all the mysteries of his wisdom,
>   the marvel of its methods,
> Then you would learn that God
>   does not remember all your guilt against you!'

(9: 5–6; Moffatt)

and the common plea of the friends has been that Job submit to the inestimable power and wisdom of God—in repentance. On this reading, God upholds the traditional wisdom of the friends, and Job's arguments against it are not so much met as brushed aside by unreasoning power and an indignant denial of Job's right to question the ways of God.

But this reading is too simple. In the first place it is explicitly denied by the epilogue, where God declares that the three friends "have not spoken of me what is right, as my servant Job has" (42: 7). Second, as we have seen, the friends have been shown by the prologue to display lack of wisdom in insisting on Job's supposed sin. And third, it runs counter to the whole movement of the work which has displayed Job's developing thought against the static background of an inadequate orthodoxy; it represents the conclusion as taking no account of this development.[43]

So let us look again at the contribution the speeches from the whirlwind make to the debate. In one important sense they add nothing; not only can they be represented as saying no more than the friends have said, but also no more than Job himself has maintained. Indeed, the speeches are often closer verbally to Job than to the friends;[44] thus the Lord asks

> 'Can you bind the chains of the Pleiades,
>   or loose the cords of Orion?
> Can you lead forth the Mazzaroth in their season,
>   or can you guide the Bear with its children?'

> (38: 31–32)

which seems a clear plagiarization of Job's description of God as he 'who made the Bear and Orion, | the Pleiades and the chambers of the south' (9: 9) of whom he had said

> 'If one wished to contend with him,
>   one could not answer him once in a thousand times.
> He is wise in heart, and mighty in strength
>   —who has hardened himself against him, and succeeded?'

> (9: 3–5)

---

[43] The first two considerations lead Stevenson and Richards to reject the authenticity of prologue and epilogue, but they ignore the third. Irwin notes the third and takes it as evidence for rejecting the divine speeches. The desire to adjust the text to fit one's own preferred reading here appears to be particularly strong.

[44] Note that it was Job, not the friends, who previously spoke of Leviathan (3: 8).

As Irwin remarks (407), in the early verses of Chapter 9 Job voices the entire theological content of the divine speeches. Their purpose can hardly be to inform Job of what he has already maintained, yet in terms of their content they do not seem to go beyond this. All of which suggests that their major significance should be seen not primarily in what is said, but in how it is said and who it is said by—and of this we find confirmation in the final words of Job; what leads him ultimately to submission and repentance is "'I had heard of thee by the hearing of the ear, | but now my eye sees thee'" (42: 5).[45] The crucial point about the divine reply is that it *is* a divine reply; the major significance of God's appearing and speaking to Job is the fact that he has done so, and it is this fact which is decisive both for Job himself and for a proper understanding of the work as a whole.[46]

When we turn back to the speeches with this in mind, we find that they are constructed in order to evoke wonder and awe rather than to convey information. Although the reader who has followed the text thus far is intended to see in them the implication that Job has claimed wisdom he could not possess—an implication Job makes explicit in his submission—no such implication is drawn in the speeches themselves, which are not concerned with rational argument. Otto saw in this theophany "the element of the mysterious displayed in rare purity and completeness", and in his analysis drew attention to its non-rational character:

In the last resort it relies on something quite different from anything that can be exhaustively rendered in rational concepts, namely, on the sheer absolute wondrousness that transcends thought, on the *mysterium*, presented in its pure, non-rational form. All the glorious examples from nature speak very plainly in this sense . . . of *strangeness* and *marvel* . . . and [together with] the whole context, tenor and sense of the entire passage . . . express in masterly fashion the downright stupendousness, the well nigh daemonic and wholly incomprehensible character of the eternal creative power; how incalculable and 'wholly other', it mocks at all conceiving but yet can stir the mind to its depths, fascinate and overbrim the heart. What is

---

[45] The contrast involved is rendered more clearly in *The New English Bible* translation: 'I knew of thee then only by report, but now I see thee with my own eyes.'

[46] Cf. Williams ((2), 31): 'The Lord declines altogether to withdraw his hand or to modify his nature. He speaks irrationally; he offers no kind of intelligent explanation. But the main point is that he has answered; he has acknowledged Job's claim even if only to rail at it. His mockeries are themselves a reply.'

meant is the *mysterium* not as mysterious simply, but at the same time also as 'fascinating' and 'august'; and here, too, these latter meanings live, not in any explicit concepts, but in the tone, the enthusiasm, in the very rhythm of the entire exposition. . . . This is incommensurable with thoughts of rational human teleology and is not assimilated to them: it remains in all its mystery. But it is as it becomes felt in consciousness that . . . Job's soul [is] brought to peace (79–80).

What we have, then, in the voice from the whirlwind is a reworking of Job's own thoughts and fears into the context of an encounter with God; Job's sheet-anchor throughout—his conviction of his innocence despite his suffering—is not disputed, but in the context of his encounter with God it no longer seems important to him, "therefore I despise myself"—a phrase in stark contrast to his final words before God's reply, "like a prince I would approach him" (31: 37). The pressure of the divine presence overawes Job—as he had feared it would—and we find the classic pattern of abasement and repentance in response to it;[47] in the context of the divine majesty, princely pretensions are mere presumption.

But not all Job's fears are realized. God does not accuse Job of sins which more than justify the suffering, as Zophar at least had predicted; nor, as his friends had also insisted, had God declined to respond to Job until he submitted. In his final speech, Job had seen his tribulations as a sign that God had abandoned him (29: 2–5), but when Job sees God this element in his sufferings disappears; he is still able to regard his troubles as undeserved, but now he bears them in the presence of God and they no longer overmaster him[48]—thereby displaying a pattern which, as we have seen, can lay claim to being paradigmatic of release from affliction. The pattern would be falsified if the release did not fulfil the earlier dread, as it would if it contributed significantly new information or attempted to falsify Job's experience of innocent suffering as if it were not innocent. The author has a clearer vision of the dynamics of human personality than many of our simplifying commentators, a vision recognized by the discerning in every age, for whom Kierkegaard

---

[47] Cf. Foster (46): '"To say: God is holy, is the same thing as to say: I am a man of unclean lips." To recognize the holiness of God *is* to repent and *vice versa*.' (The embedded quotation is from J. Zink in *Sontagsblatt*.)

[48] Cf. Rowley (2), 20: 'If he had found God only after his restoration, the book would have been spiritually far inferior. It is of the essence of its message that Job found God *in* his suffering, and so found relief not *from* his misfortunes, but *in* them.'

spoke when he remarked, 'I read this book as it were with my heart. . . . Everything about him is so human' ((1), 121–2).[49]

But the experience of reading the Book of Job is not the same as the experience of Job as presented in the book; the pattern of the work is not yet complete. Throughout the discourses we have seen Job rejecting the traditional wisdom of the friends as inadequate, and struggling to find a new understanding of God which will admit both his justice and Job's innocence; failing in this task, he demands that God explain himself. God's response is hardly an explanation, but rather a demonstration of the incapacity of wisdom to compass him—but his commendation of Job in the epilogue proclaims that the latter has been right in rejecting the wisdom of the friends, who "have not spoken of me what is right, as my servant Job has" (42: 7).[50]

Having "listened in the council of God" by reading the prologue, we are provided with a resolution for this particular case—the suffering is a form of testing of the disinterestedness of Job's integrity. But it is not a general solution; the prologue makes it clear that it was Job's very uniqueness, "that there is none like him on the earth" (1: 8) that made him liable for this test, so the author seems

---

[49] See also Simone Weil's comment that "The Book of Job is a pure marvel of truth and authenticity from beginning to end. As regards affliction, all that departs from this model is more or less stained with falsehood" (*Waiting on God*, 66). Her understanding of this model is further developed elsewhere, especially in her war-time correspondence; for example: 'The outward results of true affliction are nearly always bad. We lie when we try to disguise this. It is in affliction itself that the splendour of God's mercy shines; from its very depths, in the heart of its inconsolable bitterness. If still persevering in our love, we fall to the point where the soul cannot keep back the cry "My God, why hast thou forsaken me?", if we remain at this point without ceasing to love, we end by touching something which is not affliction, which is not joy; something which is the central essence, necessary and pure; something not of the senses, common to joy and sorrow; something which is the very love of God' (37–8).

[50] Cf. Driver and Gray, lviii–lix: 'Certainly the speech of Yahweh does not contain what Job had not demanded, a positive theory of the meaning or purpose of suffering—and doubtless for the very good reason that the author himself had no such theory; had he had, he would probably have represented Job discovering this theory through suffering, and God at last approving Job's theory as against that of the friends; as it is, he is content to make clear the truth of Job's and the falseness of the friends' assertion as to the fact of Job's integrity. What Job had demanded was that God should formulate the charges of sin for which his sufferings had been sent; and to this God replies in the only possible way (cp. i 8) by formulating no such charge. The speech of Yahweh contains a charge, it is true; but it is a charge of a different kind; and the Epilogue in the most direct terms pronounces Job in the right and the friends in the wrong.'

not to be attempting a general "justification" of innocent suffering here. Rather, he uses the old folk-tale to provide a possible example —not, indeed, a very satisfactory one—of the way in which innocent suffering might be permitted by a just God. His *general* thesis is merely that such resolutions of apparent incompatibles are possible. The wisdom of the friends is wrong, for although God is just there is no necessary connection between sin and suffering; any claim to knowledge based on this supposed connection represents an illegitimate attempt to confine God within the confines of human wisdom, as indeed would any general theory of why God runs the world as he does.[51]

Through holding fast to his conviction of innocence, Job is led to recognize that the assumption, common to himself and his friends, that there must be this nexus is mistaken, and his rebellion ends.[52] He is no longer concerned for himself, for his faith has been purified from such concerns through contending with the paradox of his position. In this struggle he has refused to lie for God (13: 7), and has been led to such affirmations as "Yet the righteous holds to his way" (17: 9) despite all discouragement; his striving reaches its fulfilment in the purifying presence of God. Kant's comment is pertinent:

In the ancient sacred book Job says to his friends: 'Will you defend God with wrong? Will you plead for God? He will punish you. No hypocrite is admitted to him.' The theory affirmed by the friends has the appearance of more rational speculation and also pious humility. . . . But the divine judgment favoured the honest man and condemned the religious flatterers.

The resolution of Job's doubts was strange, as it consisted in showing up his ignorance. This method could only establish faith in the soul of a man who was able to say in the midst of his sufferings: 'Until my death I shall not budge from my piety.' His morality was not the result of his faith, but his faith was the result of his morality. He did not base his religion on currying favour with God but on a good life ((3), 234–5).

As the closing verse of the "chorus" on wisdom puts it, "Behold, the fear of the Lord, that is wisdom; and to depart from evil is understanding" (28: 28).

[51] Cf. Terrien, 21: 'The poet of Job did not attempt to solve the problem of evil nor did he propose a vindication of God's justice. For him, any attempt of man to justify God would have been an act of arrogance. But he knew and promoted in the immediacy of God's confrontation *a mode of life*.'

[52] Cf. Rowley (2), 19: 'A false theology sapped the springs of religion, when religion was most needed. Job was sure in his own conscience that his suffering was innocent, but he did not realise the corollary of this until the end of the book.'

The epilogue, therefore, plays a crucial part in our understanding of the whole—preventing us from resting in over-simple solutions. It portrays God coming down decisively against the wisdom of the friends and commending the strugglings of Job,[53] so that the salvation of the friends is made dependent on the prayers of the rebel.[54] It also represents God as restoring Job's prosperity and happiness; whatever the significance of this in the old folk tale, in context it is required to demonstrate God's continuing concern with justice; given the terms of the trial in the prologue, now the verdict has been given in Job's favour the suffering must cease.[55] The

---

[53] Cf. Driver and Gray, lxi: 'In inventing charges against Job they have told lies to maintain their theory of God; in repudiating these charges and denying that his calamities are God's accusation of wickedness in him, Job has spoken right.'

[54] Cf. Williams (2), 32: '"And the Lord turned the captivity of Job, when he prayed for his friends; also the Lord gave Job twice as much as he had before." It is the intercession, then, which marks the moment of return. . . . But it was Job's philosophical impatience of angry curiosity that brought him to such a moment.'

[55] As Peake (1) puts it, "the compensation given to Job is to clear God's character, not in any way to re-affirm the old theory that the righteous must be fortunate" (102). See also Rowley (2) 343: 'The author recognised that the cause of human suffering cannot be deduced by man, and in the case of Job says that it was to vindicate God's trust in him. But if the sufferings were now continued, they would no longer be for that purpose, but would merely be the expression of God's arbitrary malice, which the author was less interested to maintain than some of his critics.'

In his 'Job: A Deconstruction', Professor Clines has recently made use of a contemporary variant of the "hermeneutics of suspicion" (cf. Ricoeur, i. ch. 2) to argue that the book deconstructs itself, in part because while its central core takes the stance that "the dogma of retribution" is false the epilogue undermines this by affirming that "Job prospers because of his piety, which is to say, that the doctrine of retribution is true". It is essential to deconstructive theory to maintain that any text can be deconstructed, so the demonstration that such an exercise can be carried through in the case of Job is hardly surprising; it would be a serious objection to the argument of this chapter, however, if it could be shown that the deconstructive reading undercut any account which did not present the text as in irreconcilable conflict with itself, but this is not the case; the plausibility of the deconstruction depends on taking the final prosperity as an endorsement of "the dogma of retribution", which is either to ignore the possibility that it is rather a sign of God's justice or to presuppose that very interdependence between God's justice and the "dogma" which on my account the work is concerned to combat. Since this study is concerned with Job primarily in terms of its influence and potential for explicating the appeal to the "heart", all that is here required is to show that the text is coherently open to the hermeneutics of faith as well as of suspicion (Ricœur 28); this I have set out to do. As for how we should judge between the two hermeneutic strategies with respect to Job outside the context of this book, Ricœur's comment is apt: 'Plato . . . said in the *Phaedo* that there remains in each of us an infant to be consoled. The question is whether the function of consolation is merely infantile, or whether there is not also . . . [an] ascending dialectic of consolation' (548). See also my 'Introduction' to *The Bible as Rhetoric*.

epilogue therefore endorses the twin poles of Job's thought; his conviction that suffering does not imply guilt, and his horror at the appearance of injustice in God. In his particular case the prologue provides what purports to be a solution; but the main body of the work insists that no general solution can be found, that true wisdom consists—so far as man is concerned—in recognizing the limits of human understanding and holding fast to one's integrity.

8. The Appeal to the "Heart"

But to portray the book as culminating in any such simple and pious "conclusion" is over-simple; this would be a fair characterization of the "chorus" on wisdom, and the latter can certainly be read as providing a commentary on the book as a whole, but there is more to the book than there is to the poem. For the poem deals in generalities, but the book is focused on an individual, and it is here that the strength of its persuasive power rests. It appears to be this priority of enactment over theory that has caused such trouble to theologians and commentators, most starkly revealed by Mac-Donald's contention that the author "did not intend to teach", for "it is not his part to tell us that A is B; he only portrays some scenes of this world's life before us" (71). Such an over-simple opposition, alien to modern literary criticism, presupposes a model of "telling" which excludes from its ambit the "showing" which examples can exhibit. It has affinities with that "geometric" disposition to drive a wedge between "scientific proof" and "imaginative discourse" we have seen Hackforth attempting to foist upon Plato in our study of the *Phaedo*. For the author of Job, "portraying" can be an integral part of "telling".

The mainspring of the book's development is the dispute between Job and his friends. Experience teaches Job the falsity of the traditional wisdom, and the chiding of his friends provides the goad that forces him on in his intellectual and emotional progress. The faithfulness of this development to a widespread pattern of human experience has enabled generations of readers to associate their own responses to affliction with those of Job, and follow him step by step. The fact that the voice from the whirlwind only uses elements already assembled in this development enables the sympathetic reader to see how such a transformation of his own condition by such an encounter might be possible.

Thus the method of the book, in Pascal's terms, is to appeal to the heart as well as the mind. This, indeed, is no accident for, as we shall see in Chapter 5, Pascal's source for his use of 'heart' is Biblical; in Job as elsewhere in Scripture, 'heart' signifies that centre of man's inwardness where he encounters God in a context where thought, feeling, will and memory are integrated. Thus the RSV's rendering of the moment when Job first counter-attacks against the "wisdom" of his friends, "I have understanding as well as you" (12: 3), uses 'understanding' where the literal translation would be 'heart'; and earlier Job has used the term of the Divine Wisdom itself, affirming that God "is wise in heart" (9: 4). As in the case of Pascal's appeals to the "heart", there is here a psychological as well as an intellectual dimension. The work presents a picture of human development in such a way that it is possible for the reader to judge its credibility; this development culminates in an experience of the numinous which integrates its various strands and leads to a conviction of the presence in the midst of innocent suffering of a God before whom it is more appropriate to repent rebelliousness than "like a prince" to demand repentance.[56] This aspect of the work stands or falls with the psychological credibility of the pattern. If it is credible, then it shows how a man can be brought by experience to such beliefs, and to the extent that Job's experience appears to the reader to resonate with his own it enables him to see how they could resolve his own perplexities. Thus far the work "appeals to the heart".

But however much such a faith might resolve one's own perplexities, it cannot be accepted if it is self-contradictory or otherwise refuted. Thus the author both tests it against the wisdom of orthodoxy, showing that in terms of faithfulness to the facts it is a better account, and sets out to guard against the charge of inconsistency. On his own terms, he does not have to show how innocent suffering is reconciled with God's justice in the divine plan (why repenting before God is more appropriate than demanding repentance of him), for he holds that such a theodicy is beyond the reach of human wisdom, but he has to claim that such a reconciliation is not impossible—and, as if to confute those of the Wise who deny the possibility, uses the old folk-tale to provide an example of a context

---

[56] Thus it is hardly surprising to find cultic literary forms in what is fundamentally a Wisdom document; the author makes use of his religious experience to enrich the concept of "wisdom", and relies on the appropriate conventions in order to do so.

in which innocent suffering and justice are reconciled; this example provides the stage machinery for the whole drama. There is some evidence that the author was not entirely happy with this example,[57] but such unease only undermines the whole if it is shown that no example could work as a matter of logical possibility.[58]

The book's central appeal then, is to the pattern of experience in adversity of a man of steadfast integrity;[59] it presents this pattern in such a way as imaginatively to evoke and develop it, and to the extent that it succeeds it may be said to have persuasive power.[60] Concession is made to intellectual wisdom, but only so far as is needed to indicate its incapacity and to guard against the charges of incoherence and empirical falsehood.[61] Criticism is accordingly possible on three types of grounds; one might dispute its intellectual thesis under any or all of its three main heads;[62] one might dispute

[57] The author was not as insensitive as he is sometimes portrayed; although all Job's goods are doubled in the epilogue, the number of children is only restored to what it was before—as if to suggest that one's children are irreplaceable.

[58] For an example to be relevant to the general problem, of course, the sufferer must not be made aware of the reason for his suffering.

[59] The scope is therefore narrower that that of Pascal's appeal to the *mondain* unbeliever, of whom steadfast integrity is not always a leading characteristic. If Dr Lake is to be followed, the psychological appeal of Job is also restricted to those of introverted personality; once again, Pascal is not so restricted—in the *Pensées* he draws on his knowledge of his companions of the gaming tables, from the Chevalier de Méré downwards.

[60] In contrast to the *Phaedo*, both pity and fear constitute significant elements of the work's persuasive power, but their use is subject to a careful control which to some degree neutralizes their propensity to mislead through emotional excess of which Plato was so critical. 'Have pity on me, O you my friends' pleads Job (19: 21); through the flawed quality of those friends' responses the reader is himself drawn into a form of solidarity with the protagonist, apprehending as apt Job's phrase "the terrors of God" and so, through recognition of the potentialities of the numinous presented through the theophany, becomes open to their transcendence in an embracing of "the fear of the Lord that is wisdom" (28: 28). What to Plato is a self-denying ordinance required of the lover of wisdom which facilitates sublimation, to the author of Job would be an evasion of the deepest layers of purely human experience which need to be plumbed, so that wisdom may be achieved through their transcendence. However, sublimation and transcendence have structural analogies; the temptation to draw too sharp a contrast between the *Phaedo* and Job should be resisted (see ch. 3, n. 16).

[61] It is therefore little wonder that Kant thought so highly of it.

[62] The main thrust of the Elihu intervention is directed against the book's intellectual thesis. According to Elihu, it is empirically false that the innocent suffer, although sufferers may sometimes falsely believe that they are innocent; human wisdom can therefore penetrate further than the author of the book would admit. Elihu may also be seen as disputing the psychological plausibility of the work, in that there is a strong suggestion that no man who responds to suffering as self-righteously as Job does could have real integrity; Elihu diagnoses Job's sin as that of pride (cf. n. 38).

its psychological plausibility, and in particular the adequacy of the theophany to Job's spiritual condition; finally, one might dispute the value of its method of procedure—and it is this methodological issue that is of primary interest here.

From the point of view of the Aristotelian model discussed in Chapter 2, in so far as the Book of Job is concerned with "fundamental principles" we can hardly require demonstrative methods to be prominent, and in fact the main attention it pays to them is to debunk them; the friends are represented as deducing conclusions from allegedly first principles which are false. In attempting to develop its own methods, it appeals to experience rather than deduction, though taking care not to fall into logical inconsistency. It takes an example of a relevant pattern of experience, and attempts to display its paradigmatic status by showing it coming recognizably to terms with fundamental human concerns in a manner that resolves both psychological and intellectual perplexity. Unless one is to rule out the relevance of religious experience altogether in the establishment of first principles in religion, such a method can hardly be excluded from the outset as inappropriate.

The pattern of experience invoked is one which recurs throughout religious literature from Isaiah to Simone Weil. In a given instance of evil, God is felt as making himself known through the evil, and questions of disavowal or affirmation are transcended in the consciousness of God's presence with the sufferer;[63] as in Gethsemane, the climax of a revulsion from suffering leads to acceptance of it as the will of God. In this case, the experience of God is felt in a context where the standing puzzle of the existence of the evil is brought alongside other cosmological puzzles, and the sufferer is lost in wonder, realizing his utter finitude; God is transcendent and incomprehensible, beyond and the "creator of" good and evil (cf. Isaiah 45: 7), but nevertheless felt as being holy. Even so specified the pattern is a familiar one, and by no means limited to Judaeo-Christian religious traditions;[64] throughout the world it has been the inspiration for many examples of "negative theology".

---

[63] Cf. Wheeler Robinson's claim that "the author of the book asks us to believe that there is innocent suffering . . . which is the necessary condition for the manifestation of the deepest piety" (175–6).

[64] The classic treatment of such experiences of the transcendent is still Otto's *The Idea of the Holy*.

The Book of Job, indeed, is characteristic of much religious thought; it takes note of intellectual constraints, but its central concern is an appeal to the "heart". Being so early in date, it does not possess the self-consciousness about its procedures of later works with a similar concern, and reveals a wholeness of engagement with both mind and heart that it is difficult now to recapture. If one starts with the presupposition that only methods which follow the canons of deductive or inductive inference are appropriate to an investigation of the truth in such matters, that rationality is solely a function of such inferences, one must conclude that Job is a fundamentally irrational work—however much some of its ideas may be open to rational reconstruction.[65] But Job is exploring a form of "wisdom" which is incompatible with this presupposition, in opposition to the traditional "wisdom" of the friends which is not; thus in order to assess its critique of that conventional wisdom adequately one either has to relinquish this presupposition—for the defendant should not be judge in his own cause—or else show that the presupposition is correct.

Pascal is clear that any such presupposition should be rejected.

---

[65] The extraction of what are seen as its "proposed solutions" which are then attacked or defended in quite other (more "logical") terms, is a well established intellectual pastime whose presuppositions are rarely questioned.

5
Pascal's Reasons of the Heart

1. "Mind" and "Heart"

The Pascalian heart is a complex organ. I sketched in my first chapter the way Pascal concedes a significant sphere of operation —the "mind" ("*esprit*")—to "geometric" reasoning, but resists the wider (Cartesian) pretensions of that "arrogant power". In place of variants of Hackforth's ingenuous opposition of "scientific proof" to "imaginative discourse", we find in Pascal an intricate and ingenious distinction between "mind" and "heart" ("*cœur*"). The ramifications of this contrast are best brought out by a series of quotations from the *Pensées*.[1]

"Judgement is what goes with *sentiment*, just as knowledge [*les sciences*] goes with mind. *Finesse* falls to the lot of judgement, mathematics [*géométrie*] to that of the mind" (L.513, B.4, S.671). But the opposition is not absolute. "All our reasoning comes down to surrendering to *sentiment*" (L.530, B.274, S.455). Part of the explanation is that

Reason's last step is the recognition that there are an infinite number of things which are beyond it. It is merely feeble if it does not go as far as to realise that.

If natural things are beyond it, what are we to say about supernatural things? (L.188, B.267, S.220)

---

[1] Translations from the *Pensées* are based on Krailsheimer (1), which follows the Lafuma (1) text and classification. Where I have departed from it I have always given the original French, either in place of an English word or phrase or in brackets after my own rendering. On occasion I have used Dr Krailsheimer's translation but also given the French, so that the nuances and interconnections of key terms—which sometimes have no exact equivalent in English—may be brought out. Further to preserve these interconnections, in this chapter translations from other Pascalian works are my own and based on the Lafuma (1) text. After each quotation from the *Pensées* I have given the classification provided by Lafuma (1), Brunschvicg, and Sellier (1) respectively, e.g. 'L.513, B.4, S.671'.

As "proof" is to the mind, so *"sentiment"* is to the heart.

Knowledge of first principles, like space, time, motion, number, is as solid as any derived through reason, and it is on such knowledge, coming from the heart and instinct, that reason has to depend and base all its argument. . . . Principles are felt [*se sentent*], propositions proved, and both with certainty though by different means. It is just as pointless and absurd for reason to demand proof of first principles from the heart before agreeing to accept them as it would be absurd for the heart to demand a *sentiment* of all the propositions demonstrated by reason before agreeing to accept them (L.110, B.282, S.142).

And with regard to "supernatural things", "It is the heart which perceives [*sent*] God and not the reason. That is what faith is: God perceived by the heart, not by the reason" (L.424, B.278, S.680). Light is thrown on this definition by the claim that "God wishes to move the will rather than the mind. Perfect clarity would help the mind and harm the will" (L.234, B.581, S.266). The latter contention points to the close association Pascal sees between cognitive and volitional elements in the heart, for

The will is one of the chief organs of belief, not because it creates belief, but because things are true or false according to the aspect by which we judge them. . . . The mind, keeping in step with the will, remains looking at the aspect preferred by the will and so judges by what it sees there (L.539, B.99, S.458).

A doctrine that gives point to the regular use of such versatile terms as 'sentiment' and 'sentir' in association with the heart.[2]

The *sentiment*/proof distinction gives rise to a psychological one: "Those who are accustomed to judge by *sentiment* have no understanding of matters involving reasoning. . . . The others, on the contrary, who are accustomed to reason from principles, have no understanding of matters involving *sentiment*" (L.751, B.3, S.622). Common usage invites a broadening of the sense of 'esprit' to

---

[2] The versatility of 'sentiment' soon became notorious. Pascal, as we shall see, developed an intellectual framework within which its subtleties could play a creative role; but in other hands its flexibility led to ambiguity or even equivocation. Locke's comment on Malebranche's use of the term is representative of the unease it provoked in several quarters: "The reader must not blame me for making use here all along of the word 'sentiment', which is our author's own, and I understood it so little, that I knew not how to translate it to any other" (Locke (1), ix, 'An Examination of P. Malebranche's Opinion of Seeing All Things in God', para. 42, p. 237) See also ch. 6, n. 1.

include both classes, thus we may speak not only of '*l'esprit de géométrie*' but also of '*l'esprit de finesse*'. It is the role of the latter to discriminate veridical from deceptive *sentiments*, and this can be an exacting task since "Men often take their imagination for their heart" (L.975, B.275, S.739). The exercise has its own procedures, however: 'The heart has its order, the mind has its own, which uses principles and demonstrations. The heart has a different one. We do not prove that we ought to be loved by setting out in order the causes of love; that would be absurd' (L.298, B.283, S.329). The latter fragment brings out once again the volitional aspect of the heart, for "The mind naturally believes and the will naturally loves" (L.661, B.81, S.544). But if the heart has its own ordered *modus operandi* then, parallel to the broadening of the meaning of '*esprit*' mentioned above, it is intelligible also to extend that of 'reason' to generate the apparent paradox that "The heart has its reasons of which reason knows nothing" (L.423, B.277, S.680).

In certain important respects, therefore, it would appear that the "heart"—together with the "order" associated with it—plays for Pascal a role analogous to that of dialectic in Aristotle's thinking. As with dialectic, part of the significance of the "heart" lies in the way it is contrasted with demonstration—the *métier* of *l'esprit de géométrie*—and its role in the establishing of those first principles from which demonstration starts. But there is also significant divergence. According to Aristotle, it is not so much in dialectic as in rhetoric that one should seek the counterparts of the heart's volitional features, and it is noticeable that Pascal makes no attempt to dissociate rhetoric from the order of the heart. On the contrary, it is the part of the latter to develop what Plato termed a "noble" rhetoric or art of persuasion, as opposed to one dominated by the "powers of deception" ("*puissances trompeuses*"; L.45, B.83, S.78) characteristic of a Gorgias or an Aristotelian eristic.

'*Eloquence*. There must be elements both pleasing and real, but what is pleasing must itself be drawn from what is true' (L.667, B.25, S.547). Plato said much the same. The key problem, of course, is how to determine what *is* true once one concedes the lack of any rhetoric-free dialectic to establish first principles. Pascal poses the problem at its starkest in what has recently been identified as an early fragment, dating from the period when he was preparing himself for his projected *Apology for the Christian Religion*, the notes for which we know as the *Pensées* (Sellier (1), 16); the first line was cited above:

All our reasoning comes down to surrendering to *sentiment*.

But *fantaisie* is like and also unlike *sentiment*, so that we cannot distinguish between these two opposites. One person says that my *sentiment* is mere *fantaisie*, another that his *fantaisie* is *sentiment*. We should have a rule. Reason is available but can be bent in any direction.

And so there is no rule (L.530, B.274, S.455).

This was far from being his last word on the matter, but it shows the propriety of a simple question. If the heart has its reasons of which reason knows nothing, how are we to tell when they are good reasons?

2. The Historical Context

To grasp Pascal's answer to this question we need to consider the nature of the sceptical challenge as he understood it, together with the conceptual resources available to him in responding.

The claim that reason "can be bent in any direction" is a direct echo of Montaigne's *Apologie de Raimond Sebond* (Montaigne (1), II. xii. 634), which is a pervasive presence within the *Pensées*. Montaigne's revival of Pyrrhonic scepticism represents Pascal's chief source on these matters, though reference is also made to Cartesian methodic doubt. For Montaigne the pretensions of human reason are absurd, even comic; it cannot be used successfully to defend religion, but then it cannot be so used to attack it either. All is changing, not least our first principles, and only the eternal God escapes the flux. There are clear affinities with fideism in the way he humbles reason to make room for faith, and it is a strand of thought with which Pascal has a good deal of sympathy.

The strongest of the sceptics' [*pyrrhoniens*] arguments . . . is that we cannot be sure that these principles are true (faith and revelation apart) except in so far as we feel them naturally within ourselves [*sinon en (ce) que nous les sentons naturellement en nous*]. Now this natural *sentiment* affords no convincing proof that they are true. There is no certainty, apart from faith, as to whether man was created by a good God, an evil demon, or just by chance, and so it is a matter of doubt, depending on our origin, whether these innate principles are true, false, or uncertain. . . .

I pause at the dogmatists' only strong point, which is that we cannot doubt natural principles if we speak sincerely and in all good faith.

To which the sceptics reply, in a word, that uncertainty as to our origin entails uncertainty as to our nature. The dogmatists have been trying to answer that ever since the world began.

(Anyone wanting ampler information about scepticism should look at their books; he will soon be persuaded, perhaps too much so.) (L.131, B.434, S.164)

The final phrase gives the game away. For Pascal, Montaigne's view of the human condition is only partial. A few years earlier he had taken Epictetus and Montaigne as representing the world's two main, and irreconcilable, philosophical persuasions—the one, dogmatic, perceiving man's greatness, the other, sceptical, his wretchedness (Pascal (2), '*Entretien avec M. de Saci*', 291–7). His position has not changed. The passage cited above is set in a section on the human condition entitled 'Contradictions', whose spirit is well brought out by the immediately preceding fragment:

> If he exalts himself, I humble him.
> If he humbles himself, I exalt him.
> And I go on contradicting him
> Until he understands
> That he is a monster that passes all understanding.

> (L.130, B.420, S.163)

The apparent endorsement of scepticism given above is part of the humbling process. For Pascal there is not only evidence of man's wretchedness (including the impotence of his reason) but also of his "greatness"; in the section so entitled he remarks that "our doubts cannot remove every bit of light any more than our natural light can dispel all the darkness" (L.109, B.392, S.141). He heads the fragment 'Against Scepticism', and follows it with the one cited earlier to the effect that knowledge of first principles, being known through the heart, "is as solid as any derived through reason" (L.110, B.282, S.680). Here we see the reverse process at work, that of man's exaltation.

From an epistemological point of view, Pascal's claim is that "the dogmatists' only strong point" is indeed a strong one, despite their inability satisfactorily to meet the sceptical counter; 'I maintain that a perfectly genuine (*effectif*) sceptic has never existed. Nature backs up helpless reason and stops it going so wildly astray' (L.131, B.434,

S.164). A synopsis of this position is provided by one of the preliminary fragments (Sellier (1), 31): '*Instinct, reason*. We have an incapacity for proving anything which no amount of dogmatism can overcome. We have an idea of truth which no amount of scepticism can overcome' (L.406, B.395, S.25). The resolution of this impasse, for Pascal, cannot be achieved in purely epistemological terms:

> Who will unravel such a tangle? This is certainly beyond dogmatism and scepticism, beyond all human philosophy. . . .
>
> Know then, proud man, what a paradox you are to yourself. Be humble, impotent reason! Be silent, feeble [*imbécile*] nature! Learn that man infinitely transcends man, hear from your master your true condition, which is unknown to you.
>
> Listen to God (L.131, B.434, S.164).

In place, therefore, of the simple opposition of "human philosophy" between assurance and doubt—the dogmatic and the sceptical tendencies—we are presented with a third term, that of submission to divine authority. But to leave the matter there would be merely to embrace another form of fideism, facing the inevitable question: Why trust this authority? As Pascal remarks: 'I see a number of religions in conflict, and therefore all false, except one. Each of them wishes to be believed on its own authority and threatens unbelievers. I do not believe them on that account. Anyone can say that' (L.198, B.693, S.229). Thus when Pascal puts words into the mouth of the "Wisdom of God" the listeners are told "'I do not demand of you blind faith'" (L.149, B.430, S.182). Discrimination is therefore necessary. The tripartite framework within which it must take place is sketched forcibly in the section entitled 'Submission and Use of Reason':

> *Submission*. One must know when it is right to doubt, to affirm [*assurer*], to submit. Anyone who does otherwise does not understand the force of reason. Some men run counter to these three principles, either affirming that everything can be proved, because they know nothing about proof [*démonstration*], or doubting everything, because they do not know when to submit, or always submitting, because they do not know when judgement is called for.
>
> Sceptic, mathematician [*géomètre*], Christian; doubt, affirmation, submission (L.170, B.268, S.201).

The term employed to characterize the required discrimination is 'judgement'. Remembering that *"Finesse* falls to the lot of judgement", the use of *'géomètre'* and *'démonstration'* in apposition to *'assurance'* here recalls the contrast between *l'esprit de finesse* and *l'esprit de géométrie*; the judgement called for in differentiating true from false authority is of a piece with that *finesse* which sorts veridical from deceptive *sentiments*. So long as 'reason' is construed in terms of *'géométrie'*, philosophy is deadlocked; the vicious circle of dogmatist and sceptic can be broken only by enlarging our conception of rationality to include *finesse*, thus making possible an appeal to the "reasons" of the "heart".

The terms in which such an appeal is couched are suspect to twentieth-century ears, being redolent of outmoded faculty psychology. But they are worth demythologizing, for in giving the "heart" a cognitive role Pascal was making a decisive break with the traditional analyses of man into separate faculties which had done much to exacerbate the epistemological impasse of his time. His terminology is often traditional, but the old bottles contain new wine.

Pascal's acknowledged soucrce for his use of 'heart' is Biblical, and it is clear that its religious associations form a large part of its attraction for him.

We shall never believe, with an effective belief and faith, unless God inclines our hearts, and we shall believe as soon as he does so.
   And that is what David knew very well: *Incline my heart unto thy testimonies* (L.380, B.284, S.412).

The same tag from Psalm 119 is invoked elsewhere in a discussion of the respective roles of reason, habit and *sentiment* in human psychology (L.821, B.252, S.661), indicating that 'heart' does not shift its meaning between theological and psychological contexts. The psalm in question is frequently cited by Pascal, and we know that it figured daily in his breviary (Sellier (1), 200), thus it seems likely that its terminology established significant resonances within his own inwardness; this is a matter to which we shall return. 'Inwardness', indeed, captures much of the force of the Biblical 'heart'—1 Peter 3: 4 invokes "the hidden man of the heart"—but is too narrow. Hebrew has no separate word for 'will', and 'direct the heart' can come close to meaning 'decide'; on the other hand, the heart can both feel and think, while 'call to heart' means 'remember'. In short, for both Old and New Testaments the heart is the seat not only of the will, but also of thought and feeling; thus "the heart is above all the central place in man to which God turns, where religious experience has its root, which determines conduct" (Kittel iii. 615).[3] As we saw in the previous chapter, the final words of Elihu's commentary on the earlier text of Job, inserted at the pivotal point where man encounters God (37: 24), are "the wise of heart". Any serious attempt to be faithful to Biblical usage is likely to play havoc with faculty psychology.

But of course Pascal read his Bible with a far from innocent eye, being imbued with the self-conscious Augustinianism of Port-Royal for which 'heart' and 'will' were closely associated—a linkage of terms taking distinctive significance from the role allotted to the will in Jansenist thinking. The great debate on grace and free will between Port-Royal and the Jesuits, in which Pascal's own *Lettres provinciales* played so notable a part, largely turned on this issue. The dispute developed in the context of the collapse of the great medieval syntheses—with the consequent attempts to find alternatives—and it is worth recalling this background in order to clarify what is at stake in Pascal's own methodology.

It had been widely held among the Scholastics that many of the different terms we use in talking about men do not merely represent convenient *façons de parler*, but reflect genuine distinctions in the human psyche. But if there is "real" differentiation between the various faculties of the soul, we are faced with the problem of how they interact. For a system like that of St Thomas, the will in its morally significant dimension belongs to the province of the "rational appetite", and thus ultimately takes its guidance from the intellect—which perceives the good at which the will aims. But the spread of voluntaristic tendencies, often associated with the Franciscan order, was a potent factor in undermining such intellectualist accounts; increasingly men insisted on the primacy of love (a function of the will) over all else, including the operations of the intellect.

The key shift in perspective can be discerned as early as Duns Scotus. For him, "nothing extrinsic to the will is the cause of volition", which is self-determining (*'Opus Oxoniense'*, II. xxv. 20–3).

---

[3] E. C. Blackman's translation in Richardson; see his whole discussion (144–6). See also Miel (1), 157–61, together with the references there given.

From St Augustine onwards, the freedom of the will had been conceived as freedom from constraint to follow its natural objects, but with Scotus

the will is divorced from its objects and becomes a subjective, arbitrary faculty, not only absolutely free but something approaching a pure but empty power. To conceive such a will in relation to the Divine Will becomes immediately more problematic; the Divine Will, if it is to be triumphant, must impose itself as one power overruling another; predestination must inevitably take on an overwhelming and sinister character, as of a tyrant imposing his will from above, or at least pushing us from behind, rather than calling or inviting as a desirable object (Miel (1), 41–2).

Although Scotus' system soon lost its charm, the liberation of the will from the intellect could not be undone. The Reformers embraced predestination on the new terms, and in reaction the Molinists began to water such old doctrines down—until they, in turn, were denounced by the disciples of Jansenius at Port-Royal.

Jansenius had maintained that whereas philosophy depends on reason, theology is founded on the authority of tradition—on the "memory". Accordingly, he proposed that theologians return to the teaching and concepts of the authoritative Patristic writings, innocent of Scholastic philosophizing. So far as issues of grace and free will went, this clearly involved a return to St Augustine whose teaching had been confirmed by successive Church Councils. In this teaching the action of grace is upon the will, liberating it from the bonds of concupiscence by presenting it with a more attractive delight or "delectation"; as concupiscence is at root self-love, we have here the basis of the seminal distinction between the Earthly City and the City of God: 'Two loves therefore have given origin to these two cities, self-love in contempt of God unto the earthly, love of God in contempt of one's self to the heavenly' (Augustine (3), xiv. 28). For Jansenius the doctrine of this double delectation was central. However, in St Augustine the "will" is the whole soul as active in loving, without benefit of "real" distinctions between willing, desiring and thinking, and it proved instructively difficult consistently to think in terms of Augustinian psychology in post-medieval Europe. The inevitable happened, and as so often "Augustinians" found themselves drawn to take sides in a debate belonging to a thought world alien to the concepts to which they were committed.

Once the faculties of will and intellect had been separated, the question of their relative priority could not be ignored. On the one side there were those who held that, while the will might well be led astray by passions, it ought to be guided by the judgement of the intellect; intellect and passion were thereby set in opposition to each other, and the possibility of a genuinely moral passion—such as the love of God—became radically problematic. Alternatively,

instead of taking the judgements of reason as the norm it is possible to disregard the reason and define the criterion of moral activity in terms of the will alone. The Augustinian distinction of the two loves and the double delectation, interpreted against the divorce of intellect and will, constituted the alternative branch of the dilemma and contained its own anomalies (Levi (1), 310).

Foremost among these is the fact that although love of God is now put at the centre of the moral picture, it appears to be at the cost of rendering it—like all actions of the will—irrational.

There is thus a tension at the heart of Jansenist theology. Its Augustinian principles lead it to speak of the love of God as involving "knowledge" ("*cognitionis*"; Jansenius, '*Liber Prooe-malis*', *passim*), but its psychology renders extremely obscure what sort of knowledge is possible to the operations of the will. Augustine was no fideist, but if faith is founded in the faculty of the will fideism seems inevitable. Some of Jansenius' disciples attempted to "camouflage the difficulty" (Levi (1), 317) by writing of the 'heart' rather than the 'will'; Biblical precedent certainly warranted a cognitive as well as volitional status to the heart. But in default of any theory uniting will with intellect, this apparent escape from the dilemma by use of a third term was purely verbal. For both Saint-Cyran and Nicole the heart, in the last analysis, turns out to be the will or an aspect of it. It was Pascal who made the required breakthrough, for "The heart, which was associated with the affec-tions and with the will, finally became in the true sense cognitive in Pascal" (Levi (1), 326).[4]

It may in part be a failure to appreciate what Pascal was trying to do, in the face of the Jansenist impasse, that leads even the most judicious critics to complain of laxity in his use of key terms: 'It can hardly be said that Pascal uses the term *le cœur* in any one clearly defined sense. Sometimes it appears to be used as synonymous with

[4] For documented analyses of Port-Royal usage see Laporte and Levi (1). I have made significant use of these works, together with France, Miel (1), and Morgan (1) in sketching the background to Pascal's thinking.

'the will'. . . . At other times *le cœur* designates a kind of knowledge or an instrument of knowing' (Copleston (1), iv. 164). Certainly there is some imprecision; few of the relevant writings, with the exception of the *Lettres provinciales*, were prepared for publication, and the crucial documents we know as the *Pensées* were composed over a period of years—during which his thought was continuously evolving—with only haphazard and very partial revision. But the general drift, even of '*le cœur*', is clear enough; Pascal is attempting to escape the rigid strait-jacket of faculty psychology to which it would appear that Fr Copleston seeks to return him.

This overall orientation is best seen by looking beyond the will/knowledge distinction. For Augustine, the three central activities of man which reveal his creation in the image of God are remembering, understanding, and willing (Augustine (2), x. 17–18), a doctrine which powerfully influenced the traditional selection of the memory, the reason, and the will as man's principal faculties.[5] Pascal lays his cards on the table in two fragments from the same early period in which he had sceptically commented on the proposition that "All our reasoning comes down to surrendering to *sentiment*", cited earlier: 'Memory is necessary for all the operations of reason' (L.651, B.369, S.536); '*Sentiment*. Memory and joy are *sentiments*, and even mathematical [*géométriques*] propositions can become *sentiments*' (L.646, B.95, S.531). Remembering the close association between "heart" and "*sentiment*", and that for Augustinians the proper object of the will is "delectation" or "joy", we can see here preparation being made for deconstructing the whole apparatus of faculty psychology. An attempt is being launched to undo the post-Augustinian separation of the leading faculties, in order to combat the related dangers of fideism and Pyrrhonic scepticism; the traditional term 'heart' is used to designate the central unifying concept in the resulting theory.

[5] For Augustine, of course, one must differentiate between '*mens*', the rational soul, and '*intelligentia*' ('understanding') which is less concerned with reasoning than with Platonic intellectual vision. Pascal's distinction between 'mind' and 'heart' is in some respects reminiscent of the earlier contrast, though the analogy should not be pressed. By the seventeenth century, however, the standard terminology had become sufficiently confused for Pascal to be able to use '*espirt*' ('mind') and '*entendement*' ('understanding') interchangeably for the seat of demonstrative reasoning (Pascal (2), '*De l'art de persuader*', 355).

Let no one say that I have said nothing new; the arrangement of the material is new. In playing tennis both players use the same ball, but one plays it better.

I would just as soon be told that I have used old words. As if the same thoughts did not form a different argument by being differently arranged, just as the same words make different thoughts when arranged differently! (L.696, B.22, S.575)

3. A Revised Epistemology

Several years before starting work on his *Apology*, Pascal had endorsed Jansenius' distinction between the sciences of memory, which include theology, and those of reason—though he added that the latter needed to be subdivided between experimental and demonstrative (Pascal (2), '*Preface sur le traité du vide*', 230–2). Later he was to employ what appears to have been standard Port-Royal terminology (Saint-Cyran, II. civ. 455–6), in consigning theological truths to the 'heart' (Jansenius' 'will' being used as an interchangeable term), and those capable of demonstration to the 'mind' (*esprit*) or 'understanding' ('*entendement*'); the former seeks a satisfaction that will give it "joy", its operative principle being either a worthy or a base love, the latter is construed on the geometrical model (Pascal (2), '*De l'art de persuader*', 355–9). It therefore follows that both memory and joy are within the province of the heart. Montaigne's scepticism casts doubt on the self-sufficiency of reason, so if a satisfactory case can be made for designating the heart—as so far characterized—as the organ concerned with establishing the required first principles of demonstration, the stage is set for an authentically Augustinian unification of the principal faculties which is more than mere verbal camouflage; the early probing of the scope of *sentiment* points the way to a revised epistemology.

A leading feature of this revision lies in its increase in flexibility over the traditional stereotypes, a flexibility dependent on the concept of different points of view. We have already seen that whereas from one perspective reason must be distinguished from *sentiment*, from another it must be acknowledged that "all our reasoning comes down to surrendering to *sentiment*"; analogously we must both distinguish imagination from the heart and acknowledge the roots of the former in the latter. In contemporary French writing it had become conventional to discard the traditional Augustinian trio of activities or faculties in favour of a new triad, with imagination displacing will (Levi (1), 319); similarly, across the Channel Bacon had recently argued that "the best division of human learning is that derived from the three faculties of the rational soul, which is the seat of learning. History has reference to the Memory, poesy to the Imagination, and philosophy to the Reason" (Bacon, '*De Augmentis Scientiarum*', II. i. 426). But for Pascal the imagination does not reflect the image of God in man in the same way as the Augustinian trinity, and thus in an important sense lies outside the ambit of the heart, though it is easy to confuse the two: 'Men often take their imagination for their heart, and often believe they are converted as soon as they start thinking of becoming converted' (L.975, B.275, S.739). The explanation seems to be that "*fantaisie* is like and also unlike *sentiment*, so that we cannot distinguish between these two opposites" (L.530, B.275, S.455); not, that is, so long as we are "too much persuaded" by the sceptics.

Given the point of view from which heart and imagination must be distinguished, it would appear that just as heart and *sentiment* go together so do imagination and *fantaisie*; the former can give knowledge "as solid as any derived through reason", but in the latter case:

Imagination. It is the dominant faculty [*partie*] in man, master of error and falsehood, all the more deceptive for not being invariably so; for it would be an infallible criterion of truth if it were infallibly that of lies. Since, however, it is usually false, it gives no indication of its quality, setting the same mark on true and false alike.

I am not speaking of fools, but of the wisest men, amongst whom imagination is best entitled to persuade. Reason may object in vain, it cannot fix the price of things.

This arrogant force, which checks and dominates its enemy, reason, for the pleasure of showing off the power it has in every sphere, has established a second nature in man. . . . How absurd is reason, the sport of every wind! . . . Reason never wholly overcomes imagination, while the contrary is quite common. . . .

Imagination decides everything; it creates beauty, justice and happiness, which is the world's supreme good (L.44, B.82, S.78).

Thus, "Each man has *fantaisies* contrary to his own good, in the very idea he has of good" (L.805, B.106, S.653).

The claim that imagination is "the dominant faculty" needs to be treated with circumspection; the whole of the relevant fragment is strongly derivative from Montaigne, is placed under the heading 'Vanity', and forms part of the sketch of the "wretchedness [*misère*] of man without God" (L.6, B.60, S.40). It thus represents how things appear from the perspective in which dogmatism and scepticism are deadlocked, which is why the contrast here is with reason —not the heart. The whole strategy of the projected *Apology* is to wean the *mondain* unbeliever away from such a perspective to one in which there is adequate scope for the "Wisdom of God" to operate: 'When we want to correct someone usefully and show him he is wrong, we must see from what point of view he is approaching the matter, for it is usually right from that point of view, and we must admit this, but show him the point of the view from which it is wrong' (L.701, B.9, S.579). Given the perspective in which the only alternative to imagination is the reason of the "dogmatists", then "How absurd is reason, the sport of every wind!" But Pascal is arguing for a different perspective, or rather for a "fixed point" (L.695, B.445, S.574; and L.697, B.383, S.576) from which other perspectives can properly be judged, which takes into account man's greatness as well as his wretchedness, and can make sense of the perception that "Thought constitutes man's greatness" (L.759, B.346, S.628). Once one allows a dimension of thought which goes beyond the reason of the dogmatists, *l'esprit de finesse* as well as *l'esprit de géométrie*, the situation is transformed. The challenge now is to show how *finesse* can distinguish between veridical *sentiments* and mere *fantaisies*.

But caution is necessary. It is not claimed that all *sentiments* are reliable while all the products of imagination are misleading. Such a contention would immediately reinstate the worst features of faculty psychology. On the contrary, we are explicitly told that imagination is not invariably deceptive, giving "no indication of its quality"; and so far as the *sentiments* of the heart are concerned: 'How hollow and foul is the heart of man!' (L.139, B.143, S.171); 'Disguise, falsehood and hypocrisy . . . are naturally rooted in his heart' (L.978, B.100, S.743). For 'The mind naturally believes and the will naturally loves, so that when there are no true objects for them they necessarily become attached to false ones' (L.661, B.81, S.544). The imagination, it would appear, is one of the leading creators of such "false objects"—though not the only one, Pascal insists that "we have plenty of other principles of error" (L.44, B.82, S.78). For

Pascal as for Augustine, the heart or will is moved either by a legitimate love—charity—or by a carnal love—concupiscence; both loves being forms of desire. From one point of view, the falsehoods purveyed by imagination are rooted in the carnality of *"l'amour-propre"* (L.978, B.100, S.743), and this theological perspective no doubt represents Pascal's underlying touchstone. But from a psychological standpoint, if we focus on the volitional aspect of the heart, discriminating between it and the imagination can be salutary. We can project for our own self-gratification the image of our authentically responding to the love of God, and fall in love with that *fantaisie*—hence men "often believe they are converted as soon as they start thinking of becoming converted", a practice fairly describable as men taking "their imagination for their heart"; the volition integral to the activities of the heart is no doubt operating, but not where it is thought to be involved. The way such adaptability of viewpoint opens up potentialities for accurate description and hence diagnosis is obvious.

But flexibility has its own dangers. Unless the proposed analyses are to risk being vacuous, a unified theory is required underlying the many-sided vocabulary. More particularly, we need to know how the Augustinian triad are united in the heart; and here the Jansenist inheritance renders pressing the integration of its volitional and cognitive aspects. Copleston puts the issue with his usual incisiveness: 'In the case of the first principles of geometry there can hardly be question of loving the principles' (Copleston (1), iv. 165). The contrast drawn is with the heart's loving apprehension of God, and it is certainly clear that the heart's relation to first principles is very different from its relation to God. But it does not follow that affective and volitional elements are wholly irrelevant even in the case of the principles. This would only be the case if the basic orientation of our soul was contemplative, as with the Cartesian ego—and this is what Pascal denies.

Descartes had attempted to anchor his metaphysics in the mind's clear and distinct idea of itself as revealed initially in the self-evidence of the *Cogito*. Pascal's comment is terse: 'Descartes useless and uncertain' (L.887, B.78, S.445). When one looks more closely it appears that the uselessness and the uncertainty are connected. We saw in Chapter 1 that Pascal is prepared to allow considerable scope to the Cartesian model of geometric reasoning; it represents the proper procedure for persuading the mind on the basis of "natural truths known to everyone, such as that the whole is greater than its part" (Pascal (2), 355), though as a matter of fact men are more often improperly persuaded of "truths within our reach" by *sentiment*, the operation of the will. But two caveats are given to this thesis. First, we should not attempt to define or prove everything, and in particular not attempt to demonstrate first principles on pain of circularity and obfuscation. Second, with regard to "divine truths", which are "infinitely above nature", the ordinary procedure does not apply, for these are properly matters of the heart or will; thus here we are rightly persuaded by *sentiment*, and may "only enter into truth by charity". We may therefore see "the normal process of human persuasion as a disordered image of the divine" (Morgan (1), 274).

Both qualifications are relevant to the *Pensées*. Being concerned with "divine truths", they eschew demonstrative argument in the strict sense, and this for two reasons. One is that, whilst reason has its place in such matters, Christianity "does not admit as its true children those who believe without inspiration" (L.808, B.245, S.655); the prime requisite is that the heart be touched, thus "Even if someone were convinced that the proportions between numbers are immaterial, eternal truths, depending on a first truth in which they subsist, called God, I should not consider that he had made much progress towards his salvation" (L.449, B.556, S.690). The other is that it is extremely doubtful whether it is possible "to prove by *raisons naturelles* either the existence of God, or the Trinity or the immortality of the soul, or anything of that kind: . . . I should not feel competent to find in nature arguments which would convince hardened atheists" (ibid.). Indeed, with regard to those who attempt to prove the existence of God from the works of nature,

Their enterprise would cause me no surprise if they were addressing their arguments to the faithful, for those with living faith in their hearts can certainly see at once that everything which exists is entirely the work of the God they worship. But for those in whom this light has gone out and in whom we are trying to rekindle it . . . to tell them that they have only to look at the least thing around them and they will see in it God plainly revealed . . . this is giving them cause to think that the proofs of our religion are indeed feeble, and reason and experience tell me that nothing is more likely to bring it into contempt in their eyes. This is not how Scripture speaks, with its better knowledge of the things of God. On the contrary it says that God is a hidden God (L.781, B.242, S.644).

"Natural truths known to everyone", it would appear, are insufficient to ground any such demonstrations; Pascal does indeed think that non-demonstrative "proofs" are available, a matter to which we shall return, but these do not fit the geometric model.

Yet while there are no arguments in the *Pensées* that fit this model as it is expounded either in '*De l'art de persuader*' or '*De l'esprit géométrique*' (Pascal (2), 348–59), there is one notorious fragment which makes use of what he elsewhere characterized as "The Geometry of Chance" (Pascal (2), '*Adresse à l'Académie Parisienne*', 101–3)—it is the "*Infini rien*" discussion of the "*pari*" or "wager", the central section of which closes with '*Cela est démonstratif*'. Of course, no attempt is made to "demonstrate" the overwhelming probability of God's existence even here. '"Either God is or he is not." But to which view shall we be inclined? Reason cannot decide this question' (L.418, B.233, S.680). The case rather is that even the demands of self-love render it sensible to seek faith in God—that the demands of reason and volition can be integrated in a single probability sum:

Which will you choose then? Let us see: since a choice must be made, let us see which offers you the least interest. You have two things to lose: the true and the good; and two things to stake: your reason and your will, your knowledge and your happiness; and your nature has two things to avoid: error and wretchedness (*ibid.*).

With only a finite stake to lose, a finite chance of winning, and a potential infinity of happiness to gain if we wager on God's existence, concupiscence points beyond itself to the desirability of that inspiration which gives rise to charity; we should, therefore, prepare ourselves to make possible the reception of such inspiration should God grant it. Probability theory, with its own canons of "demonstration", is thus invoked to help shift the free-thinker's perspective to one open to the demands of faith.

But the projected integration of reason and volition cuts deeper than this. Like any demonstration, the argument depends on first principles; thus it opens with a comment on the basic elements out of which the operative finite/infinite distinction is constructed: 'Our soul is cast (*jetée*) into the body where it finds number, time, dimensions; it reasons about these things and calls them natural, or necessary, and can believe nothing else' (*ibid.*). Here we have tersely presented the familiar deadlock of "all human philosophy";

the thesis is that of "the dogmatists' only strong point, which is that we cannot doubt natural principles," but it is expressed in such a way as to remind us of the sceptic: 'This natural *sentiment* affords no convincing proof that they are true. There is no certainty, apart from faith, as to . . . whether these innate principles are true, false, or uncertain' (L.131, B.434, S.164). With these first principles, as with that initial orientation we call faith, reason by itself is at a loss. But just as the promptings of the human heart can be combined with reason in the case of faith to force a decision, so here "nature backs up helpless reason and stops it going so wildly astray". In short, the basic orientation of our soul is not contemplative but practical, and the Cartesian ego is a misleading abstraction.

The incompatibility of the two perspectives is focused when Pascal permits the free thinker to advocate a detached position: The right thing is not to wager at all.' The response is immediate: 'Yes, but you must wager. There is no choice, you are embarked (*embarqués*)' (L.418, B.233, S.680). *'Jetée'* and *'embarqués'*; these are the watchwords. At its most basic level our thinking is a product of the human condition, and this is not one of disinterested contemplation but of life in the world—a doctrine with several twentieth-century analogues.

Nothing stands still for us. This is our natural state and yet the state most contrary to our inclinations. We burn with desire to find a firm footing (*assiette*), an ultimate, lasting base on which to build a tower rising up to infinity, but our whole foundation cracks and the earth opens up into the depth of the abyss (L.199, B.72, S.230).

The natural order provides no such *assiette*, yet we need to act and think; life imposes choices that cannot be evaded any more than death can be evaded; if we do not wager for God we wager against him.

Yet although it is impossible to demonstrate first principles, this shows neither that it is irrational to credit those which are inescapable, nor that we cannot assess rationally the choices imposed upon us; we are only tempted towards such sceptical conclusions by improperly divorcing mind from will. "Man's true nature, his true good and true virtue, and true religion are things which cannot be known separately" (L.393, B.442, S.12), for "The mind, keeping in step with the will, remains looking at the aspect, preferred by the will, and so judges by what it sees there" (L.539, B.99, S.458). If our

will is properly adjusted to our true condition, aiming at that which
is capable of giving genuine satisfaction, then concepts and assumptions necessary for achieving our desires cannot be misleading; they
accurately reflect the structure of man's estate and lead toward the
possibility of our enjoying authentic fulfilment. Further, any first
principles which are inescapable whatever the tendency of our will
are also trustworthy—for if they are indeed necessary to us we
shall need them to understand and respond to the reality of our
condition. On the other hand, our wills are usually misdirected:

It is untrue that we are worthy to be loved by others. It is unfair (*injuste*)
that we should want such a thing. If we were born reasonable and impartial,
with a knowledge of ourselves and others, we should not give our wills this
bias. However, we are born with it, and so we are born unfair.

For everything tends towards itself: this is contrary to all order.

The tendency should be towards the general, and the bias towards self is
the beginning of all disorder. . . .

The will is therefore depraved (L.421, B.477, S.680).

Accordingly, assumptions which are part of this bias fall into the
category of "*puissances trompeuses*" (powers of deception) (L.45,
B.83, S.78).

The ideal of contemplative detachment is thus abandoned as a
mirage, and the deadlock of "human philosophy" reinterpreted in
terms of Augustine's two loves:

The will of man is divided between two principles: cupidity and charity. It is
not that cupidity and faith in God are incompatible, not that charity and
earthly blessings never go together, but cupidity makes use of God and
delights in the world while charity does just the opposite.

Now things are described in relation to ultimate purpose. (L.502, B.571,
S.738)

While, "God should govern everything and everything should be
related to him" (L.933, B.460, S.761). An accurate grasp of our lot
will therefore be God-centred, descriptions which cannot ultimately be analysed in such terms will be misdescriptions, and the
sentiments on which our assurance of first principles is founded are
functions of our loves. Only that love we call 'charity' grounds
reliable judgement, and that ground is sufficient: 'God diversified
this single precept of charity to satisfy our curiosity, which seeks
diversity, through a diversity which always leads to the one thing
that is necessary for us' (L.270, B.670, S.301). Any account of the
heart which permits a divorce between cognitive and volitional

elements therefore stands condemned: 'We make an idol of truth itself, for truth apart from charity is not God, but his image and an idol that we must not love or worship. Still less must we love or worship its opposite, which is falsehood' (L.926, B.582, S.755).

By embracing the Christian identification of the proper direction of the will as the love of God, Pascal is able to secure the integration of the remaining element of the Augustinian triad—the memory —into his account of the heart. For the appropriate specification of man's true state and goal comes not, as was only to be expected, from his imagination—but from historical revelation as recorded in authoritative Scripture. And the study of ancient documents, like that of history and languages, falls within the province of memory, whose "authority has its principal force in theology" (Pascal (2), 'Preface sur le traité du vide', 230). Memory should not be uncritical, of course, and very early in the preparation for his *Apology* we find Pascal analysing and appraising his Biblical sources—a process he continued almost to his death (Sellier (1), 15–18 and 203–7). Indeed, a proper grasp of hermeneutic principles in this context enables us to authenticate the credentials of the Christian revelation, and thus show it to be true. When Pascal writes of "the proofs of our religion" it is to the evidences of historical revelation that he is referring; these "proofs" belong to the sphere of memory, not the mind, and hence do not aspire to the geometric model. We have here an adumbration of that methodological distinction between natural and human sciences which was to play so important a role in later thought.

The projected *Apology* was to be a work of the heart in two senses. It arose, at least in part, from the promptings of charity (L.418 *ad fin.*, B.233, S.680), and was designed to move the readers' hearts in such a way as to render them open to the inspiration of God. The last of Pascal's preliminary fragments outlines the project in terms of the heart's three dimensions—understanding, will, and memory:

Order. Men despise religion. They hate it and are afraid it may be true. The cure for this is first to show that religion is not contrary to reason, but worthy of reverence and respect.

Next make it attractive, make good men wish it were true, and then show that it is.

Worthy of reverence because it really understands human nature.

Attractive because it promises true good (L.12, B.187, S.46).

And true, of course, because proved by Scripture and history. Epistemological principle, Augustinian theology, psychological analysis, and rhetorical strategy are all here focused.

4. Memory, Understanding, and Will

In Pascal's thinking the three dimensions of this work of the heart could not finally be separated; Augustine had long ago used the integration of his triad as an image of the divine Trinity, three in one with neither confounding of the Persons nor division of the Substance (Augustine (2), ix–xv). But the fragments available have not worn equally well; those concerned with the proofs of memory have today little more than curiosity value, while those designed to show that Christianity "understands human nature" and "promises true good" still hold men's attention. This fact in itself puts in question the role memory can play in the Pascalian heart. Unless analogous "proofs" of greater adequacy can be constructed, we appear to be faced with two alternatives. Either it is human conjecture rather than divine revelation that specifies, if anything can, man's true state; in which case imagination displaces memory in the workings of the heart. Or else the line between memory and imagination has been wrongly drawn.[6]

Pascal is not without defences even here. His "proofs" are only discernible as such to those whose eyes have been enlightened; the volitional aspect of the heart is no more irrelevant to its operation in the field of memory than in the field of reason. 'The proofs drawn from Scripture by Jesus and the Apostles are not conclusive [*démonstratives*]' (L.840, B.843, S.425). Here as elsewhere God is a hidden God; the prophecies need to be taken figuratively, which is why the Jews have failed to interpret them as pointing to Jesus Christ; thus

---

[6] The present state of Biblical scholarship holds little promise of plausible "proofs". The best serious exploration of the alternatives, from the point of view of Christian theology, is still to be found in the work of the late Dr Farrer; see especially Farrer (2) and (5). No doubt contemporary Biblical scholarship is not itself beyond criticism; indeed, Farrer writes with some plausibility and authority of it as being dominated by "great systems of organized and cooperative folly" (Farrer (5), 162)—and Pascal might well describe those systems as "carnal" (cf. L.256, B.662, S.288 and L.270, B.670, S.301).

God has appointed visible signs in the Church so that he shall be recognised by those who genuinely seek him, and . . . has none the less hidden them in such a way that he will only be perceived by those who seek him with all their heart (L.427, B.194, S.681).

There is enough light for those who desire only to see, and enough darkness for those of a contrary disposition (L.149, B.430, S.182).

This is why appeal to such proofs is only to be made after religion has been shown to be both intellectually respectable and humanly attractive. In the "*Infini rien*" fragment reference is made to turning up "the cards" of "Scripture and the rest" only after the argument of the wager has been concluded with "*Cela est démonstratif*". If all three dimensions of the heart are designed to work together, then resistance at one level—that of "memory"—may be a symptom of a wider disorder. If contemporary scholarship is an obstacle to accepting the "proofs" as proofs, we should remember that the Messiah came "to blind the wise and learned" (L.487, B.727, S.734).

But such a rejoinder can achieve little more than damage limitation. At the early stage at which he conceded that the proofs drawn from Scripture were not conclusive, he still thought that they became "sufficient" when buttressed by miracles, "therefore all faith rests on miracles" (L.846, B.808, S.429); this was in the first flush of the enthusiasm generated by the miracle of the Holy Thorn at Port-Royal, which probably provided the impetus for the inception of his *Apology* (Sellier (1), 16). But experience soon disillusioned him, even the best attested miracles could be interpreted in more than one way, and by the time he started work on the *Apology* in earnest he had a more sophisticated interlocking apparatus: '*Proofs of religion*. Morality/Doctrine/Miracles/Prophecies/Figures' (L.402, B.290, S.21). 'The three signs of religion; perpetuity, godly life, miracles' (L.894, B.844, S.448). "Perpetuity" relates to the claim that the fundamental "Doctrine" of Fall and Restoration, common to Jews and Christians, "has always existed on earth" (L.281, B.613, S.313); "morality" to the spiritual "secret force" of Christianity, leading men to "godly life" (L.338, B.724, S.370). "Miracles" relates both to those recorded in Scripture, and to those since wrought in the Church. The remaining two terms can be taken together; with regard to the Old Testament prophecies of the Messiah, "The time was foretold clearly, while the manner was figurative" (L.255, B.758, S.287).

The weakness of any case built out of such materials is obvious enough. The claims to perpetuity are grounded in the literal truth of the Book of Genesis, long since undermined. Those regarding godly life and miracles can be paralleled outside Christianity, and in the latter case any attempt to rule out pagan miracles by doctrinal considerations is self-defeating: 'If doctrine determines miracles, miracles are useless for doctrine' (L.832, B.803, S.421). Figures can be read in more than one way, if they are admitted at all,[7] while with regard to the time of the Christ being "foretold clearly", even Pascal is forced to admit that there is an ambiguity in the interpretation of one of the key prophecies—and one's confidence is not increased when he attempts to dismiss the difficulty with the comment: "But the difference only amounts to 200 years" (L.341, B.723, S.373). Of free thinkers Pascal writes:

In order really to attack the truth they would have to protest that they had made every effort to seek it everywhere, even in what the Church offers by way of instruction, but without any satisfaction. If they talked like that they would indeed be attacking one of Christianity's claims. But I hope to show here that no reasonable person could talk like that. I even venture to say that no one has ever done so (L.427, B.194, S.681).

To twentieth-century ears this sounds like bluster; failure to recognize proofs such as these as "sufficient" cannot simply be dismissed as a sign that the seeker is not "genuine" or "reasonable". Such claims for the proofs of "memory" are indeed refuted on their own ground, the evidence of historical fact.

And that ground itself has shifted. The development of archaeology, geology, and related sciences has not merely, and notoriously, played havoc with the chronology of the Book of Genesis; it has so transformed our conception of historiography that it requires a considerable mental effort to think of history as a science of the

---

[7] Pascal has a highly sophisticated set of hermeneutic principles, showing a nuanced appreciation of the importance of context of utterance (see his '*Écrits sur la grace*', Pascal (2), 310–48, and the discussion in Miel (1), ch. 2). However, his exploitation of these principles to justify the figurative interpretation of the Old Testament (L.257, B.684, S.289 and L.501, B.659, S.737) rests on the assumption that Scripture is divinely inspired—which needs to be shown. The contemporary reluctance of Biblical scholars to allow any but a very limited figurative interpretation of the Old Testament appears to reflect the presupposition either that it is not so inspired, or that the relation between the inspiration of God and the creativity of the human imagination is not as Pascal conceived of it. For detailed discussion of the Port-Royal exegetical tradition, see Wetsel.

memory.[8] For Pascal the role of memory, in its relation both to the classification of the sciences and to human psychology, was one of the less problematic parts of his intellectual inheritance. Although this role was under implicit challenge from the Jesuits, it would appear from the *Lettres provinciales* and related writings that Pascal was unimpressed by such critiques. His main intellectual energies, in so far as he was concerned with redrawing the conceptual map of his time, were directed more towards the relation of understanding to will than towards that of memory to either. But what for Pascal was the most secure part of his apparatus is for us the least defensible, and of less contemporary interest than his innovations. The reputation of the *Pensées* rests not on its "proofs of religion" drawn from Scripture and history, but on its endeavours to "show that religion is not contrary to reason" and to "make good men wish it were true". These twin endeavours of "understanding" and "will" respectively are, as we should expect, interconnected; and the procedure employed is instructive.

From a methodological point of view, the challenge is to provide criteria for discerning when the will is properly adjusted to man's true condition. Those suggested by Christianity will be acceptable if it can be shown that it "really understands human nature" and "promises true good". Thus Pascal's overall strategy is to lead the reader to acknowledge the authenticity of a perspective such that

As soon as the Christian religion reveals the principle that men are by nature corrupt and have fallen away from God, this opens one's eyes so that the mark of this truth is everywhere apparent; for nature is such that it points at every turn to a God who has been lost, both within man and without, and to a corrupt nature (L.471, B.441, S.708).

The presentation of the doctrine of man's divided will, a function of human corruption, as resolving the sceptical deadlock is characteristic of his procedure. In similar fashion he analyses the self-defeating nature of human restlessness (L.136, B.139, S.168) and self-love (L.978, B.100, S.743) as revealing a tension in the human

---

[8] The point of designating a group of studies as dependent on the memory lies in the data available being confined to people's actual memories or to written records —conceived as an extension of the human faculty. Such studies are concerned with "matters where we are only concerned to know what the authors have written, . . . since everything we can know about them is contained there" (Pascal (2), '*Preface sur le traité du vide*', 230). Examples other than history offered by Pascal as candidates for this status include jurisprudence, the study of languages, and such matters as "where geographers place the first meridian".

condition that bids fair to be constitutive; once we have been led to see the facts of human psychology in such a perspective, the doctrine of the Fall renders intelligible what would otherwise be baffling and the promise of Redemption offers hope where in human terms there can only be either self-deception or despair. The power of such fragments on the human condition lies partly in the precision of observation and partly in their range and scope which produce a cumulative effect. In epistemology, psychology, ethics, politics, the law, and even such matters as choice of career, Pascal attempts to show that an honest and accurate account of the facts requires concepts which invite interpretation in terms of man's "wretchedness" ("*misère*") or "greatness" ("*grandeur*") or, more often, of the tension between the two; 'Man's greatness comes from knowing he is wretched: a tree does not know that it is wretched. | Thus it is wretched to know that one is wretched, but there is greatness in knowing one is wretched' (L.114, B.397, S.146).

The opposition of *grandeur* to *misère* straddles the reason/will divide. If we insist on the latter dichotomy, the emphasis of *grandeur* is on the potentialities of man's reason—'All our dignity consists in thought' (L.200, B.347, S.232)—while that of *misère* is on the frustrations of the will: '*Misère*. Solomon and Job have known and spoken best about man's wretchedness, one the happiest, the other the unhappiest of men; one knowing by experience the vanity of pleasure, and the other the reality of afflictions' (L.403, B.174, S.22). But of course Pascal's case depends on the dichotomy being a false one. The limitations of our thought frustrate our will, 'Anyone is unhappy who wills but cannot do. Now he wants to be happy and assured of some truth, and yet he is equally incapable of knowing and of not desiring to know. He cannot even doubt' (L.75, B.389, S.110). Again, the misdirection of the will corrupts our thought, for "the will is one of the chief organs of belief" (L.539, B.99, S.458). Thus both cognitive and volitional phenomena can be related to the tension between *grandeur* and *misère*. We have seen why at the most fundamental level we are, except by reference to the divine, "incapable of knowing"; the parallel argument about happiness is summarized in a preliminary fragment:

The Stoics say: 'Withdraw into yourself, that is where you will find peace.'
And that is not true.

Others say: 'Go outside: look for happiness in some diversion.' And that is not true: we may fall sick.

Happiness is neither outside nor inside us: it is in God, both outside and inside us (L.407, B.465, S.26).

In short, 'We desire truth and find in ourselves nothing but uncertainty. We seek happiness and find only wretchedness and death. We are incapable of not desiring truth and happiness and incapable of either certainty or happiness' (L.401, B.437, S.20). And this tension is presented as pointing beyond itself:

Man's greatness is so obvious that it arises [se tire] even from his wretchedness, for what is nature in animals we call wretchedness in man, thus recognizing that, if his nature is today like that of the animals, he must have fallen from some better state which was once his own (L.117, B.409, S.149).

In 1658 Pascal gave an account of his work on the *Apology* to friends at Port-Royal, and what are usually thought to be notes for this play the role of pivot in his arrangement of the fragments, as revealed by the contents table we find in the two *Copies* (L.149, B.430, S.182).[9] The notes start by apparently pointing back to the deadlock of "all human philosophy"; God and his operations may be beyond our comprehension, "and yet, but for this mystery, the most incomprehensible of all, we remain incomprehensible to ourselves" (L.131, B.434, S.164). The note "after explaining incomprehensibility" may also refer to his response to the obvious objection: 'We know that the infinite exists without knowing its nature, just as we know that it is untrue that numbers are finite. . . . | Therefore we may well know that God exists without knowing what he is' (L.418, B.233, S.680). 'Everything that is incomprehensible does not cease to exist' (L.230, B.430, S.262: repeated with reference to L.418 later in L.149). There are, it would appear, degrees of incomprehensibility, and even "the most incomprehensible of all" is not totally unintelligible; the notes end with

[9] All serious contemporary study of the *Pensées* leans heavily on two "*Copies*" made of the relevant papers in the order they were found at Pascal's death. Even those who object that their "authority has in recent years come to be accepted too uncritically" concede that "that authority remains real none the less" (Topliss, 164; see also Hubert). The work of Louis Lafuma (see especially Lafuma (2)) proved decisive in authenticating these *Copies*, but gave precedence to the *Première Copie*. The recent investigations of Philippe Sellier (Sellier (1) and (2)) seem to have rendered this ordering untenable, and I have treated his arguments defending the priority of the *Seconde Copie* as conclusive, together with the consequences they appear to imply for the chronology of the fragments.

the remark 'There is enough light for those who desire only to see, and enough darkness for those of a contrary disposition.' The framework of the whole section thus represents the familiar transition from understanding to will, the two elements being seen as interdependent.

After the reference to "incomprehensibility" the notes continue:

> Man's greatness and wretchedness are so evident that the true religion must necessarily teach us that there is in man some great principle of greatness and some great principle of wretchedness.
>
> It must also account for such amazing contradictions. . . .
>
> It must teach us the cure for our helplessness and the means of obtaining this cure. Let us examine all the religions of the world on that point and let us see whether any but the Christian religion meets it.

To avoid begging the question, the standard philosophical systems are accounted potential candidates for the desiderated "true religion", as much as that of "the Moslems", and we are told that "The philosophers . . . do not know what your true good is, nor what your true state is. | How could they provide cures for ills which they did not even know?" Reason is thus presented as pointing beyond itself, and man's aspirations to understanding and happiness— understood as reflecting the tension between *grandeur* and *misère* —suggest criteria that any proposed resolution must meet.

The immense perplexity men have encountered in grappling with these issues strongly suggests that any proposed solution worth taking seriously will, at least in part, transcend our mental capacity:

> For, after all, what is man in nature? A nothing compared to the infinite, a whole compared to the nothing, a middle point between all and nothing, infinitely remote from an understanding of the extremes; the end of things and their principles are unattainably hidden from him in impenetrable secrecy. . . .
>
> All the sciences are infinite . . . in the multiplicity and subtlety of their principles, for anyone can see that those which are supposed to be ultimate do not stand by themselves, but depend on others, which depend on others again, and thus never allow of any finality. . . .
>
> And what makes our inability to know things absolute is that they are simple in themselves, while we are composed of two opposing natures of different kinds, soul and body. . . . Man is to himself the greatest prodigy in nature, for he cannot conceive what body is, and still less what mind is, and least of all how a body can be joined to a mind. This is his supreme difficulty, and yet it is his very being. 'The way in which minds are attached

to bodies is beyond man's understanding, and yet this is what man is.'
(L.199, B.72, S.230; the concluding quotation is from St Augustine.)

This, we are told, is "where unaided [*naturelles*] knowledge brings
us"; there is a "disproportion" between man, together with his
capacities, and the reality of which he is a part. "The Christian
religion", of course, is well placed to meet the implied requirement:

What do the prophets say about Jesus Christ? That he will plainly be God?
No, but that he is a truly hidden God. . . .
    Let us not then be criticised for lack of clarity, since we openly profess it
(L.228, B.751, S.260).
God being thus hidden, any religion that does not say that God is hidden is
not true, and any religion which does not explain why does not instruct.
Ours does all this (L.242, B.585, S.275).

As for the more positive criteria, deriving from the conflicting
tendencies in man, "Follow your own impulses. Observe yourself,
and see if you do not find the living characteristics of these two
natures."
    Thus the notes for Port-Royal, from which the last passage
quoted is again taken, present us in short compass with an outline of
Pascal's characteristic procedure. While they certainly refer to
historical "miracles and proofs", the heart needs to be made ready
to recognize these. With respect to this preparation, the personified
"Wisdom of God" claims the capacity "to reconcile these contradictions"; '"I do not mean you to believe me submissively and without
reason; I do not claim to subdue you by tyranny. Nor do I claim to
account to you for everything."' We are invited to "observe", and
"find" for ourselves how aptly that "Wisdom" is proportioned to
our condition, an investigation in which both understanding and
aspiration play an interconnected part.
    One of the most remarkable features of this procedure is the way
it renders explicit the underlying structure of a widespread form of
argument often regarded as dialectical. The late Dr Farrer provided
a pithy account and defence of this structure:

If the world is in God, it is likely that those who habitually look at it have
some crypto-theism in some parts of their interpretation of it, some
sub-awareness of certain aspects of the divine activity. If we wish to enlarge
the vision of these persons, we shall do ill to throw a formulated theology at
their heads, set out according to the *ordo essendi*; we had much better start
from their scraps of crypto-theism and show how these can only be upheld

in a full theistic position, and how the denial of such a position removes them wholly. Such a proceeding is what one finds in almost every proof of God known to history, and we call it dialectic reasoning (Farrer (1), 10).

The "heretical argument of Anselm" is admitted to be an exception, but the other classic "proofs" are all argued to fit—some despite appearances—this non-demonstrative pattern. Characteristically, the theist

exhibits his account of God active in the world and the world existing in God, that others may recognise it to be the account of what they themselves apprehend—or, if you like, that others may find it to be an instrument through which they apprehend, for perhaps apprehension here is not separable from interpretation.

But such apprehension is not necessarily forthcoming at once, for it is evident that deity is, like other things, e.g. the unity and freedom of the self, obscure to our vision, and may need some straining of the eyes before it is brought into focus.

Dialectic is the required procedure for arriving at "a convincing interpretation"; 'we can go no further than to challenge men to recognise that, with theology and its consequences rigidly excluded, we must exclude from our account of the world things which in our thoughts and actions we cannot but assume to be there' (ibid. 9–12). The final recourse, therefore, is "to apprehension and to judgment".

But this admission points to a lacuna in the presentation. "The man who continues in disbelief will regard such dialectic as an argument which sets out to make men through and through as bad as their worst inherited prejudices." Even so, it might be argued, a wavering nationalist—brought up to believe in "a metaphysical superpersonal entity called the Race"—might have his doubts removed by a dialectic that focused on the way that those concepts which for him "appeared to enlighten, dignify or dramatise the real world" belonged to an ideology that presupposed the existence of the racialist chimaera. Such dialectic might be genuinely informative, for as one grows accustomed to construing events in terms of ideologically interrelated concepts, so it can happen that "the relative predicates lose their conscious relatedness, and the chimaera drops more and more out of sight. As . . . a Public School master who has long debated whether he believed in God or not, may compromise in middle life, and opt for a system of Absolute Values." Such considerations show what a difficult game the dialectic is; for we shall have not only to make our appeal to crypto-theism, we shall need also to show that the theistic vision arises out of a pure metaphysical interest in Being, in contrast to various idolatries whose impure motives can be seen. Indeed dialectic, to be complete, would have to do battle with every rival; and if every system were of equal importance, and if nature were not strong and the soul *naturaliter deicola*, we should certainly never produce conviction (ibid.).

Of course, not every system was of equal importance to the *mondain* unbeliever of seventeenth-century France, and Pascal is properly selective in his examination of "all the religions of the world"; he also trusts both in the strength of nature, which "backs up helpless reason and stops it going so wildly astray" (L.131, B.434, S.164), and in the natural bent of the soul towards God—'If man was not made for God, why is he only happy in God?' (L.399, B.438, S.18)—though with the important *caveat* "If man was made for God, why is he so opposed to God?" (ibid.). But above all, he sees the need for an interrogation of motive in the dialectical assessment of "apprehension" and "judgment". His criticism of "the Moslems, who offer nothing else for our good than earthly pleasures, even in eternity" (L.149, B.430, S.182; the Port-Royal notes) is precisely designed to contrast the Christian faith with an "idolatry whose impure motives can be seen". Pascal is honest enough to concede that there are

Two kinds of men in every religion. . . .
   Among the Jews those who were carnal and those who were spiritual, the Christians of the old law.
   Among the Christians the gross ones, who are the Jews of the new law.
   The carnal Jews awaited a carnal Messiah, and the gross Christians believe that the Messiah has dispensed them from loving God. True Jews and true Christians worship a Messiah who makes them love God (L.286, B.609, S.318).

Thus it is open to the Moslems to attempt to show that a similar distinction is available within Islam, as it is to the Jesuits (whom he clearly has in his sights; see the tenth of the *Lettres provinciales*) to argue that he has misrepresented their position—or indeed that he has misdescribed what it is to be a "gross Christian". Such debates are familiar enough; but however much they may have progressed in the last three hundred years, Pascal's importance lies in his perception of their integral relation to the rest of the dialectical enterprise. In pioneering the integration of understanding and volition, he pointed to the need in assessing argument about first principles for some such concept as Kierkegaard's "Purity of Heart"—or its secular cousin "authenticity".[10]

5. *L'Esprit de Finesse*

> Is it wrong for me to be guided in my actions by the propositions of physics? Am I to say I have no good ground for doing so? Isn't precisely this what we call a 'good ground'?
>
> Supposing we met people who did not regard that as a telling reason. Now, how do we imagine this? Instead of the physicist, they consult an oracle. (And for that we consider them primitive.) Is it wrong for them to consult an oracle and be guided by it?—If we call this "wrong" aren't we using our language-game as a base from which to combat theirs?
>
> And are we right or wrong to combat it? Of course there are all sorts of slogans which will be used to support our proceedings.
>
> Where two principles really do meet which cannot be reconciled with one another, then each man declares the other a fool and heretic.
>
> I said I would 'combat' the other man,—but wouldn't I give him *reasons*? Certainly; but how far do they go? At the end of reasons comes *persuasion*. (Think what happens when missionaries convert natives.)
>
> (Wittgenstein (3), paras. 608–12)

For Pascal, too, persuasion takes over where reason fails to resolve conflict of principles—and he would accept the religious analogy as paradigmatic. He concedes that we hanker after something better, a mode of argument which is properly demonstrative on the geometric model yet able to establish its own principles and concepts without circularity—enabling us "to define all terms and prove all propositions". However, this ideal is one which "men can never achieve. Certainly this method would be admirable [*belle*], but it is absolutely impossible"; geometry cannot do without primitive terms and first principles, and so long as we adhere to its standards of demonstrability we find that "whatever transcends geometry transcends us". If we dismiss the ideal of this *"veritable ordre"*, "it

---

[10] As discussed in, for example, Trilling. For "Purity of Heart" see Kierkegaard (2).

does not follow that we should abandon any sort of *ordre*"; orderly procedures are available which lead to results which are perfectly "certain" (Pascal (2), '*De l'esprit géométrique*', 348–55).

We have seen that the first principles of geometry are "natural truths known to everyone", but also that these are insufficient to ground demonstrations according to the order of *l'esprit de géométrie* concerning the fundamental issues of human life. With regard to that order, 'I know something about it and how few people understand it. No human science can keep it. St. Thomas did not keep it. Mathematics keeps it, but it goes so far as to be useless' (L.694, B.61, S.573). Pascal concedes that Descartes attempted to apply the geometric order far beyond mathematics, but is not impressed by the results: '*Descartes*. In general terms one must say: 'That is the result of figure and motion,' because it is true, but to name them and assemble the machine is quite ridiculous. It is useless [*inutile*], uncertain, and arduous' (L.84, B.79, S.118). "Uncertain", of course, because the application of theory to the recalcitrant world involves the intervention of more principles than those of figure and motion. So far as men are concerned, at least, we need also consider the will—and here he speaks with the authority of one who, by inventing *la Pascaline*, had literally "assembled the machine"; 'The adding-machine produces effects closer to thought than anything done by the animals, but it does nothing to justify the assertion that it has a will like the animals' (L.741, B.340, S.617). As we saw earlier, Descartes's uselessness and uncertainty are for Pascal connected; in trying to grasp our condition we need an apparatus which connects goodness with truth, will with reason, utility with certainty —we need, in effect, the Pascalian heart. At the end of reasons, certainly, come the persuasions of the heart; but "it does not follow that we should abandon any sort of *ordre*", for "the heart has its reasons" of which *l'esprit de géométrie* knows nothing.

Once the relevance of the will is admitted, however, we enter a region of the "art of persuasion" which is "incomparably more difficult, more subtle, more useful and more admirable" than that part modelled on geometry; while he is happy to systematize the rules governing geometric thinking, it is otherwise here. The reason given is that he finds himself incapable of doing so; 'and I feel myself so utterly disproportioned to the task, that I believe the matter to be absolutely impossible' (Pascal (2), '*De l'art de persuader*', 355–6). He admits that there are rules here as "certain" ("*sûres*") as those for demonstrative reason, but believes that it is impossible "to know and employ them perfectly", let alone systematize them, because men are too variable and inconstant.

Inconstancy. We think playing upon man is like playing upon an ordinary organ. It is indeed an organ, but strange, shifting and changeable. Those who only know how to play an ordinary organ would never be in tune on this one. You have to know where the keys are (L.55, B.111, S.88).

But if perfect knowledge is impossible here, it does not follow that no guidance is available, nor that there may be more or less competent practitioners. The systematizing approach of *l'esprit de géométrie* is inappropriate, but this does not prevent Pascal attempting in practice—with some success—what he could not schematize in theory; the *Pensées* are a classic product of *l'esprit de finesse*.

The principles which are the concern of *les esprits fins*, we are told, are "felt" (the verb is *sentir*)

rather than seen, and it is with endless difficulty that they can be communicated [*faire sentir*] to those who do not feel them for themselves. These things are so delicate and numerous that it takes a sense of great delicacy and precision to feel and judge correctly and accurately from this *sentiment*: most often it is not possible to set it out in orderly fashion [*démontrer par ordre*] as in *géométrie*, because the necessary principles are not ready to hand, and it would be an endless task to undertake . . .

The principles are so intricate and numerous, that it is almost impossible not to miss some. Now the omission of one principle can lead to error, and so one needs very clear sight to see all the principles as well as an accurate mind [*esprit juste*] to avoid drawing false conclusions from known principles (L.512, B.1, S.670).

For an example of the intricacy of the principles, so far as the project of the *Apology* is concerned, it is worth recalling that "Man's true nature, his true good and true virtue, and true religion are things which cannot be known separately" (L.393, B.442, S.12). This insistence on the interconnection of the principles involved in trying to grasp our condition is echoed by Wittgenstein's more recent grappling with the way we assess our own assumptions:[11]

---

[11] It is also, of course, a central feature of much of the best Christian apologetic since Pascal's time. Compare, for example, Archbishop William Temple's insistence that "By religious experience we ought to mean an experience which is religious through and through—an experiencing of all things in the light of the knowledge of God. It is this, and not any moment of illumination, of which we may say that it is self-authenticating; for in such an experience all things increasingly fit together in a single intelligible whole" (Temple, 25).

We do not learn the practice of making empirical judgments by learning rules: we are taught *judgments* and their connection with other judgments. A *totality* of judgments is made plausible to us.

When we first begin to *believe* anything, what we believe is not a single proposition, it is a whole system of propositions. (Light dawns gradually over the whole.)

It is not single axioms that strike me as obvious, it is a system in which consequences and premises give one another *mutual* support. . . .

There are countless general empirical propositions that count as certain for us. . . .

Experience can be said to teach us these propositions. However, it does not teach us them in isolation: rather, it teaches us a host of interdependent propositions. If they were isolated I might perhaps doubt them (Wittgenstein (3), 140–2 and 273–4).

Attempts have recently been made to trivialize Pascal's account of "finesse" (e.g. Miel (1), 165); the Wittgensteinian parallel should perhaps encourage us to treat these efforts with some scepticism.[12]

But we should be careful not to exaggerate in the opposite direction. Pascal throws some light on why he feels so "disproportioned to the task" of systematizing the reasons of the heart in his discussion of the "disproportion of man";

If man studied himself, he would see how incapable he is of going further. How could a part possibly know the whole? But perhaps he will aspire to know at least the parts to which he bears some proportion. But the parts of

[12] Wittgenstein's later work, indeed, represents a powerful expression of *l'esprit de finesse* (compare Bambrough (3) and Levi (2), but see also ch. 8, n. 1). It is often read as supporting conceptual, and hence cultural, relativism (see ch. 1, nn. 17 and 18), but this is over simple. See, for example, Hinman, who aligns Wittgenstein's accounts of differing "forms of life"—and hence "language games"—with Gadamer's version of hermeneutics but, unlike Rorty (1) and (2), without drawing relativistic conclusions in his interpretation of Wittgenstein.

In the work quoted in the text, Wittgenstein likens the belief in God to that of members of a tribe who believe that "people sometimes go to the moon (perhaps that is how they interpret their dreams), and who indeed grant that there are no ordinary means of climbing up to it or flying there" ((3), paras. 106–7; the passage was written, of course, long before space travel became practicable). Of this tribe he remarks: "We say: these people do not know a lot that we know. And, let them be never so sure of their belief—they are wrong and we know it. |If we compare our system of knowledge with theirs then theirs is evidently the poorer one by far" (((3), 286). His final paragraph suggests that we should not read the "for that we consider them primitive" ((3), 609) quoted in the text (at the start of this section) as simply an expression of cultural bias. It is not as clear as is often thought that Wittgenstein closes the door on the sort of cross-cultural comparisons envisaged by Pascal; only if we interpret his distinction between "reasons" and "persuasion" ((3), 612) in terms of the geometric model's devaluation of "persuasion" are we forced to resolve his nuances into a straightforward cultural relativism.

the whole are all so related and linked together that I think it is impossible to know one without the other and without the whole. . . .

Thus, since all things are both caused and causing, assisted and assisting, mediate and immediate, providing mutual support in a chain linking together naturally and imperceptibly the most distant and different things, I consider it as impossible to know the parts without knowing the whole as to know the whole without knowing the individual parts (L.199, B.72, S.230).

One influential commentator has taken this as providing "the clearest possible expression both of Pascal's own attitude and that of any dialectical thinker", and expressing the point of view from which "we can and should" try to understand Pascal's work as a whole—thereby seeing that work as embodying "The Tragic Vision". (Goldmann (1), ch. 1) But this is to give insufficient weight to the fact that the pessimistic account of the human condition in question is explicitly presented as "where unaided knowledge brings us"; it is part of a section entitled 'Transition from knowledge of man to knowledge of God', and represents an aspect of man's *misère* without God. It represents, for Pascal, an important truth, but it is balanced by others which point to a conception of knowledge richer than that which generates the impasse. Pascal is certainly, as we have seen, in some sense a "dialectical thinker", and his dialectic wrestles with the problems generated by man's "disproportion"; but to take the "impossibility" of knowledge as presented here as his last word, in terms of which we should interpret the rest of his work, is seriously to distort it.[13]

[13] By reading Pascal in the light of Lukács, Goldmann's perversely brilliant interpretation falls, ironically but precisely, under the condemnation he reserves for others: "Certain partial elements of a work are taken out of context and transformed into independent and autonomous wholes; the existence of similar elements in the work of another author is then noted, and a parallel is established; a wholly factitious analogy is then set up, which either consciously or not fails to take account of the context in which these elements are originally to be found, and which gives them a completely different and even contradictory meaning to the one which they originally had" (Goldmann (1), 10–11). For detailed analysis of the misreadings involved see Blanchet, Lafuma (4), and Goldmann (2); also Miel (1), 114–15 and 161.

More recently Paul de Man has argued that Pascal's avowal that he finds it "impossible" to systematize the "art of persuasion" is a symptom of the incoherence of that art: "Even in the transcendental realm of revealed language in Holy Writ, the necessary choice between seduction and truth remains undecidable" ('Pascal's Allegory of Persuasion' 23, in Greenblatt). The implication would seem to be that we are trapped in what for Pascal would count as *misère*. However, although de Man rightly sees that the *Pensées* "helps to undo the tendencious and simplistic opposition between knowledge and faith which is often forced upon Pascal" (7), the undecidability in question appears to depend on attributing to Pascal just such a "simplistic opposition".

Pascal presents the epistemological perplexities of part and whole in the context of an analogous problem about "principles"; "those which are supposed to be ultimate do not stand by themselves, but depend on others, which depend on others again, and thus never allow of any finality" (ibid.). The way out of the impasse, it appears, is through abandoning the attempt to find self-evident axioms, and so changing our perspective that we grasp these principles within a Wittgensteinian framework "in which consequences and premises give one another mutual support". As Pascal puts it, "The thing must be seen all at once, at a glance, and not as a result of progressive reasoning, at least up to a point" (L.512, B.1, S.670). The final phrase reflects the obvious fact that not all the operations of *l'esprit de finesse*, which is here being discussed, are instantaneous; the operation of the projected *Apology* in changing the perspective of readers is the most immediate example. In the first instance the significance of the contrast lies in the rejection of "progressive reasoning" ("*progrès de raisonnement*"), the drawing of successive consequences from first principles characteristic of *l'esprit de géométrie*, in favour of the model of "light dawning over the whole", whether or not the dawn comes "gradually" or "all at once".

However, the suggestion that seeing things "at a glance" is characteristic of *les esprits fins* reflects a truth on which Pascal may have had only an insecure hold. In planning his *Apology* he considered a number of different strategies; ordering it by means of dialogues or by letters being the favourite candidates—the *Lettres provinciales*, of course, had employed both. A form which it seems he did not seriously envisage using was that of the aphorism, yet the accident of history has led to the bulk of the fragments known as the *Pensées* approximating more closely to that model than to any other. A few decades earlier, Bacon had advocated their use:

For aphorisms, not to be ridiculous, must be made out of the pith and heart of sciences. For illustration and excursion are cut off; variety of examples is cut off; deduction and connexion are cut off; descriptions of practice are cut off; so there is nothing left to make the aphorisms of but some good quantity of observation. . . . Aphorisms, representing only portions and as it were fragments of knowledge, invite others to contribute and add something in their turn (Bacon, '*De Augmentis Scientiarum*', VI. ii. 531).

The power the *Pensées* have exerted over men's minds is partly a function of such characteristics; the mind is not sidetracked from the "good quantity of observation" by elaborate deductions—save in the notorious example of *Infini rien* which is a dialogue, not an aphorism—and the invitation to "observe yourself" of the Port-Royal notes is reinforced by the use of the "short and dispersed sentence". These are indeed ideally suited to *l'esprit fin*; but the most obvious characteristic of the aphorism is its brevity, its ability to enable the reader to grasp the matter in question "at a glance". The juxtaposition of many such fragments, encouraging a sequence of such "glances" within a coherent but non-deductive framework, is ideally suited to those operations of *l'esprit de finesse* which bring it about that "Light dawns gradually over the whole". Pascal's early death may have brought about the publication of a work which is both more effective and more faithful to his own account of *finesse* than any *Apology* structured along the lines he was in fact planning.

But if there is evidence of incompleteness of thought in the analysis of *finesse*, it is also apparent when we consider the relation between the two *esprits*. We are assured that it is best to combine the two, though it is very difficult to do so, but the account of what this would involve is left at the level of metaphor. The notion of *"justesse"* may be intended to supply a link. It has been plausibly argued that the extremely obscure account of *"l'esprit de justesse"* (L.511, B.2, S.669) locates it as a subdivision of *l'esprit de géométrie* (Brunschivicg, xii. 16–17); yet we have seen that *l'esprit juste* is also a desirable property of *l'esprit de finesse*. But if a link between *"justesse"* and *"juste"* was intended, it has not been provided. Again, the most systematic account of *l'esprit géométrique* is careful to point out that it is expounding only the method of synthesis; analysis, "the art of discovering unknown truths", is explicitly omitted (Pascal (2), 348). Pascal characterizes the principles with which *l'esprit de finesse* is concerned as "in ordinary usage and there for all to see", which is a fair characterization of the traditional starting-point of geometric analysis; as he nowhere else discusses analysis, one is tempted to see *finesse* as a version of it.[14] However,

---

[14] There seems to be some tension between the claim that the principles of *finesse* are "there for all to see" and that they are "not ready to hand". Presumably the two theses are supposed to be reconciled by the contention that "the principles are so intricate and numerous that it is almost impossible not to miss some" (L.512, B.1, S.670), but it must be admitted that Pascal falls far below his usual standard of clarity here—a further indication that in the analysis of *finesse* he died with business still unfinished.

analysis is clearly characterized as belonging to *l'esprit géométrique*, and it is a leading feature of Descartes's method which is so harshly criticized. The relation between *finesse* and the "analytic" side of *géométrie* remains unworked out, and it cannot be said that the brief discussion of analysis in the *Port-Royal Logic* (Arnauld, iv. ch. 2) sheds much light on the matter.

Instead, the *Pensées* subsumes the problem within a threefold framework which depends more on theological than epistemological considerations. The contemporary orthodoxy that this structure holds the key to Pascal's thinking (see, for example, Broome, Davidson (2), Krailsheimer (2), Miel (1), Nelson) has been elegantly undermined by Janet Morgan (Morgan (2)), but the trichotomy still has a certain explanatory value. It is developed most fully in two fragments, of which the one based on Jansenius appears to be the earlier (Sellier (2), 169–96). This fragment presents that earthly, fallen, love we call 'concupiscence' as operating in

three orders of things: flesh, mind [*l'esprit*] and will.
The carnal are rich men and kings. Their interest is in the body.
Inquirers and scholars; their interest is in the mind.
The wise; their interest is in *la justice*.

The characteristic form of concupiscence besetting the wise is pride, "for you cannot grant that a man has become wise but that he is wrong to glory in it, for it is right that he should.│Therefore God alone bestows wisdom, and that is why: 'He that glorieth, let him glory in the Lord'" (L.933, B.460, S.761). A number of familiar themes are here being woven together; the two loves of St Augustine, the alignment of the will with a wisdom that transcends the mental operations of the detached scholar, and the contradictions inherent in such wisdom so long as it remains at the purely human level. Thus it should come as no surprise to find the other fragment putting a more distinctively Pascalian stamp on the initial Jansenist analysis; the "geometrical" books of Archimedes are taken as paradigmatic of the order of *l'esprit*, we learn that wisdom is perceived by "the eyes of the heart"—operating in the order of supreme importance—and instead of concupiscence the focus is on the "heavenly" love, charity, thus balancing the "wretchedness of man without God" of the earlier fragment with the "happiness of man with God":

The infinite distance between body and mind symbolizes the infinitely more infinite distance between mind and charity, for charity is supernatural. . . .

They are three orders differing in kind. . . .

There are some who are only capable of admiring carnal greatness, as if there were no such thing as greatness of the mind. And others who only admire greatness of the mind, as if there were not infinitely higher greatness in wisdom.

All bodies, the firmament, the stars, the earth and its kingdoms are not worth the least of minds, for it knows them all and itself too, while bodies know nothing.

All bodies together and all minds together and all their products are not worth the least impulse of charity. This is of an infinitely superior order.

Out of all bodies together we could not succeed in creating one little thought. It is impossible, and of a different order. Out of all bodies and minds we could not extract one impulse of true charity. It is impossible, and of a different, supernatural, order (L.308, B.793, S.339).

The supreme exemplar of the order of charity is, of course, Jesus Christ.

We have already seen how Pascal would defend the thesis that the eyes of the heart may be blinded or enlightened according to the disposition of the will towards self-love or charity respectively; an accurate grasp of our lot must be God-centred. Since the heart is the place where God may be known, and also provides the potential for us to understand our condition, it is not surprising to find that when it is enlightened—operating according to the principle of charity —it represents the culminating point of man's *grandeur*. The threefold structure of the heart provides a perspective in terms of which another triple pattern may be discerned and assessed, a pattern in which the heart is itself but an element. The wisdom that is a function of the integration of will and understanding is to be distinguished from the knowledge that comes from "geometrical" scholarship; it very much looks as if we here have a reformulation in theological terms of the epistemological discrimination between *finesse* and *géométrie*. These orders "differ in kind" and yet may be ranked in the same scale; the apparent paradox may well echo his work at the "geometrical" level on the way different orders of magnitude may at one and the same time be discontinuous—that is, disproportionate to each other—and yet be ranked hierarchically (Pascal (2), '*Potestatum Numericarum Summa*', 90–4). Within a given order we can resolve the problem of discontinuous ranking without too much difficulty, but when we are presented with such ranking between the orders it is a different matter; having, as it would appear, no epistemological resolution ready to hand, he characteristically presents the matter as a brute fact, reformulates it in a theological context, and provides an analogy.

This is derived from what "unaided knowledge" finds its "supreme difficulty"; the relation between body and mind (L.199, B.72, S.230). "All our dignity consists in thought" (L.200, B.347, S.232), it is a sign of man's *grandeur* and superior to the order of the body in which "man is only a reed, the weakest in nature"; but our "disproportion" is such that unaided we cannot conceive "how a body can be joined to a mind", for they are "opposing natures of different kinds". But this "infinite distance . . . symbolizes the infinitely more infinite distance" between *l'esprit géométrique* and the proper operation of the heart. We begin to see why the account of the difficult though desirable unification of *finesse* and *géométrie* within a single mind is left in such an unsatisfactory state, and why Pascal feels himself "so utterly disproportioned to the task" of systematizing the principles of that art of persuasion which plays on all the organ stops of man's "inconstancy".[15]

6. *"Infini Rien"* and Finesse

Pascal, then, has a well developed account of the threefold structure of the heart, but only a somewhat impressionistic one of its relation to the other two orders which with it constitute the human condition. But these impressions are sufficient to provide guidelines for his *Apology*; it must be focused primarily upon the heart, but must not ignore wholly the other orders of reality—for the workings of concupiscence operate in all three.

The most sophisticated attempt to mount a three-pronged assault

[15] By the time of the *Pensées* Pascal clearly combined within himself both *esprits*, even if he could give only the sketchiest account of their integration. The picturesque legends which depict him developing out of the narrowness of a mere *géomètre* under the tutelage of the Chevalier de Méré do not bear scrutiny (see Mesnard (2)), but Méré certainly stood in Pascal's mind as a paradigm of *l'esprit fin*, as Archimedes and Descartes did in the case of *géométrie*. Méré was also the pattern of an *honnête homme*, and the versatility of that ideal is both reflected in the *Pensées* (cf. L.647, B.35, S.532) and helps reinforce Pascal's conviction that *finesse* is essentially many-sided; the cited fragment may even be seen as pointing to the possibility that *finesse* at its fullest could incorporate *l'esprit de géométrie*.

of this nature is "*Infini rien*". The initial partition of possibilities in terms of which the wager operates is "Either God is or he is not", together with the concomitant utilities about salvation for the faithful specified by the orthodox conception of God (L.418, B.233, S.680). Given this partition, the ensuing exercise in 'The Geometry of Chance' is perfectly valid; it moves at increasing levels of sophistication from an argument from dominance, to one from expectation, to the clinching "demonstration" from dominating expectation. (For detailed analysis from the standpoint of probability theory, see Hacking (1) and (2) ch 8.) *L'esprit géométrique* is wooed even in terms of its own concupiscence with the strongest persuasion available to that order: '*Cela est démonstratif*'; even geometrical reasoning points to the need for a faith that transcends it. But there are two caveats that must be entered, corresponding to the two other "orders". One concerns the initial partition. Pascal does not think this can be given "geometrically"; most of the rest of the *Pensées*, as we have seen, is concerned to establish it by reasons which appeal to the "heart". A different conception of God, it has often been urged, will undermine the whole argument; but this is why Pascal is at pains elsewhere to draw from his analysis of the human condition certain criteria that any acceptable characterization of God must meet.[16] In his notes for Port-Royal, it will be remembered, he suggests one such and goes on: "Let us examine all the religions of the world on that point and let us see whether any but the Christian religion meets it" (L.149, B.430, S.182). Here we have an example of the heart providing a first principle required for a geometrical demonstration which is not one of the "natural truths known to everyone", though these latter (concerning "number, time, dimensions") also play their appointed role in the argument. The "eyes of the heart" belong to an order "infinitely superior" to that of *l'esprit géométrique*, thus it is appropriate that the latter's most sophisticated demonstrations turn out to be dependent on their clear-sightedness.

The other reservation concerns the order of the body, and turns on the weakness of the flesh in matters of the spirit.

[16] See Geoffrey Brown's 'A Defence of Pascal's Wager' (477): "Although theoretically Pascal claims that an infinite number of options ought to make no difference, he is really assuming that the reader has reached the point at which his mind is poised between Christianity and atheism: the purpose of much of the remainder of the *Pensées* is to bring him to this point." Brown argues that, even without this appeal to context, the problem about the initial partition can be met at the technical level.

'I am being held fast and am so made that I cannot believe. What do you want me to do then?'—'That is true, but at least get it into your head that, if you are unable to believe, it is because of your passions, since reason impels you to believe and yet you cannot do so. . . . Learn from those who were once bound like you and who now wager all they have. . . . They behaved just as if they did believe, taking holy water, having masses said, and so on. That will make you believe quite naturally, and *abêtira* you.

The power of habit is taken up elsewhere;

Outward penance creates a disposition to inward penance, and humiliations dispose us to be humble (L.936, B.698, S.751).

For we must make no mistake about ourselves: we are as much automaton as mind. As a result, demonstration is not the only instrument for convincing us. How few things can be demonstrated! Proofs only convince the mind; habit [*coutume*] provides the strongest proofs and those that are most believed. It inclines the automaton, which leads the mind unconsciously along with it. . . . In short, we must resort to habit once the mind has seen where the truth lies. . . . When we believe only by the strength of our conviction and the automaton is inclined to believe the opposite, that is not enough. We must therefore make both parts believe: the mind by reasons, which need to be seen only once in a lifetime, and the automaton by habit, and not allowing it any inclination to the contrary: 'Incline my heart' (L.821, B.252, S.661).

The power of the human unconscious is here brought into the open, and aligned with the order of the body; following St Augustine it is understood in terms of habit, and reference is also made to passion and inclination. Any adequate *Apology*, therefore, must make provision for the automaton in terms of these considerations; not in order to create faith—for we know that this is a gift of God, it is of little use to "believe without inspiration" (L.808, B.245, S.655) —but so that the reader may be impelled to prepare himself in such a way that God, in the words of Psalm 119, may "incline my heart". There are, we are told, "three ways to believe: reason, habit, inspiration" (L.808, B.245, S.655); "*Infini rien*", like the *Pensées* as a whole, makes provision for all three.

But it will be noticed that there seem to be almost as many loose ends left by Pascal's account of the order of the body as by that of *finesse*. It arises out of the theological notion of the "flesh" ("*chair*") with the associated "carnal" ("*charnel*"); to have an "interest in the body [*corps*]" in this sense is to be concerned with power and riches, and those dominated by these concerns typically disregard the things of the mind and spirit. But we also find that "out of all bodies together we could not succeed in creating one little thought", thus moving from a theological distinction to one in the philosophy of mind. And by then considering "thought" ("*pensée*") in terms of fully conscious human thought we find a psychological contrast drawn with the workings of the "automaton" which seem to operate at the level of the beasts ("*abêtira*"). Here Fr Copleston's unease about the slipperiness of Pascal's terms seems much more justified than in the case of the "heart", and the unfinished character of the work needs more than usually to be pleaded in mitigation. But the criticism should not be pressed too far. If we attempt to interpret the three "orders" as if they were a reworking of faculty psychology—that classic construct of *l'esprit de géométrie* —we soon run into anomalies. But we have seen that Pascal was working his way towards a greater flexibility, even *finesse*, than such rigid categories allowed. There are obvious family resemblances between the concepts of carnality, the flesh and the body, and the resulting interconnected web of associations has lain at the heart of Christianity ever since St John declared that "the Word became flesh". From one perspective flesh/mind/will represents an intelligible hierarchy, from another body/mind/charity, and from a third habit/reason/inspiration. We have seen something of how all three hierarchies can be used in different ways to illuminate the same basic grasp of the human condition, and Pascal might well reply to his critics that, so long as they do not invalidate each other, we should not ask for more. A network of interlocking points of view, focusing on the same reality, is more representative of the reasons of the heart than analysis based on a single and rigid set of categories—whether we are dealing with the body or *finesse*.

The greatest problems in aligning the different hierarchies come, as we might expect, when we consider the interrelationship of the two elements formally most distant from each other, body and heart. Here there is evidence that Pascal's thought continued to develop to a very late stage. The fragment about the automaton is found in one of the later *liasses* (Pascal (6), 338), and after "Incline my heart" he has drawn a line and added in much smaller writing (Pascal (4), 271)—presumably some time afterwards—the following paragraph:

Reason works slowly, looking so often at so many principles, which must always be present, that it is constantly nodding or straying because all its principles are not present. *Sentiment* does not work like that, but works instantly, and is always ready. We must then put our faith in *sentiment*, or it will always be vacillating (L.821, B.252, S.661).

Here we have the reason/*sentiment* distinction developed in a way strongly reminiscent of that between the two *esprits*—a further ground for associating *finesse* with the heart, which has just been invoked. But we have seen that in the rest of L.821 it is the operation of the automaton that prevents faith from vacillating, thus suggesting an intimate connection between the order of the body and the *sentiment* that moves the heart. Yet if we remember the centrality of will to the heart, and treat the hierarchy of the three orders as a sometimes dispensable speculative instrument rather than a classification of fundamental ontological levels, this connection is not surprising. "Passions" and "inclinations" may be mastered by "habit", and all at the unconscious level. When such forces act on the will they are called '*sentiments*', and it was to be the business of the *Apology* to bring the most powerful ones to full consciousness —once revealed to "the eyes of the heart" that organ's capacity for understanding could be taught how to value them;

Abraham took nothing for himself but only for his servants. Thus the righteous [*juste*] man takes nothing from the world or its applause for himself, but only for his passions, which he uses like a master, saying to one 'Go' and (to another) 'Come'. 'Thou shalt rule over thy desire [*appetitus*].' Thus mastered his passions become virtues; avarice, jealousy, anger, even God ascribes these to himself. And they are just as much virtues as mercy, pity, constancy, which are also passions. We must treat them like slaves, and give them food but prevent the soul feeding on it. For, when passions are in control they become vices, and then they give their food to the soul, which feeds on it and is poisoned (L.603, B.502, S.500).

The concluding note to the discussion of the automaton thus points to another way of envisaging the role of the heart. In an early fragment Pascal had sketched man's condition without God in terms of a

Civil war in man between reason and passions.
   If there were only reason without passions.
   If there were only passions without reason.

But since he has both he cannot be free from war, for he can only be at peace with the one if he is at war with the other.

Thus he is always torn by inner divisions and contradictions (L.621, B.412, S.514; see also L.410, B.413, S.29).

We have seen how the perpetual strife between dogmatist and sceptic is resolved in the heart; similarly the war between reason and passions is overcome by the *"juste"* man, and we know that the sphere of *"justice"* is that of the will or heart. And the parallel can be pressed further. The dogmatist's final resort is to "nature" or "instinct" (L.131, B.434, S.164; and L.406, B.395, S.25), but there is a close connection between instinct and passion; "Our instinct makes us feel [*sentir*] that our happiness must be sought outside ourselves. Our passions drive us outwards, even without objects to excite them" (L.143, B.464, S.176). On the other hand, that knowledge of first principles—deriving from nature or instinct—on which the dogmatist insists, can in a proper perspective be seen as part of the operation of the heart; we are told that it comes "from the heart and instinct . . . with certainty" (L.110, B.282, S.142), hence the *aide-mémoire*

Heart
Instinct
Principles (L.155, B.281, S.187).

From Scholastic times the passions had been associated with *appetitus*, and the will defined as belonging to its province—whether or not the appetite was also "rational". And this association is wholly congenial to Pascal's outlook; if the heart is drawn by "delectations", and should properly seek joy in God, then its volitional and affective elements cannot be divorced—and any purported *"Apology"* that lacked emotive appeal would be seriously deficient. *"Infini rien"*, as one might expect, does not neglect this side of the matter:

End of this address.

'Now what harm will come to you from choosing this course? You will be faithful, honest, humble, grateful, full of good works, a sincere, true friend. . . . It is true you will not enjoy noxious pleasures, glory and good living, but will you not have others?

'I tell you that you will gain even in this life, and . . . in the end you will realize that you have wagered on something certain and infinite for which you have paid nothing.'

'How these words fill me with rapture and delight!' (L.418, B.233, S.680)

Not for nothing does Pascal use 'sentiment' as his favourite term for the operations of the heart.

The power of "Infini rien" turns on the integrated many-sidedness of its appeal. All three aspects of the heart are involved, cognitive, volitional, and—in the reference to "Scripture and the rest"—mnemonic; the centre-piece is a demonstration designed for l'esprit de géométrie; and once this has done its work provision is made for the weakness of the flesh. Even a disciplined use of the imagination is employed—its products, as we know, are not invariably deceptive—to paint a picture of the life of faith so that the emotions may be touched, but only at the "end of this address" —"once the mind has seen where the truth lies". Although it is unclear to what use Pascal intended finally to put "Infini rien" in the structure of his Apology, it thus comes close to providing an epitome of the Pensées as a whole.

But while it comes close, there is one element which, of its very nature, is lacking from the fragment. The uncharacteristic prominence given to l'esprit de géométrie leads to its form being that of sequential "progressive reasoning"; in this respect it is lacking in finesse. And this missing feature is one by which Pascal set a good deal of store; the reasons of the heart characteristically demand a form that is "digressive" rather than "progressive":

Order. Against the objection that there is no order in Scripture.

The heart has its order, the mind has its own, which uses principles and demonstrations. The heart has a different one. We do not prove that we ought to be loved by setting out in order the causes of love; that would be absurd.

Jesus Christ and St Paul possess the order of charity, not of the mind, for they wished to humble, not to teach.

The same with St Augustine. This order consists mainly in digressions upon each point which relates to the end, so that this shall be kept always in sight (L.298, B.283, S.329).

Where we are concerned to move the will—either in the direction advocated by self-love or, on the contrary, to humble the self—we need to employ an art of persuasion different from that appropriate to géométrie. What is required is a technique of digression, with a periodical return to a central point which is thereby thrown into relief; as Professor Broome has pointed out, this "explains why the simplest conceivable way of editing the Pensées, which is to assemble all the passages dealing with the same themes, can never give a convincing impression of Pascal's unwritten book" (Broome, 136).

The reason for this requirement, as we should expect, has to do with human inconstancy.

Language.
The mind must not be led off on to something else except for relaxation, but at the right time; give it relaxation when it is due and not otherwise. Relaxation at the wrong time wearies it and wearying it at the wrong time relaxes it, for we just give everything up (L.710, B.24, S.588).

Continual eloquence is tedious. . . . Continuity in anything is tedious (L.771, B.355, S.636).

The metaphysical proofs for the existence of God are so remote from human reasoning and so involved that they make little impact, and, even if they did help some people, it would only be for the moment during which they watched the demonstration, because an hour later they would be afraid they had made a mistake (L.190, B.543, S.222).

Men being what they are, the concentrated intensity of *"Infini rien"* would be counterproductive if significantly prolonged; the reader must be permitted a legitimate degree of relaxation in his focus and attention, so long as these digressions and changes of tone are purposive, keeping the end "always in sight". In this way a network of associations and reasonances can be built up, reinforcing our grasp on that ultimate "end" by enabling us to relate it to a multitude of different phenomena and considerations. Ideally, each new perspective should combine clarity with simplicity: '*Proofs of Jesus Christ.* Jesus said great things so simply that he seems not to have thought about them, and yet so clearly that it is obvious what he thought about them. Such clarity together with such simplicity is wonderful [*admirable*]' (L.309, B.797, S.340). At their best, the more aphoristic of the *Pensées* have this luminous character. By carefully ordering the sequence of such synoptic "glances", the apologist aims to carry the reader with him so that "light dawns gradually over the whole".

The relationship with the reader is thus a co-operative one. Devices like that of the letter or dialogue are well placed to exploit it, and it is clear that it was much in Pascal's mind. "When some passion or effect is described in a natural style, we find within ourselves the truth of what we hear, without knowing it was there" (L.652, B.14, S.536). This is important because "We are usually convinced more easily by reasons we have found ourselves than by those which have occurred to others" (L.737, B.10, S.617). These two factors taken together explain the haunting power Montaigne's *Essais* had on Pascal's thinking, despite their radical differences; 'It is not in Montaigne but in myself that I find everything I see there' (L.689, B.64, S.568), a comment which ironically echoes, of course, Montaigne's own dictum about Plato (Montaigne (1), I. xxvi. 162). The apologist needs, therefore, to emulate Montaigne's "natural style", with an "Eloquence which persuades gently, not imperiously, as a tyrant" (L.584, B.15, S.485). In this connection it is worth recalling Pascal's definition: 'Tyranny consists in the desire to dominate everything regardless of order. . . . We pay different dues to different kinds of merit; we must love charm [*agrément*], fear strength, believe in knowledge [*science*]' (L.58, B.332, S92–1). The imperious tone of "*Cela est demonstratif*" has its place in the order of *science*, of *géométrie*, but is merely tyrannical if employed to move the will; here we require the gentler promptings of the order of charity, which are in the long term much more effective. The anomalous position in which this places "*Infini rien*" is one which Pascal sees the need to take extreme steps to mitigate, unparalleled elsewhere in the *Pensées*:

If my words please you and seem cogent, you must know that they come from a man who went down upon his knees before and after to pray this infinite and indivisible being, to whom he submits his own, that he might bring your being also to submit to him for your own good and for his glory; and that strength might thus be reconciled with lowliness. (L.418, B.233, S.680)

The authority of the demonstration thus resides ultimately not in the "geometry of chance" but in "this infinite and indivisible being", and the apparent "tyranny" is to be "reconciled with lowliness"; such is the tribute *géométrie* must pay *finesse* when it trespasses into the order of charity. More representative of the reasons of the heart is: 'Follow your own impulses. Observe yourself, and see if you do not find the living characteristics of these two natures' (L.149, B.430, S.182).

The contrast is at this point strikingly similar to the well-known distinction drawn by the late Dr Leavis between the procedures characteristic of philosophy and those of literary criticism. When the philosopher trespasses into the field of literary criticism, it is suggested, he is apt to speak of "norms" in terms of which one "measures every poet"; he has, it appears, many of the character-istics of *l'esprit de géométrie*. Against this idealization is set another, that of the critic:

The critic's aim is, first, to realize as sensitively and completely as possible this or that which claims his attention; and a certain valuing is implicit in the realizing. As he matures in experience of the new thing he asks, explicitly and implicitly: 'Where does this come? How does it stand in relation to . . . ? How relatively important does it seem?' And the organization into which it settles as a constituent in becoming 'placed' is an organization of similarly 'placed' things, things that have found their bearings with regard to one another, and not a theoretical system or a system determined by abstract considerations. . . .

Of course, the process of 'making fully conscious and articulate' is a process of relating and organizing, and the 'immediate sense of value' should, as the critic matures with experience, represent a growing stability of organization. . . . On testing and re-testing and wider experience, . . . what map or chart of English poetry as a whole represents my utmost consistency and most inclusive coherence of response? . . .

The cogency I hoped to achieve was to be for other readers of poetry —readers of poetry as such. I hoped, by putting in front of them, in a criticism that should keep as close to the concrete as possible, my own developed 'coherence of response', to get them to agree (with, no doubt, critical qualifications) that the map, the essential order, of English poetry seen as a whole did, when they interrogated their experience, look like that to them also. . . .

My whole effort was to work in terms of concrete judgements and particular analyses. 'This—doesn't it?—bears such a relation to that; this kind of thing—don't you find it so?—wears better than that', etc. (Leavis (1), 'Literary Criticism and Philosophy', 212–5).

Mutatis mutandis we find here concentrated many of the leading features of *l'esprit de finesse*. What is being sought is an individual's "utmost consistency and most inclusive coherence of response", through "testing and re-testing and wider experience" of a variety of concrete instances which one comes to "place" in relation to each other. If one is true to one's experience, one finds that "abstract" distinctions between fact and value dissolve, "a certain value is implicit in the realizing", in much the same way as does that between cognition and volition in Pascal—which is, indeed, a version of the same dichotomy.

The agreement sought is a discriminating one, but is not finally subject to validation or "measurement" by "norms" provided by the "theoretical" systems constructed by *l'esprit de géométrie*, other than that of "consistency"; the particularity and diversity of the considerations involved preclude this, as in the case of *finesse*. Instead, the final test of "cogency" is that provided by the serious "interrogation of experience" by those whose integrity, width of experience, attention to the particular, and preparedness to enter with sensitivity into the ensuing dialogue renders them fit to judge. Pascal's "Observe yourself, and see if you do not find" is very close to the literary critic's "This—don't you find it so?". Elsewhere, Dr Leavis endorses T. S. Eliot's characterization of literary criticism as

'The common pursuit of true judgment': that is how the critic should see his business, and what it should be for him. His perceptions and judgments are his, or they are nothing; but, whether or not he has consciously addressed himself to cooperative labour, they are inevitably collaborative. Collaboration may take the form of disagreement, and one is grateful to the critic whom one has found worth disagreeing with (Leavis (1), 'Preface', v).

One is reminded both of Pascal's insistence on finding "within ourselves the truth of what we hear", and of his collaborative "Let us see what the wisdom of God will do"—which prefaces "Follow your own impulses [*mouvements*]. Observe ourself" (L.149, B.430, S.182).[17]

"To realize as sensitively and completely as possible"; this is the first requirement for Pascal as it is for Leavis. The *Apology*, it appears, was intended to impel the reader to discover within himself the truth of what he reads, at all the different levels of his being; tensions created by the polarities which constitute the human condition could thereby be brought to consciousness, and the enquirer predisposed to respond positively to the transcendence of those polarities made possible by the "Wisdom of God". The fullness, "completeness", of the response—cognitive, volitional,

---

[17] An indication of how, for Pascal, the collaboration might work is provided by the comments of Nicole, one of the leading *solitaires* at Port-Royal. Nicole argues that Pascal's analysis of the relation between *divertissement* and *ennui* is "perhaps more subtle than solid. . . . *Tristesse* and *ennui* are different impulses [*mouvements*]. . . . M. Pascal confuses them" (Brunschvicg, xiii, 65–6). However, the distinction between *tristesse* and *ennui* appears to be grounded in a "system determined by abstract considerations", and this feature provides Pascal with an obvious opening for further clarification (see Morgan (1), 276–7). There is considerable evidence that Pascal's relationship with his colleagues at Port-Royal was genuinely collaborative.

emotional, even imaginative—is thus essential; 'When we believe only by the strength of our conviction and the automaton is inclined to believe the opposite, that is not enough' (L.821, B.252, S.661). This is why the persuasions of the heart are "incomparably more difficult, more subtle, more useful, and more admirable" than those of *l'esprit géométrique*.

If an analogy is required, we should look not to "*Cela est démonstratif*", but rather to those "proofs" which Pascal classified as belonging to the workings of memory—and thus falling within the province of the heart. These ultimately turn on his interpretation of Scripture, which is also seen as involving the reconciliation of polarities:

Contradictions. A good portrait can only be made by reconciling all our contradictory features, and it is not enough to follow through a series of mutually compatible qualities without reconciling their opposites; to understand an author's meaning all contradictory passages must be reconciled.

Thus to understand Scripture a meaning must be found which reconciles all contradictory passages; it is not enough to have one that fits a number of compatible passages, but one which reconciles even contradictory ones.

Every author has a meaning which reconciles all contradictory passages, or else he has no meaning at all (L.257, B.684, S.289).

Setting aside the controversial assumption about the unity of Scripture, and allowing for a certain element of exaggeration, this is a recognizable characterization of the interpretative element in literary criticism, comparable to Dame Helen Gardner's

If it is a passage which we are interpreting, the final test is always the consistency of the interpretation of the passage with the interpretation of the work as a whole. If we are attempting the interpretation of a single complete work, the test is the reverse of this: does our interpretation of the whole make sense of all the parts? (Gardner, 53)

L'esprit de finesse, we remember, is concerned with principles which "are so delicate and so numerous that it takes a sense of great delicacy and precision to feel and judge correctly" (L.512, B.1, S.670); "I consider it as impossible to know the parts without knowing the whole as to know the whole without knowing the individual parts" (L.199, B.72, S.230). Not only the evaluative element in literary criticism stressed by Dr Leavis, but also the hermeneutic constituent, fit Pascal's model admirably.

Of course, the unbeliever's initial response is likely to be the denial that there is any "author's meaning" to be understood; that if the fiction of an author be maintained for the sake of the analogy, then life should be construed as "told by an idiot, . . . signifying nothing". But whether or not there is an overall interpretation of our lot which reconciles all the apparent "contradictions", enabling us to see life both steadily and whole, is not a matter that can be established a priori; and if there is one, then we should not continue blankly to affirm that there is "no meaning at all". Pascal is concerned to show that if we persist in our refusal seriously to entertain the possibility of an "author", and think and will only in terms of "Man without God", then—in Farrer's words—"we must exclude from our account of the world things which in our thoughts and actions we cannot but assume to be there". The criteria appropriate to establishing this "must" are all the multifarious considerations which we have seen to govern the "reasons of the heart".

7. Dialectic, Rhetoric, and Finesse

At the very time, then, when Descartes was establishing the geometrical pattern of reasoning as a model for philosophy, with the consequences we noticed in Chapter 1, Pascal was forming a resistance movement centred on Port-Royal. As was only to be expected, many of the resources he employed to oppose the Cartesian *géomètre* had been familiar since Classical times; but "Let no one say that I have said nothing new; the arrangement of the material is new" (L.696, B.22, S.575). Among these traditional elements we find the need for a mode of reasoning other than the demonstrative in order to establish first principles, a mode which takes its starting-point from the interrelation of a number of diverse elements which themselves need to be subjected to critical scrutiny, and proceeds by attempting to bring out underlying principles which will reconcile apparent "contradictions" among these elements; even Aristotle's preference for the ἔνδοξα of "the many" (especially as enshrined in common linguistic usage) over those of "the wise" is paralleled by Pascal's claim that the principles of *finesse*, unlike those of *géométrie*, "are in ordinary usage and there for all to see".

But this familiar picture of Aristotelian dialectic is revolutionized by the introduction of the Augustinian theme of the centrality of the will, itself a version of the importance the Bible assigns to the "heart". If the human situation is fundamentally that of being *embarqué*, any framework of thinking that centres round the ideal of detached contemplation is radically defective; "truth apart from charity is . . . an idol" (L.926, B.582, S.755). Concepts and judgements to which we are tempted, but which do not accurately reflect our situation, are likely to hinder the search for genuine fulfilment, and cannot in any case be necessary to it. But by the same token, a perverse will is liable to give rise to perverse beliefs. Hence the analyses of *divertissement*, diagnosing its origins, examining its typical ways of thinking, and attempting to bring out its ultimately self-frustrating character. We need to probe the inclinations of our hearts to discern whether they are directed towards what can properly be characterized as their good, for "The mind, keeping in step with the will, remains looking at the aspect preferred by the will and so judges by what it sees there" (L.539, B.99, S.458).

If "the bias towards self is the beginning of all disorder" (L.421, B.477, S.680), then apparent first principles that are functions of self-love are mere "powers of deception". To show that this tendency is indeed a disordering bias, Pascal presents a series of observations drawn from the most pervasive features of human life, and challenges the reader to recognize their uncomfortable accuracy, representative nature, and cumulative significance. These observations are drawn from the fields both of understanding and of aspiration, as commonly distinguished; to the extent that we acknowledge their convergence on the same perspective—the perversity of self-love—we are provided with criteria that enable us to discriminate between *sentiment* and *fantaisie*, so long as "the eyes of the heart" are not blinded by that perverse but pervasive bias and we allow ourselves to judge authentically.

The authenticity required, both to assess the validity of the observations presented and to recognize their implications, involves all the levels of our being—each of the three orders; thus any work designed to evoke it should pay significant regard to matters that Aristotle designated as falling within the sphere of rhetoric, though the model required is closer to that of Plato's "noble" rhetoric than to its deceptive analogue—and closer to the *Phaedo* than either. Rather as Socrates there urges us "before all things" to

beware misology, yet shows how a persuasive "spell" may nevertheless be both legitimate and rational, so Pascal specifies "Two
excesses: to exclude reason, to admit nothing but reason" (L.183,
B.253, S.214), and attempts to show that "Reason's last step is the
recognition that there are an infinite number of things which are
beyond it" (L.188, B.267, S.220)—yet beyond the reasons of the
géomètre lie the reasons of the heart. The testing of these latter
"reasons", like the legitimation of the "spell" of the *Phaedo*, is a
co-operative endeavour; and rather as Simmias, Cebes and, by
implication, the reader are urged to "follow up the argument", so
Pascal's reader is exhorted to "observe yourself, and see".

But here the Platonic model, like the Aristotelian, begins to fail
us. Socrates provides us with an account of methodic cross-
questioning, in terms of which we may "follow up the argument".
Pascal is doubtful about the practicability of any such systematiza-
tion; it is implausible to assimilate the workings of *finesse* to
Socrates' hypothetical method. The preferred "digressive" procedure appears in practice to involve presenting the reader with a
multitude of interrelated vignettes of the human condition and
saying, in effect, "This—doesn't it?—bears such a relation to that";
and in response to the expected "Yes, but . . ." we find sketched
another cluster of phenomena that relate to the "but". There are
also religious perceptions designed to fit in with the other observations, so that we may be led to see how Revelation completes our
best fragmentary intimations in ways which satisfy the most deep-
seated aspirations at once of our understanding and of our will. The
analogy with Job is here stronger than with the *Phaedo*. Pascal's
procedure is that of comparing case with case, so that gradually
illumination may dawn. The initial vignettes are chosen for their
relevance to the supposed condition of the reader; to the extent that
they are not so relevant, the procedure has no value.

In this interrogation of one's experience, testing perspective
against perspective, successive layers of self-deception about the
security of our judgements and the nature of our desires are
gradually stripped away, and the poverty or otherwise of our own
inwardness laid bare. Thus Pascal exposes his own sensibility to
us—fed by such diverse sources as his breviary, Montaigne, St
Augustine, and his companions at the gaming table—seeking his
own "utmost consistency and most inclusive coherence of response", and finding in it a mode of making creative use of the

pressures imposed by the polarities that appear to constitute it. The intention is so to intensify such pressures within the reader that he is impelled to match his own inwardness with that presented to him, "find within himself" something of what has been depicted, and respond with integrity;

> If he exalts himself, I humble him.
> If he humbles himself, I exalt him.
> And I go on contradicting him
> Until he understands
> That he is a monster that passes all understanding.
>
> (L.130, B.420, S.163)

The theological perspective that Pascal will ultimately offer is, of course, suitably nuanced to match this enigma; 'Perfect clarity would help the mind and harm the will' (L.234, B.581, S.266). 'Everything that is incomprehensible does not cease to exist. . . . | There is enough light for those who desire only to see, and enough darkness for those of a contrary disposition' (L.149, B.430, S.182).

But a reader whose sensitivity, integrity, and depth of inwardness has led him to recognize in himself Pascal's "monster that passes all understanding", may yet remain unconvinced by the proposed resolution of the contradictions—however nuanced. Successive generations of serious readers have felt able to identify themselves with the *mondain* unbeliever to whose condition Pascal addresses himself,[18] without submitting themselves to the "Wisdom of God". For this state of affairs there are two obvious explanations. At the volitional level, even sensitivity and integrity can be subverted by self-love; '*Reasons for not believing*. . . . Lack of charity' (L.834, B.826, S.422). 'The will is . . . depraved' (L.421, B.477, S.680). The requirement that one should "desire only to see" is a stringent one. At the cognitive level, incredulity doubtless has much to do with the inadequacy of the "proofs" provided belonging to the sphere of the "memory", together with the outdated assumptions which so

[18] Rather fewer readers have been happy to see themselves as *libertins*, but this widespread characterization of Pascal's intended readership, though not without point, is in certain respects misleading; Robert Nelson's otherwise sensible argument to this effect (Nelson, 250–2) is unfortunately marred by failure to consider L.179 (B.256, S.210), but his conclusion is still sustainable.

classifying them reveals.[19] To these considerations can be added the obvious fact that our identification with Pascal's intended readership can never be more than partial; we are not seventeenth-century Frenchmen, and we share their thought patterns and aspirations only to a very approximate degree.

This last circumstance points to a matter of considerable epistemological significance. Pascalian *finesse*, of its very nature, starts from principles that are "there for all to see"—as Aristotelian dialectic does from ἔνδοξα. But such starting-points vary from culture to culture and historical period to historical period; this is part of the force of Wittgenstein's question about "the propositions of physics". If the Pascalian touchstone is ultimately that of experience, one may legitimately ask whether there is such a thing as "human" experience as such—let alone "the human situation". Much of the force of the *Pensées* derives from the reader being part of a culture deeply influenced by Christian assumptions; the analyses of *grandeur* and *misère* might look rather different in a Buddhist society. Dr Farrer's parallel of the puzzled nationalist, whose concepts are shaped by his ideology, is in point here; Pascal may be able to show with some plausibility that there is what we might call a "God-shaped" blank in our experience, but his may tell us more about our cultural inheritance than about the *Deus Absconditus*.

Yet this claim, too, needs to be tested. Pascal expressed himself ready to interrogate "all the religions of the world" if necessary, with the suggestion that any which did not provide what he represents the "Wisdom of God" as providing were seriously deficient. Perhaps some cultures are more impoverished than others; it is worth recalling Wittgenstein's "And for that we consider them primitive"—perhaps there is enough constancy in human experi-

---

[19] Obsolete assumptions and signs of incompleteness are also to be found elsewhere, notably in the important fragment on the 'Disproportion of man' (L.199, B.72, S.230). Since Cantor its handling of "infinity" has looked a little archaic, and many logical eyebrows have been raised by the way it implies the availability of an argument, which is not given, "from incongruity of dimension to epistemological impotence" (Topliss, 213); the two issues are not unconnected. But to leave the matter there would be to reject the invitation to collaboration; the important question is whether such weaknesses can be made good in the present state of knowledge, and since the discovery of new problems of commensurability surrounding the Gödelian numbering not all the dice are weighted against Pascal.

ence for physics to be preferred over the oracle.[20] To decide this we must look and see, comparing case with case in a co-operative endeavour which owes much to *finesse*. And ultimately, doubtless, we must compare complete systems of thought, aspiration, and experience with each other. But this has much in common with Cicero's practice in attempting to "lay before my readers the doctrines of the various schools". Of course, the practice is not identical with that of cross-cultural comparison, but is designed to circumvent problems about commensurability very closely analogous to those which bedevil the wider enterprise; considerations which bear upon the relative adequacy of "the various schools" are likely to have their relevance in assessing the relative poverty of differing cultures.

It is this ancient model of philosophical enquiry which was exploited by David Hume in his *Dialogues concerning Natural Religion*, for purposes very similar to those of Cicero.

[20] For Professor Rorty such a hypothesis implies either that "language does *not* go all the way down, or that, contrary to the appearances, all vocabularies are commensurable" (Rorty (2), xxx). He rejects both alternatives, characterizing the issue between himself and "the intuitive realist" as "one about whether philosophy should try to find natural starting-points which are distinct from cultural traditions, or whether all philosophy should do is compare and contrast cultural traditions"; he embraces the conclusion that "in the process of playing vocabularies and cultures off against each other, we produce new and better ways of talking and acting—not better by reference to a previously known standard, but just better in the sense that they come to *seem* clearly better than their predecessors" (xxxvii).
Against such cultural relativism Professor Rosen argues that the claim "that mathematical physics, or modern science, is an expression of the western European linguistic *Lebensform* [is] . . . a vacuous response. Those who live in ignorance of the laws of gravity and thermodynamics are not living in some other world (except in a metaphorical sense); they are living in ignorance. What we require is an explanation of why the western European *Lebensform* is adequate to an explanation of the work of the world, whereas nonwestern forms of life either produce no such adequate account, or else do produce parts of such an account. . . . To be told that science is a consequence of our life form is to be told that, finally, science is on a par with Babylonian creation myths. For these, too, are consequences of a life form, and how are we to choose between life forms? In fact, such a choice is relatively simple, since once we perceive the diversity of life forms, we are in a position to understand the superiority of one to another. To say that this understanding is again a consequence of one's own life form is to speak truly. But it casts no light upon whether one's own life form enables one to speak truly" (Rosen, 320–1). It is this latter issue that is the concern of Pascal. See also n. 12 and ch. 8.2.

6

Hume and the Education of Pamphilus

1. Philosophy, Sentiment, and the Ciceronian Model

> Philosophical decisions are nothing but the reflections of
> common life, methodized and corrected.

(Hume (6), 1st Enquiry, 162)

Hume sets this epitome of his recommended "mitigated scepticism" in opposition to such rival models of philosophizing as the
Cartesian, which recommends that we follow

a chain of reasoning, deduced from some original principle, which cannot
possibly be fallacious or deceitful. But neither is there any such original
principle, which has a prerogative above others, that are self-evident and
convincing: or if there were, could we advance a step beyond it (ibid. 150).

Hume's formula, indeed, is strikingly reminiscent of Aristotelian
dialectic which subjects the ἔνδοξα of "the many" to critical
scrutiny, and of Pascalian *finesse* whose principles "are in ordinary
usage and there for all to see". The distinctive features of Hume's
thinking emerge when we ask in what "common" life consists, what
counts as satisfactory "method", and hence what criteria are available to distinguish correct from incorrect "reflections".

At the heart of common life, it appears, are "the primary instincts
of nature" which give rise to beliefs and feelings comprising "a
species of natural instincts, which no reasoning or process of the
thought and understanding is able either to produce or prevent"
(152 and 46–7). "Excessive" scepticism can indeed raise doubts
even here, showing in any given instance that we are only led to such
a belief by "custom or a certain instinct of our nature; which it is
indeed difficult to resist, but which, like other instincts, may be
fallacious and deceitful" (159). But to seek to upset the "reflections
of common life" merely on the ground that no Cartesian first
principles are available is indeed excessive:

The great subverter of *Pyrrhonism* or the excessive principles of scepticism is action, and employment, and the occupations of common life. . . . Though a Pyrrhonian may throw himself or others into a momentary amazement and confusion by his profound reasonings; the first and most trivial event in life will put to flight all his doubts and scruples;

for "mankind", we are reminded, "must act and reason and believe" (158–60).

So far there is close agreement between Hume and Pascal. The latter, it will be remembered, maintained that "a perfectly genuine sceptic has never existed. Nature backs up helpless reason and stops it going so wildly astray" (Pascal, Pensées, L.131, B.434, S.164). It is in their responses to this common diagnosis that the radical differences between the two start to emerge. For Pascal the tension between instinct and reason leads to an impasse; 'Who will unravel such a tangle? This is certainly beyond dogmatism and scepticism, beyond all human philosophy. . . . Listen to God' (ibid.). For Hume, on the contrary, this tension points not towards religion but away from it; the moral is that we should limit "our enquiries to such subjects as are best adapted to the narrow capacity of human understanding", and "never be tempted to go beyond common life".

While we cannot give a satisfactory reason, why we believe, after a thousand experiments, that a stone will fall, or fire burn; can we ever satisfy ourselves concerning any determination, which we may form, with regard to the origin of worlds, and the situation of nature, from, and to eternity? (Hume (6), *1st Enquiry*, 162)

The Pascalian counter to this is obvious. If the tangle is indeed "beyond all human philosophy", then from a rational standpoint religion is in no worse condition than "common life", and if the one may be rehabilitated by reference to instinct or *sentiment* so may the other. To understand how Hume seeks to evade the force of such objections, we need to consider his own—entirely secular—attempt to "unravel" the tangle, and in particular his account of the forms of reasoning whereby we may "methodize" and "correct" the deliverances of our instincts.

The Pyrrhonian, thinks Hume, uses the admitted fact that there is no manner of establishing beliefs "which cannot possibly be fallacious or deceitful" to cast doubt on belief as such. But such considerations only warrant the doubt given an unduly limited model of justified certainty in terms of the demonstration of conclusions "deduced from some original principle". Several readers of the *Treatise*, dominated by such a model, had attributed excessive scepticism to Hume, especially in respect of the causal principle. But both in public and in private he rejected both the imputation and the assumptions about rationality on which it was based.

It is common for Philosophers to distinguish the Kinds of Evidence into *intuitive, demonstrative, sensible*, and *moral*; by which they intend *only* to mark a Difference betwixt them, not to denote a Superiority of one above another. *Moral Certainty* may reach as *high* a degree of Assurance as *Mathematical*; and our Senses are surely to be comprised amongst the clearest and most convincing of all Evidences. Now, it being the Author's Purpose . . . to examine the Grounds of that Proposition; he used the Freedom of disputing the common Opinion, that it was founded on *demonstrative* or *intuitive Certainty*; but asserts, that it is supported by *moral Evidence*, and is followed by a Conviction of the same Kind with these Truths, *That all Men must die*, and that *the Sun will rise To-morrow*. Is this any Thing like denying the Truth of that Proposition, which indeed *a Man must have lost all common Sense to doubt of?* (Hume (4), *Letter from a Gentleman*, 22)

And again,

Allow me to tell you, that I never asserted so absurd a Proposition as *that any thing might arise without a Cause*: I only maintain'd, that our Certainty of the Falsehood of that Proposition proceeded neither from Intuition nor Demonstration; but from another Source. *That Caesar existed, that there is such an Island as Sicily*; for these Propositions, I affirm, we have no demonstrative nor intuitive Proof. Would you infer that I deny their Truth, or even their Certainty? There are many different kinds of Certainty; and some of them as satisfactory to the Mind, tho perhaps not so regular, as the demonstrative kind (Hume (2), *Letters* i. 187).

It is in this spirit that he finds fault with the classifications of his predecessors;

Mr. Locke divides all arguments into demonstrative and probable. In this view, we must say, that it is only probable all men must die, or that the sun will rise to-morrow. But to conform our language more to common use, we ought to divide arguments into *demonstrations*, *proofs*, and *probabilities*. By proofs meaning such arguments from experience as leave no room for doubt or opposition (Hume (6), *1st Enquiry*, 56).

To deny that a principle "cannot possibly be fallacious or deceitful" is merely to deny its necessity; necessity is a function of demonstrative, not of moral reasoning; but if "*Moral Certainty* may reach as *high* a degree of Assurance as *Mathematical*" then the fact that "proofs" from experience employ principles which "may be fallacious and deceitful" does not show that they cannot convey a form of certainty "as satisfactory to the Mind . . . as the demonstrative kind".

Intuition and sense-experience are only in an extended sense to be counted as forms of reasoning, thus characteristically Hume presents a simple dichotomy. 'All reasonings may be divided into two kinds, namely, demonstrative reasoning, or that concerning relations of ideas, and moral reasoning, or that concerning matter of fact and existence' (Hume (6), *1st Enquiry*, 35). Notoriously, these two subordinate clauses, classifying together mode of reasoning and type of subject matter, provide Hume with a sharp cutting edge to his mitigated scepticism.

It seems to me, that the only objects of the abstract science or of demonstration are quantity and number, and that all attempts to extend this more perfect species of knowledge beyond these bounds are mere sophistry and illusion. . . .

All other enquiries of men regard only matter of fact and existence; and these are evidently incapable of demonstration. Whatever *is* may *not be*. No negation of a fact can involve a contradiction. The non-existence of any being, without exception, is as clear and distinct an idea as its existence. . . .

The existence, therefore, of any being can only be proved by arguments from its cause or its effect; and these arguments are founded entirely on experience. . . . Such is the foundation of moral reasoning, which forms the greater part of human knowledge, and is the source of all human action and behaviour (ibid. 163–4).

Thus in considering how we may "methodize" and "correct" our common reflections we may look either to mathematics or, more importantly, to arguments grounded in our experience of cause and effect.

These considerations indicate how we may, methodically, enlarge our knowledge of the world around us. The "reflections of common life" provide our touchstones, but we can go beyond them by employing principles that have their grounding in those reflections. This, thinks Hume, is the ultimate justification of Newtonian science which so immensely enlarged the bounds of our knowledge and provided one of the main models for his own enquiries; its principles are grounded in our common experience of cause and effect.

It is entirely agreeable to the rules of philosophy, and even of common reason; where any principle has been found to have a great force and energy in one instance, to ascribe to it a like energy in all similar instances. This indeed is Newton's chief rule of philosophizing (Hume (6), *2nd Enquiry*, 204).

Following this rule of analogy we may safely pursue "experimental reasoning concerning matter of fact and existence" (Hume (6), *1st Enquiry*, 165) without Pyrrhonic scruples; for such moral reasoning is securely rooted in "action, and employment, and the occupations of common life".

Hume's dismissive remarks about claims concerning "the origin of worlds, and the situation of nature, from, and to eternity" are at least in part directed against theologians and other upholders of "the religious hypothesis" of God as the eternal Creator of all things. Such opponents have a variety of ripostes open to them. They may accept Hume's challenge on its own terms, and attempt to show that the Newtonian principle of analogy securely grounds the religious hypothesis, as indeed Newton thought it did. In contrast, they may reject the notion of 'hypothesis' here and, with it, the fundamental Humean dichotomy between forms of reasoning; the existence of God, it may be said, provides a counter-example to the claim that "Whatever *is* may *not be*", for it can indeed be demonstrated. A third possibility is to admit that religious belief is not grounded in either of Hume's two types of reasoning, but nevertheless claim that it possesses its own type of certainty "as satisfactory to the Mind, tho perhaps not so regular" as in the case of Hume's preferred categories; the Pascalian position. Hume, indeed, purports to offer the religious a combination of the first and third escape routes:

Divinity or Theology, as it proves the existence of a Deity, and the immortality of souls, . . . has a foundation in *reason*, so far as it is supported by experience. But its best and most solid foundation is *faith* and divine revelation (Hume (6), *1st Enquiry*, 165).

But this gift-horse needs to be looked in the mouth. In the immediately preceding section of the *1st Enquiry* Hume has made it abundantly clear that he regards the support in experience for either doctrine as seriously defective, so all the weight of Hume's concession is carried by *"faith* and divine revelation". Further, that section is preceded by another in which the credibility of reports of miracles and fulfilled prophecies, the traditional guarantors of "divine revelation" (Pascal's 'proofs of memory'), is systematically undermined. This "best and most solid foundation" thus turns out to be simply faith, unbuttressed by its traditional supports.

If one then asks about its epistemological status, the obvious place to look is among those "natural instincts, which no reasoning or process of the thought and understanding is able to produce or prevent", with an eye to including the deliverances of faith among "the reflections of common life". If this enquiry were to succeed we could then conclude that arguments from cause and effect, guided by Newton's "chief rule", do not exhaust the proper scope of our explorations concerning "matter of fact and existence". According to Hume, "reason is nothing but a wonderful and unintelligible instinct in our souls, which carries us along a certain train of ideas, and endows them with particular qualities, according to their particular situations and relations" (Hume (5), *Treatise*, 179). Faith might be another such instinct, and Hume's distinction between the two serve "*only* to mark a Difference betwixt them, not to denote a Superiority of one above another".

The point may be sharpened by reference to a key term Hume shares with Pascal—'sentiment'. For both writers the word has application to thought as well as feeling,[1] thus Hume might seem especially vulnerable to the Pascalian definition of 'faith' in terms of *'sentiment'*. Hume goes a long way, indeed, in this direction; having been concerned to argue that "belief is more properly an act of the sensitive, than of the cogitative part of our natures" (Hume (5), *Treatise*, 183), he later is prepared to "conclude, that belief consists merely in a certain feeling or sentiment; in something, that depends not on the will, but must arise from certain determinate causes and principles, of which we are not masters" (ibid. Appendix 624). Despite this explicit separation of belief from the will, Hume's exposition of belief in terms of sentiment remains closely parallel to

[1] For a full discussion of Hume's use of 'sentiment' see Jones (2); note especially his claim that "the ambiguity in the French term *sentiment*, deplored by French and English writers alike, is precisely mirrored in Hume's term 'sentiment', by which he sometimes means 'emotion, passion', and sometimes 'judgment, opinion'" (98).

that of Pascal; for the latter, we are not entirely "masters" of our wills—hence the discussions of habit and the unconscious—, while Hume is quite prepared to admit that we can by judicious use of education and habit modify our sentiments (Hume (1), iii, 'The Sceptic', 223), a matter to which we shall return. Further, once again paralleling Pascal, the distinction between the "sensitive" and the "cogitative" parts of our "natures" is not absolute. Using the term 'probable reasoning' in the Lockean manner he was later to criticize to cover all non-demonstrative argument (Hume (5), *Treatise*, 124), Hume declares that

all probable reasoning is nothing but a species of sensation. 'Tis not solely in poetry and music, we must follow our taste and sentiment, but likewise in philosophy. When I am convinc'd of any principle, 'tis only an idea, which strikes more strongly upon me. When I give the preference to one set of arguments above another, I do nothing but decide from my feeling concerning the superiority of their influence. Objects have no discoverable connexion together; nor is it from any other principle but custom operating upon the imagination, that we can draw any inference from the appearance of one to the existence of another (ibid. 103).

If "custom operating upon the imagination" may properly ground "Newton's chief rule of philosophizing" and all the apparatus of "moral reasoning", then it would appear prima facie that faith may invoke the same principle, insisting that we follow sentiment in religion as in "philosophy".

The difficulty is obvious; sentiment, like custom, "may be fallacious and deceitful". As Pascal put it, "All our reasoning comes down to surrendering to *sentiment*. But *fantasie* is like and also unlike *sentiment*, so that we cannot distinguish between these two opposites" (*Pensées*, L.530, B.274, S.455). For Hume, the principles of "moral reasoning" may be secured against this Pyrrhonic attack by reference to "action, and employment, and the occupations of common life"; mankind "must act and reason and believe". (Hume (6), *1st Enquiry*, 158–60) As Philo and Cleanthes agree, "To whatever length any one may push his speculative principles of scepticism, he must act, I own and live, and converse like other men; and for this conduct he is not obliged to give any other reason than the absolute necessity he lies under of so doing" (Hume (7), *Dialogues*, 134). The parallel between faith and reason can only be made out if the principles of faith, too, are governed by a like necessity; but that this is so is by no means obvious. The deliverances of our natural instincts are universally credited, because we cannot but act on them in our daily lives, but religious beliefs do not appear to be similarly universal:

The belief of invisible, intelligent power has been very generally diffused over the human race, in all places and in all ages; but it has neither perhaps been so universal as to admit of no exception, nor has it been, in any degree, uniform in the ideas, which it has suggested. Some nations have been discovered, who entertained no sentiments of Religion, . . . and scarce any two men, have ever agreed precisely in the same sentiments. It would appear, therefore, that this preconception springs not from an original instinct or primary impression of nature. . . . The first religious principles must be secondary; such as may easily be perverted by various accidents and causes (Hume (10), *Natural History of Religion*, 21).

If faith is to be counted as a "first religious principle", and it is difficult to see how within Hume's framework this classification can be avoided, it follows that this "best and most solid foundation" is epistemologically far from solid; the religious rhetoric, as so often in Hume, is markedly ironic.

If religion indeed has a foundation in reason as well as faith, as Hume purports to believe in the passage quoted earlier, then the status of faith as a secondary principle might provide the required solidity, for "where reason is lively, and mixes itself with some propensity, it ought to be assented to" (Hume (5), *Treatise*, 270). But if this is not the case, we are faced with the delicate and difficult task of attempting to assess the degree of credibility we should afford to a "propensity" which, "if not an original instinct", is "at least a general attendant of human nature" (Hume (10), *Natural History of Religion*, 75), being grounded in secondary principles. In this enterprise, the fact of our ability to shape sentiments by means of education and habituation becomes a pressing issue. Hume focuses the problem in a letter to Gilbert Elliot written when he was composing the first draft of his *Dialogues Concerning Natural Religion*:

Your Notion of correcting Subtilty of Sentiment is certainly very just with regard to Morals, which depend upon Sentiment; & in Politics & natural Philosophy, whatever Conclusion is contrary to certain Matter of Fact must certainly be wrong, and there must some Error lie somewhere in the Argument, whether we be able to show it or not. But in Metaphysics or Theology, I cannot see how either of these plain and obvious Standards of Truth can have place. Nothing there can correct bad Reasoning but good

Reasoning: and Sophistry must be oppos'd by Syllogism. About seventy or eighty Years ago, I observe, a Principle like that which you advance prevail'd very much in France amongst some Philosophers & *beaux Esprits*.

The principle, it turns out, is that the "plain and obvious Standard of Truth" for faith, lies in "Sentiment", a doctrine Hume traces to a controversy centred on Port-Royal.[2]

The Comparison of these controversial Writings begot an Idea in some, that it was neither by Reasoning nor Authority we learn our Religion, but by Sentiment. And certainly this were a very convenient Way, and what a Philosopher wou'd be very well pleas'd to comply with, if he could distinguish Sentiment from Education. But to all Appearance, the Sentiment of Stockholm, Geneva, Rome antient & modern, Athens, & Memphis, have the same Characters. And no thinking man can implicitly assent to any of them; but from the general Principle, that as the Truth in these Subjects is beyond human Capacity, & that as for one's own Ease he must adopt some Tenets, there is more Satisfaction & Convenience in holding to the Catechism we have been first taught. Now this I have nothing to say against. I would only observe, that such a Conduct is founded on the most universal & determin'd Scepticism, join'd to a little Indolence. For more Curiosity & Research gives a direct opposite Turn from the same Principles (Hume (2), *Letters* i. 150–2).

Elsewhere, Hume writes of "the irresistible contagion of opinion" in religious matters (Hume (10), *Natural History of Religion*, 76). It would appear that all the bombast about "*faith* and divine revelation" only serves to mask the conviction that religious belief is a matter of convenience, education and habituation without independent epistemological standing.

Hume was well aware that such an inference would prove unpalatable. If the distinction between sentiment and education in this field could be made out, the conclusion could also be resisted. The theologian might attempt to argue that the near universality of the religious propensity should secure it against the attacks of mitigated scepticism, as the necessity and complete universality of the "original instincts" does against Pyrrhonism; the exceptions, whether national or individual, being symptoms of some deficiency. The wide variation in religious ideas and beliefs could then be traced to

---

[2] The letter is dated 1751, which places the controversy referred to near the 1670s—the decade which opened with the first (Port-Royal) publication of Pascal's *Pensées*. Hume singles out Nicole, one of the editors, as the originator of the controversy, without apparently recognizing the Pascalian influence.

variety of circumstances and education without undermining the credibility of religious conviction as such, any more than in the case of morality which is similarly grounded in sentiment.

The Rhine flows north, the Rhone south; yet both spring from the *same* mountain, and are also actuated, in their opposite directions, by the *same* principle of gravity. The different inclinations of the ground, on which they run, cause all the difference of their courses. . . .

The principles upon which men reason in morals are always the same; though the conclusions which they draw are often very different. That they all reason aright with regard to this subject, more than with regard to any other, it is not incumbent on any moralist to show. It is sufficient, that the original principles of censure or blame are uniform, and that erroneous conclusions can be corrected by sounder reasoning and larger experience (Hume (6), *A Dialogue*, 333–6).

It might be hoped that detailed cross-cultural comparison, of the sort adumbrated at the close of my last chapter, would show that some religious systems are more true to the original impulse, more enlightened, and grounded in "larger experience" than others —and hence more worthy of credit.

The Natural History of Religion is written, in part, to block this move. Hume has few qualms about the commensurability of different cultures, since "as far . . . as observation reaches, there is no universal difference discernible in the human species" (Hume (1), iii, 'Of the Populousness of Ancient Nations', 382; see also Hume (6), *1st Enquiry*, 83). Indeed, he is perfectly prepared to make overall evaluative judgements between ancient and modern civilizations, stigmatizing "the humour of blaming the present, and admiring the past" (Hume (1), iii. 443). But he argues that investigation reveals that the fundamental religious impulses are disreputable.

The first ideas of religion arose not from a contemplation of the works of nature, but from a concern with regard to the events of life, and from the incessant hopes and fears, which actuate the human mind. . . .

Agitated by hopes and fears . . . especially the latter, men scrutinize, with a trembling curiosity, the course of future causes, and examine the various and contrary events of human life. And in this disordered scene, with eyes still more disordered and astonished, they see the first obscure traces of divinity (Hume (10), *Natural History of Religion*, 27–8).

Fear, disorder, and astonishment provide an unpromising base for religion, very different from the first principles of morality; prima facie, it would appear that it is the possession rather than the lack of impulses so grounded that provides evidence of human deficiency. This presumption can be and has, of course, been challenged (for example by Otto), but Hume has done enough to show the treacherous nature of any simple appeal to sentiment as a ground for faith.

But more complex appeals to this principle may still retain plausibility. One might discriminate more from less reputable religious sentiments, and rest the religious case on the way men are so generally "led into the apprehension of invisible, intelligent power by a contemplation of the works of nature" (Hume (10), *Natural History of Religion*, 26), either as a self-sufficient propensity on its own, or as supported by reason—and treat deviations from this norm as symptoms of immaturity or barbarism on the one hand, or of corruption or decadence on the other. The near universal acceptance of "the religious hypothesis" among Hume's contemporaries, whether in theistic or deistic form, would have made this line of thought especially attractive. In combating it, Hume was attempting "to root out a whole vision of reality" (Morrisroe (2), 967), and at this level of debate—as we have seen in earlier chapters—it is very difficult decisively to oppose "Sophistry" with "Syllogism".

What is here needed is a complex and sophisticated presentation of the conflicting conceptual frameworks available, so that the representative reader may recognize his own predisposition (whichever it be) as accurately characterized, and yet be sufficiently distanced from it fairly to judge between probabilities. In other words, what is required is some approximation to Cicero's practice of attempting to "lay before my readers the doctrines of the various schools" so that they may reach "the nearest possible approximation to the truth" (Cicero (1), *DND* I. vi. 13; *Academica* II. iii. 7).

His "original imitation" (Battersby (1)) of the latter's *De Natura Deorum* is Hume's attempt to meet this requirement.

2. The Characters of the Dialogues

One of the more puzzling features of Hume's *Dialogues Concerning Natural Religion* is the treatment of Demea. Of the three main characters, he has the best title to represent orthodox religion, but the Christian reader is hardly encouraged to see in him a reliable champion. We first hear of Demea in terms of "the rigid inflexible orthodoxy" of his disposition (Hume (7), *Dialogues*, 128); he is portrayed as too slow-witted to recognize the ironic nature of Philo's ostensible agreement with his opening remarks (132); and when at length he grasps the underlying import of Philo's arguments this defender of "established opinions" departs in high dudgeon (213).

The style of discourse assigned to him reinforces this negative impression. At the start of Part 2 he opens the main debate in prose remarkable for its uneasy broken syntax: 'I must own, CLEANTHES, said DEMEA, that nothing can more surprise me, than the light, in which you have, all along, put this argument. . . . No man; no man, at least, of common sense, I am persuaded, ever entertained a serious doubt . . .' (141). After this stuttering start he soon falls back on the Biblical cadences of traditional pulpit oratory: 'adore in silence his infinite perfections, which eye hath not seen, ear hath not heard, neither hath it entered into the heart of man to conceive them' (ibid.). Pulling himself up short "lest you should think, that my *piety* has here got the better of my *philosophy*", he takes refuge in a somewhat wordy quotation from Malebranche. The pithy and light-footed nature of Philo's response comes as a welcome contrast:

Nothing exists without a cause; and the original cause of this universe (whatever it be) we call God; and piously ascribe to him every species of perfection. . . . But as all perfection is entirely relative, we ought never to imagine, that we comprehend the attributes of this divine Being. . . . Our ideas reach no farther than our experience: We have no experience of divine attributes and operations: I need not conclude my syllogism: You can draw the inference yourself (142–3).

Even Cleanthes' dogged recourse to common sense compares favourably with the erratic rhetoric of Demea:

Not to lose any time in circumlocutions, said CLEANTHES, addressing DEMEA, much less in replying to the pious declamations of PHILO; I shall briefly explain how I conceive this matter. Look round the world: Contemplate the whole and every part of it: You will find it to be nothing but one great machine . . . (143).

Controversy has long raged concerning whether Cleanthes is indeed, as Hume once claimed (Hume (2), *Letters* i. 153), "the Hero of the Dialogue", or whether Philo more properly deserves that accolade; but it would be a perverse reader indeed who proposed Demea for the role.

This suggests that Hume was not seriously concerned to use the distinctive persuasive capacities of a Ciceronian dialogue to entice upholders of "our vulgar theology" (Hume (7), *Dialogues* 213) into unbiased weighing of probabilities. In part, possibly, he had reservations about the effectiveness of such gentle persuasions in weaning men from "the prevailing systems of superstition" (Hume (7), 'Letter from Adam Smith', 245); hence Demea's alleged inflexibility, contrasting with Cleanthes' preparedness to cut his theological coat according to the philosophical cloth available —even at the price of heresy (Hume (7), *Dialogues*, 203). But, more significantly, it would appear that he did not think he needed such indirect means to assault Demea's version of orthodoxy.

There are three planks to Demea's platform: the "incomprehensible nature of the divine Being" (212), the "unhappiness of man" (193), and "that simple and sublime argument *a priori*, which, by offering to us infallible demonstration, cuts off at once all doubt and difficulty" (188). Without the third element, or some substitute for it,[3] the other two are compatible with "all the topics of the

---

[3] Pascal provides the threefold substitute of arguments from memory, the wager, and *finesse*. Hume has elsewhere attempted to discredit the first of these (Hume (6), *1st Enquiry*, s. 10); in a passage inserted on revision, Hume challenges the partition on which the wager is based (Hume (7), *Dialogues*, 226–7); the operations of *finesse* are effectively neutralized by restricting Demea's other two contentions to what, from the point of view of orthodoxy, are dangerous half-truths. First, in place of the Pascalian "There is enough light for those who desire only to see, and enough darkness for those of a contrary disposition" (*Pensées* L.149, B.430, S.182) Demea insists only, and without proper explanation, on God's incomprehensibility. Second, his emphasis on the wretchedness of man gives no scope to the latter pole of the *misère/grandeur* opposition which powers the Pascalian dialectic; the only challenge to this bias is provided by Cleanthes who misguidedly, but characteristically, denies *misère* instead of acknowledging it and countering this side of human experience with that of *grandeur*.

Demea's invocation of human suffering and divine incomprehensibility, taken together with his avowed suspicion of human reasoning and insistence on the importance of submission in religion, may seem to align him rather closely with the author of the Book of Job; however his reliance on the "argument a priori" makes clear the distance between them—it is Job's comforters who have recourse to the a priori. It would be more accurate to note that the weakness of Demea points to potential inadequacies in the procedures of Job for establishing first principles. The full development of *finesse* is only achieved when Classical perceptions are combined with Biblical—as in Pascal who is intellectually far removed from Demea. No doubt Pascal, like the author of Job and Demea himself, has an underlying religious motivation for his distrust of human reason, but the arguments he gives derive from Classical scepticism (mediated through Montaigne) and his reformulation of reason in terms of the heart draws on secular as well as religious sources.

greatest libertines and infidels" (213) and Philo enthusiastically accepts them. But Cleanthes' uncharacteristically sharp assault on that crucial third component is one of the most devastating passages in the *Dialogues*:

There is an evident absurdity in pretending to demonstrate a matter of fact, or to prove it by any arguments *a priori*. Nothing is demonstrable, unless the contrary implies a contradiction. Nothing, that is distinctly conceivable, implies a contradiction. Whatever we conceive as existent, we can also conceive as non-existent. There is no Being, therefore, whose non-existence implies a contradiction. Consequently there is no Being, whose existence is demonstrable. I propose this argument as entirely decisive, and am willing to rest the whole controversy upon it (189).

Behind this, of course, lies the dichotomy between demonstrative and moral reasoning we encountered earlier; Demea's attempt to extend demonstrative reasoning to matters of fact inevitably involves "sophistry and illusion". The burden of proof is thus thrown firmly back on Demea's shoulders and, as we saw, this can only be sustained by a successful challenge to the fundamental Humean distinction between forms of reasoning with their associated subject matters. This distinction Hume sees as firmly grounded in considerations far closer to "the reflections of common life" than the "abstract reasoning" (191) of a Demea, and he does not believe it can be subverted.

But this by itself might be thought to smack of dogmatism, thus Cleanthes adds certain further arguments and then Philo, in a passage inserted on revision of the work, contributes a fall-back position in case any such challenge is sustained. There is a certain tension in Hume's thinking between the empiricist dichotomy mentioned above, which apparently excludes necessity from applying to matters of fact, and his recognition of causes as involving "necessary connection" together with rejection of all appeals to chance;[4] 'We must certainly allow, that the cohesion of the parts of matter arises from natural and necessary principles, whatever difficulty we may find in explaining them' (Hume (5), *Treatise*, 401). If a principle may be necessary and yet have factual application, a Demea might well ask, why not God? To such a demand Philo here

---

[4] See Anderson, ch. 14–16. For an attempt to show that this tension is more apparent than real see Wright, especially ch. 4.

provides (part of)[5] Hume's answer. Consider one of the more remarkable patterns of mathematics:

To a superficial observer, so wonderful a regularity may be admired as the effect either of chance or design; but a skilful algebraist immediately concludes it to be the work of necessity. . . . Is it not probable, I ask, that the whole œconomy of the universe is conducted by a like necessity, though no human algebra can furnish a key which solves the difficulty? And instead of admiring the order of natural beings, may it not happen, that, could we penetrate into the intimate nature of bodies, we should clearly see why it was absolutely impossible, they could ever admit of any other disposition? So dangerous is it to introduce this idea of necessity into the present question! And so naturally does it afford an inference directly opposite to the religious hypothesis! (Hume (7), *Dialogues*, 191)

This response is constructed, of course, with more than half an eye to the arguments a posteriori of Cleanthes—with its appeal to "design" and "the order of natural beings".[6] But it provides a distributive counterpart to Cleanthes' second challenge to Demea's argument: "why may not the material universe be the necessarily existent Being, according to this pretended explication of necessity?" (190), and serves to protect an otherwise uncomfortably exposed flank of the Humean position against attack.

In Hume's thinking, therefore, arguments a priori for "the religious hypothesis" can be decisively refuted,[7] thus their

---

[5] Philo has already given the rest of Hume's reply at the end of pt. 4, a passage also inserted on revision (Hume (7), 164): ultimate causes or principles are general in nature, not particular. This contention is open to objection on purely scientific grounds (see Swinburne (1), 208, and Pike, 161), but even if granted only has force if God is taken to be a particular. The anthropomorphically inclined Cleanthes, indeed, does assume this, for he "operates throughout the *Dialogues* only with the notion of particular cause" (Nathan, 142); how close this brings him to conceiving of God as a part of the world of which we too are parts is hidden from him only through a lack of precision in his uses of the terms 'world' and 'universe' (see Grave, 72). Demea appears to have too insecure a hold on the doctrine of the "incomprehensible nature of the Deity" to be in a position to challenge this assumption.

[6] Indeed, part of the passage is a close paraphrase of Philo's remarks at the close of pt. 6 (Hume (7), 174–5), which are unambiguously directed against Cleanthes.

[7] In Kantian terms, of course, neither Demea's argument nor that of Samuel Clarke which it summarizes is "a priori" in the "pure" sense of "absolutely independent of all experience" (Kant (1), 43). Although Clarke terms his argument 'a priori', he has little trust in ontological arguments and does not deploy one (Clarke (2), 20–1); he, like Demea, proposes a form of cosmological argument (understandably misclassified by Kemp Smith (1), 115) which starts "from experience of existence in general" (Kant (1), 500). But for Hume this is not the main point, which is that the argument is proposed (following a tradition heavily influenced by Locke) as demonstrative. According to Locke, the "evidence" for God's existence is "equal

footnote continued overleaf

representative may play the secondary roles of foil, butt, and stalking-horse in the economy of the *Dialogues*, whose main thrust is towards exploring attempts to base that "hypothesis" or arguments a posteriori and on sentiment—if the latter, indeed, can be distinguished from education. It is Cleanthes and Philo who must appear to have heroic stature, such that the reader will respect their presentations, not Demea.

Light is thrown on this complex interrelationship by considering Hume's Ciceronian prototype, the *De Natura Deorum*. Here too there are three main characters, one of whom is presented as intellectually a good deal weaker than the other two. Velleius the Epicurean is the first to present his case, and does so in a manner designed to alienate the reader;

> Hereupon Velleius began, in the confident manner (I need not say) that is customary with Epicureans, afraid of nothing so much as lest he should appear to have doubts about anything. One would have supposed he had just come down from the assembly of the gods in the intermundane spaces of Epicurus (Cicero (1), I. viii. 18).

The case is concluded by half way through the first book, and is bitingly rebutted by Cotta the Academic sceptic in the second half. At the outset of the next book Velleius expresses himself "rash" to have joined issue with him and drops out of the discussion. Balbus the Stoic is given the whole of the second book to deploy his position, which he does with some skill, and Cotta takes the whole of the third and final book to reply, treating the Stoic position with considerably more respect than he had the Epicurean. At the close Cotta looks forward to Balbus' answer on some other occasion, expressing himself "confident that you can easily defeat me"; Velleius expresses doubts about this, but in an intemperate manner

---

footnote 7 cont.

to mathematical certainty", involving a "regular deduction" from "some part of our intuitive knowledge" (Locke (2) IV. x. 1–6). For Locke the knowledge in question is that of our own existence, for Clarke that of "Something actually existing without me" (Clarke (2), 21; but see 8–11), for Demea that of the existence of at least something. Hume argues that demonstration is of its nature a priori, "concerning relations of ideas", and the necessity involved applies only to "quantity and number"; thus the claims of this Lockean tradition must embody "sophistry and illusion". It is on the indemonstrability of matters of fact that Cleanthes' critique of Demea's argument turns, not on the (derivative) issue of its classification as 'a priori'—a term used in the pre-Kantian sense in which "the ideal of *a priori* knowledge of nature was a real but unattainable ideal" (Wright, 31).

which suggests chagrin rather than dispassionate assessment. And finally Cicero himself as narrator and silent spectator, although himself an Academic, concludes 'Here the conversation ended, and we parted, Velleius thinking Cotta's discourse to be the truer, while I felt that that of Balbus approximated more nearly to a semblance of the truth' (Cicero (1), III. xl. 95). An ending which invites comparison with that of Hume's *Dialogues*, as expressed by his narrator Pamphilus:

> CLEANTHES and PHILO pursued not this conversation much farther; and as nothing ever made greater impression on me, than all the reasonings of that day; so I confess, that, upon a serious review of the whole, I cannot but think, that PHILO's principles are more probable than DEMEA's; but that those of CLEANTHES approach still nearer to the truth.

If we add to these considerations the fact that in considerable part Hume bases the character of Cleanthes on that of Balbus and Philo on Cotta (Price (1) and (2)), it begins to appear that Hume is using a good deal of the machinery provided by Cicero in the presentation of Velleius for his own, rather more sophisticated, presentation of Demea.

The conclusions of the two works, taken together, provide a clue to what is most important for Hume in this machinery. Cicero provides a framework in which one may distinguish between philosophical disputes where the impartial observer can properly judge one side clearly to have won the argument from others where this is not so. There has been long debate about whether Cicero's final comment should be taken at face value or not, but even if we accept Hume's view that it is not to be taken literally and that Cicero was himself "a great sceptic in matters of religion" (Hume (1), iii, 'Of the Rise and Progress of the Arts and Sciences', 189), its existence —together with the dubious value of Velleius' opposing judgement and Cotta's expressed "desire to be refuted"—helps to counterbalance the fact that Balbus has been given no opportunity to reply to Cotta's searching critique. The implication is that the matter remains unresolved; indeed, although many of Cotta's criticisms are highly pertinent, "in some instances they may be directly answered from the speech of Balbus" already delivered (Mayor, III. xxiv). Professor Pease's magisterial judgement is to be accepted so far as it goes:

> Cicero desires to give the impression of impartiality, which would not be produced by two Academics voting alike at the end. He also wishes to show

the reader an example of Academic method rather than of a dogma which might have been (even though wrongly) inferred from the consensus of two Academics, and to suggest that an Academic might use his individual liberty to select and accept any practical working principle, no matter from what school (Pease (2), i. 36).

But this impartiality is not, as we have seen, extended to the Epicurean school, for which Cicero had little intellectual respect and considerable antipathy. In laying "before my readers the doctrines of the various schools", it would appear, he aims to lead us to see that Epicureanism in much less defensible than Stoicism or Academic Scepticism.

Whether the closing judgement of Hume's *Dialogues* is ironic has been similarly debated, hence the controversy about whether Cleanthes or Philo is "the Hero of the Dialogue". There is an element of balance between these latter which does not apply to Demea, a discrepancy which is clearly intentional. Hume is exploiting the pattern established by Cicero to enact the difference in kind on the one hand of the debate between mitigated or "Academic" scepticism and a religion dependent on "arguments a priori", and on the other of that between such scepticism and religions otherwise grounded. The very pretensions of "arguments a priori" to "infallible demonstration" are their undoing; if fallacious, they can be decisively shown to be so. But when we content ourselves with reasonings more appropriate to matters of fact, "there are all imaginable degrees of assurance, from the highest certainty to the lowest species of moral evidence" (Hume (6), *1st Enquiry*, 110); in assessing these, more subtle means are called for.

In exploring them, Hume departs from his Ciceronian model in a number of significant ways. He provides a set of indicators of his intentions with the names he gives to his characters, all of which save one have Ciceronian antecedents.[8] In the *De Natura Deorum* both Cotta and Cicero himself are described as "disciples of Philo" (Cicero (1), I. vii. 17; see also I. iii. 6). The Philo in question was the founder of the Fourth or "New" Academy with much of whose underlying methodology—as the *Academica* makes clear—Cicero was in broad sympathy; he had, indeed, been taught by Philo

---

[8] The Ciceronian bias of eighteenth-century education would justify Hume in assuming that his clues were sufficiently obvious to a contemporary "man of letters" (Hume (7), 228); as he remarks elsewhere, "The fame of Cicero flourishes at present; but that of Aristotle is utterly decayed" (Hume (6), *1st Enquiry*, 7).

personally at a formative stage. Hume himself terms his recommended mitigated scepticism "Academic" (e.g. Hume (6), *1st Enquiry*, v. 1; also xii. 3), and in so doing appears to have Philo's Academy in mind. Philo accepted the arguments of his predecessors Arcesilas and Carneades, to the effect that no perceptions are self-authenticating but that we may nevertheless discriminate between probabilities on the basis of our experience, and to them added the claim that a high degree of probability gives us knowledge; we have seen how Hume, in similar fashion, allows non-demonstrative "proofs" from experience—which Locke would classify as merely probable but in fact "leave no room for doubt". Thus we should antecedently expect the sceptical "Philo" of Hume's *Dialogues* to represent Humean principles; it would not follow, of course, that his actual arguments and conclusions are Hume's, any more than Cicero represents himself as being in agreement with Cotta's "discourse" (*"disputatio"*). But here a highly significant discrepancy between the conclusions of the two works becomes important; whereas Cicero purports to endorse the *"disputatio"* of Balbus rather than Cotta, which is explicable along the lines suggested by Professor Pease, for Pamphilus it is the "principles" of Cleanthes which are to be preferred. This alone is sufficient to cast doubt on Pamphilus' reliability in the economy of the *Dialogues*.

Cleanthes himself has an important pedigree. Cicero's Balbus refers to him as "our master Cleanthes" (*"Cleanthes noster"*; Cicero (1), II. v. 13) and frequently cites him. He was, in fact, the successor of Zeno—the founder of the Stoic school—and the teacher of the historical Balbus. We should thus expect to find significant parallels between Cicero's Balbus and Hume's Cleanthes, and so indeed it proves: "Both employ the argument from design; both argue by analogy; they use parallel examples; the structure of their arguments, their language is often similar; and they insist upon the moral orientation of the world" (Price (1), 261). The argument a posteriori championed by Cleanthes in Hume's *Dialogues* had been pioneered by the Stoics of antiquity, as the "philosophical" scepticism recommended by his Philo (Hume (7), *Dialogues*, 228) finds its Classical counterpart in the Academy. Now the underlying principles of Stoics and Academics were radically opposed; the sceptical attack led by Arcesilas of the Academy against the claims of any perceptions to be self-authenticating was inspired by the insistence of Zeno on just such a standard of truth—the φαντασία καταληπτική. The appeal of the Humean Cleanthes to the authority of "your own feeling" (154) echoes this dogmatic tendency in Stoicism, as the "sceptical and metaphysical subtilty" (202) of Hume's Philo does the characteristic tendencies of the Academy. Thus, so far as historical precedents go, it would appear that in endorsing the principles of Cleanthes, Pamphilus is rejecting those of Philo.

Historical precedents are not everything, and there is evidence that Hume thought such a conclusion needed amendment. "It seems evident", we read late in the *Dialogues*, "that the dispute between the sceptics and dogmatists is entirely verbal" (219). This is a passage to which we shall return, but before we can grasp its full import we need to see how this thesis departs from that of the Ciceronean prototype.

Cicero had studied under the Academic Antiochus as well as Philo, and absorbed from him a tendency to eclecticism. In the *De Natura Deorum* Cotta, in conversation with the character 'Cicero' speaks of the claim of "our master Antiochus" ("*Antiochi nostri*"; Cicero (1), I. vii. 16) that "the doctrines of the Stoics, though differing in form of expression, agree in substance with those of the Peripatetics". Balbus, not surprisingly, rejects this claim— referring to their differences in ethics—but as the topic is introduced by Cotta as a reason for holding that "you have no need to regret the absence" of a Peripatetic representative from the discussion, and there was in fact a good deal in common between the two schools in matters of theology, there is reasonable precedent in the dialogue for regarding apparent differences between them in matters concerning the nature of the gods as "entirely verbal" in a way in which the differences between Epicurean, Stoic, and Academic are not. In these matters, at least, it would appear that the Peripatetics are seen as natural allies of the Stoics against the other two schools.

This leaves only one other major school unrepresented—the Platonic. The fact that the Academics look back to Plato as their original founder may lead us to overlook this, but there was a strong constructive side to Plato's thought which played little role in the Fourth Academy. It is this aspect of Plato that Velleius has in mind when he classifies the theology of the *Timaeus* with that of the Stoics in order to attack both (ibid. I. viii–x. 18–24). And it is this dogmatic, religious Plato who lies behind the portrait of 'The Platonist' which Hume contrasts with that of 'The Sceptic' in his essays of those names (Hume (1), iii. 210–31). Thus in the *Dialogues* Philo can oppose "STOICS, PLATONISTS, and PERIPATETICS" to "PYRRHONIANS and ACADEMICS" (Hume (7), 139); it is clear from the context that whereas Philo sees Cleanthes as belonging to the former camp, Cleanthes himself would place Philo in the latter. Now an individual with the name of Hume's narrator, Pamphilus, is referred to in the *De Natura Deorum* (Cicero (1), I. xxvi. 72–3), and it is hardly surprising to find that he is there identified as a "Platonist"—a potential ally of Cleanthes and hence likely to endorse his principles rather than those of Philo in his closing remarks.[9]

But there is one other character in Hume's *Dialogues* as yet unmentioned; often overlooked, his perceptions nevertheless throw a long shadow over the work and the vexed history of its interpretation: Hermippus. Pamphilus, a pupil and near "adopted son" of Cleanthes, is represented as recounting to his friend Hermippus a conversation between the three main characters at which "my youth rendered me a mere auditor of their disputes" (Hume (7), 127–30). Hermippus himself is represented as already having commented on "the remarkable contrast in their characters": "You opposed the accurate philosophical turn of CLEANTHES to the careless scepticism of PHILO, . . . compared either of their dispositions with the rigid inflexible orthodoxy of DEMEA" (128). Pamphilus does not dispute this characterization, and there is evidence from his subsequent comments that he endorses it (ibid. 132, 150, 155, 199, 213, 228), but we have already seen that Pamphilus' impartiality is questionable, thus the weight we are to place on the crucial contrast between Cleanthes' accuracy and Philo's carelessness—and how we are to interpret it—turns on the authority of Hermippus.

The fact that Hermippus is absent from the discussions no doubt reflects the fact that he is nowhere mentioned in the *De Natura Deorum*, but of course there was a famous scholar of Peripatetic leanings with that name, Hermippus of Smyrna, a near contemporary of Cleanthes. Thus on a formal level Hume's threefold alliance of "STOICS, PLATONISTS, and PERIPATETICS" is reflected by

---

[9] For useful discussions of the significance of Pamphilus' Platonic associations for the *Dialogues* see Price (3), 127–32, and Mossner (3).

Cleanthes, Pamphilus, and Hermippus respectively; the agreement between the latter two that Cleanthes has the "accurate philosophical turn" is only what is to be expected, and in no sense a neutral assessment—it is grounded on a convergence of view remarked by the *De Natura Deorum* itself.

But an educated contemporary of Hume might well be expected to recognize a further dimension to the Humean irony. Hermippus of Smyrna is, on the face of it, an odd choice as representative Peripatetic, for he was more biographer than philosopher. But there is another Hermippus, one who plays a role elsewhere in the Ciceronian corpus, and the coincidence of names appears to have given Hume his cue. In the speech in defence of Flaccus, Hermippus appears as "a learned man, . . . an old friend and guest of mine", who gets swindled through misreading the character of a man with whom he "should have been thoroughly acquainted" (Cicero (12), *Pro Flacco*, xx. 46–8); in a private letter to his brother, Cicero indicates that this friendship was merely politic on his own side but Hermippus lacked the insight to recognize his true feelings, even though coming from a nation which "has a natural aptitude for deceit" (Cicero (13), *Epistulae Ad Quintum Fratrem*, I. ii. 4). The choice of the name 'Hermippus' for Pamphilus' correspondent, in a Ciceronian dialogue, should surely make us pause before we take his reading of character at face value.

We know that Hume took great pains over a long period in the preparation of his *Dialogues*, and near the end of his life wrote that "On revising them (which I have not done these 15 Years) I find that nothing can be more cautiously and more artfully written"; he also remarked that "Some of my Friends flatter me, that it is the best thing I ever wrote". (Hume (2), *Letters* ii. 334 and 232). The choice of names for the characters is one aspect of that artfulness, which needs to be taken into account in assessing their different roles —not least the reliability of Hermippus as a reader of men's "dispositions".

In one of the best, though brief, recent discussions of the *Dialogues*, Professor Sutherland perceptively remarks that Pamphilus has a tendency towards "coming near to but not quite grasping the truth" (Sutherland, 184). This applies, too, to the understanding he shares with Hermippus of the main figures in the debate, as may be brought out by considering the case of Philo. Here the claim that his scepticism is "careless" is splendidly ambiguous; the "care" that is lacking could either be the sort that makes for Cleanthes' (alleged) accuracy or that which is associated with anxiety. Some years earlier, in discussing a notorious sceptic, a character in Berkeley's *Alciphron* had remarked that "it is natural for careless writers to run into faults they never think of " (Berkeley, iii. 204); this is the first form of "carelessness", and the contrast Hermippus draws with "accuracy" suggests that it is this that he has in mind. Indeed, there are elements of this type of carelessness in Philo's discussions. His initial praise of scepticism appears to be of the extreme sort, applying "even in subjects of common life and practice" and insisting on "the errors and deceits of our very senses" (Hume (7), 131), until he is brought up short by Cleanthes and agrees to distinguish extreme from mitigated scepticism (134–5). Again, his objection that we could have no empirical evidence of a Designer of the universe unless "we had experience of the origin of worlds" (149–50) is quietly dropped after Cleanthes' counter-examples in Part 3 (see Wadia). Further, when imbued (at least according to Pamphilus) "with an air of alacrity and triumph" he challenges Cleanthes to tell "By what phenomena in nature can we pretend to decide" about the unity of the Deity (166–8); but when discussing that Deity's moral attributes he is happy enough to invoke "the uniformity and steadiness of general laws" to oppose the suggestion that they are "mixed" without any consideration of the significance of this contention for his earlier challenge. Even leaving aside the problematic final section of the *Dialogues*, there are signs of Philo "running into faults" he had not anticipated (see also Bricke, s. 2).

But to rest one's account of Philo on passages such as these would be grotesque. Much more representative are the passages of great subtlety in which Cleanthes' arguments are undermined by a judicious blend of logical analysis and parallel reasoning, reminiscent of Hume's own argumentation at its best. And here it becomes relevant that for Hume (as opposed to Berkeley) "carelessness" in a philosopher is a virtue. This, of course, is 'carelessness' in the second sense of the word, that used by Pope in his description of Voiture as "wisely careless, innocently gay" (Pope, 'Epistle to Miss Blount', 169). Hume recommends the "innocent satisfaction" of those who philosophize with a "easy disposition", free of "spleen" and "indolence"; "The conduct of a man, who studies philosophy in this careless manner, is more truly sceptical" than that of one who allows himself to be "over-whelm'd with doubts and scruples"

(Hume (5), *Treatise*, 273).[10] This temper is characteristic of the Philo who can speak of "the freedom of my conversation" and disdains the "cautious" approach to natural religion "because I know that I can never, on that head, corrupt the principles of any man of common sense" (Hume (7), 214), the Philo who impresses Pamphilus as "somewhat between jest and earnest" (150). From the point of view of an ally of Cleanthes, Philo may well appear "careless" in the pejorative sense; but Hume is insinuating that the sense in which this term is most properly applied to the character is his own preferred favourable one. Hermippus, like Pamphilus, is "coming near to but not quite grasping the truth".

Philo, indeed, displays many of the characteristics of his creator, and the overlap of views is so marked that ever since Professor Kemp Smith's classic discussion (Kemp Smith (1)) it has been customary to see Philo as Hume's spokesman. Although there have been dissenting voices, the standard orthodoxy has recently been powerfully reasserted by Parent (2) and by Gaskin (2) (159–66). But while Philo's temper and principles are indeed very close to those of Hume himself, there are cases where the two appear to be at variance and the standard recourse to irony is inappropriate. The most obvious instance is that where Philo solemnly declares "my unfeigned sentiments" (Hume (7), *Dialogues*, 219) and goes on to argue that God's moral attributes must not be judged by human standards, thus reinforcing his earlier denial that "our ideas any wise correspond to his perfections" (142), and to claim that God's moral attributes are "infinitely perfect, but incomprehensible" (199). Elsewhere, however, Hume—speaking in his own voice of "the Divine standard of merit and demerit"—declares that "to suppose measures of approbation and blame, different from the human, confounds every thing" (Hume (1), iv, 'Of the Immortality of the Soul', 402) and attacks religions which divorce human from divine criteria of goodness as "daemonism" and "superstition" (Hume (10), *Natural History of Religion*, 67). Indeed, in a private letter Hume suggests that God cannot properly be said to have any moral attributes at all:

I wish from my Heart, I could avoid concluding, that since Morality, according to your Opinion as well as mine, is determined merely by

---

[10] This recommendation of "carelessness" has deep roots in what has been called Hume's "epistemology of ease" (Battersby (2) 51–2).

Sentiment, it regards only human Nature & human Life. This has been often urg'd against you, & the Consequences are very momentous (Hume (2), *Letters* i. 40).

Although the date of this declaration of "unfeigned sentiments" is early (1740), there is every reason to believe that Hume continued to hold to these "momentous" consequences throughout his life.

But such discrepancies are only puzzling if we accept the ortho-dox opinion that Philo unambiguously "speaks for Hume", despite the fact—pointed out by Professor Laird sometime ago—that "the Ciceronian type of dialogue that Hume chose does not permit such canons of interpretation" (Laird (2), 206). Philo himself hints at the true situation in his concluding remarks; his final paragraph begins:

If the whole of natural theology, as some people seem to maintain, resolves itself into one simple, though somewhat ambiguous, at least undefined proposition, *that the cause or causes of order in the universe probably bear some remote analogy to human intelligence* . . . (Hume (7), *Dialogues*, 227).

Leaving aside the content of this "undefined proposition" two interconnected elements of this opening deserve comment. First, it is hypothetical. The fact that by the end of the paragraph the hypothesis has become sufficiently developed for it to serve as the foundation for Philo's recommendation to Pamphilus, indicates that it is one to which Philo is sympathetic, and of course it fits in excellently with all he has argued before. But simply to assert the proposition would smack more of the dogmatist than the "sceptic" with whom Philo identifies himself, who "has himself no fixed station or abiding city, which he is ever, on any occasion, obliged to defend" (186–7). Instead—and this is the second consideration —Philo indirectly aligns himself with a tradition which is radically sceptical of the pretensions of natural theology, invoking "some people" who "seem to maintain" (rather than clearly assert) that "the whole of natural theology . . . resolves itself" into a prop-osition which is religiously useless, leaving the "inquisitive, con-templative, and religious man" with "some contempt of human reason, that it can give no solution more satisfactory with regard to so extraordinary and magnificent a question" (227). In having Philo conclude by gesturing to the tradition, with which he is in general sympathy, Hume is indicating the matrix within which we are to place his character—and, to the extent that Hume shares Philo's standpoint, Hume himself.

Here, once again, Hume is following his Ciceronian model, and developing a parallel between Cleanthes and Philo. Cleanthes' roots in the Stoic tradition of Balbus are supplemented by borrowings from eighteenth-century empirical deists and theists influenced by Newtonian science, such as Maclaurin and (probably) Bishop Butler (Price (1), Mossner (1) and (3), Hurlbutt (1) and (2), Jeffner, ch. 6). Philo also has his Ciceronian prototype, Cotta (see Price (2)), and likewise his modern counterparts—of whom the most obvious is Bayle, one of the great influences on Hume's own thought and a figure to whom we shall return.[11] Cicero was concerned to "lay before my readers the doctrines of the various schools", including those of the Academic one with whose principles he was in general agreement—though his overall alignment did not involve endorsement of every contention of its leaders. Similarly for Hume, a character who represents a tradition whose principles he himself endorses need not at all points represent his own opinions. We shall consider in the next section some of the ways in which he is able to exploit this "semi-detached" status of Philo to render him a character of much greater subtlety than is comprehensible to Pamphilus.

As one might expect, the "accurate philosophical turn" attributed to Cleanthes by Hermippus and Pamphilus also represents only a partial truth. Cleanthes' initial presentation of the "argument a posteriori" is pithy and judicious (Hume (7), 143), but the subsequent discussions show that reservations must be entered about its "accuracy"; Cleanthes himself soon finds himself defending arguments he acknowledges to be of an "irregular nature" (155). His criticism of Demea's "argument a priori" (189–91) is, as

---

[11] Cleanthes identifies Bayle as the leader of the sceptical school to which he is most opposed early on in the *Dialogues* (Hume (7), 138). Hendel (305, 325, 331, and 352), Kemp Smith (1) (see especially app. B), and Jeffner (204–9) have detailed a number of specific parallels between Bayle's arguments and those of Philo; the latter, indeed, goes so far as to identify Philo with Bayle. Bayle's position was expressly, if sometimes somewhat ironically, fideistic and phrases like "sound, believing Christian" sound more at home on his lips than on those of Hume. The corpus of Bayle's writings (usually misinterpreted) represents one of the great formative influences on eighteenth-century scepticism, and Hume was under its influence very early on (Kemp Smith (2), ch. 14, app. C; Mossner (2), 78). But Bayle was probably not the only modern "source" for Philo—Wright (186), for example, has recently pointed to an instructive parallel with Diderot—and Cicero's Cotta is a very strong classical presence; Philo, like Cleanthes and Demea, speaks for a tradition and is not simply to be identified with any figure within that tradition.

we have seen, masterly, and his "accurate turn" is also displayed in
the checks he gives to Philo, mentioned above; but much more often
he flounders in the nets Philo casts for him, sometimes failing to
understand the force of the sceptical criticisms (as with the distinction between "general" and "particular" causes (164; see Nathan,
142)), and sometimes taking refuge in generalities:

> So great is your fertility of invention, that I am not ashamed to acknowledge
> myself unable, in a sudden, to solve regularly such out-of-the-way difficul-
> ties as you incessantly start upon me: Though I clearly see, in general, their
> fallacy and error. . . . Such whimsies, as you have delivered, may puzzle,
> but never can convince us (181).

When in the later sections he is driven "to deny absolutely the
misery and wickedness of man" he embraces a position which is, as
Philo remarks, "extremely doubtful", and Cleanthes' reference to
"computation" here smacks more of the trappings of accuracy than
the real thing (200).

I shall return to Philo and Cleanthes in the next section, but
before we consider more precisely the nature of the debate between
them there is one further aspect of the presentation of Demea that
needs to be considered. Alone among Hume's characters, Demea
has no significant Ciceronian namesake. We have seen that he plays
a role in Hume's *Dialogues* analogous to that of Velleius the
Epicurean in the *De Natura Deorum*; but the leading Epicurean
arguments in natural theology were dead by Hume's time, unlike
many of those of the Stoics and Academics, and Demea is used to
present aspects of contemporary "vulgar theology" (213) which
were without Ciceronian parallel. Now Cicero normally incorporated into his dialogues a good deal of material drawn from
representatives of the schools he was portraying, so that their
doctrines could be laid before his readers as fairly as possible; the
less sympathy he had for a doctrine, the more he relied on his
sources. Similarly, Hume has Demea quote extensively in support
of his major contentions. That God's nature is "altogether incomprehensible and unknown to us" is supported by a long quotation
from "Father MALEBRANCHE" (141–2); his "argument a priori"
(188–9), which has roots at least as far back as St Thomas Aquinas,
is an epitome of the argument of Samuel Clarke, the Boyle Lecturer
(Clarke (2), 8–17; see also Mossner (1), 335–8, and Rowe, esp.
117), whom Cleanthes ironically quotes in his reply; and although

the "unhappiness of man" is said to need no "authorities", since it represents "the united testimony of mankind", we are treated not only to some stock pulpit "eloquence and strong imagery" but also to quotations from Milton and Dryden (193–8)—Philo, mischievously and characteristically, contributes a reflection to the same effect strongly reminiscent of Lucretius' Epicurean assault on "superstitious terrors" (195; compare Lucretius, i. 62–111). 'Demea', derived from the word for 'common people'[12], is the name given to the character who advocates what he calls the "common" argument for the existence of God (188), supports "submission" to "the most established doctrines and opinions" (131), whom Cleanthes criticizes for employing "the injudicious reasoning of our vulgar theology" (213), and who represents "orthodoxy" to Hermippus and Pamphilus. Hume, as we have seen, believes himself to have a clear and decisive counter to that "common" argument, but he also holds that the "orthodox" position is internally incoherent. By weaving three of its main strands together through the mouth of Demea, and exposing them to the crossfire of Cleanthes and Philo, he is attempting to convey this thought to the reader. The plausibility of this insinuation cannot rest on the credibility of Demea, which is systematically undermined, but on that of his different sources—hence the need for quotation and appeal to "authorities".

Demea calls on Philo to assist him "in proving the adorable mysteriousness of the divine nature" (145). Philo purports to do so, but this support turns out to be highly tendentious; the only "proofs" he accepts are of "mysteriousness" and give only the most equivocal support to the claim that the "cause or causes of order in the universe" are indeed worthy of "profound adoration" (186–7, 212, 214, 219, 227). Demea insists, with some justification, that "the

[12] Here at least Smith's etymological key is in place (ii. 524). Mossner (1), 338, objects "Who, it may well be asked, has ever heard the masses argue to 'a necessarily existent Being'?"; but this misses the point, which is that the orthodoxy nominally accepted by the masses appears to presuppose such a Being and that the different elements of Demea's position are supposed to represent essential elements of that orthodoxy. There can be a "vulgar theology" without the vulgar being theologians. Professor Mossner (ibid. 345) prefers Laird's (1) (294–5) suggestion that Hume's Demea is to be identified with the Demea of Terence's *Adelphi* who "stands for orthodox opinion"; but Terence is not otherwise an influence on the *Dialogues* and, save for the common devotion to received opinion indicated by the etymology of the name, the parallel is misleading. Terence's character learns from experience to retort his opponents' stratagems against themselves, but when the veils are lifted from the eyes of that of Hume, *his* Demea gives up.

theory of religion becomes altogether useless" if we are uncertain "whether the Deity or Deities, to whom we owe our existence, be perfect or imperfect"; for religion is concerned with such matters as trust, worship, veneration, and obedience (170). His problem is to show that a theology which maintains the incomprehensibility of God is not thereby rendered "useless". Cleanthes, indeed, presses this difficulty on him:

> The Deity, I can readily allow, possesses many powers and attributes, of which we can have no comprehension: But if our ideas, so far as they go, be not just and adequate, and correspondent to his real nature, I know not what there is in this subject worth insisting on. . . . How do you MYSTICS, who maintain the absolute incomprehensibility of the Deity, differ from sceptics or atheists, who assert that the first cause of All is unknown and unintelligible? (158)

The way the sceptical Philo joins forces with Demea in combatting Cleanthes' "anthropomorphism" (160) lends ironic force to this objection.

In Western tradition the difficulty is often met by distinguishing between the nature and attributes of God.[13] "No created mind", maintains St Thomas, "can attain the perfect sort of understanding that is intrinsically possible of God's essence", and in this sense endorses Dionysius' claim that "All find it completely impossible to comprehend him" (Aquinas, 1a, 12, 7 and 1); it follows that we cannot properly imagine the manner or "*modus*" in which he exists. Now when we predicate of something, the nature of the subject in question will determine the manner in which the attribute we are assigning can apply; a man and a dog can both display faithfulness, but not in exactly the same manner. The inevitable limitations in our knowledge of the divine nature thus place strict limits on our grasp of the manner in which his perfections are possessed by God, though they need not rule out the possibility of our being able to know that he does indeed possess them in some "analogous" sense—whether by argument a priori or a posteriori, by inner illumination, or by revelation. Berkeley had defended much of this tradition in his *Alciphron* (Berkeley, iii. 163–70), and Demea's own source for his argument a priori is clear that although we can demonstrate many of God's attributes we cannot comprehend the

---

[13] The Palamite distinction of Eastern Christendom between God's essence and his energies plays a related but not quite identical role.

divine essence (Clarke (2), 38–43)—a distinction that lies behind his discussion of God's omnipresence:

> As to the *particular Manner* of his being Infinite or every where present, in opposition to the manner of Created Things being present in such or such finite Places; This is as impossible for our finite Understandings to comprehend or explain, as it is for us to form an adequate Idea of Infinity (Clarke (2), 46).

That this appeal to the finite nature of our understandings is not to be used as a licence for conceptual irresponsibility is shown by his rejection of traditional construals of God's eternity in terms of timelessness as unintelligible (Clarke (2), 43; see Rowe 224).

Demea's presentation, however, virtually ignores such considerations. Instead of discriminating *modus significandi* from *res significata* in the ascription of attributes to God, with the mysteriousness of the former (derived from the mystery of the divine nature) being contrasted with the comparative intelligibility of the latter, Demea flatly denies that we have any "adequate idea of his nature and attributes" (Hume (7), 155). Right from the start, it is not only "the essence of that supreme mind" and "the manner of his existence" that is said to be "altogether incomprehensible and unknown to us", but also "his attributes" (141). Demea's defence of "that perfect immutability and simplicity, which all true theists ascribe to the Deity" (159) is innocent of any of the apparatus by means of which competent theologians over the centuries have striven to give content to such doctrines, thus opening himself to Cleanthes' rejoinder:

> I can readily allow . . . that those who maintain the perfect simplicity of the supreme Being, to the extent in which you have explained it, are complete *mystics*, and chargeable with all the consequences which I have drawn from their opinion. They are, in a word, atheists, without knowing it (159).

The reasons for Demea's weakness here are not far to seek. The coherence of the Thomist doctrine of analogous predication depends on the metaphysical doctrine of the analogy of being, taken together with an Aristotelian account of causality which posits a necessary similarity between cause and effect; these considerations both ensure that only "perfections" can properly be predicated of God, and give sufficient indirect clues to his nature for the *modus* in which he possesses his attributes to be at least partially intelligible. But the metaphysical doctrine had been losing its grip on men's minds with the progress of the scientific revolution, and contemporary theologians had encountered great difficulties in finding a suitable substitute.[14] The perhaps inevitable result was that those most impressed by that revolution construed the analogical element in theology in scientific terms, denying any difference in meaning between terms as applied to the world and to God, and—if concerned to remain orthodox—admitted with Cleanthes that we could not have knowledge of all God's attributes; this was approximately Butler's position (Butler (1), i. 4, 37; ii. 190–202), and Hume is concerned to show through the figure of Cleanthes that it is inherently unstable, leading to heresy or scepticism. Those, on the other hand, who saw such an approach as the high road to Deism laid stress on the inadequacy of human understanding and, while insisting on the orthodox formulae, denied that we can understand how they apply to God; in default of an adequate replacement for the Thomist machinery, however, they were open to the charge of scepticism levelled in the Fourth Dialogue of Berkeley's *Alciphron*, or that directed at "Mystics" by Cleanthes. Hume's analysis of causation, furthermore, knocks the other crucial prop from the intellectual structure lying behind the traditional theology; if there is no necessary likeness between cause and effect (see, e.g. Hume (6), *1st Enquiry*, s. 7), then our knowledge of the creation affords no insight into the sense in which terms may properly be applied to its first cause. Finally, the Humean theory of meaning, grounded as it is in ideas which "reach no farther than our experience" (Hume (7), *Dialogues*, 142–3), allows little scope for distinguishing *modus significandi* from *res significata*. with regard to that which transcends our experience. It is little wonder that for Hume classical orthodoxy was broken-backed.

Now in discussing the traditional accounts of theological language, Berkeley had felt it necessary to "ask your pardon for having dwelt so long on a point of metaphysics, and introduced such unpolished and unfashionable writers as the Schoolmen into good company" (Berkeley, iii. 170). Hume saw himself as "a Kind of Resident or Ambassador from the Dominions of Learning to those of Conversation", hence his use of the dialogue and essay form, but as a tactful one who "chiefly" used for his materials whatever is

---

[14] For an excellent sketch of some of the relevant background see Jeffner, ch. 7. St Thomas summarizes his theory at Aquinas, iii. 1a, 13.

"furnish'd by Conversation and common Life" (Hume (1), iv, 'Of Essay Writing', 368–9). Such an aspiration appears to lie behind the warning he puts into Pamphilus' mouth about the danger that the dialogue form may, if injudiciously handled, "convey the image of *pedagogue* and *pupil*",[15] the very fault for which Berkeley's character offers his excuses. Hume takes steps to avoid this pitfall; instead of having Demea attempt the necessary discriminations, and then using Philo or Cleanthes to undermine them and point unwelcome consequences, he simply presents Demea as an innocent stalking-horse for the scepticism of Philo. The onus of proof is now on the reader to provide a contemporaneously credible account of discourse about God which will avoid the charges Cleanthes levels at Demea's "Mysticism", while avoiding Cleanthes' own "Anthropomorphism", and successfully blocking Philo's "infidel" ascription to God of attributes which are very far from being "perfections" (Hume (7), 212–13).[16]

Hume is confident this cannot be done. It is a function of the "*artfulness*" of the *Dialogues* that the point is not laboured. Demea is an eighteenth-century figure, capable of expounding not only Clarke and Malebranche (Wright, 185–6), but also Hume's own account of "the soul of man" (Hume (7), 159; compare Hume (5), *Treatise*, 207); his weakness reflects the contemporary weakness of a position which, as Philo points out, is strongly reminiscent of "all the sound, orthodox divines almost, who have treated of this subject" (160). Demea's "rigidity" in clinging to the ancient formulae in a modern context leads to consequences which those "sound divines" who developed the formulae would reject.[17] The informed

[15] Pamphilus characteristically clouds Hume's perception by first rejecting any attempt "to deliver a SYSTEM in conversation" and then commending his conversationalists for displaying their "various systems" (Hume (7), 127–8); here as elsewhere we see him "coming near to but not quite grasping the truth" (Sutherland, 184). For the significance of Pamphilus' own role as "pupil" see the next section.

[16] Demea's recognition of Philo's incipient blasphemy (Hume (7), 212–13) should be read in the light of his earlier insistence that God's "attributes are perfect, but incomprehensible" (156); it is little wonder that "Demea did not at all relish the latter part of the discourse" (213). In pt. 12 Philo purports, in somewhat ambiguous syntax, to allow "the supreme Being . . . to be absolutely and entirely perfect" (219), but we have already been alerted to the real worth of a sceptic's readiness "to bestow on him as many sublime eulogies and unmeaning epithets, as you shall please to require" (158).

[17] Compre the fortunes of the Augustinian formulae in post-medieval Europe, discussed in ch. 5.2.

Christian reader may be expected to see the point and, so Hume doubtless intends, discouraged by the unceremonious manner in which the cosmological argument has been shot from under him, take his cue from Philo's "almost", abandon the unpromising labour of attempting to salvage a Demea-like "orthodoxy", and align himself with Cleanthes.

In doing so, he plays into Hume's hands.

3. Education and its Effects

> After I joined the company, whom I found sitting in CLEANTHES'S library, DEMEA paid CLEANTHES some compliments, on the great care which he took of my education.
>
> (Hume (7), *Dialogues*, 130)

Pamphilus' opening to Part 1 adumbrates the topic which is to dominate, explicitly or implicitly, the whole of the first section: the role of education—as opposed to reason—as a principle upon which religion may properly be grounded. The importance of the issue is stressed by Philo as the part closes; 'At present, when the influence of education is much diminished, . . . if we distrust human reason, we have now no other principle to lead us into religion' (139).

Thereafter the topic appears to drop largely, though not completely, out of sight until the close of the penultimate section, and instead of education we have feeling as the alternative to reason. Thus on the rebutting of Demea's "argument a priori" Part 10 opens: 'It is my opinion, I own, replied DEMEA, that each man feels, in a manner, the truth of religion within his own breast' (193).[18] Similarly, the far-reaching criticisms Philo urges in Part 2 against Cleanthes' presentation of the "argument *a posteriori*" are met (in part) by Cleanthes urging Philo "Tell me, from your own feeling, if the idea of a contriver does not immediately flow in upon you with a force like that of sensation" (154). And Philo himself contrasts the difficulty of inferring the moral attributes of God with the way in which "the beauty and fitness of final causes strike us with such

---

[18] Demea is not abandoning Clarke here, despite appearances, for the latter admits that the argument a priori cannot "be made obvious to the *Generality* of Men" (Clarke (2), 489).

irresistible force, that all objections appear (what I believe they really are) mere cavils and sophisms" (202).

But at the close of Part 11 Philo again raises the significance of education as an important issue (213), opening the next and final section with a response to Cleanthes' earlier challenge which is subtly ambiguous between an appeal to feeling and to education: 'Notwithstanding the freedom of my conversation, and my love of singular arguments, no one has a deeper sense of religion impressed on his mind' (214). Philo goes on to invoke "reason" in relation to the belief in "a supreme intelligence" (215), and thereupon Cleanthes pulls together the three threads; the "religious hypothesis" is "supported by strong and obvious reason, by natural propensity, and by early education"—in such circumstances "suspense of judgment" is impossible (216). Philo purports to agree, though it emerges that his understanding of the content of that hypothesis is remarkably attenuated.

The climax comes in the final speech where Philo, recommending that we be "seasoned with a just sense of the imperfections of natural reason", concludes as follows:

> To be a philosophical sceptic is, in a man of letters, the first and most essential step towards being a sound, believing Christian; a proposition which I would willingly recommend to the attention of PAMPHILUS: and I hope CLEANTHES will forgive me for interposing so far in the education and instruction of his pupil (227–8).

This peroration is a familiar interpretative crux, for Hume had no sympathy for Christianity and Philo, as we have seen, is widely regarded as speaking for him; but surprisingly little attention has been paid to the significance of the latter part of it, reminding the reader of the importance of education.

At the most obvious level this comment on Pamphilus' status prepares the way for his concluding endorsement of the "principles" of Cleanthes; quite apart from the Ciceronian associations of his name, he is a biased witness—unlike the studiedly impartial 'Cicero' of the De Natura Deorum. Cleanthes has earlier expressed his dissatisfaction with Philo's proposal "to erect religious faith on philosophical scepticism" (132 and 136), thus Pamphilus' mind is unlikely to have been "seasoned with a just sense of the imperfections of natural reason" in the sense Philo advocates; he is unlikely, therefore, to endorse the principles of philosophical scepticism. That this expectation is fulfilled should suggest to the attentive reader that the conclusions we draw from philosophical debates concerning natural religion will depend on who we are and what we bring to those debates in the first place. This apparently innocuous upshot has, of course, a subversive aspect; we saw earlier that Hume held that the "Convenience in holding to the Catechism we have been first taught" is a highly insecure basis for religion (Hume (2), *Letters* i. 152). If "more Curiosity & Research gives a direct opposite Turn from the same principles' (ibid.), then the reader of a Ciceronian dialogue may respond in a manner rather different from that of the youthful Pamphilus. The *Dialogues* appear to be directed primarily at those sharing Cleanthes' predispositions and, it has been well remarked, "the Cleanthes of this world had to be woo'd with subtlety" (Sutherland, 186).

A further dimension of this subtlety becomes apparent when we consider the reasons Philo gives for recommending scepticism as a foundation for faith. He suggests that the reasonings of natural theology cannot establish any religious proposition save one which can "afford no inference that affects human life, or can be the source of any action or forbearance" (in an earlier draft Hume went so far as to write "steady sentiment" in place of "forbearance" Hume (11), 260)). Such a proposition is, of course, in Demea's terms "useless", and we remember that Philo has earlier claimed that in default of the influence of education "if we distrust human reason, we have now no other principle to lead us into religion" (Hume (7), *Dialogues*, 170 and 139). But now the gap between reason and devotion thus opened up is filled by a seemingly different *tertium quid*;

What can the most inquisitive, contemplative, and religious man do more than give a plain, philosophical assent to the proposition, as often as it occurs; and believe that the arguments, on which it is established, exceed the objections which lie against it? . . . But believe me, CLEANTHES, the most natural sentiment, which a well-disposed mind will feel on this occasion, is a longing desire and expectation, that Heaven would be pleased to dissipate, at least alleviate, this profound ignorance, by affording some more particular revelation to mankind, and making discoveries of the nature, attributes, and operations of the divine object of our Faith. A person, seasoned with a just sense of the imperfections of natural reason, will fly to revealed truth with the greatest avidity (227).

But we have already seen what such blandishments are worth in Hume's thinking. 'Divinity or Theology . . . has a foundation in *reason*, so far as it is supported by experience. But its best and most solid foundation is *faith* and divine revelation' (Hume (6), *1st Enquiry*, 165). In the *Dialogues* as in the *Enquiry* the experiential foundation in reason is "altogether useless". Section 10 of the *1st Enquiry*, 'Of Miracles', attacks "the ultimate refuge of religion, revelation: for revelation is, on the ordinary theory, proved by miracles" (Wollheim, 26), and we have seen the difficulties attendant upon attempting to give faith any other grounding—such as natural sentiment. The *Dialogues* are concerned with natural, not revealed, religion, but Philo's remarks have several indications of the epistemological insecurity of the appeal to revelation—reminiscent of the technique of "assent and modification" (Sutherland, 182) he has established in his earlier discussions.

First, even the "useless" proposition of natural theology, "that the cause or causes of order in the universe probably bear some remote analogy to human intelligence" (Hume (7) *Dialogues*, 227) is only said to be conceded by the "religious man"; one who, it has been suggested, "out of antecedent prejudice in favour of the evidence in support of his religious beliefs, elects upon nonrational grounds to accept the favored conclusion" (Hurlbutt (2), 168). Philo has already shown what any propensity towards accepting the proposition he may display is worth by telling us that "no one has a deeper sense of religion impressed on his mind" (Hume (7), *Dialogues*, 214); thus any consequences he draws from its acceptability are equally insecure. Second, the credibility of "some more particular revelation" is said to depend on "natural sentiment", which gives the science of man rather than that of theology an arbitrating role, and the authority which universality normally gives to "natural sentiment" is immediately removed by restricting it to a "well-disposed mind"—that is, given the context, a religious one; not for nothing had Hume toyed with having Philo remark that the "useless" proposition could not be the source of any "steady sentiment". Third, the reference to being "seasoned with a just sense of the imperfections of natural reason" should remind us of the earlier occasion on which the metaphor of "seasoning" is used. Demea then, like Philo now, is discussing Pamphilus' education, and he gives an account of the method he observes with his own children: 'To season their minds with early piety is my chief care; . . . I imprint deeply on their tender minds an habitual reverence for all the principles of religion' (130). Philo, we remember, has also had a "sense of religion impressed on his mind", and there is no reason to suppose that the "tender mind" of Pamphilus—who despite the course of the argument endorses Cleanthes' principles—has not been similarly "seasoned" by his master. The use of this metaphor in this context should remind the reader that education as well as feeling has been invoked as grounding religion when reason fails, that the two have not been clearly distinguished, and that education has been said to be capable of "taming" the mind to "a proper submission" which will render it impervious to philosophical temptations to infidelity (130–1). As Hume remarks elsewhere, through the mouth of a "Sceptic" with whom he is in general sympathy: "The prodigious effects of education may convince us, that the mind is not altogether stubborn and inflexible, but will admit of many alterations from its original make and structure" (Hume (1), iii, 'The Sceptic', 223).

Finally, for those familiar with Hume's other writings, there is evidence that Philo possibly, and certainly Hume himself, is subtly distancing himself from the concluding fideistic exhortation. The reference to the "imperfections of natural reason" is reminiscent of an earlier passage, cited in the previous section, in which Philo apparently sets out his "unfeigned sentiments" (Hume (7), *Dialogues*, 219):

We have reason to infer that the natural attributes of the Deity have a greater resemblance to those of man, than his moral have to human virtues. But what is the consequence? Nothing but this, that the moral qualities of man are more defective in their kind than his natural abilities. For, as the supreme Being is allowed to be absolutely and entirely perfect, whatever differs most from him departs the farthest from the supreme standard of rectitude and perfection.

Both natural reason and human virtue, it would appear, are defective guides in matters of religion. But Philo also launches an attack on the tendencies of "superstition or enthusiasm" to declaim "against morality" and "virtue in human behaviour" (221–2); if it is "revelation" which "allows" that God's "nature, attributes and operations" are "entirely perfect", and thus inculcates a distrust of man's "moral qualities", one may wonder whether it suffers guilt by association with "superstition or enthusiasm". This suspicion gains added force from Hume's essay 'Of Superstition and Enthusiasm' where "enthusiasm" is attacked as a state in which "Human reason, and even morality, are rejected as fallacious guides; And the fanatic madman delivers himself over . . . to inspiration from above" (Hume (1), iii. 145). In the *Dialogues*, as elsewhere, "superstition and enthusiasm" are contrasted with "true religion" (Hume (7), 223), but if the "sound believing Christianity" of the "man of letters" recommended to Pamphilus is both to be grounded in "some more particular revelation" and to be other than that of "the fanatic madman", the content of that revelation is liable to be slight indeed. As Cleanthes, indeed, admits

The proper office of religion is to regulate the heart of men, humanize their conduct, . . . and as its operation is silent . . . it is in danger of being overlooked. . . . When it distinguishes itself, and acts as a separate principle over men, it has departed from its proper sphere (220).

If revelation establishes no "separate principle" and true religion is essentially concerned with "humanizing" men's conduct, then the dangers of "enthusiasm" are indeed avoided, but at the cost of divorcing the recommended "Christianity" from most of its traditional or "vulgar" content; trust, worship, veneration, and obedience all appear to be jettisoned, in so far as these derive from some "separate principle", and Demea—had he still been present— might well have objected that on this account "the theory of religion becomes altogether useless" (170), as useless indeed as the sole "proposition" of natural theology allowed by Philo. The more Pamphilus thinks through Philo's final recommendation to him in the light of Cleanthes' own principles, which he upholds, the less content he will find in any step beyond that "first and most essential" one of being "a philosophical sceptic". And the same consideration should strike those religious Moderates of Cleanthes-like sympathies at whom the *Dialogues* appear to have been principally aimed; the Ciceronian web is woven with skill, "artfulness", and subtlety.

This subtlety is also apparent in the way Hume exploits a further element of his Classical model to combat the influence of "early piety" on the minds of those predisposed to be religious. The Ciceronian convention, noted in the previous section, whereby each speaker represents a tradition, and even the spokesman for the author's own "school" need not be taken as speaking for the writer at all points, enables Hume to strengthen the appeal of the *Dia-*

logues to the prospective reader in a number of ways. For example, discrepancies in the sceptical tradition can be incorporated into Philo's discourse so that he appears "careless" in the pejorative sense, thus providing opportunities for the strengthening of Cleanthes as a character.[19] But more importantly Philo can go further than Hume himself would wish to in "rejecting as fallacious guides" "human reason, and even morality", so turning against itself a popular line of religious thinking. Further, he can give stronger support to Demea's characterization of the human condition as "cursed and polluted" (194).

This final point is worth expansion. In his initial statement of the argument a posteriori, as we have seen, Cleanthes opens with: 'Look round the world: Contemplate the whole and every part of it: You will find it to be nothing but one great machine . . .' (143). As Philo approaches the peroration of his final counterblast, he recalls that starting-point:

Look round this universe. What an immense profusion of beings, animated and organized, sensible and active! You admire this prodigious variety and fecundity. But inspect a little more narrowly these living existences, the only beings worth regarding. How hostile and destructive to each other! How insufficient all of them for their own happiness! How contemptible or odious to the spectator! The whole presents nothing but the idea of a blind nature, impregnated by a great vivifying principle, and pouring forth from her lap, without discernment or parental care, her maimed and abortive children.

Here the MANICHAEAN system occurs as a proper hypothesis to solve the difficulty . . . (211).

This passage has with some justice been called 'both a shattering artistic parody and a shattering philosophical rebuttal of Cleanthes' prototype of the analogical argument' (Mossner (3), 11). But it has an un-Humean ring. As Professor Kemp Smith remarked, 'Coming in the dramatic setting of the *Dialogues*, this view of Nature may not, however, be taken to be Hume's own. No other passage in any of his writings is on these lines' (Kemp Smith (2), 564). It is, of course, far more reminiscent of Bayle's article on the Manichaeans (Bayle, iii. 302–7), hence Philo's reference to them, Bayle's *Dictionnaire* is, indeed, a powerful influence on the imagery as well as

---

[19] For examples of Philo's carelessness, beyond those cited in the previous section, see Bricke, s. 2.

the argument of the sections (10 and 11) on God's moral attributes. And the imagery is important in the rhetorical economy of the *Dialogues*;

The idea of the neutrality or indifference of the universe was new to Hume's readers, and Hume had to compensate for their prejudices. His cataloguing of imagery for effect—to create an impact something like a sense impression—is similar to the use of imagery found in some of the romantic poets. It is calculated for a net effect. Specifically, it is aimed to counterbalance the picture of order and harmony presented in the design argument. When Hume has Demea exaggerate the ills and horrors of the world, it is merely compensation for the propensity of the mind toward Cleanthes' argument (Morrisroe (2), 972).

By having Philo incorporate into his sceptical vision the Demea-like bleakness of so much contemporary religious thinking, Hume is able to engage many of his readers much more nearly than if he had had Philo simply replicate his own rather more "optimistic" outlook (Kemp Smith (2), 564). There is nothing intellectually disreputable about this, for Hume holds that even on the most optimistic account the fact of suffering invalidates Cleanthes' attempt to infer God's benevolence from his creation—as he is careful to have Philo point out: 'But allowing you, what never will be believed; at least, what you never possibly can prove, that animal, or at least, human happiness, in this life, exceeds its misery; you have yet done nothing' (Hume (7), *Dialogues*, 201). But by using the darker sceptical perceptions, Hume strengthens the *Dialogues*' potential for rooting out that whole theistic outlook on reality which he was concerned to combat.[20]

[20] It has been urged that "Philo and Philo alone is Hume's spokesman" (Mossner (3), 3–4 and 12) on the ground that Hume himself once maintained that "In every Dialogue, no more than one person can be supposed to represent the author" (Hume (2), *Letters* i. 173). But this is shaky support for the claim that a Humean dialogue must always have a character who unambiguously represents the author's views in all respects. Indeed, although in the dialogue under discussion in Hume's letter the two characters have antithetical views one of which is clearly recognizable as that of the author, it would be disingenuous to apply Hume's contention to s. 11 of the *1st Enquiry*, which is also in dialogue form and addresses one of the central issues of the *Dialogues*; here the "friend" certainly speaks for Hume for most of the Section, but the final, distinctively Humean, consideration is put into the mouth of the narrator.

Of the recent attempts to read Philo as Hume, that of Parent (2) virtually ignores the difference in their relative "optimism" noted by Kemp Smith, and invokes essays where Hume is not speaking in his own voice to find parallels to Philo's eulogies on the incomprehensibility of the divine perfections. (Parent (1) may go some—though not all—of the way towards showing that Philo is self-consistent, but does little to

We have seen that the imaginative power of this religious perspective is a recurrent theme of the *Dialogues*; in responding to it Philo displays an instructive shift of emphasis.[21] In Part 1 he argues that "theological reasonings" are "quite beyond the reach of our faculties . . . and run wide of common life"; with such "speculations", "the most refined scepticism comes to be upon a footing with them, and is able to oppose and counterbalance them. The one has no more weight than the other. The mind must remain in suspense between them; and it is that very suspense or balance, which is the triumph of scepticism" (135–6). Again, he sums up the argument of Parts 5 to 8 with "All religious systems, it is confessed, are subject to great and insuperable difficulties. Each disputant triumphs in his turn. . . . A total suspense of judgment is here our only reasonable resource" (186–7). But in the final section Cleanthes maintains that

suspence of judgment . . . can never be steadily maintained against such striking appearances as continually engage us into the religious hypothesis. A false, absurd system, human nature, from the force of prejudice, is capable of adhering to with obstinacy and perseverance: But no system at all, in opposition to a theory, supported by strong and obvious reason, by natural propensity, and by early education, I think it absolutely impossible to maintain or defend.

To which Philo replies: 'So little . . . do I esteem this suspense of judgment in the present case to be possible, that I am apt to suspect there enters somewhat of a dispute of words into this controversy, more than is usually imagined' (216). Although, that is, scepticism

---

[21] For Yandell (111) this shift involves a clear inconsistency which shows that Philo "does not always speak for Hume".

---

strengthen the case that he consistently speaks for Hume.) Gaskin (2), 160–2, notes that in a Ciceronian dialogue "one may ask which of the opinions expressed command the author's sympathy", but fails to distinguish between a character having "Hume's favour" and being a "mouthpiece" for him; coming from so normally careful a writer, the identification of "Philo as Hume if only on the negative ground that there is no one else he could be: Philo has no matrix outside his creator's mind" is somewhat bizarre.

In contrast, Penelhum (2), 179, remarks 'Perhaps we are all wrong in being as ready to identify Philo with Hume as we have been since Kemp Smith.' Jones (2), 169, correctly points out that "Hume valued the dialogue form partly because it allowed the full expression of rival views." Various forms of the case that we should read the *Dialogues* in terms of the clash of these views, rather than looking for Hume's mouthpiece, have recently been made by Butler (2), Noxon, Jeffner (204–9), Capaldi, Bricke, Yandell, and Battersby (1), amongst others.

may "triumph" over theological *"reasonings"*, and "suspense of judgment" in religious matters be *"reasonable"*, once faced with the appropriate "striking appearances" what may be reasonable turns out not to be "possible". Speaking as one than whom "no one has a deeper sense of religion impressed on his mind", he remarks the way we are led "almost . . . insensibly to acknowledge a first intelligent Author" (214–15).[22]

His diagnosis of this state of affairs develops in two stages. He first contrasts theist and atheist, maintaining that their contention lies in the degree to which each stresses the likenesses and differences (which all must acknowledge) between observable phenomena and "the original principle of order" or, which comes to the same thing, "the first and supreme cause".

But there is a species of controversy, which, from the very nature of language and of human ideas, is involved in perpetual ambiguity, and can never, by any precaution or any definitions, be able to reach a reasonable certainty or precision. These are the controversies concerning the degrees of any quality or circumstance. . . . Because the degrees of these qualities are not, like quantity or number, susceptible of any exact mensuration, which may be the standard in the controversy. That the dispute concerning theism is of this nature, and consequently is merely verbal, or perhaps, if possible, still more incurably ambiguous, will appear upon the slightest enquiry (217–18).

Because there is no "exact mensuration" available to serve as a "standard", "the disputants may here agree in their sense and differ in the terms, or *vice versa*; yet never be able to define their terms, so as to enter into each other's meaning." But, as we saw in Chapter 2, these are precisely the considerations which led Cicero to experiment with the dialogue form in which "the sole object of our discussions is by arguing on both sides to draw out and give shape to some result that may be either true or the nearest possible approximation to the truth" (Cicero (1), *Academica*, II. iii. 7). A result which may show that two apparently antithetical schools,

---

[22] These apparently positive religious utterances of Philo near the start of pt. 12 sound much more like Bayle, for whom the piety of his childhood was a continuing influence, than Hume. To a remarkable degree Hume emancipated himself from his religious upbringing, although there is evidence of occasional "lapses into belief" (Battersby (1), 252; see Mossner (2), 217). In line with his established technique of "assent and modification" (Sutherland, 182), Philo gradually evacuates his concessions of most of their significance as Baylean tendencies are extended in a Humean direction.

"while agreeing in doctrine differed in name" (ibid. I. iv. 17), or "though differing in form of expression, agree in substance" (Cicero (1), *De Natura Deorum*, I. vii. 16). Hume's exploitation of the dialogue form to handle such controversies has good Ciceronian warrant.

After a brief interlude, discussed above, on the incomprehensibility of the divine perfections, Philo (or Hume) moves on to the second stage of diagnosis.[23] Philo has never admitted to atheism, only to scepticism, but now "the dispute between the sceptics and dogmatists" is placed on the same basis as the other and also claimed to be "entirely verbal", since it

regards only the degrees of doubt and assurance, which we ought to indulge with regard to all reasoning: And such disputes are commonly at the bottom, verbal, and admit not of any precise determination. . . . The only difference, then, between these sects, if they merit that name, is, that the sceptic, from habit, caprice, or inclination, insists most on the difficulties; the dogmatist, for like reasons, on the necessity (Hume (7). *Dialogues*, 219).

The impossibility of steadily maintaining "suspense of judgment" in "the dispute concerning theism" is thus a function of "habit, caprice, or inclination", which leads the man who has a deep "sense of religion impressed on his mind" to prefer theistic language to equally eligible alternatives in his account of the universe and its "original principle of order".[24]

But the terms 'habit' and 'inclination' have significant

[23] By placing Philo's account of the divine perfections between the two passages on verbal disputes, Hume appears to underline the problematic nature of the apparent concession. Kemp Smith (1), 219, prints the second discussion as a footnote, leading Noxon to characterize it as the single occasion on which Hume "speaks for himself in the twelfth Dialogue" (259). In fact, although Hume appears at first to have intended it as a note, there is evidence that on revising the *Dialogues* he incorporated it into Philo's speech (Colver and Price, 250–1; supported by Stewart, 51). Nevertheless, the probability that Hume initially intended the passage as a note strongly suggests that in the final draft Philo is at this point acting as his creator's mouthpiece. (See also Duerlinger.)

[24] It is important to realize that theistic language is only equally eligible for Philo so long as it stresses the "great and immeasurable, because incomprehensible, difference between the *human* and the *divine* mind" (218), and insinuates no separate principle over men" (220). The argument of the preceding sections has been designed to block all attempts to give the religious hypothesis any significant content. This is fully in accord with Hume's own position, which finds objections "to every thing we commonly call Religion, except the Practice of Morality, and the Assent of the Understanding to the Proposition *that God exists*" (Hume (2), *Letters* i. 50; Hume (3), *New Letters*, (12–13).

associations in Hume's thinking. 'Habit', 'custom', 'repetition', and 'education' represent the leading concepts of a set which may rival those of reason and experience;

All those opinions and notions of things, to which we have been accustom'd from our infancy, take such deep root, that 'tis impossible for us, by all the powers of reason and experience, to eradicate them; and this habit not only approaches in its influence, but even on many occasions prevails over that which arises from constant and inseparable union of causes and effects. . . . The frequent repetition of any idea infixes it in the imagination. . . .

If we consider this argument from *education* in a proper light, . . . upon examination we shall find more than one half of those opinions, that prevail among mankind, to be owing to education, and that the principles, which are thus implicitely embrac'd, over-ballance those, which are owing either to abstract reasoning or experience (Hume (5), *Treatise*, 116–17; cf. 422–4).

The repetitions of custom are unflatteringly compared with those of liars, and we are informed that "education is an artificial and not a natural cause".

The word 'inclination' points in a similar direction. In a letter to Elliot about the *Dialogues* Hume writes:

I cou'd wish that Cleanthes' Argument could be so analys'd, as to be render'd quite formal & regular. The Propensity of the Mind towards it, unless that Propensity were as strong & universal as that to believe in our Senses & Experience, will still, I am afraid, be esteem'd a suspicious Foundation. Tis here I wish for your Assistance. We must endeavour to prove that this Propensity is somewhat different from our Inclination to find our own Figures in the Clouds, our Face in the Moon, our Passions & Sentiments even in inanimate Matter. Such an Inclination may, & ought to be controul'd, & can never be a legitimate Ground of Assent. (Hume (2), *Letters* i. 155)

As Professor Norton, commenting on this passage, puts it, 'Although we can in theory distinguish between a mere "Inclination" and what is more significant, a "Propensity", in any given case we must prove that what seems like a propensity is not merely an inclination, for inclinations provide no ground for assent' (Norton, (1) 201–2). Hume is not always as consistent in his vocabulary as this might suggest, but by yoking 'inclination' and 'caprice' together in his diagnosis of the impossibility of "suspense of judgment" in the Dialogues, he gives a strong indication that it is this use he has in mind.

The imaginative power of the religious perspective, which serves to prevent "the triumph of scepticism", is thus given a damaging analysis. Elsewhere we have been told that the "first religious principles must be secondary", for they do not stem either from "an original instinct or primary impression of nature" (Hume (10), *Natural History of Religion*, 21), and that the attempt to found religion on "sentiment" is bedevilled by the difficulty of distinguishing sentiment from education and habituation (Hume (2), *Letters* i. 150–2); education, being a species of habit, is said to be "an artificial and not a natural cause", which is never "recogniz'd by philosophers" and provides no securer epistemological base than that we allow to "liars, by the frequent repetition of their lies" (Hume (5), *Treatise*, 117); "strong and universal" "propensities", reminiscent of "original instincts", are apparently to be contrasted with mere "inclinations" (Hume (2), *Letters* i. 155). Now, as the *Dialogues* draw to their close, we are invited to see those "sentiments" which Philo shares with Cleanthes (Hume (7), *Dialogues*, 219), and hence with the intended readership, as grounded in "habit, caprice, or inclination", on a par with finding "our Face in the Moon"; Philo may find that he had a deep "sense of religion impressed on his mind", but we remember that "the frequent repetition of any idea infixes it in the imagination", and that those with the care of children in a culture such as Hume's "imprint deeply on their tender minds an habitual reverence for all the principles of religion" (130).

In his summing up Pamphilus appears to ignore Philo's attempted reconciliation of his principles with those of Cleanthes on a foundation inimical to religion, and to endorse those of the latter in the face of all the argument; in doing so he reveals that his mind has indeed been well "seasoned" with "early piety". But the reader who, similarly seasoned, might be inclined to echo such sentiments finds that in doing so he is identifying himself not with the point of view of a respected philosopher, as in the *De Natura Deorum*, but with that of a mere pupil—an identification which is not merely factitious, but can be seen on reflection to be of a piece with the development of the entire work. This break with Ciceronian precedent thus facilitates a final ironic twist which sets the power of the religious vision in an unflattering light, that of the "prodigious effects of education" (Hume (1), iii, 'The Sceptic', 223).

4. The Role of "Irregular" Arguments

With a few notable exceptions, commentators on the *Dialogues* have concentrated their attention on the discussion of the capacity of reason to "lead us into religion", and paid far less attention to what the work is concerned to convey about the available alternatives—education and feeling.[25] This preoccupation with the detail of the theistic arguments has led one recent interpreter to complain that Part 1 is a section "which none of us seems to read" and Part 12 one "which none of us seems to understand" (Penelhum (1), 270)—for it is in sections 2 to 11 that the main logical analysis is to be found. The parallel with recent selective discussions of the *Phaedo* is striking.

This is not the place to assess the intrinsic strength of Cleanthes' argument a posteriori with its various ramifications, and of Philo's numerous counters;[26] for present purposes it is sufficient to note that Hume himself appears to have thought that he had shown through Philo that it could be reduced to triviality, at least in so far as it could be given a "quite formal and regular" shape. Indeed, so conscious was he of this that he asked Elliot for assistance "to strengthen that Side of the Argument";

I have often thought, that the best way of composing a Dialogue, wou'd be for two Persons that are of different Opinions about any Question of Importance, to write alternately the different Parts of the Discourse, & reply to each other. By this Means, that vulgar Error would be avoided, of putting nothing but Nonsense into the Mouth of the Adversary: And at the same time, a Variety of Character & Genius being upheld, woud make the whole look more natural & unaffected. Had it been my good Fortune to live near you, I shou'd have taken on me the Character of Philo, in the Dialogue, which you'll own I coud have supported naturally enough: And you woud not have been averse to that of Cleanthes. I believe, too, we coud both of us have kept our Temper very well (Hume (2), *Letters*, i. 153–4).

---

[25] The most significant discussions of the role of feeling in the *Dialogues* are those of Butler (2) and Pike; the topic of education has been almost entirely neglected.

[26] That Philo's critique is less powerful than is often thought, gaining its plausibility from inadequacies in Cleanthes' presentation, has been interestingly argued by Swinburne (1) and (2), and countered by Olding (1) and (2). Swinburne's (3) generalization of the thesis has been responded to on the same level by Mackie. Jeffner's historically informed assessment of the issues repays study.

This concern with what he elsewhere calls the "spirit of dialogue" and that there be "a tolerable equality maintained among the speakers" (Hume (1), iii, 'Of the Rise and Progress of the Arts and Sciences', 189),[27] represented a widely accepted ideal which such writers as Dryden had invoked to unify classical tradition and modern thinking in the name of impartiality; defending a dialogue of his own he writes

I must crave leave to say, that my whole discourse was sceptical, according to that way of reasoning which was used by Socrates, Plato, and all the Academics of old, which Tully and the best of the Ancients followed, and which is imitated by the modest inquisitions of the Royal Society. . . . You see it is a dialogue sustained by persons of several opinions, all of them left doubtful, to be determined by the readers in general (Dryden, i, 'A Defence of an Essay of Dramatic Poesy', 124).

Demea's opinions, as we have seen, are rhetorically and argumentatively discounted; thus if the "spirit of dialogue" is to be preserved in Hume's composition it is important that Philo's virtuosity should not completely overshadow the figure of Cleanthes.

Elliot was able to afford Hume little help,[28] and in the text as we have it two types of strategy are employed to offset the weakness of Cleanthes' main argument. The first is rhetorical. Hume remarks to Elliot that "I make Cleanthes the Hero of the Dialogue" (Hume (2), *Letters* i. 153), and the concessions Philo makes in Part 12, together with Pamphilus' concluding judgement, give colour to his disingenuous claim about the work that "I there introduce a Sceptic, who is indeed refuted, and at last gives up the Argument, nay confesses that he was only amusing himself by all his Cavils" (Hume (2), *Letters* ii. 323). Philo's "confession", of course, must be treated

---

[27] The quotation comes from a footnote, deleted in the later editions, in which Hume ascribes the "spirit of dialogue" to Cicero's *De Natura Deorum* and *De Oratore*. It is worth remarking that Hume describes the characters in the former work as "disputing concerning the being and nature of the gods", although officially it is supposed to be concerned only with their "nature", their existence being assumed (see, for example, Cicero (1), *De Natura Deorum*, I, vi. 13: II. v. 13; III. iv. 9; III. xxxix. 93). Thus when Pamphilus makes a similar distinction between God's "being" and "nature", claiming that only the latter is at issue in the ensuing conversation (Hume (7), 128), we have additional reason to be wary of his acumen; for the misleading nature of Pamphilus' claim, see Mossner (3), 14 and 21.

[28] To Hume's request for assistance Elliot at least drafted a reply, copies of a part of which have come down to us (Colver and Price, app. A); on this evidence Dr Price's comment is apt: "Like many men of his intellectual calibre, Hume had the kindly failing of overestimating his friends' abilities" (Price (1), 263).

with some reserve (Parent (1)), and the reference to Cleanthes is ambiguous. Indeed, with some reservations it may be said that

> Cleanthes is the dramatic center of the dialogue, but Philo is the intellectual victor. Hume could not have allowed Philo to be the hero of the *Dialogues*. If Philo had been given the emphasis which Cleanthes received, Hume would have been accused of championing Philo's position. . . . Had Hume not made Cleanthes an impressive figure at the outset of the dialogue, there would have been little dramatic and intellectual rationale for the prolonged attacks which Philo directs at his position (Morrisroe (3), 103).[29]

Further, the divergent characters of the two enable Hume to bring out how such matters as "habit, caprice or inclination" can shape one's outlook:

> There is . . . a deep-seated personality conflict between Philo and Cleanthes which Hume obviously wants to stress. While Philo is naturally disposed to be critical and cannot help but emphasize the difficulties which attend human reasoning, Cleanthes is naturally inclined to play down these difficulties and to accept unquestioningly all beliefs confirmed by experience and natural good sense. The dispute between them regarding the proper degree of confidence to have in the arguments of experimental theism stems from temperamental differences (Parent (2), 105).

In bringing out this conflict Hume modifies his Ciceronian model. The *De Natura Deorum* is comparatively "static", dominated by set speeches, but Hume's *Dialogues* are much more dramatic and "conversible", with interplay between the characters, thereby bringing the issues to the bar of "Experience, where alone it is to be found, in common Life and Conversation" (Hume (1), iv, 'Of Essay Writing', 367–8). In such a context the sympathetic presentation of Cleanthes can achieve a disproportionate effect, especially when reinforced by the preliminary half-truths of Hermippus and Pamphilus about the main figures' respective characters.

The personality difference thus brought out facilitates Hume's other strategy for counterbalancing the weakness of Cleanthes' main argument *a posteriori*—the appeal to "common sense and the

---

[29] For those familiar with the 'Conclusion' to Hume's *2nd Enquiry* the associations of Cleanthes' name would serve to increase the attractiveness of the upholder of the argument a posteriori; "The Cleanthes of the *Dialogues* is not unlike the Cleanthes of the *Enquiry Concerning the Principles of Morals* who possesses all of the natural virtues and none of the monkish vices. Cleanthes represents the position of the intelligent layman and liberal theologian of Hume's time" (Capaldi, 195).

plain instincts of nature" (Hume (7), *Dialogues*, 154). This is the touchstone upon which Cleanthes insists when pressed by Philo: 'Consider, anatomize the eye: Survey its structure and contrivance; and tell me, from your own feeling, if the idea of a contriver does not immediately flow in upon you with a force like that of sensation' (ibid.). Philo's "love of singular arguments" (214) makes it "natural and unavoidable" for him to raise "doubts and objections" (181), even "cavils and sophisms", but we have seen that he is ultimately prepared to concede the "irresistible force" (202) of the appeal to his "own feeling". Thus the reader is encouraged to suppose that Cleanthes' argumentative weakness masks a deeper strength—the power of authentic feeling.

That appeal to this touchstone marks something of a retreat from the presentation of a "formal and regular" argument operating according to "all the rules of analogy" (143) is indicated by Cleanthes himself:[30]

> Some beauties in writing we may meet with, which seem contrary to rules, and which gain the affections, and animate the imagination, in opposition to all the precepts of criticism, and to the authority of the established masters of art. And if the argument for theism be, as you pretend, contradictory to the rules of logic: its universal, its irresistible influence proves clearly, that there may be arguments of a like irregular nature. Whatever cavils may be urged; an orderly world, as well as a coherent, articulate speech, will still be received as an incontestable proof of design and intention. (155)

But such "irregular" arguments are not taken to be altogether beyond assessment. When later Cleanthes is again pressed hard by Philo and challenged "to tug the labouring oar" (202), he responds by presenting the doctrine of the finitude of God as a means of meeting the problem of evil and invites Philo's "opinion of this new theory; and if it deserve our attention, we may afterwards, at more leisure, reduce it into form" (203). Formal considerations, it would appear, are not the only or even the decisive ones in establishing the value of an argument; Philo, indeed, makes his rejoinder in terms of his "sentiments", using irony (Hurlbutt (2), 164), rhetorical questions, example, hyperbole, and parody mixed in with his analysis, thereby reminding the reader of his earlier contention that on this

---

[30] The importance to Cleanthes of "irregular" arguments has been explored by Pike (222–9).

topic "a talent of eloquence and strong imagery is more requisite than that of reasoning and argument" (193). Once one moves from "regular" considerations, as we have seen in earlier chapters, dialectic and rhetoric cannot be finally divorced.

Indeed, Cleanthes' comparison of "the argument for theism" with aesthetic discriminations explicitly invokes the importance of "the affections" and "the imagination". Later he returns to such matters: 'Forfeit not this principle, the chief, the only great comfort in life; and our principal support amidst all the attacks of adverse fortune. The most agreeable reflection, which it is possible for human imagination to suggest, is that of genuine theism' (224). Philo responds by highlighting the dark side of popular religion, and evacuating "genuine theism" of most of its imaginative and passionate content so that it is only "alluring" in a somewhat bloodless sense.

We are here back with the practice of "correcting Subtilty of Sentiment" and of attempting to apply it "in Metaphysics or Theology" (Hume (2), *Letters* i. 150–1), and hence with the problems surrounding the lack of universality in its deliverances. Cleanthes endeavours to circumvent them by defending this "irregular" argument's "universal, its irresistible influence" against the sort of evidence adduced in *The Natural History of Religion*; he maintains that the fact that such reasonings "have not their due influence on an ignorant savage and barbarian" is "not because they are obscure and difficult, but because he never asks himself any question with regard to them" (Hume (7), *Dialogues*, 155). But this at best, for Hume, only establishes "the first religious principles" as "secondary" (Hume (10), *Natural History of Religion*, 21), and hence open, as we saw earlier, to genuinely subversive enquiry into their origins. Even Philo may admit the "irresistible force" of the appeal to his "feeling", though he is careful to limit its scope to the support of what has been called "attenuated deism" (Gaskin (1), 311; cf. (2), 166–73), but this does not preclude the raising of questions about how it is that the "sense of religion" is "impressed on his mind" (Hume (7). *Dialogues*, 214).

As so often, the *De Natura Deorum* suggests the direction to be followed. Far from being an atheist, the sceptical Cotta is a functionary of the traditional religion. Commenting on Balbus' attempt, despite disclaimers, to prove "the divine existence" he remarks, "For my part a single argument would have sufficed, namely that it has been handed down to us by our forefathers. But you despise authority, and fight your battles with the weapon of reason. Give permission therefore, for my reason to join issue with yours" (Cicero (1), III. iv. 9). His "reason", of course, goes nearly as far to undermine that of Balbus as Philo's does in the case of Cleanthes, thus his position is close to that of the "Conformist Sceptical Fideist", for whom religious meaning "has been evaporated by the process of argument for and against the dogmas that are supposed to support it, and he is able to return to the traditional rites and practices in a detached and unanxious manner, flowing with the local stream but with his head above it" (Penelhum (2), 175–6). But this is to embrace "the general Principle, that as the Truth in these Subjects is beyond human Capacity, & that as for one's own Ease he must adopt some Tenets, there is more Satisfaction & Convenience in holding to the Catechism we have been first taught" (Hume (2) *Letters* i. 151–2). This principle Hume is not prepared to rest on; "such a Conduct is founded on the most universal & determin'd Scepticism, join'd to a little Indolence. For more Curiosity & Research gives a direct opposite Turn from the same Principles." Whether or not it would be fair to describe Cleanthes as "indolent", "curiosity" is the hallmark of Philo as, indeed, of Hume himself. Hence Philo's attack on the "priestcraft" of "ignorant ages" which forbade "the presumptuous questioning of received opinions";

Education had then a mighty influence over the minds of men, and was almost equal in force to those suggestions of the senses and common understanding, by which the most determined sceptic must allow himself to be governed. But at present, when the influence of education is much diminished, and men, from a more open commerce of the world, have learned to compare the popular principles of different nations and ages, . . . if we distrust human reason, we have now no other principle to lead us into religion (Hume (7), *Dialogues*, 139).

By the end of the *Dialogues* we have had displayed to us good cause for distrusting "human reason", at least as represented by "regular" arguments, as a means for leading us into religion. Cleanthes has joined with Philo in associating faith indissolubly with reason (138–9), and any counter to this alliance that might be derived from the "mystical" tendency in Demea's thought has been firmly discredited. We are left with attempting to construe the recurrent appeal to "feeling" in terms of "reason". As Philo purports to accept attentuated deism at least partly on grounds of reasoning he has shown not to be defensible in any "regular" fashion, there is at least the hint of the possibility that religion is "reasonable" in the Pickwickian sense of representing "the inescapable conclusion of an argument which he has shown, and knows he has shown, to be a complete philosophical failure—except in the one respect that when we encounter it we cannot help assenting to its conclusion" (Penelhum (2), 171). But such a subversive conclusion would be unattractive to a Cleanthes-like reader, who would doubtless prefer an alternative, and this is offered by Cleanthes himself.

The latter sees Philo's religious scepticism as subject to the difficulties of scepticism generally. He claims

with regard to you, PHILO, and all speculative sceptics, that your doctrine and practice are as much at variance in the most abstruse points of theory as in the conduct of common life . . . Your own conduct, in every circumstance, refutes your principles; and shows the firmest reliance on all the received maxims of science, morals, prudence and behaviour (Hume (7), *Dialogues*, 136–7).

Thus the "reasonable sceptic" is bound "to adhere to common sense and the plain instincts of nature; and to assent, wherever any reasons strike him with so full a force, that he cannot, without the greatest violence, prevent it. Now the arguments for natural religion are plainly of this kind" (154). It follows that however many "out-of-the-way difficulties" Philo may raise which cannot be "regularly" solved, he must nevertheless recognize "that common sense and reason is entirely against you, and that such whimsies, as you have delivered, may puzzle, but never can convince us" (181).[31] The "received maxims" of religion are no doubt open to sceptical attack, but are grounded on "common sense and the plain instincts

---

[31] The concluding phrase is inspired by Berkeley, whose sceptical Alciphron objects to Demea-like arguments a priori that "they may perhaps puzzle, but never will convince me" (Berkeley, III, 142). Philo expresses similar reservations in different words in response to Demea (Hume (7), 191–2), but Hume here inverts the context of the phrase by directing it *against* the sceptic. That this is more than an academic joke can be seen from the way he elsewhere turns the objection against Berkeley himself, associating him with Bayle; "That all his arguments, though otherwise intended, are, in reality, merely sceptical, appears from this, *that they admit of no answer and produce no conviction*. Their only effect is to cause that momentary amazement and irresolution and confusion, which is the result of scepticism" (Hume (6), *1st Enquiry*, 155).

of nature" and hence no less rational than those of "science, morals, prudence and behaviour": 'You defy me to solve the difficulties, or reconcile the repugnancies, which you discover in them. I have not capacity for so great an undertaking: I have not leisure for it: I perceive it to be superfluous' (137). As Philo agrees, in acting on the principles of common sense, a man "is not obliged to give any other reason than the absolute necessity he lies under of so doing" (134). Both Cleanthes and Philo agree that it is "absolutely impossible" to retain a sceptical attitude in the face of "such striking appearances as continually engage us into the religious hypothesis" (216), and this impossibility provides all the "reason" we need to "lead us into religion".

Hume, however, is concerned to turn the flank of this last ditch. The "absolute necessity" Philo admits as justifying "the reflections of common life" is associated with the need "to act, . . . and live, and converse" (134), and this universality does not apply in the case of religion. The "arguments for natural religion" are felt as compelling by one who has a "sense of religion impressed on his mind" (214), but we have been warned at the outset of the importance of education in religion; without it there is the danger of one's charges "neglecting or rejecting altogether" the "principles of religion", but with suitable "seasoning" one may "imprint" their minds so "deeply" that there is henceforth no danger of them being seduced into infidelity by "that assuming arrogance of philosophy" (130-1). The capacity of a man to remain sceptical is a matter of "habit, caprice, or inclination" (219), and the reference to education at the end reminds us of the likelihood that whatever the "most inquisitive, contemplative, and religious man" (227) may find himself constrained to accept will be coloured by his early "seasoning"; but to treat such imprinted inclinations as "almost equal in force" to the deliverances of "the senses and common understanding" is a characteristic of "ignorant ages"—and Hume is writing for the Enlightenment.

Parts 2 to 11 of the *Dialogues* lay out the weaknesses of the arguments a priori and a posteriori for theism, and suggest an alternative mode of "irregular" argument that appeals to "feeling", "the affections" and "the imagination". The first and final Parts press the suggestion that this alternative collapses into a merely sceptical recourse to convention because of the difficulties attendant on any attempt in this area to "distinguish Sentiment from

Education". But this suggestion can only be expected to strike home to the readership if alternative ways of construing the agreed data are made imaginatively accessible. Parts 5 to 8 are designed to do precisely this. Philo remarks that "In this little corner of the world alone, there are four principles, *reason*, *instinct*, *generation*, *vegetation*, which are similar to each other, and are the causes of similar effects" (178). Even "reason", he argues in Part 5 can be interpreted in a radically heretical manner, and the next three sections systematically explore cosmogonies based on the other principles; as they are grounded on the same data, the differences in these imaginatively competing visions are rationally equivalent and controversy concerning them, one may suppose, "entirely verbal". Similarly, but with greater rhetorical power, Parts 10 and 11 present alternatives to "the most established doctrines and opinions" based on moral considerations, such that even "the MANICHAEAN system occurs as a proper hypothesis" (211).

It is this persuasive presentation of apparently diverse options which most markedly distinguishes these central sections of the *Dialogues* from Hume's other discussions of natural religion. Much of the demolition of the argument a priori can also be found in the *Treatise* (1. iii.) and the *1st Enquiry* (4 and 12); the weakness of the inference to divine benevolence is insinuated in the *1st Enquiry* (8. ii, and 11); and much of the logical critique of the argument a posteriori mounted by Philo in Part 2 of the *Dialogues* is paralleled in Section 11 of the *1st Enquiry*. But in Part 3 Cleanthes proposes the possibility of "irregular" argument and presents a couple of thought-experiments that apparently conflict with Philo's analysis in Part 2 but appear to have some cogency (see Wadia). In response Philo (Part 4) provides the general objections, first that Cleanthes' approach—if allowed—can be made to lead to conclusions incompatible with the religious hypothesis, and second that the infinite regress involved can only be shrugged off by failing to distinguish particular from general causes. The next four sections elaborate on that general response, with Parts 10 and 11 providing a coda, and it is here that the main burden of the attempt "to root out a whole vision of reality" (Morrisroe (2), 967) lies. The reader, through identification with the figure of Cleanthes, is forced to grapple with alien conceptions and through them see the force—however reluctantly—of Philo's cry: "We have no *data* to establish any system of cosmogony" (177); the more vividly we are aware of the many alternatives available on the basis of the same data, the more embarrassing our need to rely on the simple generalized assertion that "common sense and reason" reject them (181). If only limited success is to be expected here in opposing Cleanthes' "Sophistry" (if that is what it is)[32] with "Syllogism" (Hume (2), *Letters* i. 151), more may be achieved by offsetting it with Philo's "fertility of invention" (Hume (7), *Dialogues*, 181). Once the availability of alternative visions is imaginatively grasped, the appeal to "feeling" is correspondingly weakened, and the thought that "common sense" may be no more than a function of education and habituation rendered a live issue.

Thus "irregular" argument needs to be matched with "irregular" argument. The flexibility of the dialogue form enables the writer both to meet "regular" arguments, where they are available, on their own terms, and to undermine the appeal of those considerations which, being but the fruit of prejudice, we cannot "reduce to form". This is the significance of Philo's reference to another influence on Hume's *Dialogues*, that of Galileo.[33]

The modern system of astronomy is now so much received by all enquirers, and has become so essential a part even of our earliest education, that we are not commonly very scrupulous in examining the reasons upon which it is founded. It is now become a matter of mere curiosity to study the first writers on that subject, who had the full force of prejudice to encounter, and were obliged to turn their arguments on every side, in order to render them popular and convincing. But if we peruse GALILAEO's famous Dialogues concerning the system of the world, we shall find, that that great genius, one of the sublimest that ever existed, first bent all his endeavours to prove, that there was no foundation for the distinction commonly made between elementary and celestial substances. The schools, proceeding from the illusions of sense, had carried this distinction very far (150–1).

The parallel with Hume's own work is obvious enough; 'It is likely that Hume hoped his *Dialogues* would have the same effect on the

---

[32] Cleanthes' first thought-experiment, borrowed from Berkeley (iii, *Alciphron*, 161), exploits the notorious sceptical problem of "other minds"; the inference involved is no more irregular, it is suggested, than the ascribing of intentions to people on the basis of their verbal behaviour. For an illuminating discussion of the underlying issue, see pt. 3 of Plantinga, who contends that "belief in other minds and belief in God are in the same epistemological boat" (viii).

[33] Mossner (3), 8, rightly points out the parallel, but provides no evidence for the claim that Galileo's *Dialogue* acts as a "model" for the "structuring" of Hume's work.

design argument as Galileo's arguments did on . . . [traditional] astronomy' (Colver and Price, 171). As with Galileo, so with Hume, the use of dialogue met the need for them "to turn their arguments on every side" in order to counter "the full force of prejudice" which stemmed from "the schools" (or their contemporary equivalents). In each case what is ultimately required for the progress of enlightenment is a change in the practice of "our earliest education".[34]

A start, Philo ironically suggests at the close, should be made with Pamphilus.

[34] Philo's account of Galileo's *Dialogue* seems designed to correct the characteristic half-truths of Pamphilus about the dialogue form. Cleanthes' pupil sees its role in "*obscure* and *uncertain*" matters as given by the fact that "Opposite sentiments, even without any decision, afford an agreeable amusement" (128). But Hume's *Dialogues*, as in the case of Galileo, do point to a "decision"; Pamphilus' final summing up indicates that he has failed to grasp what it is.

7
Nietzsche's Philosophical Hammer

1. Perspectivism and the "Winning" of Truth

> Supposing truth is a woman—what then?
>
> (Nietzsche (7), *Beyond Good and Evil*, Preface)[1]

With Nietzsche an idiosyncratic voice enters philosophy; mocking, outrageous and questioning, but also affirmative, passionate and oracular: 'Unconcerned, mocking, violent—thus wisdom wants *us*: she is a woman and always loves only a warrior' (Nietzsche (7), *Genealogy of Morals*, Epigraph to Third Essay, quoted from *Zarathustra*, I. vii). Commentators have had great difficulty in doing justice to both aspects, but whichever one is emphasized Nietzsche's penchant for expressing abstractions in concrete terms presents the reader with provocative juxtapositions, of which the above are among the more notorious. Reactions to the numerous and very uneven references to women range from the embarrassed distaste of Stern (59), through the apologies to the women's movement of Parsons (187), to the somewhat excessive enthusiasm of several French scholars led by Derrida (1); further, as the latter has shown, Heidegger's simple expedient of ignoring such remarks creates its own interpretive pitfalls. The arousal of such obvious unease is, indeed, part of Nietzsche's strategy but, despite Professor Stern's insistence here that "embarrassment . . . heightens one's

---

[1] Translations of Nietzsche are normally those of the late Professor Kaufmann, where available. Where I have modified the cited rendering the original German is also given, using the Colli-Montinari edition of Nietzsche's text, although for reasons analogous to those given in the case of Pascal citation of the original does not always indicate such a modification. The Kaufmann translation of the *Götzen-Dämmerung*, the work primarily at issue in this study, is taken from *The Portable Nietzsche*, trans. Walter Kaufmann; copyright 1958 by The Viking Press, Inc., copyright renewed (c) 1982 by Viking Penguin Inc.; all rights reserved; reprinted by permission of Viking Penguin Inc. Unless otherwise specified, references to works by Nietzsche are to sections.

perception", an "unconcerned" yet discriminating attention to some of this material points the way to the heart of the Nietzschean enterprise, to how subversive and creative elements may be united once it is shown "How one philosophizes with a hammer" (Nietzsche (6), Subtitle to *Twilight of the Idols*).

'Truth' and 'Wisdom' are alternative designations of the philosopher's goal, so one proposed answer to "What then?" is "Warfare", and this is indeed a prominent theme in *Twilight* to which we shall return; but in the work where the question is posed a more indirect answer is returned:

Are there not grounds for the suspicion that all philosophers, insofar as they were dogmatists, have been very inexpert about women? That the gruesome seriousness, the clumsy obtrusiveness with which they have usually approached truth so far have been awkward and very improper methods for winning a woman's heart? What is certain is that she has not allowed herself to be won—and today every kind of dogmatism is left standing dispirited and discouraged (Nietzsche (7), *BGE*, 'Preface').

Derrida (1) (47) glosses this reply with "Woman (truth) will not be pinned down" and the sequel shows that he takes this to amount to the claim that truth is "unwinnable", but this is not what the text says; rather,

the point Nietzsche seeks to make here is that 'truth' is something requiring to be *won*, by means quite other than the 'awkward and very improper methods' of those who think it something needing only to be seized to be possessed (or already theirs as some kind of gift) (Schacht (1), 115).

The dogmatist tradition, Nietzsche claims, has dominated European thought since Plato, encouraging the building of "unconditional philosophers' edifices" depending on supposed "cornerstones" which turn out on investigation to be projections of "all too human facts", "superstition" or "seduction by grammar"; further, "the worst, most durable, and most dangerous of all errors so far was a dogmatist's error—. . . it meant standing truth on her head and denying *perspective*, the basic condition of all life, when one spoke of spirit and the good as Plato did" (Nietzsche (7), *BGE*, 'Preface'). It is the conception of truth as "unconditional", untouched by the perspective of the enquirer and the conditions of his life, that Nietzsche sees as the dogmatist's hallmark, accounting for his inept methods, and stigmatizes as a sign not only of "childishness" but also of self-deception. Such philosophers all pose as if they had discovered and reached their real opinions through the self-development of a cold, pure, divinely unconcerned dialectic; . . . while at bottom it is . . . most often a desire of the heart that has been filtered and made abstract—that they defend with reasons they have sought after the fact. . . .

Consider the hocus-pocus of mathematical form with which Spinoza clad his philosophy—really "the love of *his* wisdom", to render that word fairly and squarely—in mail and mask, to strike terror into the heart of any assailant . . . : how much personal timidity and vulnerability this masquerade of a sick hermit betrays! (Nietzsche (7), *BGE*, 5)

The beginning of wisdom is the honest recognition of the horizons of one's own perspectives and the role of one's "desires of the heart" in constituting them; only then is it possible so to set about evaluating, modifying and transcending those perspectives that one may move beyond that beginning: 'Every step forward in knowledge, *follows* from courage, from hardness against oneself, from cleanliness in relation to oneself' (Nietzsche (7), *Ecce Homo*, 'Preface', 3).

Philosophical understanding, therefore, is not to be construed simply as the intellectual acceptance of propositions which can be shown in some "unconditional" manner to correspond to perspective-free facts; Nietzsche is scathing about the supposition that "distinct from every perspective kind of outlook or sensual-spiritual appropriation, something exists, an 'in-itself'. . . . The psychological derivation of the belief in things forbids us to speak of 'things-in-themselves'" (Nietzsche (8), *Will to Power*, 473).[2] Any attempt to specify that "true reality" to which veridical propositions, on the "dogmatist's" view of things, correspond must itself be bound by a perspective; and the Kantian attempt to overcome this impasse by means of a critique of pure reason is itself incoherent. It is in this context that Nietzsche's famous fragment should be read: 'A critique of the faculty of knowledge is senseless: how should a tool be able to criticise itself when it can use only itself for the critique?' (ibid. 486) Assessment of the knowledge drive and the associated "will to truth", which figures significantly in Nietzsche's writings, must take account of their self-referential character and "psychological derivation", thereby abandoning as a chimera the

---

[2] The fragments, which Nietzsche had not prepared for publication, collected in *The Will to Power* need to be treated with extreme caution (see, for example, Montinari and Alderman). But where material unpublished by Nietzsche puts more pithily than elsewhere themes and theses that can be discerned in his published work, I have not hesitated to make use of it.

ideal of "absolute knowledge" (ibid. 473). For the lover of wisdom there is a delicate internal relationship between wooer and wooed, for "truth . . . is a woman: she should not be violated" (Nietzsche (7), *BGE*, 220).[3]

An alternative model for the seeking and winning of truth is required from that of the "dogmatic" tradition, and Nietzsche sketches part of it in his portrait of the desiderated "new philosophers":

> They will certainly not be dogmatists. It must offend their pride, also their taste, if their truth is supposed to be a truth for everyman—which has so far been the secret wish and hidden meaning of all dogmatic aspirations. "My judgment is *my* judgment": no one else is easily entitled to it—that is what such a philosopher of the future may perhaps say of himself (ibid. 43–4).

Further, they may be expected to possess "that genuinely philosophical combination, for example, of a bold and exuberant spirituality that runs *presto* and a dialectical severity and necessity that takes no false step (ibid. 213). Part of what is at stake in the first part of this combination has already been exemplified. Nietzsche often associates the *presto* spirit with lightness of touch—in opposition to the "spirit of gravity" (e.g. Nietzsche (6), *Zarathustra*, iii. 11)—and this is what we find in the 'Preface' to *Beyond Good and Evil*;

> Both the lightness of tone and the questioning are essential to the intended refutation of dogmatism. Since dogmatism is objectionable in part because of its clumsiness, refutation of it must be "light"; dogmatism cannot be refuted dogmatically. The preface anticipates the book in its abundance of question-marks, dashes, and such qualifying words as "perhaps". Nietzsche does not even assert that truth *is* a woman, but merely *supposes* that truth is a woman (Dannhauser, 180).

Light, bold, and exuberant questioning as opposed to the "gruesome seriousness" of those who attempt to build "unconditional edifices" which they defend clad in the "mail and mask" of "the

---

[3] At this point Nietzsche's metaphor may be thought to become misleading. If there is an internal relationship between lover of wisdom and wisdom itself, then the wooer/wooed model which gives point to characterizing truth as a "woman" would seem to be less appropriate than one which characterizes the metaphysical quest as hermaphroditic. Nietzsche would no doubt regard such literal-minded objections as insufficiently free-spirited and in any case disabled by their tendency to overlook the way in which the idea of "woman" presupposed by the wooer is itself (at least in part) a masculine projection: "Man has created woman—out of what? Out of a rib of his god—of his 'ideal'" (Nietzsche (6), *Twilight*, i. 13).

hocus-pocus of mathematical form"; as in any good caricature, the figures are exaggerated but recognizable, and if all the available "cornerstones" are friable the former attitude is clearly superior. But "lightweight" has pejorative connotations, and it is to exclude these that we are presented with "dialectical severity and necessity that takes no false step". Behind this requirement lies an exacting discipline;

it may be necessary for the education of a genuine philosopher that he himself has also once stood on all these steps on which his servants, the scientific laborers of philosophy, remain standing. . . . Perhaps he himself must have been critic and skeptic and dogmatist . . . and seer and "free spirit" and almost everything in order to . . . be *able* to see with many eyes and consciences. . . . But all these are merely preconditions of his task (Nietzsche (7), *BGE*, 211).

In place of the ideal of "absolute knowledge", unconditioned by human presuppositions, we have here suggested a model of truth-seeking where the goal is internally related to the capacity to master multiple perspectives. This suggestion is made explicit in the work which is presented as intending "to Supplement and Clarify" *Beyond Good and Evil* (Nietzsche (7), p. 439):

Henceforth, my dear philosophers, let us be on guard against the dangerous old conceptual fiction that posited a "pure, will-less, painless, timeless knowing subject"; let us guard against the snares of such contradictory concepts as "pure reason", "absolute spirituality", "knowledge in itself": these always demand that we should think of an eye that is completely unthinkable, an eye turned in no particular direction, in which the active and interpreting forces, through which alone seeing becomes seeing *something*, are supposed to be lacking; these always demand of the eye an absurdity and a nonsense. There is *only* a perspective seeing, *only* a perspective "knowing"; and the *more* affects we allow to speak about one thing, the *more* eyes, different eyes, we can use to observe one thing, the more complete will our "concept" of this thing, our "objectivity", be (Nietzsche (7), *Genealogy of Morals*, iii. 12).

This radical rethinking of the notion of "objectivity" is explicitly presented as part of Nietzsche's "exegesis" of the aphorism quoted earlier characterizing wisdom as a woman (ibid. 'Preface', 8). Disinterested love of wisdom (philosophy), like disinterested love of woman, is an absurdity (cf. also *BGE*, 220); in both cases will and feelings are involved. On the other hand, a certain "unconcern" is required, a readiness to sit loosely to any single perspective or affect while recognizing its potency, so that one may be "*able* to see with many eyes and consciences"; both thinker and warrior need to be at once sure-footed and light-footed, thus at this point the required combination of severity with exuberance becomes imaginable: 'One has to be *very light* to drive one's will to knowledge into such a distance and, as it were, beyond one's time, to create for oneself eyes to survey millenia and, moreover, clear skies in these eyes' (Nietzsche (5), *Gay Science*, v. 380). To achieve those clear skies, the "objectivity" which comes with sure-footedness in a multiplicity of perspectives, much is required:

The thinker needs imagination, self-uplifting, abstraction, desensualiza-tion, invention, presentiment, induction, dialectics, deduction, the critical faculty, the assemblage of material, the impersonal mode of thinking, contemplativeness and comprehensiveness, and not least justice and love for all that exists (Nietzsche (4), *Daybreak*, 43).

As the dogmatists have found, truth is a woman not easily won; their presuppositions about her character and bluffly straightforward procedures disable them from the start, for "nature has hidden behind riddles and iridescent uncertainties. Perhaps truth is a woman who has reasons for not letting us see her reasons?" (Nietzsche (5), *Gay Science*, 'Preface', 4). Different presuppositions and a more broadly conceived strategy lie behind the nuanced approach of the "Don Juan of knowledge" (Nietzsche (4), *Daybreak*, 327).

There is no need to follow Nietzsche's rapidly ramifying metaphor into all its transformations. Lying behind it is the thought that "Man has created woman—out of what? Out of a rib of his god—of his 'ideal'" (Nietzsche (6), *Twilight*, i. 13). The image of "woman" he is exploiting is itself the projection of a "desire of the heart", with many of the elusive subtleties one finds in his preferred analysis of truth. By reading the two "ideals" in terms of each other (for some of the complex interplay see, for example, *Gay Science*, 60 and 64) he both draws attention to the similarity between the "will to truth" and other drives, and suggests a model for the attaining of the elusive in terms of which a new conception of the philosophical activity can be developed. Of course part of the persuasive force of the metaphor depends on the authenticity of Nietzsche's conception of that "ideal" of femininity, and notori-ously his perceptions here are too often second-hand hangovers from the otherwise outgrown period of Schopenhauerian influence, but altogether too much can be made of this. Ultimately the analyses of truth and "genuine" philosophy do not stand or fall with the vehicle of Nietzsche's metaphor, yet to the extent that we can imaginatively enter into his image of "woman" we are enabled to grasp some of the more intricate subtleties of his most central philosophical analyses. Indeed, the very ambivalence of the metaphor, at once glamorizing and making fun of the philosophical activity, exemplifies that union of positive and negative in Nietzche's thinking which so baffles the commentators (cf. Williams (5), 'Nietzsche's Masks', 96).

Further, the use of metaphor itself is symptomatic of the view of language that underlies the attack on "dogmatists" and the revised conceptions of "truth" and "objectivity". In an early essay the old sceptical arguments are taken as seriously as in Pascal or Hume, pushed to their limits, and given a linguistic twist. We find it difficult, Nietzsche suggests, to admit to ourselves that

the insect or the bird perceives an entirely different world from the one that man does, and that the question of which of these perceptions of the world is the more correct one is quite meaningless, for this would have to have been decided previously in accordance with the criterion of the *correct perception*, which means, in accordance with a criterion which is *not available*. But in any case it seems to me that "the correct perception"—which would mean "the adequate expression of an object in the subject"—is a contradictory impossibility. For between two absolutely different spheres, as between subject and object, there is no causality, no correctness, and no expression; there is, at most, an *aesthetic* relation: I mean, a suggestive transference, a stammering translation into a completely foreign tongue (Nietzsche (2), 'On Truth and Lies in a Nonmoral Sense', p. 86).

In later writings even this tentative recourse to aesthetic criteria is put in question, as revised conceptions of truth are developed to cope with the ramifying perspectivism we see here in embryo with the problem of "stammering translation" between incommensurables, an issue which earlier in the essay is handled in terms of "metaphor":

What is a word? It is the copy in sound of a nerve stimulus. But the further inference from the nerve stimulus to a cause outside of us is already the result of a false and unjustifiable application of the principle of sufficient reason. If truth alone had been the deciding factor in the genesis of language, . . . how could we still dare to say 'the stone is hard', as if 'hard' were something otherwise familiar to us, and not merely a totally subjective stimulation! . . . The various languages placed side by side show that with words it is never a question of truth, never a question of adequate expression; otherwise, there would not be so many languages. The "thing in itself" (which is precisely what the pure truth, apart from any of its consequences, would be) is likewise something quite incomprehensible to the creator of language. . . . This creator only designates the relations of things to men, and for expressing these relations he lays hold of the boldest metaphors. To begin with, a nerve stimulus is transferred into an image: first metaphor. The image, in turn, is imitated in a sound: second metaphor. And each time there is a complete overleaping of one sphere, right into the middle of an entirely new and different one (ibid. pp. 81–2).

The conception of truth as "adequate expression" (a strong version of the Correspondence Theory, recently denominated "correspondence-as-congruity" and associated with the early Wittgenstein; see Pitcher (10–11) and Grimm (49–52)) provides the necessary foil for exploiting the underlying etymology concerning transference of 'metaphor' to enlarge its sphere of use. A "literal" statement purports to give "adequate expression" of its referent; only elements in commensurable "spheres" can "adequately express" each other, thus where a linguistic item is used to refer to a non-linguistic one there can be no adequacy and hence no literal truth—there is at best transfer, or "stammering translation" from one sphere to another, in short "metaphor". The only area where linguistic items can approximate to literal truth, so conceived, is in giving "adequate expression" of other such items—that is, in tautologies—and this is precisely what Nietzsche concludes in notes dating from the same period:

There is no "real" expression and *no real knowing apart from metaphor.* . . .

Knowledge, strictly speaking, has only the form of tautology and *is empty.* All the knowledge which is of assistance to us involves the *identification of things which are not the same*, of things which are only similar. In other words, such knowledge is essentially illogical (Nietzsche (2), 'The Philosopher', 149–50).

The latter claim is elaborated in the essay:

Every word instantly becomes a concept precisely insofar as it is not supposed to serve as a reminder of the unique and entirely individual original experience to which it owes its origin; but rather, a word becomes a concept insofar as it simultaneously has to fit countless more or less similar cases—which means, purely and simply, cases which are never equal. . . . Every concept arises from the equation of unequal things. Just as it is certain that one leaf is never totally the same as the other, so it is certain that the concept "leaf" is formed by arbitrarily discarding these individual differences and by forgetting the distinguishing aspects. This awakens the idea that, in addition to leaves, there exists in nature the "leaf" (Nietzsche (2), 'On Truth and Lies', p. 83).

This evocation of Berkeley's problem about abstract general ideas is used further to undermine the "adequacy" conception of truth and the literal:

What then is truth? A movable host of metaphors, metonymies, and anthropomorphisms; in short, a sum of human relations which have been poetically and rhetorically intensified, transferred, and embellished, and which, after long usage, seem to a people to be fixed, canonical, and binding. Truths are illusions which we have forgotten are illusions; they are metaphors that have become worn out and have been drained of sensuous force (ibid. p. 84).

Out of such forgetfulness, Nietzsche suggests, arises the idea of a "true world", transcending the "appearances" of the senses, which grounds the idea of the "thing in itself" and lends plausibility to the ideal of "adequate expression";

Everything which distinguishes man from the animals depends upon this ability to volatilize perceptual metaphors in a schema, and thus to dissolve an image into a concept. For something is possible in the realm of these schemata which could never be achieved with the vivid first impressions: the construction of a pyramidal order, . . . a new world, one which now confronts that other vivid world of first impressions as more solid, more universal, better known, and more human than the immediately perceived world. Whereas each perceptual metaphor is individual and without equals and is therefore able to elude all classification, the great edifice of concepts displays the rigid regularity of a Roman columbarium and exhales in logic the strength and coolness which is characteristic of mathematics. Anyone who has felt this cool breath . . . will hardly believe that even the concept —which is as bony, foursquare, and transposable as a die—is nevertheless merely the *residue of a metaphor* (ibid. p. 84–5).

In pursuit of knowledge, Nietzsche comments, an "impression" is "captured and stamped by means of concepts. Then it is killed, skinned, mummified, and preserved as a concept" (Nietzsche (2), 'The Philosopher', 149).

These early writings are immature, and Nietzsche himself became dissatisfied with some of the formulations. In place of the opposition literal/metaphorical he came to prefer fact/interpretation; 'Against positivism, which halts at phenomena—"There are only *facts*"—I would say: No, facts is precisely what there is not, only interpretations. We cannot establish any fact "in itself": perhaps it is folly to want to do such a thing' (Nietzsche (8), *Will to Power*, 481). Hence, having sketched his own favoured account of the world in terms of "will to power" he is happy to comment, 'Supposing that this also is only interpretation—and you will be eager enough to make .this objection—well, so much the better' (Nietzsche (7), *BGE*, 22). The advantage of this formulation is that hard intellectual discipline is relevant to the assessment of interpretations; 'Forgive me as an old philologist who cannot desist from the malice of putting his finger on bad modes of interpretation' (ibid. 22).

Indeed, the whole set of virtues he ascribes to 'We Scholars' in the section so entitled in *Beyond Good and Evil* is to the point in judging Nietzsche's claim that "Morality is merely an interpretation of certain phenomena—more precisely, a misinterpretation" (Nietzsche (6), *Twilight*, vii. 1; see also Nietzsche (7), *Genealogy of Morals*, note to conclusion of 'First Essay'). The association of metaphor with illusion in the earlier writings gave rise to an uneasy tension with respect to their own status which even the most scrupulous of commentators have sometimes incautiously seen as infecting the later works, and characterized as involving the "Epimenidean predicament" ("If his assertion is correct, it is a fiction": Kaufmann (5), 204–7). At a verbal level the terminological shift marks a maturer appreciation of the issues here.

But while there are obvious faults in the early discussions, their underlying argument remains powerful. One cannot, for example, simply undercut it by accepting some weaker version of the Correspondence Theory of Truth which involves only one-to-one mapping (Professor Pitcher's "correspondence-as-correlation"), for Nietzsche argues in his later work that—so long as truth is conceived in these.terms at all—something stronger is required. The early writings use as an analogy for the transition from "sphere" to "sphere", which motivates the talk of "metaphor", Chladni's sound figures (sand patterns made by sonic vibrations): 'The images are related to the underlying nervous activity which agitates them in the same way that Chladni's acoustical figures are to the sound itself'

(Nietzsche (2), 'The Philosopher', 64; cf. also 'On Truth and Lies', pp. 82–3). On the relaxed Correspondence Theory the analogue of precise correlation between shape and sound suffices to establish truth. But Nietzsche argues that more than such correlations are required if one is to have any warrant for believing that one is talking—truly or falsely—about the subject at issue at all, save in so far as it is constituted by those same correlations. Suppose one considers

a piece of music according to how much of it could be counted, calculated, and expressed in formulas: how absurd would such a "scientific" estimation of music be! What would one have comprehended, understood, grasped of it? Nothing, really nothing of what is "music" in it! (Nietzsche (5), *Gay Science*, 373).

For all its absurdity, Nietzsche seems to be suggesting, the old ideal of "adequate expression" was pointing to a linguistic requirement that less full-blooded Correspondence Theories evade. And his own mature model of sifting better from worse interpretations through the dialectically "severe" yet creatively imaginative mastery of multiple perspectives is designed to point the way to the notion of an adequacy-relation which is not self-refuting; 'This contradictory creature has in his nature . . . a great method of acquiring knowledge: he feels many pros and cons, he raises himself to justice—to comprehension' (Nietzsche (8), *Will to Power*, 259).

More seriously, the immature discussions presuppose a referential theory of language with words taking their sense from the images they "imitate", an account which has drawn heavy twentieth-century fire. But the mature writings cut themselves largely free from this incubus, and once again the substitution of the notion of "interpretation" for that of "metaphor" helps Nietzsche to see his way. The deceptions of language are now seen less in terms of the distortion of "original experience", and more as residing in the ways grammatical structures actually affect that experience—providing constraints in terms of which we interpret our lives and all that impinges on them.

The strange family resemblance of all Indian, Greek, and German philosophizing is explained easily enough. Where there is affinity of languages, it cannot fail, owing to the common philosophy of grammar—I mean, owing to the unconscious domination and guidance by similar grammatical functions—that everything is prepared at the outset for a similar development and sequence of philosophical systems; just as the way seems barred against certain other possibilities of world-interpretation. It is highly probable that philosophers within the domain of the Ural-Altaic languages (where the concept of the subject is least developed) look otherwise "into the world", and will be found on paths of thought different from those of the Indo-Germanic peoples and the Muslims (Nietzsche (7), *BGE*, 20).

This variant of the Sapir-Whorf hypothesis looks forward to the twentieth century as clearly as the earlier discussions are part of the nineteenth. The later position is most memorably epitomized in one of the last published works: ' "Reason" in language—oh, what an old deceptive female she is! I am afraid we are not rid of God because we still have faith in grammar' (Nietzsche (6), *Twilight*, iii. 5).

The epigram points, however, to an analogue of the "Epimenidean predicament" which is far more pressing in the later writings than is the pure version, and of which Nietzsche is acutely aware; the very language in which the warning against grammar is couched is, inevitably, itself grammatical.

I shall repeat a hundred times; we really ought to free ourselves from the seduction of words! . . .
   Is it not permitted to be a bit ironical about the subject no less than the predicate and object? Shouldn't philosophers be permitted to rise above faith in grammar? All due respect for governesses—but hasn't the time come for philosophy to renounce the faith of governesses? (Nietzsche (7), *BGE*, 16 and 34)

The difficulty of freeing ourselves here is rendered acute by the close interdependence of language and thought;

The development of language and the development of consciousness . . . go hand in hand. . . . Language serves as a bridge between human beings . . . The emergence of our sense impressions into our own consciousness, the ability to fix them and, as it were, exhibit them externally, increased proportionately with the need to communicate them to *others* by means of signs. . . . Our thoughts themselves are continually governed by the character of consciousness (Nietzsche (5), *Gay Science*, 354).

Thus, "where words are lacking, we are accustomed to abandon exact observation because exact thinking there becomes painful; indeed, in earlier times one involuntarily concluded that where the realm of words ceased the realm of existence ceased also" (Nietzsche (4), *Daybreak*, 115).

In the Preface to *Twilight of the Idols*, Nietzsche describes himself as a "pied piper", a figure who leads those normally under the supervision of governesses out of their accustomed city, and in the first sustained discussion in that work attempts to take the measure of Socrates, elsewhere described as the "pied piper of Athens" (Nietzsche (5), *Gay Science*, 340). The Socratic example shows that effective piping is possible, but Nietzsche is under no illusions about its difficulty; in the other published use of this image the pied piper is a god (*BGE*, 295) and at the start of his career Nietzsche characterizes the whole Socratic phenomenon as "the one turning point and vortex of so-called world history" (Nietzsche (7), *Birth of Tragedy*, 15). The most sophisticated attempt at such piping is made in *Twilight of the Idols*, to which we shall return, but mention has already been made of some of the essential elements. As with Socrates, irony is an essential weapon (hence wisdom wants us "mocking"), for it is the rhetorical mode above all in which by saying one thing one conveys what is formally incompatible with the utterance. Again, the insistence on multiple perspectives, on attempting to see with "*more* eyes, different eyes", is of a piece with drawing attention to the potentialities of alternative grammatical structures in the attempt to shake our faith in our own. And finally, even the use of bold metaphors—not yet become "fixed, canonical, and binding"—can help to break the grip of the standard linguistic tramlines, juxtaposing abstract with concrete and general with particular in order to teach "the doltish and rash hand to hesitate and reach out more delicately"—a prime aim of the divinized pied piper (Nietzsche (7), *BGE*, 295). Lest there be any danger of the characterization of truth as a woman becoming "captured and stamped, . . . killed, skinned, mummified, and preserved as a concept", a different equivalence is thrown into the ring exerting its own field of force on that with which truth (and "reason") is elsewhere juxtaposed: "Yes, life is a woman" (Nietzsche (5), *Gay Science*, 339). The "riddles and iridescent uncertainties" of Nietzsche's style are designed to evoke those of "nature" herself (ibid. 'Preface', 4), and it is by following the interconnected nuances of such metaphors, reading Nietzsche—as he insists—"slowly, deeply, looking cautiously before and aft, with reservations, with doors left open, with delicate eyes and fingers" (Nietzsche (4), *Daybreak*, 'Preface', 5), that one is led by this pied piper out of conventional categories into accounts of language and truth which are intended to be more adequate to that world which no schematism can fully capture—which Nietzsche calls the "open sea" (Nietzsche (5), *Gay Science*, 343; cf. 124, 283, 289, 291 for some of the ramifications of *this* metaphor).

Just as *Twilight of the Idols* summarizes the new picture of language in an epigram, so too it does that of truth: ' "All truth is simple [*einfach*]." Is that not doubly [*zwiefach*] a lie?' (Nietzsche (6), *Twilight*, i. 4). In the first place truth is not simple on account of those multi-perspectival considerations I have sketched; 'An isolated judgment is never "true", never knowledge; only in the connection and relation of many judgments is there any surety' (Nietzsche (8), *Will to Power*, 530). Hence, 'One rarely rushes into a single error. Rushing into the first one, one always does too much. So one usually perpetrates another one—and now one does too little' (Nietzsche (6), *Twilight*, i. 30). On the second count, it is for Nietzsche misleading to generalize about "all truth": 'What are man's truths ultimately? Merely his *irrefutable* errors' (Nietzsche (5), *Gay Science*, 265). But we are warned against embracing "the fanatical faith 'All is false' " (Nietzsche (8), *Will to Power*, 1). Again, 'Truth is the kind of error without which a certain species of life could not live' (ibid. 493). Yet, 'A thinker is now that being in whom the impulse for truth and . . . life-preserving errors clash. . . . The impulse for truth has proved to be also a life-preserving power' (Nietzsche (5), *Gay Science*, 110). And further, 'That it does not matter whether a thing is true, but only what effect it produces—absolute lack of intellectual integrity' (Nietzsche (8), *Will to Power*, 172). Indeed, 'How much truth does a spirit *endure*, how much truth does it *dare*? More and more that became for me the real measure of value' (Nietzsche (7), *Ecce Homo*, 'Preface', 3). The widespread tendency to read what Nietzsche claims about "man's truths" as applying indiscriminately to "All truth", and censure (or celebrate) him for inconsistency as a result, is a symptom of failure to take seriously a "maxim" that might otherwise have led the "rash hand to hesitate and reach out more delicately".

"Man's truths", roughly speaking,[4] are those concerned with ordinary human life and its specialized offshoots. Although

---

[4] For more precise analysis of Nietzsche's different types of "truths" and their mutual interrelationship, see the excellent and detailed account in Schacht (1), especially ch. 2.

remarkably heterogeneous amongst themselves they can be broadly divided into two classes—those that do and those that do not purport to relate to the world. In the case of the former, any true proposition is partly constituted as such by the rules governing the domain of discourse in which it is expressed, that domain being itself partly constitutive of a human "perspective" in terms of which a form of life is carried on. These rules provide criteria for establishing whether the state of affairs referred to obtains (to this extent the Correspondence Theory points to something important), but for our experience to be able to determine whether this is so it has itself to be shaped in large part by that perspective, and here practical rather than theoretical considerations play the dominant role, for "the value for *life* is ultimately decisive" (Nietzsche (8), *Will to Power*, 493)—here the Pragmatist strain in Nietzsche's thought is to the fore. This contention may seem relatively traditional in the case of normative judgements, but Nietzsche is concerned to extend the analysis to all "interpretations" of phenomena;

the development of language and the development of consciousness . . . go hand in hand. . . . The emergence of our sense impressions into our own consciousness, the ability to fix them and, as it were, exhibit them externally, increased proportionately with the need to communicate them to *others* by means of signs. . . .

Consciousness does not really belong to man's individual existence but rather to his social or herd nature; . . . it has developed subtlety only insofar as this is required by social or herd utility (Nietzsche (5), *Gay Science*, 354).

Thus it is in terms of the concepts of the "herd", as shaped by the available language, that one interprets one's experience; indeed, "we cease to think when we refuse to do so under the constraint of language" (Nietzsche (8), *Will to Power*, 522).

The other category of these truths, "formal science, a doctrine of signs, such as logic and that applied logic which is called mathematics" (Nietzsche (6), *Twilight*, iii, 3), is—as we have seen—characterized as being concerned with "tautology"; such truths are "empty" in the sense that they do not of themselves tell us about the world. Here the linguistic rules wholly determine a proposition's truth value ("coherence" is the criterion), and the force of the rules derives from that of the relevant perspective. In so far as the rules of logic shape our thinking they play an important role in the conditions of our life, however, and may be assessed accordingly;

Logic is bound to the condition: assume there are identical cases. In fact, to make possible logical thinking and inferences, this condition must first be treated fictitiously as fulfilled. That is: the will to logical truth can be carried through only after a fundamental *falsification* of all events is assumed. . . .

Our subjective compulsion to believe in logic only reveals that, long before logic itself entered our consciousness, we did nothing but introduce its postulates into events: now we discover them in events—we can no longer do otherwise—and imagine that this compulsion guarantees something connected with the truth. It is we who created the "thing", the "identical thing", subject, attribute, activity, object, substance, form. . . . The world seems logical to us because we have made it logical. . . .

Rational thought is interpretation according to a scheme that we cannot throw off (Nietzsche (8), *Will to Power*, 512, 521 and 522).

"Man's truths", it will be noticed, bear a strong relation to Hume's "reflections of common life" when "methodically" extended; but whereas the Scottish philosopher was ultimately prepared to rest content with "common Sense" and "common reason" (cf. ch. 6.1 above), Nietzsche was sufficient of a Pyrrhonist to regard such contentment as "human, all too human". For Pascal's response to the sceptical challenge he had some respect; in an early work he cited Pascal as one of the eight thinkers with whom "I must come to terms" (Nietzsche (7), *Mixed Opinions and Maxims*, 408), and in one of his last letters describes him as "the only *logical* Christian" (Nietzsche (9), 'Letter 187', 20 Nov. 1888). But his response Nietzsche held to be no longer an available option; the existence of God, he maintained, had suffered its "definitive refutation" (Nietzsche (4), *Daybreak*, 95), and "the greatest recent event" was "that 'God is dead', that the belief in the Christian god has become unbelievable" (Nietzsche (5), *Gay Science*, 343). Hume's secular alternative, on the other hand, cut insufficiently deep, for the "Moral Certainty" on which he rested his case was still construed in terms of the very model of truth which sponsored those "dogmatic" metaphysical edifices both Nietzsche and Hume sought to undermine. From a Nietzschean point of view, those agonized wrestlings with Pyrrhonism that cast such a lurid light over the later pages of Book 1 of Hume's *Treatise* are a symptom of this superficiality.

The most durable and dangerous of the dogmatists' errors, it will be remembered, is held by Nietzsche to be "standing truth on her head and denying *perspective*, the basic condition of all life"

(Nietzsche (7), *BGE*, 'Preface'). So long as truth is conceived of as correspondence to some "true reality" of perspective-free facts, men are tempted to seek some "unconditional" method in the form of "a cold, pure, divinely unconcerned dialectic" which will lead to knowledge of this "true world" lying behind appearances, whether conceived of as that to which our concepts can give "adequate expression" or as the religious "beyond"; indeed, the two projections support each other, for "Christianity is Platonism for 'the people'" (ibid.). Here we have a set of alleged "truths" to which Nietzsche is unremittingly hostile; his account of 'How the "True World" finally became a Fable' is subtitled 'The History of an Error' (Nietzsche (6), *Twilight*, iv), and he insists that "The reasons for which 'this' world has been characterised as 'apparent' are the very reasons which indicate its reality; any other kind of reality is absolutely indemonstrable" (ibid. iii. 6). What needs to be investigated, thinks Nietzsche, is why these reasons have been so regularly misconstrued; and here psychological considerations come into play, so much so that in his later work the self-description he prefers is "psychologist". The "Platonic" and "Christian" impulses do not merely give each other mutual support, but can be traced to a common attitude towards the human condition; a lack of preparedness to acknowledge the human origins of our perspectives, whether conceptual, moral, religious, or even aesthetic (Nietzsche is scathing about the slogan *'l'art pour l'art'*: ibid. ix. 24), by denying that they all are just perspectives, a denial that reveals at once a dissatisfaction with our human condition (the world of mere "appearance") and a lack of preparedness to take responsibility for assessing, modifying, and attempting to create new perspectives on no other basis than one's own will; faith in "the will of God" is an illuminating symptom of human decline, a form of weakness most nakedly exposed in the response of "the only *logical* Christian" to the sceptical dilemma: 'Who will unravel such a tangle? This is certainly beyond dogmatism and scepticism, beyond all human philosophy. . . . Listen to God' (Pascal *Pensées*, L.131, B.434, S.164). Against this whole tendency we have the diagnosis of the "old psychologist":

To invent fables about a world "other" than this one has no meaning at all, unless an instinct of slander, detraction, and suspicion against life has gained the upper hand in us. . . .

Any distinction between a 'true' and an 'apparent' world . . . is only a suggestion of decadence, a symptom of the *decline of life* (Nietzsche (6), *Twilight*, 'Preface' and iii. 6).

With the recognition of the perspectival character of existence a number of discriminations become possible. In the first place, we can distinguish the so-called "truths" of the dogmatists, which purport to give a perspective-free account of "reality", from "man's truths" which of themselves carry no such presupposition. Within their own frames of reference the latter may often be perfectly acceptable, even humanly inescapable, thus in a thoroughly Humean passage he distinguishes the empirical from formal varieties of "science" (*Wissenschaft*) and maintains that "The rest is miscarriage and not-yet-science—in other words, metaphysics, theology, psychology, epistemology" (ibid. iii. 3). Second, within the realm of "man's truths" we may distinguish between those which are inescapable because they help constitute human thought as such, as logic appears to come close to doing, from those whose grip on us turns out on analysis to be a function of our acculturation to a particular perspective (note that "all sense perceptions are permeated with value judgments" (*Will to Power*, 505))—no doubt our thought will always be bounded by grammar, but that of the "Ural-Altaic languages" may provide "other possibilities of world-interpretation" from that of our own. And third, whereas in the case of logic the recognition that all is perspectival may do no more than liberate us from the shadow of the Platonic forms, in other instances it may also encourage us critically to assess our cultural inheritance, and to seek to replace our less satisfactory perspectives with others.

In attempting such assessments Nietzsche uses a complex battery of techniques, but most of them may be generally characterized as exploring either the internal coherence of a perspective or its past and present role in human life; in the latter case a "genealogical" investigation of its origins and development often proves his most favoured weapon. Thus the Christian perspective which, with the Platonic, he is most centrally concerned to discredit, is both seen as self-refuting—'what . . . really triumphed over the Christian god . . . [was] Christian morality itself' (Nietzsche (5), *Gay Science*, 357)—and as discredited by its origins, 'The idea of a God is disturbing and humiliating as long as it is believed, but how it *originated* can at the present stage of comparative ethnology no longer admit of doubt; and with the insight into this origination that belief falls away' (Nietzsche (10), *Human, All Too Human*, cxxxiii. p. 170). The latter contention is later expanded:

Historical refutation as the decisive refutation.—In former times, one sought to prove that there is no God—today one indicates how the belief that there is a God could *arise* and how this belief acquired its weight and importance: a counter-proof that there is no God thereby becomes superfluous.—When in former times one had refuted the 'proofs of the existence of God' put forward, there always remained the doubt whether better proofs might not be adduced than those just refuted: in those days atheists did not know how to make a clean sweep (Nietzsche (4), *Daybreak*, 95).

The status of such "genealogical" claims is a matter of some delicacy. On the face of it, "historical refutation" is simply a form of the genetic fallacy. Some have attempted to rebut this charge by pointing out that for Nietzsche there is more to a conceptual system than that which gave rise to it,[5] but this only serves to highlight the gap between showing the genesis to be disreputable and using that finding to discredit the system. An analogy with Hume may be helpful. We have seen how the latter's "genetic" account of fundamental religious impulses is used to discredit the latter in a context where basic human "propensities" are allowed some epistemological status (ch. 6. 1), that context providing the link necessary to avoid fallacy. The analogous connection for Nietzsche is provided by his perspectivism; only if truth is conceived as "unconditional", untouched by the perspective of the adherent or enquirer, must there always be an unbridgeable gap between the "desire of the heart" of those who originate a conceptual system and that system's credibility. Whether in any given instance that gap can be bridged is a matter to be considered on a case-by-case basis. For Nietzsche all perspectives have their pedigree, and some are more discrediting than others. One of his last books, *The Anti-Christ*, is a sustained attempt to show that that of Christianity is incriminating; the work is full of faults, shrill, exaggerated, dated in its scholarship, and often unconvincing, but is testimony to Nietzsche's conviction that reason was needed to establish that "what is now decisive

---

[5] Compare Alderman (58): 'Whereas Nietzsche's descriptions of conceptual systems in terms of underlying value commitments are reductive, they by no means involve the genetic fallacy. A genetic reduction becomes fallacious if and only if it says in effect that some one object is *nothing but* that to which it is reduced. . . . It was always Nietzsche's intent to avoid this fallacious form of reduction in his self-acknowledged genetic accounts of the nature of conceptual systems.'

against Christianity is our taste, no longer our reasons" (Nietzsche (5), *Gay Science*, 132)—the paradox, of course, is more apparent than real.

The reference to taste here is an indication that at this level of analysis value considerations are decisive, and here wide-ranging considerations about the overall role of a perspective in human existence are in place, the key question for Nietzsche being whether it is life-preserving or enhancing on the one hand, or is a function of the "decline of life" on the other. Indeed, "every individual may be scrutinized to see whether he represents the ascending or the descending line of life" (Nietzsche (6), *Twilight*, ix. 33), and the quality of his thought is to an important degree a function of such considerations for, as we have seen, "every step forward in knowledge, follows from courage" (a sign of ascending life) whereas Spinoza's "hocus-pocus of mathematical form" betrays the "personal timidity and vulnerability . . . of a sick hermit". Preparedness to subject even one's most deeply ingrained perspectives to critical scrutiny, both with reference to internal coherence (including the correspondence of its posited entities to what by its own criteria count as the facts) and to their role in human life, is one aspect of this courage; another is the preparedness to "attempt" new perspectives (cf. for example Nietzsche (7), *BGE*, 42 and 210), to play one off against another (perhaps by learning to think with the grammar of "the Ural-Altaic languages" as well as that of "the Indo-Germanic peoples") in the consciousness that "the *more* affects we allow to speak about one thing, the *more* eyes, different eyes, we can use to observe one thing, the more complete will our 'concept' of this thing, our 'objectivity', be" (Nietzsche (7), *Genealogy of Morals*, iii. 12). Thus there is an internal and reciprocal relationship between will to truth and the ascending form of life; 'How much truth does a spirit *endure*, how much truth does it *dare*? More and more that became for me the real measure of value' (Nietzsche (7), *Ecce Homo*, 'Preface', 3).

Here we encounter yet another variety of "truth", which is neither at the level of "man's truths" (the "irrefutable errors"), nor to be rejected as the slanders of decadents unable to face the perspectival character of existence, but with genuine claims to (relative) objectivity. The objectivity is relative because there is "no limit to the ways in which the world can be interpreted" (Nietzsche (8), *Will to Power*, 600), and hence to the potential perspectives capable of being mastered, but objectivity is to a degree possible because the lack of interpretative finality need not deter "an old philologist . . . from putting his finger on bad modes of interpretation" (Nietzsche (7), *BGE*, 22). The philological model is, indeed, closer to Nietzsche's thinking here than is that of the physical sciences; rather as a text is, *qua* text, constituted by its relationship to various linguistic conventions into which the interpreter seeks to enter, so more generally it is "quite idle" to suppose "that a thing freed from all relationships would still be a thing" (Nietzsche (8), *Will to Power*, 560); the very notion of "thing" is a projection of "the metaphysics of language" (Nietzsche (6), *Twilight*, iii, 5) and thus that of the "thing-in-itself" radically incoherent. Hence,

our multiply perspectival access to things and the world . . . turns out to accord with their fundamental character, and to be a condition of the possibility of—and a means of arriving at—a relatively comprehensive interpretation of them that would do something approaching justice to them. If the nature of something is a function of the various ways in which it admits of being encountered and the forms of interaction into which it is capable of entering, and if these are discernable only from a variety of specific standpoints, then to the extent (and only to the extent) that one is capable of making the appropriate shifts of perspective, that nature becomes accessible to one. (Schacht (1), 101)

There is an important and often overlooked development here between the early writings and the mature ones. In his celebrated essay Nietzsche writes of different "perceptions of the world" as belonging to "absolutely different spheres" between which there is at best "an aesthetic relation" (Nietzsche (2), 'On Truth and Lies in a Nonmoral Sense', p. 86), a relation in which he soon loses confidence. Reading the later work in this light, many writers have interpreted Nietzsche as a radical Kuhnian before his time, insisting on the incommensurability of scientific (and not only scientific) paradigms, and embracing "the epistemological conclusions which are inherent to his position" but which "Kuhn declines to draw" (Grimm, 196). But in the later writings although "introducing truth" is seen "as a *processus in infinitum*" (Nietzsche (8), *Will to Power*, 552), the revision of the notion of objectivity in terms of "more eyes", the incitement to "drive one's will to knowledge . . . beyond one's time" (Nietzsche (5), *Gay Science*, 380), the notion that "the strength of a spirit should be measured according to how much of the 'truth' one could still barely endure" (Nietzsche (7),

BGE, 39), and the claim that man has "a great method of acquiring knowledge: he feels many pros and cons, he raises himself to justice" (Nietzsche (8), *Will to Power*, 259) all point rather in the direction of the "verisimilitude" of Sir Karl Popper, whose position is often regarded as the antithesis of that of Professor Kuhn. For Sir Karl,

The task of science constantly renews itself. . . . Although I do not think that we can ever describe, by our universal laws, an *ultimate* essence of the world, I do not doubt that we may seek to probe deeper and deeper into . . . properties of the world that are more and more essential, or of greater and greater depth. . . . I believe that this word 'deeper' defies any attempt at exhaustive logical analysis, but that it is nevertheless a guide to our intuitions (Popper, 194–7).

As a perceptive commentator has remarked,

This might well be taken as a statement of Nietzsche's belief. . . . The consequence seems to be that, just as some philosophers have suggested that we must always analyse the word 'good' in terms of 'better', so we must analyse the word 'true' in terms of 'more true', 'less false' or 'possessing more depth of insight' (Warnock (2), 58–9).

The analogy with Popperian philosophy of science extends beyond the characterization of the goal, to include (though of course go beyond) some of the methods advocated; Nietzsche's outline sketch of the way one might properly be led to his favoured characterization of the world in terms of "will to power" has at the heart of its "conscience of method" something very close to the principle of "simplicity", so familiar from contemporary discussions. Supposing, as ever since his early writings he had maintained to be the case, that

nothing else were "given" as real except our world of desires and passions, . . . for thinking is merely a relation of these drives to each other: is it not permitted to make the experiment and to ask the question whether this "given" would not be *sufficient* for also understanding on the basis of this kind of thing the so-called mechanistic (or "material") world? . . .

In the end not only is it permitted to make this experiment; the conscience of *method* demands it. Not to assume several kinds of causality until the experiment of making do with a single one has been pushed to its utmost limit, . . . that is a moral of method which one may not shirk today. . . .

Suppose, finally, we succeeded in explaining our entire instinctive life as the development and ramification of *one* basic form of the will—namely, of the will to power, as *my* proposition has it . . .—then one would have gained the right to determine *all* efficient force univocally as—*will to power*. The world . . . defined and determined according to its "intelligible character"—it would be "will to power" and nothing else (Nietzsche (7), *BGE*, 36; cf. also 13).

There are many weak spots in this outline argument, as Nietzsche is well aware, which elsewhere he seeks to rectify; for example, the whole notion of "causality" is for him exceedingly problematic (both Hume and Kant are mentioned in this connection; *Gay Science*, 357; see also *Twilight*, vi), as is that of the "will" itself (see *BGE*, 19 and *Gay Science*, 127). But several of the weaknesses derive from the problem of summarizing intelligibly a radically subversive line of thought while using traditional language with its associated concepts. The obscurities surrounding the notion of "Will to Power" itself partly arise from such difficulties. If the "intelligible character" of the world is such that there is "no limit to the ways in which the world can be interpreted", if the introduction of truth here is "a *processus in infinitum*", and if it is the grammatical constraint exerted by our language which "forces us to posit unity, identity, permanence, substance, cause, thinghood, being" (Nietzsche (6), *Twilight*, iii. 5) though other languages might impose different constraints, then any attempt to characterize that which is constituted by "the various ways in which it admits of being encountered" (any other elements are, by definition, not intelligible) will be radically problematic. In describing it as "a monster of energy, . . . a play of forces and waves of forces, at the same time one and many, . . . eternally changing, . . . out of the play of contradictions back to the joy of concord" (Nietzsche (8), *Will to Power*, 1067), Nietzsche is obviously attempting to exclude those categories which are projections of the "metaphysics of language", but in doing so is forced to use others which need to be carefully qualified if they are not also to provoke the reaction "Words lie in our way!" (Nietzsche (4), *Daybreak*, 47). The terms and qualifications preferred are designed to point to the radical openness required by his accounts of language and truth, to the extent that even a sympathetic commentator is led to complain that Nietzsche's account "seems to possess no specific meaning of the kind obviously intended" (Hollingdale (3), 137).

The objection is exaggerated (see, for example, Schacht (1), ch. 4) but points to a danger of which Nietzsche had long been aware;

his early essay is concerned with the way that someone beginning to grasp the true context and nature of his life either "grows dumb, or else he speaks only in forbidden metaphors and in unheard-of combinations of concepts, . . . shattering and mocking the old conceptual barriers" (Nietzsche (2), 'On Truth and Lies', p. 90), an activity described as "creative" and associated with the "artist". In the later writings this creative artist is subsumed under the figure of the "new philosopher". To a very considerable degree "the spirit's power to appropriate the foreign stands revealed in its inclination to assimilate the new to the old, to simplify the manifold, and to overlook or repulse whatever is totally contradictory— . . . to file new things in old files" (Nietzsche (7), *BGE*, 230); this is the typical, and wholly necessary, activity of the "philosophical labourers" who "determine and press into formulas . . . data . . . which have become dominant and are for a time called 'truths'. It is for these investigators to make everything that has happened and been esteemed so far . . . intelligible and manageable, . . . to *overcome* the entire past" (ibid. 211). But the "old files", the "old conceptual barriers" ultimately need to be transcended, "manageability" is not the ultimate criterion of truth; new perspectives need to be created and, indeed, insisted on:

Genuine philosophers, however, are commanders and legislators: they . . . have at their disposal the preliminary labour of all philosophical labourers, all who have overcome the past. With a creative hand they reach for the future, and all that is and has been becomes a means for them, an instrument, a hammer. Their "knowing" is *creating* (ibid).

If "the nature of something is a function of the various ways in which it admits of being encountered", then to create new concepts, new perspectives, new ways of encountering the world is not merely to create new possibilities of knowledge, but "it is enough to create new names and estimations and probabilities in order to create in the long run new 'things'" (Nietzsche (5), *Gay Science*, 58).

It is important to note that such creativity is only a way to truth when subject to strict constraints; a "genuine philosopher" must himself serve his apprenticeship as a "philosophical labourer" as well as, among other things, "poet" and "moralist" (Nietzsche (7), *BGE*, 230); the 'seeker after knowledge . . . insists on profundity, multiplicity, and thoroughness, with a *will* which is a kind of cruelty of the intellectual conscience and taste. Every courageous thinker

. . . is used to severe discipline' (ibid. 230). The philosophers of the future, whom Nietzsche attempts to some extent to emulate (but among whom he does not count himself (*BGE* 44)), will make full use of all the strengths now integrated into "scientific thinking; . . . for example, that of the impulse to doubt, to negate, to wait, to collect, to dissolve". But they will need to go further, and marry the artist of the early essay with the scientist and scholar in a creativity that is also objectivity and knowledge;

Even now the time seems remote when artistic energies and the practical wisdom of life will join with scientific thinking to form a higher organic system in relation to which scholars, physicians, artists, and legislators—as we know them at present—would have to look like paltry relics of ancient times (Nietzsche (5), *Gay Science*, 113).

This image of the man who has so overcome in himself the "all too human" that he represents what may be called "a higher organic system" appears frequently in the later writings; the image helps to illuminate Zarathustra's dictum, "The *Übermensch* is the meaning of the earth" (Nietzsche (6), *Zarathustra*, 'Prologue', 3). "The ultimate question about the conditions of life", Nietzsche suggests, is "To what extent can truth endure incorporation?" (Kaufmann (3), 110). For the "all-too-human" even the recognition of the perspectival nature of "man's truths" may be too much, for "Truth is the kind of error without which a certain species of life could not live" (Nietzsche (8), *Will to Power*, 493); thus, "Perhaps truth is a woman who has reasons for not letting us see her reasons?" (Nietzsche (5). *Gay Science*, 'Preface', 4). But there are truths beyond "man's truths", and here the issue is "How much truth does a spirit *endure*, how much truth does it *dare*? (Nietzsche (7), *Ecce Homo*, 'Preface', 3) As Zarathustra puts it: 'Brave, unconcerned, mocking, violent—thus wisdom wants us: she is a woman and always loves only a warrior' (Nietzsche (6), *Zarathustra*, I vii).

2. *Twilight of the Idols* and Finesse

But in Nietzsche's most subtle work the rhetoric of warfare is balanced by a quieter, oddly familiar note. Behind all the assessments of perspectives, as we have seen, lies Nietzsche's recurrent query whether they—and the individuals most representative of them—display "the ascending or the descending line of life". On the face of it this would appear to require a (challengeable) judgement about the value of life, and at a certain stage we find an incautious formulation to this effect: 'a philosopher . . . demands of himself, a judgment, a Yes or No, . . . about life and the value of life' (Nietzsche (7), *BGE*, 205). But by the time of *Twilight of the Idols* he sees that the issue of the status of the underlying principle which guides the search for truth is more complex: 'One must by all means stretch out one's fingers and make the attempt to grasp this amazing finesse, *that the value of life cannot be estimated*' (Nietzsche (6), *Twilight*, ii. 2). At last the turth is out. To the question "Supposing truth is a woman—what then?" one important answer is "She needs to be wooed with *finesse*."

Despite Nietzsche's love–hate relationship with Pascal it is unlikely that he had the latter's usage specifically in mind in using this term, but it is nevertheless highly appropriate. The principles of *les esprits fins*, it will be recalled, are such that

it is with endless difficulty that they can be communicated. . . . These things are so delicate and numerous that it takes a sense of great delicacy and precision to feel and judge correctly and accurately . . . most often it is not possible to set it out in orderly fashion as in *géométrie* (Pascal, *Pensées*, L.512, B.1, S.670).

The need for "delicacy" in the wooing of truth is insisted on by Nietzsche when he speaks of 'that filigree art of grasping and comprehending in general, those fingers for *nuances*' (Nietzsche (7), *Ecce Homo*, i. 1); indeed he goes so far, in self-mocking vein, as to remark 'alas, I am a *nuance*' (ibid. 'The Case of Wagner', 4). *Géométrie* is above all the province of the "philosophical labourer", which the "genuine philosopher"—like Pascal himself—seeks to transcend, and Nietzsche is as conscious as his predecessor of the difficulty of "setting it out in orderly fashion" when *géométrie* provides the paradigm of order. Pascal's sense of the need to integrate "numerous" diverse elements that themselves need to be subjected to critical scrutiny is fully shared by his opponent, and even the requirement that for *finesse* "The thing must be seen all at once, at a glance . . . at least up to a point" (*Pensées*, L.512, B.1, S.670) is to a certain extent matched by Nietzsche's invocation of the "exuberant spirituality that runs *presto*" (Nietzsche (7), *BGE*, 213). All these elements are on exemplary display in *Twilight of the Idols*.

In letters Nietzsche describes this book as "my philosophy in a nutshell" and "a very stringent and subtle expression of my whole *philosophical heterodoxy*—hidden behind much gracefulness and mischief" (Nietzsche (9), Letters 181 and 177', 20 Oct. and 14 Sept. 1888). It spans, indeed, the positive and negative poles of Nietzsche's thinking. The commentary on his works in *Ecce Homo* contrasts the "Yes-saying" of *Thus Spoke Zarathustra* with the "No-saying" of *Beyond Good and Evil*, the latter being seen as a "recuperation" from the writing of *Zarathustra* but also as the setting in hand of "the revaluation of our values so far, the great war" (Nietzsche (7), *Ecce Homo*, 'Beyond Good and Evil', 1–2). The 'Preface' of *Twilight* represents that work in two lights; on the one hand it is itself a "convalescence" from this latter task, a "run into the sun" from its "shadows" and "all-too-heavy seriousness", a "recreation"; on the other hand it is "a great declaration of war" on both "idols of the age" and "eternal idols", the very "No-saying" task of revaluing values. The paradox is resolved by the suggestion that the very wounds of warfare can themselves provide re-creation, "*Increscunt animi, virescit volnere virtus*"; it is a thought familiar elsewhere in Nietzsche—"we philosophers" are "constantly trans-forming all that we are into light and flame—also everything that wounds us" (Nietzsche (5), *Gay Science*, 'Preface', 3), and to his own sickness he owes "a *higher* health—one which is made stronger by whatever does not kill it. *I also owe my philosophy to it*" (Nietzsche (6), *Nietzsche contra Wagner*, 'Epilogue', 1). The balance aimed at is set out in the opening words of the Preface: "Maintaining cheerfulness in the midst of a gloomy affair", and he is self-conscious about it in the body of the work; on the one hand "My taste, which may be the opposite of a tolerant taste, is . . . far from saying Yes indiscriminately: it does not like to say Yes; rather even No; but best of all, nothing" (Nietzsche (6), *Twilight*, x. 1); but on the other "My style, which is *affirmative* and deals with contradic-tion . . . and criticism only as a means, only involuntarily" (ibid, viii, 6). The contrast between "taste" and "style" here is suggestive, pointing to a rather subtle integration of the "Yes" and the "No". Immediately after the remark about his affirmative style Nietzsche insists on the importance of an element in *finesse* that Pascal had also advocated: 'Learning to *see*—accustoming the eye to calmness, to patience, to letting things come up to it; postponing judgment, learning to go around and grasp each individual case from all sides.

That is the *first* preliminary schooling for spirituality.' One is reminded of that divine pied piper "who silences all that is loud and self-satisfied, teaching it to listen . . . who teaches the doltish and rash hand to hesitate and reach out more delicately" (Nietzsche (7), *BGE*, 295), and that in the Preface to *Twilight* Nietzsche describes himself as "an old psychologist and pied piper". It would be rash indeed after these warnings blankly to overlook the difference between "style" and "taste", assume the incompatibility of a preference for the "affirmative" style with a taste which "does not like to say Yes", and conclude that there is simple incoherence here—that the claims for a positive as well as negative role for "philosophizing with a hammer" represent a mere sham.

It is worth elaborating on this point, both to gain a clearer insight into Nietzsche's "whole philosophical heterodoxy" and because *Twilight* has often been so badly read. Reading the final works, it has been suggested, is like "watching the work of some engine of war which is no longer governed by the hand of man. . . . His lucidity is extreme, but disastrous, since it exercises itself only to destroy" (Halévy, cited approvingly by Lea, 316); the claims to affirmation in this context are "almost laughable"—the "mere juxtaposition" of the two passages juxtaposed above is supposed to "tell a tale" of insincerity—and far removed from the "Yes-saying" of *Thus Spoke Zarathustra* a few years before.

Create, and destruction will take care of itself: that is the gospel of *Zarathustra*. Destroy, and creation will take care of itself: that is the gospel of *The Twilight of the Idols*. . . .

The cruelty of Nietzsche's final period is sublimated sadism—and not always sublimated. The Dionysus of *The Twilight of the Idols* is the deity of the Babylonian Sacaea (Lea, 317–20).

But this is to misread both *Zarathustra* and *Twilight*, casting the author of the former as a "seer" and of the latter as—on the most charitable interpretation—a participant in the "pandemonium of all free spirits" (Nietzsche (6), *Twilight*, iv. 6). As we have seen, while the "genuine philosopher" may indeed have "once stood on all these steps" which include those of "seer and 'free spirit' and almost everything", nevertheless "all these are merely preconditions of his task" (*BGE*, 211). Both *Zarathustra* and *Twilight* attempt in this sense to be "genuine".

In the last work he wrote, Nietzsche presents "the concept of Dionysus himself" in terms of Zarathustra rather than any Baby-

Ionian figure; a way to understanding it, he suggests, is given by considering "the psychological problem in the type of Zarathustra": 'how he that says No and *does* No to an unheard-of degree, to everything to which one has so far said Yes, can nevertheless be the opposite of a No-saying spirit' (Nietzsche (7), *Ecce Homo*, 'Thus Spoke Zarathustra', 6). This notion of integrated duality is spelled out in Zarathustra's own teaching: 'Whoever must be a creator in good and evil, verily, he must first be an annihilator and break values. Thus the highest evil belongs to the highest goodness: but this is creative' (Nietzsche (6), *Zarathustra*, ii. 12). Held together in Zarathustra, the two elements fall apart in those respective parodies of Zarathustra and Dionysus—the ape and the ass. Zarathustra's ape "had gathered something of his phrasing and cadences and also liked to borrow from the treasures of his wisdom" but is purely destructive, is filled with the spirit of *ressentiment*, speaks of "the slaughterhouses and ovens of the spirit", and indeed displays barely sublimated sadism; Zarathustra silences him: ' "Out of love alone shall my despising and my warning bird fly up, not out of the swamp. . . . With your grunting you spoil for me my praise of folly. . . . Where one can no longer love, there one should *pass by*" ' (ibid. iii. 7). Long before, it will be recalled, the thinker had been said to require "justice and love for all that exists" (*Daybreak*, 43), and "slander . . . against life" is still denounced in *Twilight* (Nietzsche (6), iii, 6). The ass, on the other hand, accepts everything uncritically, and whatever burdens it is given brays 'Yea-Yuh'; the "litany of the ass" puts it like this: 'What hidden wisdom it is that he has long ears and only says Yea and never No! Has he not created the world in his own image, namely, as stupid as possible?' (Nietzsche (6), *Zarathustra*, iv. 17) As Professor Deleuze argues,

The yes which does not know how to say no (the yes of the ass) is a caricature of affirmation. This is precisely because it says yes to everything which is no, because it puts up with nihilism it continues to serve the power of denying—which is like a demon whose every burden it carries. The Dionysian yes, on the contrary, knows how to say no: it is pure affirmation, it has conquered nihilism and divested negation of all autonomous power. But it has done this because it has placed the negative at the service of the powers of affirming. To affirm is to create, not to bear, put up with or accept (Deleuze, 185–6).

In terms of the first part of this chapter, the ass accepts "man's truths" at face value, unprepared also to recognize them as "errors", and hence is debarred from that creativity of the "new philosophers" which alone will earn the love of wisdom. To distinguish an unproblematically affirmative *Zarathustra* from a merely negative *Twilight* in the manner suggested is to read the one as the ass and the other as the ape—and neglect altogether the need to "place the negative at the service of the powers of affirming", the need to join the critical element of "dialectical severity" with "exuberant spirituality" for a "genuinely philosophical combination" (Nietzsche (7), *BGE*, 213). The "taste" of *Twilight* is severe to the extent that it is "far from saying Yes indiscriminately" like the ass; it is in this sense that it "may be the opposite of a tolerant taste" and "does not like to say Yes; rather even No; but best of all, nothing". Note the concluding phrase, reminiscent of "Where one can no longer love, there one should pass by"; the passage in *Twilight* continues: "That applies to whole cultures", the context is "What I owe to the Ancients", and the implication is that one needs to discriminate much more than is customary: 'At bottom it is a very small number of ancient books that counts in my life; the most famous are not among them. . . . To the Greeks I do not by any means owe . . . strong impressions . . . their manner is too foreign' (Nietzsche (6). *Twilight*, x. 1–2); where this is so one cannot love—"one should pass by".

But all this severity is in the service of discriminating positively, of "a very serious ambition for a *Roman* style, for the *aere perennius* in style" (ibid.), the zenith of affirmation, "to create things on which time tests its teeth in vain" (ibid. ix. 51). And when it is neither "taste" nor "style" that is in question, but he himself as an integration of all his perspectives Nietzsche has no doubt where he stands: 'We immoralists have . . . made room in our hearts for every kind of understanding, comprehending, and *approving*. We do not easily negate; we make it a point of honour to be *affirmers*' (ibid. v. 6). Professor Deleuze is again to the point;

To be confused with his ape; this is what Zarathustra feels as one of the frightful temptations held out to him. . . . Critique is not a re-action of *re-sentiment* but the active expression of an active mode of existence; attack and not revenge. . . . This way of being is that of the philosopher precisely because he intends to wield the differential element as critic and creator and therefore as a hammer (Deleuze, 3).

The "hammer", indeed, is the symbol for the union of critic and creator, and its transformation governs the shape of *Twilight*. The

work is subtitled 'How One Philosophizes with a Hammer' and in
the Preface the critical aspect of the image is brought out—together
with the need for delicacy, even *finesse*. One way of seeing his
"essay", Nietzsche suggests, is in terms of the activity of "sounding
out idols";

> There are more idols than realities in the world: that is *my* "evil eye" for this
> world; that is also my "evil *ear*". For once to pose questions here with a
> *hammer*, and, perhaps, to hear as a reply that famous hollow sound which
> speaks of bloated entrails—what a delight for one who has ears even behind
> his ears, for me, an old psychologist and pied piper before whom just that
> which would remain silent must become outspoken. . . .
>   Regarding the sounding out of idols, this time they are not just idols of
> the age, but eternal idols, which are here touched with a hammer as with a
> tuning fork.

The very phrase that celebrates *finesse* itself exemplifies it; "ears
even behind his ears" characteristically presents a concrete image to
focus an elusive phenomenon, breaks with the metaphors traditionally drawn from the language of vision for this purpose (which
have "become worn out and . . . drained of sensuous force") by
using that of sound, delicately echoes the Biblical "he that hath ears
to hear . . ." (for Nietzsche the author of that phrase was also a
"symbolist", "disposing of . . . the Judaism of the concepts" (Nietzsche (6), *Antichrist*, 33–4)), and invokes the down-to-earth craft of
bell-tuning to remind one that discrimination is possible between
sound and unsound even in elusive matters without invoking any
other world beside the apparent one—'the reasons for which "this"
world has been characterised as "apparent" are the very reasons
which indicate its reality' (Nietzsche (6), *Twilight*, iii. 6). Similarly,
the initially curious diagnosis of unsoundness—"that famous hollow sound which speaks of bloated entrails"—operates on several
levels. In the first place, by yoking a physiological image incon-
gruously with a campanological one an attempt is made to prevent
the mind from settling too easily into any over-simple perspective
for conceiving the matter (compare balancing "truth is a woman"
with "life is a woman"), and to render it open-minded and curious
about what may be envisaged here. In the second, we are provided
with a framework for interpreting the body of the text, whereby the
way that the "emptiest" concepts are shown "reverence" (ibid. iii.
4) is argued to arise out of the overwhelming *ressentiment*, "instinct
of slander", of the "sick" deriving from the "decline of life" (ibid.

iii. 4, 6) ("hollow", "idols", "bloated entrails"), thus lending point
to the various psychological and even physiological diagnoses of the
"old psychologist" of the Preface, who is there yoked with the "pied
piper"—thus retaining the balance between medical and musical
associations.

But for a psychologist diagnosis should lead on to treatment. The
Socratic pied piper of old had "seemed to be a physician", but the
remedy he offered—"rationality at any price . . . in opposition to
the instincts"—proved to be only "another expression of decadence. . . . To *have* to fight the instincts—that is the formula of
decadence" (ibid. ii. 11). The figure of the divine pied piper in
Beyond Good and Evil owes much to the figure of Socrates (295; see
Kaufmann's note) but goes beyond it, transforming the "instincts"
rather than fighting them. He not only teaches "rough souls" to
"listen" (to, as it were, grow "ears behind the ears", so necessary
for critical discrimination), but also "lets them taste a new desire";
he

> guesses the concealed and forgotten treasure . . . and is a divining rod for
> every grain of gold that has long lain buried in the dungeon of much mud
> and sand; the genius of the heart from whose touch everyone walks away
> richer . . . in himself, newer to himself than before, broken open, blown at
> and sounded out by a thawing wind . . . full of hopes that as yet have no
> name, full of new will and currents.

Nietzsche thought this passage sufficiently significant to quote it in
its entirety—"to give an idea of me as a psychologist"—as the
lead-in to the review in *Ecce Homo* of his entire published corpus
(Nietzsche (7), *Ecce Homo*, iii. 6). In its original context in *Beyond
Good and Evil* he goes on to identify the figure as "the god
Dionysus", that great ambiguous one and tempter (*Versucher*)
god", and himself as "the last disciple and initiate of the god
Dionysus". The tone immediately changes to the sardonic as he
addresses himself to the imaginatively flat-footed who complain
that they—with, of course, Nietzsche himself—"no longer like to
believe in God and gods" (it is worth recalling the "contempt" he
expressed for those who originally read Jesus' "symbols" as "dogma" (*Antichrist*, 34–8)); 'even that Dionysus is a philosopher, and
that gods, too, thus do philosophy, seems to me to be a novelty that
is far from innocuous and might arouse suspicion precisely among
philosophers'. But in *Twilight* he is addressing himself to those who

are prepared to attempt to listen "with ears even behind their ears", thus it is not surprising to find Dionysus first invoked with increasingly complex layers of association and significance (Nietzsche (6), *Twilight*, iii. 6; ix. 19 and 49), and his "symbolism" then expounded" (x. 4). Finally—as the concluding affirmation reaches its climax—the pied piper of the Preface displays his colours: 'I, the last disciple of the philosopher Dionysus—I, the teacher of the eternal recurrence' (x. 5); and at this, "The Hammer Speaks".

Up until now it has been Zarathustra who has been "the teacher of the eternal recurrence" (Nietzsche (6), *Zarathustra*, III. xiii. 2), thus it is entirely in keeping that the final section of *Twilight*—which is represented as the voice of the hammer—turns out to be a substantial quotation, slightly modified, from *Thus Spoke Zarathustra*. After revealing the hollowness of so many idols, at last the sounding hammer rings true as it strikes against the doctrine of Dionysus, the teaching of Zarathustra with his "new tablets" (ibid.), so that the "nutshell" of *Twilight* is "broken open . . . full of new will and currents", and the anonymously archaic wisdom of the Preface—"*Increscunt animi, virescit volnere virtus*"—which has governed the balance of the entire work, revealed as the Dionysian touchstone itself: 'If your hardness does not wish to flash and cut and cut to pieces (*zerschneiden*), how can you one day create with me?' (Nietzsche (6), *Twilight*, xi).

3. The Dionysian "Hammer"

> If you want a quick idea how before me everything stood on its head, begin with this essay. What is called *idol* on the title page is simply what has been called truth so far. *Twilight of the Idols*—that is: the old truth is approaching its end.
>
> (Nietzsche (7), *Ecce Homo*, 'Twilight of the Idols', 1)

But if we are invited to start with *Twilight*, the text itself prevents us having any excuse for stopping there. By closing with a clearly identified but obscure oracle of *Zarathustra* we are pointed to that work, and the mysterious mention for the first time of "eternal recurrence" as the key to the hammer's ringing true leads in the same direction and beyond—to, indeed, the whole corpus. Of an earlier work Nietzsche had written,

If this book is incomprehensible to anyone and jars on his ears, the fault, it seems to me, is not necessarily mine. It is clear enough, assuming, as I do assume, that one has first read my earlier writings and has not spared some trouble in doing so: for they are, indeed, not easy to penetrate (Nietzsche (7), *Genealogy of Morals*, 'Preface', 8).

The enticing stylistic brilliance of *Twilight*, with its apparent air of clarity, which makes it so suitable an entry point into Nietzsche's work, masks a level of depth and complexity unequalled in the *Genealogy*; the earlier work well represents "dialectical severity" but *Twilight* joins to that severity an "exuberant spirituality that runs *presto*"—it is much more fully a work of *finesse*, with multiple interconnections and subtleties that are only discernible by those who take Nietzsche's advice for reading the *Genealogy* more generally to heart. Increasingly in the later years we are urged "to read *well*, that is to say, to read slowly, deeply, looking cautiously before and aft, with reservations, with doors left open, with delicate eyes and fingers" (Nietzsche (4), *Daybreak*, '1886 Preface', 5; see also *Ecce Homo*, iii. 5); without such cooperation one can hardly hope to be "broken open . . . sounded out by a thawing wind" and so enabled to "taste a new desire" and transform the instincts instead of fighting them. For Nietzsche, as for Plato, Job, Pascal, and even Hume, philosophy (love of wisdom) and psychology ultimately run into each other—new ways of seeing are associated with a change of heart.

"Broken open"/"new desire", "cut to pieces"/"create"; the transformations are, of course, Dionysian:

Dionysus versus the "Crucified": there you have the antithesis. It is *not* a difference in regard to their martyrdom—it is a difference in the meaning of it. . . . The god on the cross is a curse on life, a signpost to seek redemption from life; Dionysus cut to pieces [*in Stücke geschnittne*] is a *promise* of life: it will be eternally reborn and return again from destruction (Nietzsche (8), *Will to Power*, 1052).

As usual the antithesis is tendentious; to such a declaration there is an obvious counter, perhaps no more tendentious than Nietzsche's: "There was a difference between self-sacrificed and un-self-sacrificed Deity; between the God who died of His own will for the salvation of men and the God who died at others' will for the reproductiveness of vegetables" (Williams (3), 87).

But for Nietzsche the application of the notion of "self-sacrifice" to the "Crucified" was a "barbarous" misunderstanding—"What gruesome paganism!" (Nietzsche (6), *Antichrist*, 41)— thus he felt free to have Dionysus teaching the doctrine of transformation through suffering.

At a human level health can only be made "higher" by that which "does not kill" (Nietzsche (6), *Nietzsche contra Wagner*, 'Epilogue', 1), but at the level of general principle at which Dionysus operates (the self-overcoming of all will to power—"my *Dionysian* world of the eternally self-creating, the eternally self-destroying" (Nietzsche (8), *Will to Power*, 1067)) no such qualifications are needed, and the metaphors encountered earlier can be given free play. Thus in commenting on his own "Dionysian dowry" Nietzsche comments: 'the perfect woman tears to pieces [*zerreisst*] when she loves.—I know these charming maenads' (Nietzsche (7), *Ecce Homo*, iii. 5). This dictum operates at a number of levels; these include, no doubt, the anti-feminist but it is more relevant to notice that he purports to be speaking about the "eternally feminine" (an allusion to the penultimate line of Goethe's *Faust* where the notion is elevated to the level of principle and frequently mocked by Nietzsche; e.g. *BGE*, 232), and that at least one "perfect woman" we have encountered, wisdom, "loves only a warrior". It is thus by no means far-fetched to read this passage in the light of Nietzsche's perspectivist insistence on "more eyes, different eyes" in the service of "objectivity" and a "truth" whose introduction is "a *processus in infinitum*" attempting to do "justice" to the world when there is "no limit to the ways in which the world can be interpreted":

By affirming the perspectivism of knowledge, Nietzsche in fact defends an ontological *pluralism*: the essence of Being is to show itself, and to show itself according to an *infinity of viewpoints*. Our experience reveals a Being that, in the mask of Dionysus, is "torn to pieces in the infinite dispersion of the universe" (Granier, 191).

As Nietzsche himself says, writing of "the all, the unity . . . something unconditioned"—the world conceived non-perspectivally in fact, thus tempting us into "baptizing it 'God'"—"One must shatter the all" (Nietzsche (8), *Will to Power*, 331). We may, then, bring together 'How much truth does a spirit *endure*, how much truth does it *dare*?' (Nietzsche (7), *Ecce Homo*, 'Preface', 3) with 'If your hardness does not wish to flash and cut and cut to pieces, how can you one day create with me? For all creators

are hard . . . This new tablet, O my brothers, I place over you:
become hard!' (Nietzsche (6), *Twilight*, xi, including final line of
work).

Further light is thrown on this conclusion by the very title of the
work as glossed by Nietzsche: "*Twilight of the Idols*—that is: the old
truth is approaching its end", "*idol* is simply what has been called
truth so far"—what we have here are "man's truths" misconstrued
non-perspectivally and used to project a "true" world by which to
measure this one.

There are altogether no older, no more convinced, no more puffed-up
idols—and none more hollow. That does not prevent them from being
those in which people have the most faith; nor does one ever say "idol",
especially not in the most distinguished instance (Nietzsche (6), *Twilight*,
close of 'Preface').

At the most obvious level one is reminded that in an earlier work
"God himself" has been thought "to be our most enduring lie"
(Nietzsche (5), *Gay Science*, 344), and this simple identification of
"the most distinguished instance" is soon supported by the text as
we hear of "the 'thing-in-itself', the *horrendum pudendum* of
the metaphysicians! The error of the spirit as cause mistaken for
reality! And made the very measure of reality! And called God!"
(Nietzsche (6), *Twilight*, vi. 3). A little earlier we similarly hear of
an "idiosyncrasy of the philosophers" which

consists in confusing the last and the first. They place that which comes at
the end—unfortunately! for it ought not to come at all!—namely, the
"highest concepts", which means the most general, the emptiest concepts,
the last smoke of evaporating reality, in the beginning, *as* the beginning. . . . Thus they arrive at their stupendous concept, "God". That
which is last, thinnest, and emptiest is put first, as *the* cause, as *ens
realissimum*. Why did mankind have to take seriously the brain afflictions
of sick web-spinners? They have paid dearly for it! (ibid. iii. 4)

All of which fits in with Nietzsche's later comment about the work
that it shows "how before me everything stood on its head"; the
traditional opposition between *ordo essendi* and *ordo cognoscendi*
is to be abolished, and the latter, perspectivally *nuanced*, used as the
measure of the former.

But this *nuance* introduces its own complexities, for "everything"
includes the very notions of truth and cognition themselves. To
think non-perspectivally, to conceive of *Wissenschaft* "without any

presuppositions", is not merely to invert the proper ordering of "truths" but is "paralogical" in a much more fundamental way —and lest the point be overlooked Nietzsche invokes his running metaphor; he who would think thus, "first needs to stand not only philosophy but truth itself *on its head*—the grossest violation of decency possible in relation to two such venerable females!" (Nietzsche (7), *Genealogy of Morals*, iii. 24). Such an inversion took place, he goes on, "because truth was posited as being, as God, as the highest court of appeal" (the *ordo essendi* given rights over the *ordo cognoscendi*), and in support he invokes that very passage in which "God himself" had been tentatively presented as "our most enduring lie". This latter passage had, in fact, associated the "lie" of "God" with that of "truth" in a passage of complex self-reflexivity:

Even we seekers after knowledge today, we godless anti-metaphysicians still take our fire, too, from the flame lit by a faith that is thousands of years old, that Christian faith that was also the faith of Plato, that God is the truth, that truth is divine.—But what if . . . God himself should prove to be our most enduring lie?—(Nietzsche (5), *Gay Science*, v. 344)

If so, of course, the very notions of truth and knowledge must be rethought, and hence even that philosophical activity that rethinks them. Such considerations lie behind the teasing opening to Part I of *Beyond Good and Evil* which puts in question both "the will to truth" and "the value of truth" and declares: "The falseness of a judgment is for us not necessarily an objection to a judgment; in this respect our new language may sound strangest" (Nietzsche (7), I and 4); yet which nevertheless permits the very next part to declare the anticipated "new philosophers" "new friends of 'truth'" (ibid. 42–4 (concluding sections of 2); the subtitle to the whole work is *Prelude to a Philosophy of the Future*). The warning quotation marks round 'truth' remind us that we are here encountering a "new language" and that the pied piper of the final part seeks to evoke "new will" ('The will to truth' is the opening phrase of Part I) and "hopes that as yet have no name" (ibid. 295). For those who find such paradoxes of the *presto* spirit "not easy to penetrate" the *Genealogy of Morals* (written to "Supplement and Clarify" the earlier work) spells out the required perspectival notion of objectivity more sedately (iii. 12), and the first part of this chapter has ventured to set out some of the epistemological ramifications of this rethinking in a manner suited to one of "the world's common run of philosophers, the moralists and other hollow pots, cabbage heads" (Nietzsche (7), *Ecce Homo*, iii. 5).

If we return to *Twilight of the Idols* with such considerations in mind a deeper layer of significance opens up. The Preface tells us that the idols "here touched with a hammer as with a tuning fork" are "not just idols of the age, but eternal idols". On one projection, we have seen, their "most distinguished instance" is God—who is conceived of *as* eternal but belief in whom is alleged to have "become unbelievable" and so, in an extended sense, "is dead" (Nietzsche (5), *Gay Science*, 343). But if the "old truth" which is "approaching its end" posits truth itself "as God" and maintains that "God is the truth" we have an identity set up which sponsors the projection of "the most distinguished instance" as embodying epistemological structures which partake of eternity in another and more profound sense.

It is at this level that we encounter that "very stringent . . . expression of my whole *philosophical heterodoxy*—hidden behind much gracefulness and mischief" on which Nietzsche commented to Paul Deussen. In the section entitled '"Reason" in Philosophy' (note the quotation marks) he invokes the most elemental form of idol worship: 'We enter a realm of crude fetishism when we summon before consciousness the basic presuppositions of the metaphysics of language, in plain talk, the presuppositions of reason' (Nietzsche (6), *Twilight*, iii. 5). And then, invoking the metaphor of femininity in terms of which he has been accustomed to structure his many-layered account of truth, '"Reason" in language—oh, what an old deceptive female she is! I am afraid we are not rid of God because we still have faith in grammar' (ibid.). This is a faith that can only be exploded from the inside. "Our language . . . is the constant advocate of error" (ibid.), yet we cannot do without it; some language, with its associated grammar, will always be necessary to sound out and reject grammar; even the nihilist's "faith 'All is false'" is seen by Nietzsche to be "fanatical" (Nietzsche (8), *Will to Power*, 1) and hence itself laying claim to unconditional truth. Here we encounter a sense of "eternal" that is indeed ominous, supporting Nietzsche's final summary of the whole work—typically balanced between positive and negative poles: 'This essay of less than 150 pages, cheerful and ominous in tone, a demon that laughs' (Nietzsche (7), *Ecce Homo*, 'Twilight of the Idols', 1).

The demon's laughter rings through the title, mocking Wagner's

Twilight of the Gods, but as usual in Nietzsche the parody has a serious point. In Wagner the era of the gods gives way to that of man; for Nietzsche Wagner's own gods, including the God of *Parsifal*, are but idols, and as they approach their end we approach a new form of understanding that is man-centred in a more stringent sense than Wagner had ever envisaged, that of "Zarathustra the godless" (Nietzsche (7), *Genealogy*, ii. 25). Not only is there no God, but not even truth is "divine" in the sense of "unconditioned"; the world's "intelligible character" is constituted by its perspectival nature, and so far as we interpreters and language users are concerned all truth and grammar is only recognizable and service-able within a humanly available perspective. Recognizing this, we can attempt to fight against "the constant advocate of error", with its tendency to misconstrue "man's truths" as absolute and hence tempt us to faith in *an* "absolute", balance perspective against perspective (even one grammatical structure against another), and try to see with "*more* eyes, different eyes" in pursuit of the "more complete"—that essentially incompletable but nevertheless significant image of "objectivity"—until it would take "a higher organic system" to avoid being "torn to pieces in the infinite dispersion of the universe".

This Antichrist and antinihilist; this victor over God and nothingness—*he must come one day.*—
But what am I saying? Enough! Enough! At this point it behooves me only to be silent; or I shall usurp that to which only one younger, "heavier with future", and stronger than I has a right—that to which *Zarathustra* has a right, *Zarathustra the godless.*—(Nietzsche (7), *Genealogy*, ii. 24–5)

Perhaps the "philosophers of the future" will be able to employ a language sufficiently subtle, rich, and many-sided for it no longer to be "the constant advocate of error", but Nietzsche must make do with those of "the Indo-Germanic peoples" with their underlying "grammatical functions" (Nietzsche (7), *BGE*, 20) and create a fifth column from within, creatively unmaking and recreating their structures of communication to undermine their constant biases so that an understanding bounded by the perspectives of these lan-guages may be "broken open" and aspirations pointed to "that as yet have no name"—though once glimpsed they may be given suitable designations.

The "name" which marks the climax towards which the whole of

Twilight moves is, of course, "eternal recurrence". As in almost all the published work this notion is not presented primarily as cosmological doctrine—the animals in *Zarathustra* so interpret it and are rebuked as "buffoons and barrel organs" for their "hurdy-gurdy song" (Nietzsche (6), *Zarathustra*, III. xiii. 2)—but as the crucial test of a genuinely life-affirming perspective.[6] "The idea of the eternal recurrence, this highest formula of affirmation that is at all attainable", writes Nietzsche, is "the fundamental conception" of *Zarathustra* (Nietzsche (7), *Ecce Homo*, 'Thus Spoke Zarathustra', 1), and in this work Zarathustra's supreme thought is overcoming his nausea at the thought of "the eternal recurrence even of the smallest", the most contemptible (Nietzsche (6), *Zarathustra*, III. xiii. 2). The issue there is not the truth of the doctrine, conceived cosmologically, but Zarathustra's ability to accept the thought that the contemptible and the noble are all part of the web of life, that without "the small man" no *Übermensch* is possible, and yet still be "Yes-saying". The idea is first introduced into Nietzsche's work hypothetically, by a "demon" with suspicious similarities to the one that laughs of *Twilight*:

What if some day or night a demon were to steal after you into your loneliest loneliness and say to you: "This life as you now live it and have lived it, you will have to live once more and innumerable times more; and there will be nothing new in it! . . ."

[6] Notoriously, Nietzsche explores the "hurdy-gurdy song" of the animals in the notes collected in *The Will to Power* (especially 1053–67) and other unpublished fragments, but the context and purpose of these disjoined remarks are entirely uncertain. Professor Deleuze has suggested that the main fragments "are 'apologetic' in a sense close to that sometimes given to Pascal's wager. It is a case of taking mechanism at its word, of showing that mechanism arrives at a conclusion which 'is not necessarily mechanistic'; . . . they are 'polemical' in an aggressive way, it is a question of defeating the *bad player* on his own ground" (Deleuze, 202, n. 23). This may be so, but the incautious formulation of *Ecce Homo* ('Birth of Tragedy', 3) casts some doubt on this proposal, and Nietzsche may well merely have been "making the experiment of turning his demon's story into an hypothesis, and considering how an attempt to prove it might go and what would have to be the case for it to be true" (Schacht (1), 266).
The arguments in the notes for the cosmological hypothesis are unsatisfactory, which may be why Nietzsche never published them, but in any case "little else is affected by it. His cosmology as a whole neither stands nor falls with it" (ibid. 265). Further, it is not merely the case, as Nehamas (333) points out, that *Twilight* is "a book in which a rigorous proof of this doctrine would have been quite in place, but from which it is totally absent", but the argument which does there bear on the invocation of "the eternal recurrence" points in a quite different direction from the variant (and not wholly consistent) cosmological speculations explored in the notes.

Would you not throw yourself down and gnash your teeth and curse the demon who spoke thus? Or have you once experienced a tremendous moment when you would have answered him: "You are a god and never have I heard anything more divine." If this thought gained possession of you, it would change you as you are or perhaps crush you. . . . How well disposed would you have to become to yourself and to life *to crave nothing more fervently* than this ultimate confirmation and seal? (Nietzsche (5), *Gay Science*, 341)

At a personal level, the thought is

that *if* my life were to recur, *nothing* about it could be at all different; a life dissimilar in any way would not be *my* life. This is a thought we shrink from; only the ideal Superman can so totally accept himself as he is, rather than indulging in the fancy that in many ways he might have been different (Annas's elegant summary (142 n. 28) of the upshot of the careful discussion of Nehamas).

With such acceptance comes liberation from any *ressentiment* about the past such as generates "suspicion against life" and "morality as anti-nature" (Nietzsche (6), *Twilight*, iii. 6, and v), and the ability to be creatively open to the future (Nehamas, 348–50). At a more general level, the symbol of "eternal recurrence" meshes with another: 'My formula for greatness in a human being is *amor fati*: that one wants nothing to be different, not forward, not backward not in all eternity. Not merely to bear what is necessary . . . but *love* it' (Nietzsche (7), *Ecce Homo*, ii. 10). To one with *this* measure of greatness the demon's suggestion comes as a delight; acceptance of the Recurrence marks the fully Dionysian transformation in which one is "changed" rather than "crushed", and able to acknowledge with joy that *"Increscunt animi, virescit volnere virtus"*. Here, indeed, we have a vision of the *Übermensch*:

the ideal of the most high-spirited, alive, and world-affirming human being who has not only come to terms and learned to get along with whatever was and is, but who wants to have *what was and is* repeated into all eternity, shouting insatiably *da capo*—not only to himself but to the whole play and spectacle, and not only to a spectacle but at bottom to him who needs precisely this spectacle (Nietzsche (7), *BGE*, 56).

Nietzsche, as we have seen, concedes that he has not in himself thus conquered "God and nothingness"; Zarathustra is "stronger" than his creator (Nietzsche (7), *Genealogy*, ii. 24–5). Thus it is fitting, and a sign of his authenticity, to find evidence of the alternative reaction to the demon in his notes: 'I do not want life *again*. How did I endure it? Creating. What makes me stand the sight of it? The vision of the *Übermensch* who *affirms* life. I have tried to affirm it *myself*—alas!' (cited and translated in Kaufmann (3), p. 19). It is in the *persona*, or "mask", of "the last disciple of the philosopher Dionysus" that he claims to be "the teacher of the eternal recurrence" (Nietzsche (6), *Twilight*, x), and proclaims the "new tablet" of Zarathustra—"become hard".

From this perspective the "hammer" takes on a new significance. Not only does it show "the eternal recurrence" to ring true, but in that exposure to that doctrine "would change you as you are" it becomes part of the creative process transforming those who can bear it into a new "greatness"—perhaps even into that "image of images" that alone "makes me stand the sight" of life:

Zarathustra once defines, quite strictly, his task—it is mine, too . . . he says Yes . . .
   'I walk among men as among the fragments of the future . . .'
Zarathustra has mastered the *great nausea* over man, too: man is for him an un-form, a material, an ugly stone that needs a sculptor . . .
   'My fervent will to create impels me ever again toward man; thus is the hammer impelled toward the stone. O men, in the stone an image is sleeping, the image of images! Alas, that it has to sleep in the hardest, ugliest stone! *Now my hammer rages cruelly against its prison.* . . . I want to perfect it; for a shadow came to me . . . The beauty of the *Übermensch* came to me as a shadow. O my brothers, what are gods to me now?'
I stress a final point: the verse in italics furnishes the occasion. Among the conditions for a *Dionysian* task are, in a decisive way, the hardness of the hammer (Nietzsche (7), *Ecce Homo*, 'Thus Spoke Zarathustra'', 8).

To create the new image the hammer must destroy. It must be "hard" for it needs to break "the hardest, ugliest stone", hence the severity of the attack in *Twilight* on the "idols"—the hammer is not just that of a bell-tuner but also of a sculptor. But here both images fail for that which is to be created is not just a statue but another —and greater—creator; that "higher system" of self-transformation for which the term '*Übermensch*' is Nietzsche's symbol. Another symbol pointing in the same direction is "genuine philosopher"; with his harnessed multiplicity of "affects" and "eyes" his "creative hand" reaches "for the future". But "all creators are hard", and so here we seek a "hardness" that transcends all else—for which the symbol is the "diamond"; and just as the diamond is a form of carbon which has softer forms, so the *Übermensch* is nothing other than transformed man.

'Why so hard?' the kitchen coal once said to the diamond. 'After all, are we not close kin?'

'Why so soft? O my brothers, thus I ask you: are you not after all my brothers?

'Why so soft, so pliant and yielding? Why is there so much denial, self-denial, in your hearts?' (Nietzsche (6), *Twilight*, xi)

Here we have the significance of "hardness" spelled out for us. On the one hand it does not "yield" pliantly to any constraints save its own (whether those of God, grammar, or morality); its perspectives are its own. On the other it is a sign of affirmation; being under no threat of "yielding" it has no need to deny—either life in general or its own self. Proclaimed in the context of "the eternal recurrence", "hardness" is yet another symbol for *amor fati*, strong or "great" enough to be free of *ressentiment* and the worship of all the "life-denying" "anti-natural" idols whose twilight has come.

But there is one final twist.

For all creators are hard. And it must seem blessedness to you to impress your hand on millenia as on wax,

Blessedness to write on the will of millenia as on bronze [*Erz*]—harder than bronze, nobler than bronze. Only the noblest is altogether hard (ibid.).

Against this should be set: 'To create things on which time tests its teeth in vain; in form, in *substance*, to strive for a little immortality —I have never yet been modest enough to demand less of myself. The aphorism, the apothegm . . . are the forms of eternity' (ibid. ix. 51). Also, 'In my *Zarathustra* one will recognise a very serious ambition for a *Roman* style, for the *aere perennius* in style' (ibid. x. 1). '*Erz*' is a standard equivalent for (and derived from) the Latin '*aes*', so the very text of Zarathustra which urges a form of inscription "harder than bronze" itself aspires to a style "more enduring than bronze", and a work which celebrates and sets out to exemplify "the forms of eternity" uses its own texture as an emblem of that which transcends it—of "hopes that as yet have no name". The "affirmative style" of viii. 6, joined to the "discriminating" taste of x. 1 which has the severity to single out the Horatian aspiration, is subsumed under the avowed intention "to be affirmers" of v. 6, and the whole projected forward to give content to that evocative but (in context) mysterious term—"eternal recurrence"—which is used to "baptize" the hitherto "nameless" aspirations of which the hammer speaks.

4. Reflexivity, Self-Interrogation, and the Affirmative Vision

This radical reflexivity lies at the heart of *Twilight*, of what it is to "philosophize with a hammer", and indeed of that "amazing finesse, *that the value of life cannot be estimated*" which one needs to "stretch out one's fingers" to grasp (Nietzsche (6), *Twilight*, ii. 2) and which guides the whole Nietzschean wooing of truth.

Throughout the work Nietzsche has been using the sensibility and multiple perspectives of "the last disciple of the philosopher Dionysus" as a touchstone against which all else is measured, in such a way that the sounds given off by the idols "touched" with the hammer are revealed as, by comparison, less than true. Only at the end, when we have learnt to trust the authenticity of this sensibility through its anonymous working is it given a Dionysian description and name, revealed as the very criterion of authenticity we have been led to use, and shown to be pointing to its own transcendence. The whole work is an exercise dedicated to the creation of new ways of seeing, new hopes, new will, a change of heart. Such "breaking open" cannot be achieved by employing "Dionysus" as yet another "cornerstone" for an "unconditional philosopher's edifice"—this would be the "clumsiness" of dogmatism and the non-Dionysian reader, rejecting the alleged first principle, would doubtless remain untouched. The reader's own authenticity needs to be challenged in its own terms, new perspectives opened up, incoherences laid bare, transformations begun, before it is appropriate to reveal the true name of that pied piper by whom he has been led out of his own twilit city into "the great noon" (Nietzsche (6), *Zarathustra*, i. xxii. 3; compare *Twilight*, iv. 6).

A useful light is thrown on what lies behind this procedure by the title Nietzsche originally intended for the work—until at a very late stage he was persuaded by Peter Gast's preference for a "more resplendent title" (Nietzsche (6), p. 464)—*A Psychologist's Idleness*, which echoes the theme of "recreation" from the Preface. The opening 'maxim' of the work, which with gentle irony presupposes this title and exploits the German proverb 'idleness is the beginning of all vices', runs: 'Idleness is the beginning of all psychology. What? Should psychology be a vice?' It is supported by the two following: 'Even the most courageous among us only rarely has the courage for that which he really knows'; and, 'To live alone one must be a beast or a god, says Aristotle. Leaving out the third case: one must be both—a philosopher.' A short-cut to discerning what is at issue here is provided by three passages from earlier works:

In the glorification of 'work' . . . I see . . . fear of everything individual. . . . Work, that hard industrousness from early till late . . . can mightily hinder the development of reason, covetousness, desire for independence. For it uses up an extraordinary amount of nervous energy, which is thus denied to reflection, brooding, dreaming, worrying, loving, hating; it sets a small goal always in sight and guarantees easy and regular satisfactions (Nietzsche (4), *Daybreak*, 173).

A: So you intend to return to your desert?—
B: I am not quick moving, I have to wait for myself—it is always late before the water comes to light out of the well of my self. . . . That is why I go into solitude—so as not to drink out of everybody's cistern. When I am among the many I live as the many do, and I do not think as I really think (ibid. 491).

Leisure and idleness. . . . One is ashamed of resting, and prolonged reflection almost gives people a bad conscience. One thinks with a watch in one's hand . . . Just as all forms are visibly perishing by the haste of the workers, the feeling for form itself . . . is also perishing. The proof of this may be found in the universal demand for gross *obviousness* in all those situations in which human beings wish to be honest with one another for once. . . . Hours in which honesty is *permitted* have become rare (Nietzsche (5), *Gay Science*, 329).

"Idleness", then, is something creative. It permits honesty, reflection and openness, room to seek below the obvious, a "feeling for form", and the associations of solitude—thinking as "I really think" (not in accordance with the "herd utility" incapsulated in language), acknowledging what one "really knows", self-reflexively breaking open the traditional alternatives established by Aristotle and finding through that rupture one's own place—that of the "philosopher" who is nevertheless (not least through the observation displayed so far) also a "psychologist". Thus it is no surprise to find that the next 'maxim' itself puts in question the traditional conception of philosophy, with that multi-layered observation we explored earlier—pointing to the integration of feelings with the light of the intellect in a complexity of perspectives: '"All truth is simple." Is that not doubly a lie?' Thereafter subversive epistemological reflection is followed by psychological as a subtle and ever richer web is woven which covers the entire subsequent work which it both illuminates and is illumined by. If one gives careful attention to that first section, entitled 'Maxims and Arrows', then before one reaches the second a "softening-up" process associated with the "great declaration of war" has already begun.

The first three maxims alone, for those with eyes to see, rehearse much that is to follow. The starting-point is a challenge to the folk wisdom of the people in whose language the challenge is issued; the traditions of the culture with which the author is most closely engaged must be the most critically scrutinized—thus a later section is entirely given over to "What the Germans lack". Further, this challenge puts in question the conventional criteria for distinguishing vice and virtue—a leading later theme—but does so non-dogmatically, with a question. And this model of questioning is designed to encourage self-interrogation of a sort that lays bare those non-cognitive elements on the search for knowledge that traditional epistemologists—though, as we have seen, not Pascal —ignore: courage, honesty, the heart and will, the province of the psychologist who is also philosopher. Such questioning may start with conventional folk wisdom, but it does not quail before even the highest authorities; even Aristotle may have failed to have the courage for that which he really knew—sponsoring a cleavage between beast and divinity that has led to a "ruining" of the "blond beast" (the leonine element in man) in the name of the Christian God (Nietzsche (6), *Twilight*, vii. 2), and is overcome in the figure of Dionysus who was himself "misunderstood . . . by Aristotle" (ibid. x. 5).

Thus the "old psychologist" ruminates in his "idleness", resisting "gross obviousness", sponsoring "honesty", "reflection, brooding" so that the reader may have evoked in him that rare "courage" to acknowledge and respond positively to a time when "the water comes to light out of the well of my self". It is in this context, the section immediately following 'Maxims and Arrows' that we are faced with this amazing finesse, *that the value of life cannot be estimated.* Not by the living, for they are an interested party, even a bone of contention, and not judges; not by the dead, for a different reason. For a philosopher to see a problem in the value of life is thus an objection to him, a question mark concerning his wisdom, an unwisdom (ibid. ii. 2).

The finesse is presented in response to the observation that "Concerning life, the wisest men of all ages have judged alike: *it is no good*" (ibid. ii. 1). It is used to support the suggestion that this unanimity does not so much support the observation, but rather warrants a psychological or "genealogical" exploration into the conditions of this unanimity with an eye to the "irreverent thought that the great sages are *types of decline.* . . . Indeed? All these great wise men—they were not only decadents but not wise at all?" (ibid. ii. 2). Once the mind is predisposed to entertain seriously this "irreverent thought", Nietzsche's work is half done. His analysis of "the problem of Socrates" and all that flows from him in terms of decadence must be taken seriously, and even if we take exception to the sweeping nature of his historical generalizations we may well do so by showing that Nietzsche's criteria do not apply in all cases in the way he thought they did—as so many Christian writers have, with some justice, argued that the "Christianity" he attacks is more Schopenhauerian Gnosticism, even Manichaeism, than orthodoxy and that his grasp on New Testament criticism is weak (e.g. Lea, Copleston (2)). To the extent that such responses acknowledge that if history or doctrine were as he declares Nietzsche's criticism would be damaging, the central Dionysian case is conceded.

'Judgments of value concerning life, for it or against it, can, in the end, never be true: they have value only as symptoms . . . in themselves such judgments are stupidities" (*Twilight*, ii. 2). But "For a philosopher to see a problem in the value of life is . . . an objection to him" (ibid.). On the face of it, the alert reader will notice, there is ground for the suspicion that there is "finesse" here in the pejorative sense; Nietzsche, with his celebration of "the ascending line of life" in the light of which decadence is cause for suspicion, is as much "an interested party" as the sages—one must beware against allowing an equivocation on what it is "to see a problem in the value of life" to warrant endorsement of the life-affirming attitude. On the other hand, Nietzsche's warning that "One must by all means stretch out one's fingers and make the attempt to grasp this amazing finesse" should lead any who have been impressed by the subtlety of the opening section to postpone judgement.

The counter to this perhaps "grossly obvious" objection is characteristically withheld until it is clearer what life affirmation involves, Zarathustra has been introduced, and the full significance of Nietzsche's response can be the more readily "grasped".

A condemnation of life by the living remains in the end a mere symptom of a certain kind of life: the question whether it is justified or unjustified is not even raised thereby. One would require a position *outside* of life, and yet have to know it as well as one, as many, as all who have lived it, in order to be permitted even to touch the problem of the *value* of life: reasons enough to comprehend that this problem is for us an unapproachable problem.

So far this is a restatement of the earlier case in terms of perspectivity, but then he goes on: 'When we speak of values, we speak with the inspiration, with the way of looking at things (*unter der Optik*), which is part of life: life itself forces us to posit values; life itself values through us when we posit values' (Twilight, v. 5). There are, that is, no criteria apart from those established by the essential nature of life itself by which life can be judged. For Nietzsche,

one is mistaken to think that the value of life is *something problematical* —an issue which remains open after the essential nature and conditions of life have been determined, and which is to be resolved by seeing how life fares when measured against a standard of value which has some other derivation. . . . The ultimate standard of value is to be conceived in terms which derive directly from a consideration of the essential nature of life itself; and if the former is given and determined by the latter, then the question of the value of life cannot arise. . . . Thus "the value of life cannot be estimated", on his view, not because life is without value, but rather because its essential nature itself determines the ultimate standard of value, and because it itself, in its highest form of development, *is* the ultimate value . . .

His contention . . . involves, not passing judgment upon the extent to which life is capable of satisfying certain antecedently determined conditions, but rather merely accepting life on its own terms, as he understands them (Schacht (2), 80–1).

One can, of course, purport to refuse such acceptance, but there are no independent criteria on which such rejection can be grounded —and the reader may be asked to consider what he "really thinks" here;

Pessimism, *pur*, *vert*, is proved only by the self-refutation of our dear pessimists: one must advance a step further in its logic and not only negate life with "will and representation", as Schopenhauer did—one must first of all negate Schopenhauer (Nietzsche (6), *Twilight*, ix. 36).

As he remarks elsewhere, "Schopenhauer, though a pessimist, really—played the flute" (Nietzsche (7), *BGE*, 186).

Further, the criteria suggested are, it is implied, the ones we acknowledge in our highest ideals, a distorted selection and mis-interpretation of which are exploited by "pessimism", for there is more to life than mere existence.

Anti-Darwin. As for the famous "struggle for *existence*", so far it seems to me to be asserted rather than proved. It occurs, but as an exception; the total appearance of life is not the extremity, not starvation, but rather riches, profusion, even absurd squandering—and where there is struggle, it is a struggle for *power*. One should not mistake Malthus for nature (Nietzsche (6), *Twilight*, ix. 14).

Here we touch that Dionysian vision of "Will to Power", ever transforming and self-transforming, that we have seen to represent for Nietzsche the essential nature of that reality of which our life is a part. 'Life is only a *means* to something; it is the expression of forms of the growth of power' (Nietzsche (8), *Will to Power*, 706). The intelligible character of the world is constituted by our human perspectives, and our self-reflexive knowledge of the life that creates these perspectives provides us with the materials for our most adequate grasp of that character. If, as Nietzsche argues, we have ultimately to analyse the very concept of force in terms of "an inner event", "an inner will", "a creative drive", then "There is nothing else for it: one is obliged . . . to employ man as an analogy to this end" (ibid. 619). Thus it is appropriate to look to human experience for those highest forms of development of life, most creatively transforming examples of will to power, which provide the only touchstones against which ideals can be tested. As there are no "facts" as "positivism" understands them, "only interpreta-tions", and all interpretations incorporate affects, Hume's fact/value fork can gain no purchase here; "life itself forces us to posit values; life itself values through us when we posit values".

As the idols are sounded out, and "skirmishes" carried through with many aspects of contemporary culture, we gradually become aware of the richness of the affirmative vision which underlies the whole project, until at the climax of the long ninth section ('Skirmishes of an Untimely Man') their leading elements are brought together not in any mythological figure but in the attainments and aspirations of a widely respected figure from recent history, Goethe—"the last German for whom I feel any reverence" (Nietzsche (6), *Twilight*, ix. 51), though even here there is no mere submission to authority and Nietzsche, the classical philologist, goes on with some justice to take him to task: "Goethe did not understand the Greeks" (ibid. x. 4) in the very central matter of the Dionysian spirit itself.

Despite such weaknesses Nietzsche endorses

all that which Goethe as a person had striven for: universality in understanding and in welcoming, letting everything come close to oneself, an audacious realism, a reverence for everything factual (ibid. ix. 50).

What he wanted was *totality*; he fought the mutual extraneousness of reason, senses, feeling and will . . . he disciplined himself to wholeness, he *created* himself (ibid. ix. 49).

Further,

Goethe conceived a human being who would be strong, highly educated, skillful in all bodily matters, self-controlled, reverent towards himself, and who might dare to afford the whole range and wealth of being natural, being strong enough for such freedom; the man of tolerance, not from weakness but from strength, because he knows how to use to his advantage, even that from which the average nature would perish; the man for whom there is no longer anything that is forbidden—unless it be *weakness*, whether called vice or virtue.

Such a spirit who has *become free* stands amid the cosmos with a joyous and trusting fatalism, in the *faith* that only the particular is loathsome, and that all is redeemed and affirmed in the whole—*he does not negate any more.* Such a faith, however, is the highest of all possible faiths: I have baptized it with the name of *Dionysus* (ibid.).

Schacht remarks of a similar description of the *Übermensch*, 'If there is any attainable form of human life that requires no independent justification to be found worthy of affirmation, and that may be considered to "redeem" mankind more generally as well, Nietzsche makes a strong case for taking it to be something of this sort' (Schacht) (1), 340).

The ensuing analysis of the original significance of Dionysus, now recovered, in the section 'What I owe to ancients' at once gives further content to the evocative symbols with which the work is to conclude, and again displays such content as being no mere invention of Nietszche's own; the wisdom of Dionysus is nothing alien, it is and always has been a part of ourselves though it has "long lain buried in the dungeon of much mud and sand" (Nietzsche (7), *BGE*, 295). As at the opening, so at the close, the preparedness to "grasp this amazing finesse" which turns us away from the negations of decadence is a judgement on the reader as well as on the work; for "Even the most courageous among us only rarely has the courage for that which he really knows." If this is a vicious circle, then the notion of "vice" must be revalued, for objectivity here is a function of the mastery of multiple perspectives which are themselves the product of "reason, senses, feeling and will"; to the extent that a "descending line of life" prevents one from entering fully in to a perspective as significant as the Dionysian one's judgement is to that extent lacking in objectivity, but if one does so enter and seeks to set against it some yet more inclusive perspective one is in danger of confirming that which one seeks to oppose, for self-transformation is at the heart of Nietzsche's vision and the note on which *Twilight* ends. The aspiration for any form of absolute is itself only part of a perspective, and insofar as it is projected as a genuine possibility an inferior one, thus Nietzsche ends that other account of Dionysian man with an elegant formula which turns any such attack into a boomerang:

the ideal of the most high-spirited, alive, and world-affirming human being
. . . who wants to have *what was and is* repeated into all eternity, shouting insatiably *da capo*—not only to himself but to the whole play and spectacle, and not only to a spectacle but at bottom to him who needs precisely this spectacle—and who makes it necessary because again and again he needs himself—and makes himself necessary—What? And this wouldn't be —*circulus vitiosus deus*? (Nietzsche (7), *BGE*, 56)

If it is objected that this is "a vicious circle made god", the reply is available: "God is a vicious circle"; the Latin will take either construction.

5. The Union of Form and Content

> Horace. . . . This mosaic of words, in which every word—as
> sound, as place, as concept—pours out its strength right and
> left and over the whole, this *minimum* in the extent and
> number of the signs, and the maximum thereby attained in the
> energy of the signs.
>
> (Nietzsche (6), Twilight, x. 1)

Here is the style for which Nietzsche has "a very serious ambition";
"*aere perennius*" is of course a Horatian tag, and in his final work
Nietzsche invokes "a reader as I deserve him, who reads me the way
good old philologists read their Horace" (Nietzsche (7), *Ecce
Homo*, iii. 5). In his Preface to the *Genealogy of Morals* he
comments on the relation of the epigraph (the Zarathustrian contention that wisdom "always loves only a warrior") standing before
the third essay (which is some one hundred times as long as the
quotation) and that essay itself.

People find difficulty with the aphoristic form: this arises from the fact that
today this form is *not taken seriously enough*. An aphorism, properly
stamped and molded, has not been "deciphered" when it has simply been
read; rather, one has then to begin its *exegesis*, for which is required an art
of exegesis. I have offered in the third essay . . . an example of what I
regard as "exegesis" in such a case—an aphorism is prefixed to this essay,
the essay itself is a commentary on it. To be sure, one thing is necessary
above all if one is to practice reading as an *art* in this way . . . *rumination*
(Nietzsche (7), *Genealogy*, 'Preface', 8).

"In certain languages", Nietzsche admits, what Horace achieved by
way of mosaic of words "could not even be attempted" (Nietzsche
(6), *Twilight*, x. 1), and he is well aware of the limitations he places
on himself in that "I write in German" (ibid. ix. 51). The "aphoristic
form", it would appear, provides a German (and to some degree
translatable) equivalent for the Horatian mosaic—it too "pours out
its strength right and left and over the whole". I have attempted to
give some hint of this process with respect to the opening maxims; if
Nietzsche's own practice is anything to go by, a proper exegesis of
Twilight of the Idols would demand a multi-volume commentary.

This "aphoristic form" is the stylistic counterpart of the theoretical rejection of the ideal of "a cold, pure, divinely unconcerned

dialectic" (Nietzsche (7), *BGE*, 5) where logical form has a standing independent of content. Indeed, it is a re-creation of that old Isocratean ideal of the union of "speaking well" with "sound understanding" the severance of which by Socrates Cicero so deplored. After the opening volley of "Maxims and Arrows", the second section of *Twilight* engages in hand to hand combat with "The Problem of Socrates"; thus it is appropriate that, before the concluding look to the future, the penultimate section should concern itself with "What I Owe to the Ancients" and celebrate "the culture of the Sophists . . . this inestimable movement amid the moralistic and idealistic swindle set loose on all sides by the Socratic schools" (Nietzsche (6), *Twilight*, x. 2). As in the case of Nietzsche himself, their symbolic representative—Thucydides—writes in such a manner that "one must follow him line by line and read no less clearly between the lines: there are few thinkers who say so much between the lines" (ibid.). In their writing, Nietzsche, Horace, and Thucydides may represent the *presto* spirit; but with respect to "grasping" their *finesses* "rumination" is needed: 'I, just as much as my book, are friends of *lento*' (Nietzsche (4), *Daybreak*, 'Preface', 5). Here, as so often, the hostile question "How *could* anything originate out of its opposite?" is shown by the Dionysian spirit to be a mere function of "prejudgment and prejudice" (Nietzsche (7), *BGE*, 2).

Indeed, if there is genuine integration between word and thought, one should find the self-transforming Dionysian spirit —"*Increscunt animi, virescit volnere virtus*"—operating at both levels, and so it proves. Perhaps Nietzsche's greatest literary achievement in *Twilight* is that accomplishment of the self-transcendence of decadence he had never before achieved.

What is the sign of every *literary decadence*? That life no longer dwells in the whole. The word becomes sovereign and leaps out of the sentence, the sentence reaches out and obscures the meaning of the page, the page gains life at the expense of the whole—the whole is no longer a whole. . . . Every time, the anarchy of atoms. . . . The whole no longer lives at all: it is composite, calculated, artificial, and artifact (Nietzsche (7), *The Case of Wagner*, vii).

This paraphrase of Bourget on Baudelaire (see Stern, 157) applies to most of Nietzsche's work since *Human, All-Too-Human*, for "I am . . . a child of this time; that is, a decadent: but I comprehended

this, I resisted it. The philosopher in me resisted (ibid. 'Preface';
cf. also *Ecce Homo*, i. 1–3). *Zarathustra* may have remained
uncompletable, but in *Twilight* this resistance bears fruit.

It marks the organic integration of no fewer than five importantly
discriminable types of literary form, thus it is misleading to use just
one term such as 'aphoristic' to describe it. Nietzsche himself uses
the terms 'aphorism' and 'apothegm' (*'Aphorismus', 'Sentenz'*) in a
remarkably relaxed way to cover both pithy sentences and page-
long essays, with many variants in between.[7] In *Twilight* he appears
to distinguish the 'maxims' (*'Sprüche'*) of the first section (the
shortest nine words long, the longest thirty-four) from the 'aphorisms' of the ninth (detached essays from a few sentences to three
pages in length entitled 'Skirmishes of an Untimely Man'). There
are also the 'verses' from *Zarathustra* (cf. Nietzsche (7), *Ecce
Homo*, 'Thus Spoke Zarathustra', 8) of the concluding eleventh
section ('The Hammer Speaks') which exploit the forms of Hebrew
poetry preserved in Luther's Bible, and the sets of sequentially
interconnected short essays around a central theme (s. 2, 3, 5, 6, 7,
8, and 10). The remaining fourth section is the famous 'How
the "True World" finally became a Fable: The History of an Error'
which for memorability and brilliance is unsurpassed in all
Nietzsche.

This section comprises six pairs of linked "aphorisms" (in an
extended sense), none of which is as much as four lines long in the
Colli-Montinari edition, laid out sequentially to tell a story; the first
of each pair providing a sketch of the idea of the "True World" at a
particular stage in its history, and the other a commentary on that
stage. It starts as being an attainable ideal, "A circumlocution for
the sentence "I, Plato, *am* the truth""; this, of course, is to transfer
into a philosophical context Christ's "I am the truth", and should be
read in the light of Nietzsche's own commentary in *The Antichrist*
(ss. 32–6). At the next stage it is "unattainable for now, but
promised . . . it becomes more subtle, insidious, incomprehensible
—*it becomes female*, it becomes Christian"; 'female' should by now
need no comment, and in the sense of 'Christian' intended St Paul,

---

[7] The most judicious examination of Nietzsche's use of the aphoristic tradition is
probably Donnellan, pt. 2. On the problems of aphorism criticism more generally,
see Stephenson. The organic unity of *Twilight of the Idols*, however, has been
generally unrecognized by the commentators—with unfortunate consequences for
the received interpretations of the later Nietzsche.

not Jesus, was for Nietzsche the first Christian (compare *The Antichrist*, 39 with 41 ff). Thereafter it becomes "unpromisable" (Kant), "unknown" (positivism) and then

useless and superfluous—*consequently*, a refuted idea: let us abolish it!

(Bright day; breakfast; return of *bon sens* and cheerfulness; Plato's embarrassed blush; pandemonium [*Teufelslärm*] of all free spirits.)

But the free spirit, it will be remembered, is only a precursor of the "genuine philosopher", so another stage is needed,[8]

6. The true world—we have abolished. What world has remained? The apparent one perhaps? But no! *With the true world we have also abolished the apparent one.*

(Noon; moment of the briefest shadow; end of the longest error; high point of humanity; INCIPIT ZARATHUSTRA.)

For one who has "read my earlier writings" the Dionysian outlook is here declared. Not only is *Zarathustra* itself invoked, but also that final aphorism of the first edition of *The Gay Science* which introduces Zarathustra with "*Incipit tragoedia*" (iv. 342) with its own echo of Nietzsche's first published work *The Birth of Tragedy*. The close of the final section of *Twilight* before the hammer "speaks" is thus prepared for, since there tragedy is associated with "saying Yes to life . . . the eternal joy of becoming, beyond all terror and pity", and that first work is invoked: 'herewith I again touch that point from which I first went forth'. The speech of the hammer is Zarathustra's own utterance, transcending the *Teufelslärm* of all free spirits.

But this, while correct so far as it goes, is to read *Twilight* inorganically, decadently, taking the sun of Zarathustra's noon from other solar systems; only with the acknowledged quotation

---

[8] It is convenient to use the same section as that which is used as a touchstone by the proponent of an influential misreading of Nietzsche to diagnose what is wrong with it. Heidegger's attempt to cast Nietzsche as a Plato despite himself is properly countered by Derrida's insistence on the subversive significance of "it becomes female" at a very early stage in the "progress" of the idea of the "True World" (Derrida (1), 47). But the latter's tendency to read Nietzsche (see Derrida (1) and (2)) as if there was no significant change in orientation from the time of the early essays onwards leads him to underestimate the mature concept of perspectival "objectivity" and hence the full significance of '*Incipit Zarathustra*'. Derridean commentary, indeed, embodies "*Teufelslärm* of all free spirits" and, to the extent that it claims Nietzschean sanction, exemplifies Maxim 30 of *Twilight of the Idols*; the Derridean misreading is an over-reaction against that of Heidegger.

from *Zarathustra* at the close does the work spontaneously open itself to the "gravitational pulls" of the other Nietzschean writings. Until then *Twilight* provides its own context for filling that "high point of humanity" which transcends the cheerful negations of the free spirits with significance; the new beginning which is here announced with the term 'Zarathustra' is one whose noon light has already chased away shadows and continues to do so. The subsection immediately before the fourth section had given, in terms of the intellect, a prefiguring of what it is to abolish the very notion of a dichotomy between "real" and "apparent" worlds (the throwing of a shadow): "the reasons for which 'this' world has been characterized as 'apparent' are the very reasons which indicate its reality", together with a psychological diagnosis: "any distinction between a 'true' and an 'apparent' world . . . is only a suggestion of decadence". The subsection immediately following the new beginning points forward to "*spiritualization* of passion" as the remedy. On the basis of these two subsections alone, the enigmatic 'Zarathustra' is given an orientation.

In microcosm this is what the structure of the first part of the work sets out to achieve. It is best read, at least so far as Nietzsche's final text is concerned, in three phases—each with its own fulcrum, and each building on what has gone before. Zarathustra is the pivot of the first, Goethe of the second, and the integration of "triumph" with "creation" of the third.

Of the three sections prior to that of which 'INCIPIT ZARATHUSTRA' is the climax, the first sends its flight of "maxims and arrows" into the enemy ranks ("Wisdom" we remember, "loves only a warrior"). Here it is the "arrows" (ideas and attitudes) that are of primary importance rather than the identity of the targets; when we are told "Man does *not* strive for happiness [*Glück*]; only the Englishman does" (maxim 12) it is irrelevant to complain that not all and only the English are psychological hedonists; what is more significant is the way it subserves the final maxim: "The formula of my happiness [*Glück*]: A Yes, a No, a straight line, a *goal*." As this section draws to its close there is a whole cluster (denominated "questions of conscience") that specialize in setting up two opposed alternatives and then break up the framework by pointing to a third, very different, possibility—reminiscent of the beast/god/ philosopher trichotomy of maxim 3 discussed earlier (maxims 37, 38, 40, 41; see also 21). And this warning of subversiveness of all established structures is at once given a self-reflexive twist: 'Those were steps for me, and I have climbed up over them: to that end I had to pass over them. Yet they thought that I wanted to retire on them' (maxim 42). With these warnings thrown out the subversion starts in earnest. The second section opens with the "finesse" about the value of life discussed above, and with this achieved the introduction of dialectics by Socrates is attacked and diagnosed. Once this is done Nietzsche has won the right to his inverted commas in the title to the third section ' "Reason" in Philosophy'; shorn of traditional methodological certainties the builders of "unconditional edifices" can be exposed as "idolators" of concepts, seduced by grammar into belief in God or at least a "true" world which more adequately matches it than that of appearance—susceptibility to the wiles of this "deceptive female" is diagnosed in terms of decadence. Thus the stage is set for section 4.

Ontology, epistemology, reason, and language; these are the areas in which "idols" are sounded in preparation for the coming of the figure of Zarathustra. But underlying all these soundings has been the "finesse" about life, and once we have been led to "that moment of briefest shadow" in which there are no absolutes, no "true" world, the Zarathustrian liberation can carry over into our living of that life, and the three sections which follow address themselves to morality and to religion in its practical aspect. In the first, "healthy morality" is characterized in terms of "an instinct of life" and "spiritualization"; but most moralities are argued to set themselves "against the instincts"—"the saint in whom God delights is the ideal eunuch". In the second the conceptual underpinnings of ordinary morality are exposed, and the section entitled 'The Four Great Errors' turns out to be an essay in philosophical psychology, centring around the way illusions concerning our inner life sponsor misguided conceptions of causality, which in turn lead us to misunderstand ourselves and the nature of responsibility in such concepts as "free will" (his own positive account of free will in terms of "maturity and mastery" is set out in the previous section). Finally Nietzsche transfers this discussion to a cultural level, and in 'The "Improvers" of Mankind' compares the effect of the imposition of Christian values with those of the Hindu caste system —"taming" with "breeding". Although he clearly prefers the latter to the former he accepts neither; projecting onto this canvas the same movement of thought to which the maxims testify, he rejects the two standard options and looks for a third of a different kind: '*all* the means by which one has so far attempted to make mankind moral were through and through *immoral*'. So far this is negative. Revealing the hollowness of the idols has given intimations of what positively is needed, but now a new technique is needed to give substance to that shadowy promise of Zarathustra. So the second phase retreats from the level of broad and often highly questionable generalizations, to concern itself with the particularities of culture. Here the centrepiece is the set of fifty-one 'Skirmishes of an Untimely Man' with his times which provide a set of perspectives for the culminating account of the "Dionysian" aspirations of Goethe, thus giving content to the phrase "high point of humanity" of the close of section 4. It is flanked on the one side by analysis of Nietzsche's own culture in 'What the Germans lack'. Here, true to his general concern with diagnosis, Nietzsche lays his final weight on defects in the educational system, which does not teach the young to "see" ("grasp each individual case from all sides"), "think" ("as a kind of dancing") or "write" (the ensuing 'Skirmishes' are offered as an object lesson here). Having distanced himself from his own culture, he flanks the other side of the 'Skirmishes' with 'What I owe to the ancients', and now at last the time has come to give names and descriptions to the various aspects of the Zarathustrian vision into which the pied piper has inveigled us and reflect on the manner of that piping. Drawing on that other, Classical, culture he knows best after the German, Nietzsche expounds the Dionysian, celebrates the '*aere perennius*' in style, and rejects those elements in the culture that have infected subsequent ages with "decadence". This is a vision not open to the sort of attacks he has made on others, for it is affirmative, perspectival, and self-transcending—thus the hammer can now speak with the voice of Zarathustra and without any more indirection.

This final section, too, has a central pivot. The central verses (4 and 5) of the eight exhibit that form of conceptual parallelism which is familiar from the Biblical Psalms (a standard technique of Hebrew poetry often exploited in *Zarathustra*): 'And if you do not want to be destinies and inexorable ones, how can you one day triumph with me? And if your hardness does not wish to flash and cut and cut through, how can you one day create with me?' At the heart of the notion of "hardness" (the topic of the first and last verses) is thus the reciprocal association of triumph (the Zarathustrian "end of the longest error") and creativity (Goethe *created himself*"), and hence the integration of the two central "moments" of the work. Further, 'triumph' (and hence 'create') is itself in apposition to 'destiny' ('fate', '*Schicksal*') in the preceding line, so this whole complex illuminates both *amor fati* ("my formula for greatness in a human being"), and that "goal" which is "the formula of my happiness" of the final maxim of Part 1. This union of happiness and greatness in Dionysian self-overcoming enacts that Yes-saying which the "amazing finesse" subserves, and focuses the entire book in a fragment from that other "most profound" (ix. 51) one to which it points. This is no "anarchy of atoms", but itself the expression of the overcoming of decadence; form and content are one.

The Socratic pied piper, it had been objected long before, "separated the science of wise thinking from that of elegant speaking, though in reality they are closely linked together." (Cicero (4), *De Oratore*, III. xvi. 60; see above ch. 2.3.) Under the figure of Dionysus, and celebrating "the culture of the Sophists . . . this inestimable movement", the new pied piper seeks to forge them into a union more enduring than that of Cicero.

6. Nietzsche versus Pascal: The Assessment of Rival Perspectives

> Anyone . . . who approached this almost deliberate degeneration and atrophy of man represented by the Christian European (Pascal for example) . . . with some divine hammer in his hand, would surely have to cry out in wrath, in pity, in horror: 'O you dolts . . . what have you done! Was that work for your hands? How have you bungled and botched my beautiful stone! What presumption!'
>
> (Nietzsche (7), *BGE*, 62)

With Nietzsche we have a figure ready to tackle Pascal head on, on his own ground because it is ground claimed by Nietzsche too. 'Pascal, whom I almost love because he has taught me such an infinite amount—the only *logical* Christian' (Nietzsche (9), 'Letter 187', 20 Nov. 1888). We have seen how many of Pascal's conceptions of *finesse* are given exemplary enactment in *Twilight*, how the hammer aspires to the unification of "reason, senses, feeling, and will" much as the Pascalian heart does, and how this is necessary because, in Pascal's words, "Our soul is cast into the body where it finds number, time, dimensions; it reasons about these things and calls them natural, or necessary, and can believe nothing else. . . . This natural *sentiment* affords no convincing proof that they are true" (Pascal, *Pensées* L.418, B.233, S.680; L.131, B.434, S.164). For Pascal, "*fantasie* is like and also unlike *sentiment*, so that we cannot distinguish between these two opposites" (ibid. L.530, B.275, S.455); for Nietzsche "a desire of the heart" is all too often deceptive (Nietzsche (7), *BGE*, 5, 23 and 191).

Given the sceptical problem, Hume advocates reliance on "the reflections of common life, methodized and corrected" (Hume (6), *1st Enquiry*, 162), using them as a touchstone for those more or less regular "moral" arguments which may be used to cast doubt on any speculations concerning "the situation of nature". But neither Pascal nor Nietzsche believe that the Pyrrhonic thrust can be stopped so easily, for different ways of conceiving of the limitations which assuredly bound "action, and employment, and the occupations of common life" both have an effect on and are affected by the character of that life; neither Pascal nor Nietzsche lived as Hume did in many of the respects they took to be most important in human life. Further, they both saw cause for specific doubt about the assumptions of a somewhat conventional *mondain* unbeliever such as Hume; the one invoking the consequences of the Fall, the other the grammatical structures of our language.

But if there is no *assiette* (Pascal), no *Grundstein* (cornerstone, Nietzsche), like that of Descartes[9] on which to build "unconditional philosophers' edifices" (Nietzsche) "rising up to infinity" (Pascal), and "common life" is a flawed and questionable touchstone, we are "floating in a medium of vast extent" (Pascal) which Nietzsche terms the "open sea". For both writers our only guide here is

---

[9] Nietzsche's view of Descartes's "cornerstone" is best summed up in *Beyond Good and Evil*: 'When I analyze the process that is expressed in the sentence, "I think", I find a whole series of daring assertions that would be difficult, perhaps impossible, to prove; for example, that it is *I* who think, that there must necessarily be something that thinks, that thinking is an activity and operation on the part of a being who is thought of as a cause, that there is an "ego", and, finally, that it is already determined what is to be designated by thinking—that I *know* what thinking is. . . . In short, the assertion "I think" . . . has, at any rate, no immediate certainty for me' (Nietzsche (7), *BGE*, 16).

finesse. We have seen that there is a close analogy between Pascal's version and that pattern of argument in literary criticism favoured by Dr Leavis, seeking an individual's "utmost consistency and most inclusive coherence of response", through "testing and re-testing and wider experience" of a variety of concrete instances which one comes to "place" in relation to each other. But this could also serve as an at least partial summary of the Nietzschean activity of "philosophizing with a hammer"—which is hardly surprising when one considers Nietzsche's philological training and conception of philosophy in terms of "interpretation". For both Pascal and Nietzsche, so far as this context is concerned, "What good is a book that does not even carry us beyond all books?" (Nietzsche (5), *Gay Science*, 248), and "even the most courageous among us only rarely has the courage for that which he really knows" (Nietzsche (6), *Twilight*, i. 2).

But although both writers, in their different ways, argue that a form of objectivity is possible here, the fact is that they disagree, radically, on what interpretation we should adopt. For all Pascal's courage, honesty, and *finesse*, Nietzsche regards his "utmost . . . coherence of response" as fatally flawed in that it is the response of a man diminished by "degeneration and atrophy"; Pascal would doubtless object that it was Nietzsche who was corrupted: '*Reasons for not believing.* . . . Lack of charity' (L.834, B.826, S.422). For Nietzsche, however, charity is no touchstone for it incorporates within it the cherishing of pity; 'Alas, where in the world has there been more folly than among the pitying? And what in the world has caused more suffering than the folly of the pitying? Woe to all who love without having a height that is above their pity!' (Nietzsche (6), *Zarathustra*, epigraph to pt. 4). Pity represents Zarathustra's last trial, and the close of *Twilight* describes the Dionysian as "beyond all terror and pity"; the "hardness" of which the hammer speaks is that of Zarathustra. But if Nietzsche rejects Pascal's criteria, Pascal would reject Nietzsche's; as a distinguished contemporary Catholic philosopher remarks:

What evidence is there for affirming that Pascal was ruined and spoilt by Christianity? . . . It is not that Christianity has *no* aristocratic ideal, but that it has a *different* aristocratic ideal . . . from that of Nietzsche himself. And the aristocratic ideal of Christianity can be called hostile to life, only if the whole Christian religion is a tissue of lies, legends, and fiction (Copleston (2), 128).

Nietzsche, of course, maintains that it is such a tissue and, further, that it is motivated by that *ressentiment* which is a symptom of the declining line of life and can be exposed by genealogical investigation. Pascal would reject the charge, pointing in his turn to the "proofs of memory" and the incorporation of man's *grandeur* as well as *misère* in the Christian vision. At this level of debate, it would appear, for each move there is a countermove; in the absence of an *assiette*, one may be tempted to ask, what do the claims for even relative objectivity in interpretation come down to?

The answer, both Pascal and Nietzsche would agree, is to be found by moving from the general to the particular; philosophy is not the same as scholarship, but scholarship is indispensable to the philosopher, as is a wide and exhaustive knowledge of life. Perhaps the philosopher, suggests Nietzsche,

> must have been critic and sceptic and dogmatist and historian and also poet and collector and traveller and solver of riddles and moralist and seer and "free spirit" and almost everything in order to pass through the whole range of human values and value feelings and to be *able* to see with many different eyes and consciences. . . . All these are merely preconditions of his task (Nietzsche (7), *BGE*, 211).

To take just the scholarly element of this complex (by which Nietzsche clearly set great store, the whole sixth part of *Beyond Good and Evil* is entitled 'We Scholars') Nietzsche's questions about the effects on cultures of a high value being bestowed on pity deserve a detailed historical response, taking account of the sort of evidence adduced in *On the Genealogy of Morals*.

For although the "arrows" of the opening of *Twilight* are of greater importance for interpreting it than their targets, if we saw reason to conclude that Nietzsche missed his target too often that judgement would affect the credibility of the whole; similarly, the "Untimely Man" must not undergo defeat in his "Skirmishes". Nietzsche, like Pascal, is forced by the very dynamic of *finesse*, of the hammer, to test out his vision widely and in detail and, although that vision clearly provides some of the criteria for evaluating the tests, its multi-perspectival nature forces it to allow the relevance of criteria which are not uniquely Dionysian. The scholar, for example, must also be allowed his say. To take an instructive recent instance, Professor MacIntyre argues that the "collapse" of the Enlightenment project of "justifying morality" reveals that ultimately the choice in ethics must come down to "Nietzsche or Aristotle" (MacIntyre, ch. 9). His choice of Aristotle is mainly motivated by his positive account of that tradition, but it is also motivated by weaknesses he sees in the Nietzschean account of the genealogy of morals. For Nietzsche's positive account of nobility (and "Only the noblest is altogether hard"; (Nietzsche (6), *Twilight*, xi) is given in terms of the transcendence of the old "healthy" moralities, and MacIntyre argues that his understanding of those pre-Christian values of "heroic" societies is fundamentally flawed:

Nietzsche had to mythologise the distant past in order to sustain his vision. What Nietzsche portrays is aristocratic *self*-assertion; what Homer and the sagas show are forms of assertion proper to and required by a certain *role*. The self becomes what it is in heroic societies only in and through its role; it is a social creation, not an individual one. Hence when Nietzsche projects back on to the archaic past his own nineteenth-century individualism, he reveals that what looked like an historical enquiry was actually an inventive literary construction. Nietzsche replaces the fictions of the Enlightenment individualism, of which he is so contemptuous, with a set of individualist fictions of his own (MacIntyre, 121–2).

He admits, of course, that "It does not follow that one could not be an undeceived Nietzschean; and the whole importance of being a Nietzschean does after all lie in the triumph of being finally undeceived, being, as Nietzsche put it, truthful at last" (ibid.). But to the extent that the final vision of the *Übermensch* trades on the independence supposed to have been actually enacted in "healthy" moralities, historical considerations of the kinds adduced here may lead us to doubt the very coherence—as a lived possibility—of the "hardness" for which Nietzsche's hammer calls and which MacIntyre stigmatizes as "moral solipsism" (ibid. 240).

Historical investigations of this sort, therefore, can in principle have a highly significant bearing on the weight we attach to criticisms of Nietzsche's neglect of what has been called "the sphere of association".

There are aspects of social life (such as the law, or politics, or economic exchange) which have a dialectic of their own and to which, therefore, immediate personal value judgments are irrelevant. Nietzsche's reflections on these topics show up the bad discontinuity of his thought. . . . The view of society *and* of the individual entailed by his reflections on social morality issue in an almost absolute individualism which does not provide an account of the way things are in the world (Stern, 132).

Such charges can be pressed at a number of levels. One may note the connections of this attitude with contemporary Romanticism, and also with the German Protestantism that stems from Luther, suggesting—in genealogical fashion—that in this respect the "untimely man" was only too "timely" and culture bound, an unself-critical fruit of the very decadence he is concerned to oppose. Again, one may attempt to use these considerations to turn into boomerangs some of those darts directed against the Christianity Pascal, with his strong sense of the organic nature of the community within which the Christian life must be lived, represents:

Tradition, dogma, formulation itself amount for [Nietzsche] to a second order of experience, a spurious, reach-me-down reality. Institutionalization as man's only protection against arbitrariness means little to him. Nowhere is this more patent than in his wholesale rejection of the Christian Church in the world, as though the word of Jesus (which he does not reject wholesale) could get around without 'two or three gathering together in his name' (ibid. 128).

And if it be objected that this ignores the "hardness" for which he calls, one may turn against Nietzsche the very example he uses in *Twilight* to illuminate the Dionysian ideal and make it appear a live option: 'For Goethe's love of custom and habit . . . for that part of the poet's genius which hallows the everyday and thereby gives it lasting value, Nietzsche seems to have no spontaneous understanding at all' (ibid. 130). No doubt ripostes are available. Professor Stern, indeed, cites as a possible counter to the final charge Nietzsche's exquisite account of what it is to "learn to love" in *The Gay Science*, s. 334—but implies that this reveals a damaging tension in his thought (ibid.). This is not the place to enter into a serious assessment of the whole Dionysian vision,[10] any more than

[10] Instructive starting-points for embarking on such an assessment, other than those mentioned in the text, can be found in Scheler, Foot (1) (esp. 167–8), and Dannhauser (272–3). Finesse needs to be employed in following them up, however. To take just the historical dimension of Nietzsche's thought for example, in the second of his *Untimely Meditations* he distinguishes "three kinds of history . . .—the *monumental*, the *antiquarian*, and the *critical*", of which the monumental is particularly prone to being "a little altered and touched up" (Nietzsche (3), *The Use and Abuse of History*, ii). All three elements play complicated roles in his later writings, and Nietzsche is sufficiently conscious that he is often working what may be termed an "inverted" vein of the monumental (the historical examples being presented negatively rather than positively) for him to remark that "Plato, for example, becomes a caricature in my hands" (Nietzsche (8), *Will to Power*, 374). In history as in portraiture caricature has its own canons of aptness, which are not easily mastered by the unimaginative.

those of Pascal, Hume, Plato, or the authors of Job. For present purposes the essential point is that considerations about "the way things are in the world" and how they have been which "have a dialectic of their own", relatively independent of Dionysus, can properly have a multi-faceted and cumulative effect on that philosophizing with a hammer which attempts to discern— with "ears even behind the ears"—whether Dionysus is god or idol. That no single argument here can be decisive by itself is no objection to the Nietzschean method; we have seen in earlier chapters that claims to the contrary should give ground for suspicion. But the openness of the Dionysian vision to subversive probings, using its own methodology, increases the credibility of that methodology and those elements of the vision which are constitutive of it—the self-transcending and many-sided openness allied to a critical severity in discriminating better from worse modes of interpretation that, despite all differences, it shares with the Pascalian.

And it is ultimately in relation to that Pascalian, Christian, perspective that the Nietzschean itself demands to be grasped and assessed. 'Have I been understood?—*Dionysus versus the Crucified.*—' runs the last line of Nietzsche's last work (Nietzsche (7), *Ecce Homo*, iv. 9), a book which takes for its title Pilate's introduction of Christ to the crowd. 'When Zarathustra was thirty years old' runs the opening line of *Thus Spoke Zarathustra*, identifying the age of the opening of his public teaching with that of Jesus of Nazareth, and later—with more than a trace of hubris and a very odd chronology—'Verily, that Hebrew died too early whom the preachers of slow death honour. . . . He himself would have recanted his teaching, had he reached my age. Noble enough was he to recant. But he was not yet mature' (Nietzsche (6), *Zarathustra*, 'Prologue', 1, and i. 21). It is this relationship that lies behind what Professor Stern has characterized as a "recurring pattern of Nietzsche's thought: the compulsion, repeated in one area of experience after another, that makes him group his reflections round an empty space—the space reserved for a grace from on high in a world where there is no grace and no on high either" (Stern 104–5). In my discussion of Pascal I suggested that he might be able to show us "a 'God-shaped' blank" in our experience (above, Ch. 5.7) though whether that told us as much about the *Deus Absconditus* as our cultural inheritance was another matter. Professor Stern's formulation helps sharpen the issue between Pascal and Nietzsche.

Nietzsche indeed acknowledges this "empty space" in his experience and provides a cultural diagnosis, but here as elsewhere he avoids the cruder forms of the genetic fallacy; in some respects the "God-shaped" blank represents a cultural strength and depth in insight which should be harnessed and transformed now "God is dead"—not abandoned. "The fight against the Christian-ecclesiastical pressure of millenia", he declares—the one side providing, presumably, the shape of the blank, the other its emptiness—

has created in Europe a magnificent tension of the spirit the like of which had never yet existed on earth: with so tense a bow we can now shoot for the most distant goals. To be sure, European man experiences this tension as need and distress; twice already attempts have been made in the grand style to unbend the bow—once by means of Jesuitism, the second time by means of the democratic enlightenment. . . . But we who are neither Jesuits nor democrats . . . we still feel it, the whole need of the spirit and the whole tension of its bow. And perhaps also the arrow, the task, and—who knows?—the *goal*—(Nietzsche (7), *BGE*, 'Preface').

Pascal's *Lettres provinciales* represent a notable effort to prevent the first attempt; the Nietzschean corpus, complete with *Twilight*'s own "arrows" and projected "goal", sets out to combat the second. For all Nietzsche's "horror", not least in the case of Pascal himself, at the effects of Christianity, Zarathustra's greatest nausea is reserved for the eternal recurrence of the "small man", whose limiting case is the "last man" of his most savage scorn (Nietzsche (6), *Zarathustra*, iii. xiii. 2, and 'Prologue', 5);

'Alas, the time is coming when man will no longer shoot the arrow of his longing beyond man, and the string of his bow will have forgotten how to whir! . . .
' "What is love? What is creation? What is longing? What is a star?" thus asks the last man, and he blinks.'

A certain style of academic criticism, of both Pascal and Nietzsche, is well epitomized here.

If one enters into the suggested perspective of "Dionysus versus the Crucified", however, there are two main types of consideration that suggest themselves; has Dionysus understood the Crucified, and what has the tradition of the Crucified to reply to the charges of Dionysus? For Nietzsche, of course, one must distinguish between the teaching of "that Hebrew who died too early" and that of the

Church (and hence Pascal). But since "the Crucified" is a symbol to be understood in terms of the latter teaching as "a curse on life" (Nietzsche (8), *Will to Power*, 1052), we can ignore Nietzsche's curious portrait of a Jesus "not yet mature". Yet "a curse on life" represents only a part of the traditional teaching, and a distorted part at that, for the cross is also supposed to be the symbol of new life in this world and not only "after death" (Nietzsche (6), *Antichrist*, 41). Further 'Nietzsche has nothing to say about the positive meaning of Christ's incarnation (1 John 4:9) as a validation of our mortality. A theology that argues the presence of God in the world does not suit his Manichean view, and is accordingly ignored' (Stern, 145). The New Testament is dominated by the complementary theologies of John and Paul; orthodox theology by the Incarnation and Redemption. In his later writings it is the second of each pair that is seen as central, taken out of the context of its balancing element, and read through the somewhat distinctive prisms of Luther and Schopenhauer. Despite his, by orthodox Catholic standards, somewhat excessive negative bias this was not the Christianity of Pascal, and some of Nietzsche's belief to the contrary appears to be grounded in straightforward historical misinformation (Donnellan, 46–7 and n. 48). If "Dionysus" is contrasted with the "Incarnate", the insistence that the former "is a promise of life" no longer makes the required contrast.

But whatever the strengths of the traditions of Christianity, it may be replied, "the belief in the Christian god has become unbelievable"—in other words, "God is dead" (Nietzsche (5), *Gay Science*, 343). If we are not to "unbend the bow", whether in the ways specified by Nietzsche or even in the ironic mode of Hume, a new symbol is needed to replace the old—that of Dionysus. But the premiss is, on Nietzsche's own terms, double-edged. What is pointed to is a feature of a society by his own account decadent; simple acceptance of the "death" of God of itself hardly represents the resistance to decadence elsewhere desiderated—belief in God is, after all, incomprehensible to the "last man". The limits of credibility within an acknowledgedly diminished culture—even supposing them to be as asserted—hardly meet the standards of "objectivity" set up by Nietzsche himself. Pascal expressed himself ready to interrogate "all the religions of the world" and confront them with the "Wisdom of God"; he could hardly concede the claim that shortcomings should be excused if they matched deficiencies in the cultures where they flourished, even when the religion was Dionysian and the culture late European.

Nor, indeed, does Nietzsche suppose otherwise. Despite some of the better known rhetoric, he believes that atheists have "decisive refutation" available in that genealogical analysis fatally discredits "belief in the Christian God". But at this point, if the genetic fallacy is to be eschewed, argument and scholarship of some depth and detail are needed—so we move once again from the level of slogans such as 'God is dead' to the more delicate analysis represented, for example, by 'What Is the Meaning of Ascetic Ideals?' (Nietzsche (7), *Genealogy of Morals*, Subtitle to 'Third Essay'). When we do this we have need of that *finesse* and historical acumen which Pascal and Nietzsche both insist on. 'For once to pose questions here with a *hammer* . . . for one who has ears even behind his ears' (Nietzsche (6), *Twilight*, 'Preface'). To such insistent interrogation both the Cross and the image of Dionysus are open.

8

Philosophical Finesse

1. 'The heart has its reasons of which reason knows nothing'

Pascal's *'l'esprit de finesse'* is a notorious crux for translators. The best recent English version of the *Pensées* offers 'the intuitive mind' (Krailsheimer (1), 512), thereby encapsulating that traditional misreading of Pascal in terms of the very geometric model whose pretensions he was concerned to combat mentioned in Chapter 1; for on this model some analogue of the Cartesian *intuitus* is required where deduction reaches its limits and first principles need to be grounded. But to the extent that the notion of "intuition" is understood to exclude that of "reasoning" it is clearly misleading as a representation of Pascalian *'finesse'*, which is introduced as a term for a distinctive type of reasoning, other than that consonant with *"l'esprit de géométrie"*. The *OED*'s 'delicacy or subtlety of manipulation or discrimination', with its citation of an application of the word to the work of Cicero, comes nearer the mark—but 'the mind of delicacy' or Warrington's (910) 'the subtle intelligence' are themselves insufficiently discriminating for what Pascal has in mind, for geometrical reasoning can itself embody delicacy and subtlety. For present purposes, 'finesse' is best treated as a term of art introduced, after the manner of Pascal, to designate a certain range of patterns of ratiocination which do not easily fit the geometric model.

We saw in Chapter 5 that Pascal's own explanation of the term is incomplete and otherwise unsatisfactory, so rather than follow his exposition I shall sketch some of the distinctive features which emerge from the non-geometric patterns of reasoning we have been considering, using the Pascalian adumbration as suggestive rather than definitive. These features are most pithily indicated in the Pascalian aphorism, "The heart has its reasons of which reason knows nothing" (*Pensées*, L.423, B.277, S.680). Here 'reason' designates reasoning construed according to the geometric model, but 'reasons' represents reasoning patterns which are in many ways reminiscent of Aristotelian dialectic, Ciceronian controversy, and the ideal of rational persuasiveness we found in the *Phaedo*. The word 'heart', on the other hand, indicates a Biblical strand in Pascal's thinking, a conception of "wisdom" which is a function of feeling and the will as well as of the understanding, a "wisdom" closer to Job's than to that of his "comforters". Pascal, then, attempts to complement the geometric model by integrating certain Classical and Biblical conceptions of rationality so that patterns of argumentation associated with them may be used in rational defence of a religious "perspective" on life. Hume and Nietzsche both take the Pascalian type of reasoning seriously and, without question-begging appeals to the authority of the geometric model, provide two very different styles of secular counter to the Pascalian move. In a sense only slightly extended from that proposed by Pascal, not only he himself but also Hume and Nietzsche may properly be said, in the works discussed above, to exemplify *"l'esprit de finesse"*; Hume, indeed, may be regarded as a Trojan horse within the gates of post-Cartesian orthodoxy—an irony which might well please him.

From a Classical point of view, the claim that the principles of finesse "are in ordinary usage and there for all to see" (*Pensées*, L.512, B.1, S.670), taken together with its employment to ground and defend basic perspectives, is strongly reminiscent of Aristotelian dialectic. Further, in both cases the procedure subjects a number of diverse but interrelated elements to critical scrutiny, attempting to bring out underlying principles which will reconcile apparent inconsistencies among these elements, and in both cases the enterprise is understood as a co-operative one—Aristotle enjoins a question and answer context, Pascal challenges "observe yourself, and see". The Socrates of the *Phaedo* also, as we have seen, is presented as engaged in a co-operative endeavour—challenging Simmias and Cebes to "follow up the argument"—where the ultimate test of conclusions is that of personal conviction. Such conviction, of course, is only decisive where it has been tested by argument conducted according to "method" by those who are fitted to judge, but for Pascal too the reasons of the heart have their own distinctive "order" which must be observed and the enquirer's will must be properly disposed—"there is enough light for those who desire only to see" (L.149, B.430, S.182). Pascal, no less than the Classical authors, is fully aware of the dangers of self-deception—of confusing veridical *sentiments* with mere *fantasies*.

It is at this point that the Biblical influence is most apparent. Aristotle's separation of rhetoric from dialectic prevented him from making significant use of the battery of psychological analyses to be found in his *Rhetoric* for distinguishing genuinely dialectical from merely eristic argument. Cicero set out to reintegrate rhetoric into philosophy, and his preferred method of controversy through laying "before my readers the doctrines of the various schools" has, as we have noted, close parallels with Pascal's comparison of the "Wisdom of God" with "all the religions of the world", but his use of psychological analysis in the conduct of such controversy is disappointingly thin. The Biblical "heart", however, provides Pascal with an integrating concept which enables him to treat understanding and will, together with *sentiment*, as interdependent—and thereby make legitimate use of his grasp of human psychology in the co-operative endeavour of testing the "Wisdom of God" against its rivals, secular as well as religious.

In similar fashion to that in which the Book of Job presents the divine wisdom as resolving at one and the same time both psychological and intellectual perplexity, Pascal's "Wisdom of God" represents a context which not only resolves the "contradictions" of the intellect but also all those other conflicts which arise from the tension between man's *grandeur* and *misère*; this tension is seen as pointing beyond itself, and accurately to discern the direction it indicates the "eyes of the heart" need to be enlightened and its "inclinations" purified. As the human situation is that of being *embarqué*, any framework of thinking which centres round the ideal of detached contemplation is defective; concepts and judgements to which we are tempted, but which do not accurately reflect our situation, are likely to mislead, and a perverse will is liable to lead to perverse beliefs. On the other hand, if our will is adequately adjusted to our condition, aspiring to that which will genuinely satisfy us, then concepts and assumptions necessary for achieving our desires will not similarly mislead—but rather accurately represent the structure of the reality within which we live. In comparing Pascal's vignettes of the human condition with each other, with the perspective of Revelation together with the perspectives of its rivals, and, above all, with our own experience, it is essential that the successive layers of our self-deception be stripped away as we aim at that integration of perception, aspiration, and reality which is today called 'authenticity'.

Hume's *Dialogues* are a classic example of the method of Ciceronian controversy, but there are a number of connections with Pascalian *finesse* which are not specifically Ciceronian. The Humean starting-point for philosophizing of "the reflections of common life" echoes the Aristotelian appeal to ἔνδοξα and Pascal's to principles which "are in ordinary usage and there for all to see", and the overall strategy of the work is designed to enable it to handle "irregular" as well as "regular" (geometric) arguments. The key irregular arguments appeal to feeling and psychological compulsion, being exemplified by Cleanthes' "Tell me, from your own feeling, if the idea of a contriver does not immediately flow in upon you with a force like that of sensation" (Hume (7), 154). They appeal, that is, to *sentiment*. Hume is happy to accept "moral" arguments which do not fit the geometric model in a "regular" way, but explicitly objects to the Port-Royal reliance on *sentiment* in this context on the ground that we are provided with no clear criterion by which we may "distinguish Sentiment from Education". The Ciceronian framework both enables the different "systems of cosmogony" to be compared with each other in the light of the available data, and helps to bring out the questionable status of appeal to *sentiment* and human aspiration among such data. For through the dynamics of controversy between his characters, Hume is able "to turn their arguments on every side" in order to counter "the full force of prejudice" which stems from "earliest education". Finesse is here used in an attempt to discriminate "the primary instincts of nature" from those which are secondary, and to allocate religious *sentiment* to the latter category—seen as epistemologically inferior—while providing an overall framework which enables us to see why one might be tempted to think otherwise. The appeal is primarily to a reader who may be inclined to identify himself with Cleanthes, and encourages him to interrogate his own thinking and feeling more searchingly than Cleanthes is represented as doing; the co-operative ideal is still active, and the ideal that of rational persuasiveness.

Nietzsche is Augustine inverted. Augustine, we saw, is the great formative influence behind Pascal's account of the proper adjustment of the will, leading him to see self-love as central among the "powers of deception", for "the bias towards self is the beginning of all disorder" (L.421, B.477, S.680). Nietzsche would agree with them about the importance of the will in authenticating our perceptions and interpretations, and could happily accept Pascal's "The mind, keeping in step with the will, remains looking at the aspect preferred by the will and so judges by what it sees there" (L.539, B.99, S.458). But for him the authentic will is self-affirming, not self-denying, and the relative valuation of Augustine's two "loves" is reversed. In order to enforce the Augustinian priority, we saw, Pascal presents a series of observations drawn from the most pervasive features of human life, and challenges the reader to recognize them as accurate, representative, and cumulatively supporting the misleading character of self-love. Nietzsche meets Pascal on his own terms, and frequently measures his approach against that of "the only logical Christian"; his vignettes are presented as cutting deeper than those of Pascal and pointing towards the self-affirmation of Dionysus rather than the self-negation of the Crucified.

As with Pascal, the Nietzschean method of "philosophizing with a hammer" aspires to the integration of "reason, senses, feeling and will". The Humean move of attempting to discriminate the "primary instincts" from *sentiments* of the type to which Pascal appeals is rejected on the ground that the former are epistemologically no more secure than the latter; for both Pascal and Nietzsche Pyrrhonism cuts deeper than Hume will allow, and we are left with the task of comparing perspectives and interpretations against each other with no *assiette* or *Grundstein*. For Nietzsche, indeed, the goal of truth-seeking is internally related to the capacity to master multiple perspectives; the "hocus-pocus of mathematical form" is useless or worse here, but we nevertheless need "dialectical severity and necessity that takes no false step", and the models which underlie such discipline are drawn from philology and psychology— embodying "that filigree art of grasping . . . nuances". For both Pascal and Nietzsche the aim is to encourage the reader's self-interrogation, and for both the difference between them is properly to be explored by moving from the general to the particular. Each seeks to provide a framework in terms of which the paradoxes involved when once one probes what is "in ordinary usage and there for all to see" may be resolved, and each aims at rational persuasiveness. For Nietzsche the key issue, which opposes his vision to

Pascal's Augustinian one, can only be grasped by an "amazing finesse" (Nietzsche (6), *Twilight*, ii. 2).

Pascal, Hume, and Nietzsche would agree that "The heart has its reasons of which reason knows nothing"; they differ on some of the criteria which purport to tell us how to tell when they are good reasons. But the investigation of such criteria is itself a matter of finesse.

2. Reason, Will, and "Dia-Philosophy"

> It has for a long time been taken for an indisputable axiom that the Mind is in some important sense tripartite, that is, that there are just three ultimate classes of mental processes. The Mind or Soul, we are often told, has three parts, namely, Thought, Feeling and Will; or, more solemnly, the Mind or Soul functions in three irreducibly different modes, the Cognitive mode, the Emotional mode and the Conative mode. This traditional dogma is not only not self-evident, it is such a welter of confusions and false inferences that it is best to give up any attempt to re-fashion it. It should be treated as one of the curios of theory.
>
> (Ryle (1), 62)

The words are those of Professor Ryle but the claim, otherwise expressed, is also that of Pascal. This is no accident. Ryle was concerned to explode the "Cartesian myth" of the mind, and the gap between the understanding (*'entendement'*) and the will (*'volonté'*)—which in the fourth *Meditation* is presented as the main cause of error (see Rodis-Lewis, 41–50)—is one of the most characteristic features of the tradition within which Descartes was working and which Pascal sought to escape. It has been plausibly argued that

> the dissociation of the will, which is alone in our power, from the intellect, whose judgements are extrinsic to it, must be related to certain phenomena of the early seventeenth century. . . . If the word 'rationalist' has any content when applied to early seventeenth-century ethical theory, including that of Descartes, it means essentially . . . the particular dissociation of intellect and will resulting from the stoic revival and the reaction it provoked (Levi (1), 306).

For Pascal, on the other hand, the mind keeps "in step with the will", and the will itself is not wholly within our power; "The mind naturally believes and the will naturally loves, so that when there are no true objects for them they necessarily become attached to false ones" (L.661, B.81, S.544). Both legitimate and illegitimate "loves" are forms of desire, and our desires are a function of the "automation"—habit, passion, and inclination—over which we have only indirect control. We saw in Chapter 5 how Pascal's account of the threefold structure of the "heart", itself set in a threefold hierarchy of "orders", represents an attempt to provide a more flexible framework than that provided by the "traditional dogma" of faculty psychology for interpreting and assessing the relevant phenomena.

The Pascalian approach is not without its modern analogues. One of the most influential recent analyses of volition, understood in terms of "the taking up of an attitude of approval to a state of affairs", subsumes the "theory of desire" within it, and presents volition as structurally isomorphic with judgement when set within an adequate "theory of mental predication" (Kenny, ch. 11). Again, Pascal's Augustinian conception of the "loves" which guide the will in terms of "delectation" is echoed by the claim that "the norm is that it becomes clear what a person wants when it becomes clear what pleases him. In short . . . the connection of desire to pleasure is not analytic, but nor is it just contingent" (Gosling, 114). Similarly, when Nietzsche conceives his version of finesse in terms of "totality" and fighting "the mutual extraneousness of reason, senses, feeling and will" (Nietzsche (6), *Twilight*, ix, 49) he is building on a similar insight to that of Ryle. The objection that the significance of the role of the will in reasoning for such writers exemplifies mere voluntarism represents a misunderstanding. The geometric model encourages the treating of "reason" as extraneous from "senses, feeling and will", providing a concept of logical content which can be given purely formal expression, though at the cost of evacuating the notion of giving good reasons for accepting a hypothesis, or acting in a certain way, of much significance (see Miller (2)). But if we once break with this model, one of the last justifications for conceiving of the intellect and the will as representing essentially dissociated modes of mental functioning is removed, and "voluntarism" becomes as archaic a concept as "intellectualism". From the point of view of finesse, we need to look and see in each case what elements in that complex, "reason, senses, feeling and will", are appropriate in the endeavour to achieve reliable judgements. To take the issue central to the texts by Pascal, Hume, and Nietzsche we have discussed, it is not at all obvious—geometric preconceptions apart—that the habitual self-deceiver is as well placed as the genuine seeker to judge the merits of what Hume terms "the religious hypothesis".

Like its ancestors, Aristotelian dialectic and Ciceronian controversy, finesse is appropriate when the assessment of first principles or of the claims of competing "schools" is in question—in more modern dress, the appraisal of Ayer's "conceptual systems" or Williams's "representations of the world"—such as is involved in the exploration of the conflict between religious and secular conceptions of reality which so concerned Pascal, Hume, and Nietzsche. If reason is conceived geometrically, rationality can only operate here in a somewhat Pickwickian sense; the lingering hold which we saw that model exerting on his thinking in Chapter 1 leads Professor Rorty to maintain that, while it is legitimate for the philosopher to "compare and contrast cultural traditions", he should not suppose that

deep down beneath all the texts, there is something which is not just one more text but that to which various texts are trying to be "adequate", . . . [nor] that there is anything isolable as "the purposes which we construct vocabularies and cultures to fulfil" against which to test vocabularies and cultures. But . . . in the process of playing vocabularies and cultures off against each other, we produce new and better ways of talking and acting—not better by reference to a previously known standard, but just better in the sense that they come to *seem* clearly better than their predecessors (Rorty (2), xxxvii). (See ch. 5, n. 20.)

Pascal and Nietzsche would agree that there is no *assiette* or *Grundstein*, but resist the conclusion that all that is left is mere "seeming"—unless that concept is given a rather richer content than Rorty's procedures appear to allow. Further, the opposition between "seeming" and testing against "a previously known standard" appears to be a product of the geometric model interpreted in terms of "algorithms" ((1), 336); it is reminiscent of the dichotomy between mere subjectivity of judgement and the "one eye on the standard" approach we quoted Dr Leavis as combatting in Chapter 5; in both cases there is room for the exercise of critical intelligence between the horns of the proposed dilemmas. As we saw in the same chapter (n. 12) Wittgenstein, one of Rorty's "heroes" (Rorty (1), 382), has no need of recourse to culture-transcendent standards to be able to affirm of a cultural grouping, "If we compare our system of knowledge with theirs then theirs is evidently the poorer one by far" (Wittgenstein (3), 286). The explanation, as we also saw, is that Wittgenstein's later thinking exhibits many (though of course not all) of the features of finesse.[1]

The activity of "playing vocabularies and cultures off against each other" has illuminating affinities with Professor Castañeda's recent, less relativistic, proposal for a programme of "dia-philosophy".

Sym-philosophical activity consists of the development of philosophical theories, i.e., systematic hypotheses about the general structure of the world and of experience. . . . The ultimate aim is the comparative study of maximal theories in order to establish, through isomorphisms among them, a system of invariances. Such comparisons and the establishment of such isomorphisms and invariances is *dia-philosophy* (Castañeda, 14–15).

The method proposed is said to be especially adequate for Castañeda's version of "phenomenological ontology", understood as

the study of both the most general structures of the world one finds oneself in and the most pervasive patterns of one's experience and thinking of that world . . . [It] is precisely adequate for the study of the structure of *one's* reality. . . .

---

[1] The role of the will in Wittgensteinian finesse is comparatively minor. However, a remarkably full-blooded attempt to make much fuller use of the Nietzschean "totality" in this context has recently been made by Professor Polanyi. Aiming to steer a course between "objectivism" and "subjectivism", he argues that, 'No intelligence, however critical or original, can operate outside . . . a fiduciary framework. While our acceptance of this framework is the condition for having any knowledge, this matrix can claim no self-evidence. . . . This then is our liberation from objectivism: to realize that we can voice our ultimate convictions only from within our convictions—from within the whole system of acceptances that are logically prior to any particular assertion of our own, prior to the holding of any particular piece of knowledge. . . . The fiduciary passions which induce a confident utterance about the facts are *personal*, because they submit to the facts as universally valid, but when we reflect on this act noncommittally its passion is reduced to *subjectivity*. . . . The "actual facts" are accredited facts, as seen within the commitment situation, while subjective beliefs are the convictions accrediting these facts as seen non-committally. . . . But if we regard the beliefs in question non-committally, as a mere state of mind, we cannot speak confidently, without self-contradiction, of the facts to which these beliefs refer' (Polanyi, 266–7 and 303–4).

He instances the sceptical dilemma, as exemplified by the Hume of the *Treatise*, as arising from pursuit of the impossible goal of "objectivism", catching him "in an insoluble conflict between a demand for an impersonality which would discredit all commitment and an urge to make up his mind which drives him to recommit himself" (304). But the proposed "personal knowledge", though "liberated from objectivism", is still seen as counting as knowledge in a much stronger sense than does Rorty's "seeming".

The methodology . . . allows for the possibility that there may be many different ontological systems of one's reality, all such systems being wholly comprehensive and mutually incompatible, but all equally valid descriptions of one's reality. It may be, thus, that no given maximal ontological system has a definite superiority over the other competing maximal systems. . . .

But then there is a sense in which something like a reality in itself lurks behind those maximal alternative ontological systems. For one thing, looking as it were through several of those systems, one would be looking at different manifestations and structurings of the same reality. One would be freeing oneself from the fetters and constraints of each particular carving out of reality in itself (18–19).

The obvious parallel here is with Nietzsche's 'There is *only* a perspective seeing, *only* a perspective "knowing"; and the *more* affects we allow to speak about one thing, the *more* eyes, different eyes, we can use to observe one thing, the more complete will our "concept" of this thing, our "objectivity", be' (Nietzsche (7), *Genealogy of Morals*, iii. 12). But Castañeda, like Nietzsche, goes further;

If there are many maximal ontological systems of one's reality all on equal footing, then it may be possible to develop a kind of *internal metaphysics*. This is what we call *dia-philosophy*. It consists of the study of isomorphisms among the maximal ontological systems of one and the same person's reality. *If* there are several such systems, then if there are isomorphisms, although perhaps only partial, across those systems, then such isomorphisms constitute a super-system of ontology that underlies the plurality of the maximal ontological systems (19).

Nietzsche's "Will to Power" would presumably represent one characterization of such a "super-system", and Pascal's probing of different systems of "order" an exploration of possible isomorphisms.

This "internal metaphysics", without any attempted recourse to a Rorty-like "previously known standard", has several further points of contact with finesse as we have sketched it. It is a co-operative endeavour, enabling different people's reality to be brought into relationship and one's projection of one's own reality to be tested against the projections of others:[2]

---

[2] Compare: 'The alternative to complete objectivity and complete subjectivity is inter-subjectivity' (Holley, 279).

Only a vital philosophical pluralism can prepare the way for dia-philosophy. Naturally, that requires that we see those philosophers working in full detail on unfashionable views, even on views that jar our sensibilities, as *partners* in the same dia-philosophical enterprise! This is not a Carnapian principle of tolerance. . . . It is, rather, both a Kantian principle of the convergence of all total and fully developed ontologies and a super-Hegelian principle of the ultimate integration of opposite ontologies—if dia-philosophy turns out, empirically, to be feasible (Castañeda, 20–1).

Again, the procedure envisaged is remarkably reminiscent of Ciceronian controversy; "the greatest philosophical illumination will come forth from the striking of those full theories against each other at their points of contrast" (ibid. 106). Further, the account of the preparatory "sym-philosophical" activity in terms of the "exegesis . . . of data" (112), taken together with the claim that "the relationship from data to theory is not deductive" (114), has significant affinities with Nietzsche's account of philosophizing in terms of "interpretation", employing exegetical principles derived from philology, and reminds us that for Pascal too the exegetical practices associated with the sphere of "memory" have a crucial role to play among the "reasons of the heart".

Given these parallels, Castañeda's more specific methodological principles are of some relevance to finesse. One has Aristotelian echoes; in somewhat similar fashion to that in which dialectic proceeds by attempting to bring out underlying principles which will reconcile apparent "contradictions" among ἔνδοξα, so one must "exegize the data very carefully, so as to bring out conflicts among the data, hidden connections among them, and patterns of conflicts and connections, all of which open up theoretical options and furnish criteria of adequacy for the proposed theories" (112). A second requires "maximal data"; "One must always propose a theory for . . . a philosophical pattern of reality or of experience, taking into account *all* the relevant data available at the time of theorization." The final one I shall cite concerns simplicity; in comparing such theories one should, in good Ciceronian fashion, compare them as wholes and only then consider "whether the two theories cater to exactly the same data and whether, assuming both to be consistent, one is really simpler than the other" (117), for "two theories can be advantageously compared for simplicity *only* to the extent that they cater to the same data" (114).

This final contention is highly questionable, for it implies that such comparisons are only in place where the criteria for individuation of data in the two theories are commensurable, and hence there is a high degree of translatability between the object languages of the theories. But while there must no doubt be some points of common reference for comparisons to be possible—in their different ways, Pascal, Hume, and Nietzsche are all concerned to answer, for example, the latter's question: "What is the meaning of ascetic ideals?" (Nietzsche (7), *Genealogy*, 'Third Essay')—Castañeda's principle appears over-stringent. It has been plausibly argued that in the sciences rational choice between theories is possible even where data are not commensurable, so long as there is agreement on "meta-level goals"; examples suggested include

maximum problem-solving ability, maximum internal coherence, simplicity and minimum anomalies. With any one of these goals in mind, we could (and some philosophers already have) generate machinery for comparing theories. None of this machinery need entail any object-level comparability between the theories under analysis. . . . Incommensurability of theories at the object-level does not entail incomparability at the meta-level. *The widely-held assumption that non-translatability leads inevitably to cognitive relativism is simply mistaken* (Laudan, 595–6; see also ch. I, n. 17).

The broader scope of finesse over that of purely scientific methodology increases the difficulty of agreement at even the meta-level, but analogues remain possible. For example, to take merely the first of the cited "meta-level goals", Professor Rapaport invokes a thoroughly Classical conception of what is at stake, 'the *process* of "doing philosophy"—of constantly challenging and questioning —is the very essence of progress', and uses it to argue that

there is progress even if the only sense in which we understand the problem better is the important one that we know what *won't* work. . . . For to know what *won't* work is to know what *would* work *if* we were willing to accept those principles whose rejection forestalls a solution. Accepting such principles allows problems to be solved (thus allowing the number of solutions to be a measure of progress).

And further, *"Knowing what our commitments must be for us to have solutions is progress"* (Rapaport, 296).

But where data are commensurable, Castañeda's criterion of

simplicity of theory relating "maximal data" has an important role to play, and his comment that such simplicity should not be "confused with the simplicity of data" (109) is salutary. Nietzsche, too, saw "method" as "essentially economy of principles" (Nietzsche (7), *BGE*, 13), but insisted on taking "maximal data" into account including those elements which fall into the traditionally distinguished categories of the "Emotional and Conative modes". If "phenomenological ontology" is to be grounded in "the most pervasive patterns of one's experience and thinking" it needs to take account of the full Nietzschean "totality; . . . reason, senses, feeling and will"; the proposed dia-philosophy, therefore, should be concerned with all these dimensions of finesse.

3. Abduction, Paraduction, and Rational Persuasion

When we consider those non-geometric inferential models developed in extra-philosophical contexts sketched in Chapter 1, we find a number of parallels with philosophical finesse. The latter provides a context within which the philosophical roles of several such proposals may be set and mutually related.

The problems we noted above concerning commensurability of data weaken the applicability of Lakatos's "research programme" model, though Castañeda's finesse-like programme of "dia-philosophy" has a number of specific features often encountered in scientific methodology. But at a more general level, the obvious inferential parallel in the field of the philosophy of science is that of Peircean abduction (see ch. 1, n. 21): 'The surprising fact, C, is observed; But if A were true, C would be a matter of course. Hence there is reason to suspect that A is true' (Peirce, v, para. 189). The drive of Aristotelian dialectic to find accounts that will resolve perplexities among ἔνδοξα has certain points of contact with the Peircean pattern, but the closest analogy from the works we have considered is that of the overall shape of Pascal's projected *Apology*: "Who will unravel such a tangle? . . . Listen to God" (L.131, B.434, S.164); the surprising tension between man's *grandeur* and *misère* is noted, but if the teaching of Revelation were true this tension would be a matter of course, hence there is reason to suspect that Revelation is true. Such an argument, as Peirce insists, merely suggests that A may be true; it does not show that it actually is the case, let alone prove that it must be so. So Pascal supplements this overall pattern with his detailed hermeneutic "proofs" drawn from the sphere of "memory", together with the challenge to find any other serious candidate but A for which C would be a matter of course:

Man's greatness and wretchedness are so evident that the true religion must necessarily teach us that there is in man some great principle of greatness and some great principle of wretchedness. . . .
Let us examine all the religions of the world on that point and let us see whether any but the Christian religion meets it. (L.149, B.430, S.182)

The force of the latter move is such that any proposed rival candidate must not be merely an *ad hoc* hypothesis dreamed up for the occasion, hence my qualifier "serious" and the way Pascal is only concerned to consider the competing claims of established systems of thought.

The abductive pattern is, indeed, characteristic of finesse, but it always needs supplementation. Hume is concerned to show both that there are many other hypotheses besides the "religious" one according to which the "surprising" facts instanced by Cleanthes would be "a matter of course", and that in the only sense in which the "religious hypothesis" has independent support it is too empty to count as an explanation of any such specific range of phenomena. Nietzsche presents a seriously worked out alternative to the Pascalian, which is no *ad hoc* hypothesis and purports to account both for the phenomena Pascal notes and a further important range which play no apparent role in his account; Nietzsche is also prepared to do battle in the order of "memory", hence his rubric 'Historical refutation as the decisive refutation' (Nietzsche (4), 95).

In this supplementation of abduction the characteristic legal procedure of "paraduction",[3] or arguing from particular to particular by reflecting on "the likenesses and dissimilarities of particular instances", plays an important role. It has been described as "the most usual mode of legal argument" (Stone, 481) but, as we saw in

---

[3] The term 'paraduction' is taken from Stone, but its roots are as Aristotelian as is Peirce's 'abduction'. Aristotle gives thumbnail sketches of induction (ἐπαγωγή), paraduction (παράδειγμα) and abduction (ἀπαγωγή) in Chapters 23, 24, and 25 respectively of the second book of his *Prior Analytics* but, as is pointed out in the text, Aristotle's analysis of paraduction—or argument by example—is significantly different from that of Wisdom; for Aristotle's account see ch. 2.2.

Chapter 1, Professor Wisdom has drawn attention to the important role this "case-by-case" procedure plays in philosophy; his most famous exposition of this argumentative mode runs as follows:

In such cases we notice that the process of argument is not a *chain* of demonstrative reasoning. It is a presenting and re-presenting of those features of the case which *severally* co-operate in favour of the conclusion, in favour of saying what the reasoner wishes said, in favour of calling the situation by the name by which he wishes to call it. The reasons are like the legs of a chair, not the links of a chain. Consequently although the discussion is *a priori* and the steps are not a matter of experience, the procedure resembles scientific argument in that the reasoning is not *vertically* extensive but *horizontally* extensive—it is a matter of the cumulative effect of several independent premises, not of the repeated transformation of one or two. And because the premises are severally inconclusive the process of deciding the issue becomes a matter of weighing the cumulative effect of one group of severally inconclusive items against the cumulative effect of another group of severally inconclusive items (Wisdom (1), 157).

He sets this account in the context of a discussion of the conflict between religious and secular conceptions of reality, and the sketch provided at the close of Chapter 7 of how—on the principles of finesse—the debate between the Pascalian and Nietzschean visions might be conducted involves this sort of "presenting and re-presenting"; for both Pascal and Nietzsche the debate can only be resolved by moving from the general to the particular. When once abduction has suggested that A may be true, but also that B has similar warrant, paraduction, the setting of "cases" side by side, may play a legitimate role in deciding between them.

Two features of Wisdom's analysis are especially worthy of note here. First, it moves from particular features to a particular conclusion—such as characterizing a situation in a particular way—as opposed to deduction's characteristic move from general to more specific, and induction's from particular to general; the temptation to assimilate the case-by-case procedure to Aristotle's quasi-inductive rhetorical argument by example (see ch. 2.2) should be resisted, for the former does not make the latter's implicit use of unstated generalizations. Second, arguments of this type are cumulative. The first point is seen by Wisdom as having very wide significance, for "the difference between deduction and argument

by parallels is merely a matter of form" (Yalden-Thomson, 62).[4]
The argument, briefly, is that

The deductive proof of C from P is no more than a case-by-case proof of C,
. . . for to prove a conclusion C from P is valid only when every investigation and every comparison required for the establishment of C is also
required for the establishment of P. . . . In cases of deductive reasoning the
conclusion is no better established . . . than it is by this process of the direct
case-by-case procedure (ibid. 64–5).

When we argue from "All men are mortal" and "Socrates is a man"
to "Socrates is mortal" we need to ask whether the case of Socrates
has been included in the establishment of the generalization; if it has
been the argument is circular, but if not we need to compare this
case with those that were so used in order to see why Socrates might
not prove an exception. Further, the validity of the form of such an
argument cannot be established by arguments of the same form, for
similar reasons (compare Haack (2)); to establish the validity of
"All arguments in form F are valid, and this is an argument in form
F, therefore this argument is valid" we need to consider paradigm
cases of valid arguments in form F and to show that this one parallels
them—in other words, to employ the case-by-case procedure
(Bambrough (5), 131–3). Induction too, it is argued, involves

[4] Characterizing the difference between deduction and argument by parallels as
"merely a matter of form" is perhaps over condensed and could be misleading. The
thesis seems to be that the obvious syntactic differences between the two modes do
not mark "parallel" semantic discrepancies. In other words, the ideal of semantic
validity associated with deduction (that it be impossible for premisses to be true and
conclusion false) also has its place in the "case-by-case" procedure; for deduction the
production of a (real or imaginary) counter-example is a decisive matter, but this can
also be the case in the other mode—though here what is to count as such an example
may be a matter for further argument. This ideal, however, represents only the
limiting case with respect to argument by parallels, for Wisdom maintains that "all
reflection comes in the end to a case-by-case procedure" (Yalden-Thomson, 62), but
not all worthwhile reflection achieves deductive cogency. The advantage of standard
(deductive) logical syntax, it would appear, is that of enabling us to recognize validity
in a quasi-mechanical ("geometric") manner; but this advantage is bought at
considerable epistemological cost.

Professor Wisdom distinguishes between reasoning by parallels and reasoning by
analogy, on the ground that the latter excludes imaginary instances. This appears to
be stipulative; in many standard classifications argument by analogy is not so
restricted.

I am most grateful to Professor Wisdom for allowing me to see an unpublished
version of his Virginia Lectures on 'Proof and Explanation', which have influenced
my handling of a number of issues. I have taken care to ensure that all quotations
from this material, and related accounts of his position, are taken from those
portions which are already in the public domain.

reasoning by parallels. (Yalden-Thomson, 63) Deduction cannot ground deduction or induction induction; "at the bar of reason, always the final appeal is to cases" (Wisdom (3), 102). One is reminded of Nietzsche's "Logic is bound to the condition; assume there are identical cases. In fact, to make possible logical thinking and inferences, this condition must first be treated fictitiously as fulfilled" (Nietzsche (8), 512).

Such paraduction is not undisciplined. According to Wisdom there are three fundamental operators: "You might as well say . . .", "Exactly so", and "But this is different". Bambrough (5), 134) points up the similarity of the role they play to Leavis's two basic operators—"This is so, isn't it?" and "Yes, but . . ."—in his similar defence of argumentation employing a high degree of particularity which we compared to Pascal's practice in Chapter 5; 'My whole effort was to work in terms of concrete judgements and particular analyses: "This—doesn't it?—bears such a relation to that; this kind of thing—don't you find it so?—wears better than that", etc.' (Leavis (1), 215). In both cases the procedure is essentially a co-operative one, with a structure sufficiently flexible to allow for many of the elements we have seen to be characteristic of finesse. Of Leavis's version Bambrough argues that

His description applies equally well to any discussion that proceeds, as all discussion does in the last resort, by comparison and contrast of particular instances with particular instances. In the last resort, wherever there is conflict about what is so, about what is true or false, good or bad, right or wrong, there is scope for the same appeal, 'This is so, isn't it?' and the same rejoinder, 'Yes, but . . .'. But this summary is faithful to the ultimate character of conflict only because it also brings to light that the conflict is between parties who also *agree*. Not only does the 'Yes' of the respondent's 'Yes, but . . .' signify agreement, but the 'but' itself draws attention to something that can also be recognised by the author of the original 'This is so, isn't it?'. The 'but' itself is a new 'This is so, isn't it?' and may call for another answering 'Yes, but . . .'. Here we have the shape that qualifies moral discussion and critical discussion and philosophical discussion and in the last resort all discussion to be called by the ancient name of *dialectic*. We can represent the complexity that such a fundamental enquiry deals with, without becoming bewildered by the maze of detail, only if we give this dialectical structure to our strivings after understanding of the detail. And this remains true whatever the scale of the operation, from the minute examination of one of Virgil's half-lines to the vast scale on which the philosopher may sometimes operate (Bambrough (5), 102–3).

The emphasis on "agreement" is further elucidated a few pages earlier:

(1) you and I cannot be known to be in conflict unless it is possible to identify a proposition that I assert with a proposition that you deny; (2) no such proposition can be identified unless there is some expression that you and I use in the same way; (3) if we use an expression in the same way then we regard the same steps as relevant to determining the truth or falsehood of what is expressed by it; for a disagreement about what *is* relevant is or involves a disagreement about what the dispute is that we are engaged in, and when such a case of cross-purposes is resolved it resolves itself either into agreement or into a disagreement to which all these conditions again apply. (87)

Elsewhere this overall pattern of agreement and dissent is argued to apply to that conflict between Nietzsche and the Christian perspective we discussed in Chapter 7 (Bambrough (2), 16).

The second feature of Wisdom's analysis of the case-by-case procedure we noted, correlative to the first, is its cumulative nature. The weighing of "severally inconclusive items", taken collectively, may prove conclusive even where—as is usual—there is no upper limit to the number of possibly relevant items; "an enquiry may be inexhaustible without being inconclusive" (Bambrough (5), 141). The non-hierarchical structure of this type of reasoning[5] facilitates

[5] 'Non-hierarchical' may recall Professor Nozick's championing of "patterning" in philosophy over the model of the "tower" with foundations (641 and 3). There are several points of contact between finesse and Nozick's account; the characterization of 'understanding' as locating something "in a network of possibility" (12) fits the case-by-case procedure well, and his discussion of the reversability of certain types of philosophical argument (9) parallels my own comments in ch. 1 on the direction of a *reductio*. However, the main body of his account is concerned with "explanation" rather than "understanding", and this appears to be associated with the way he still seems to think in terms of deduction as the fundamental paradigm—his preferred "explanation" is presented as the mirror image of deductive "proof" (13).

Another recent discussion which comes close to seeing the importance of finesse is that of Professor Rescher; in considering debate between different philosophical "systems" he points out the "pivotal role of analogy" and insists that "the 'logic' of analogical reasoning becomes a paramount consideration for philosophy" (98–100). He gives prime position to "the *degree of analogy* in terms of the relative importance (weight, significance) of the various similarities and disimilarities" (100), but after this promising start he resolves the issue into one concerning "cognitive values" which "reflect an intellectual predilection" and fall foul of the "fact/value distinction" so that such disputes "cannot be resolved objectively" (102–15). For an excellent critique of this invocation of "cognitive values" see Haack (5).

A further parallel to my own account is adumbrated in Anthony Quinton's sympathetic discussion of "the kind of unmethodical, accumulative procedure by which a mass of sensitive responses are precipitated into a philosophical belief, . . . a

the incorporation into it of widely diverse types of instance, taken from the whole Nietzschean "totality" where appropriate, so long as there are informatively discussable parallels between them; on the other hand, they may be so closely related—as we noted in considering Cohen's axiomatization of the convergence of circumstantial evidence in Chapter 1.5—that the "independence" Wisdom speaks of is of a very weak kind. Further, such argument may lead one to revise conventional opinion about the relative degrees of independence; by use of it Bambrough is led to "deny that there are any moral questions which are not also questions of fact or questions of logic or mixtures of questions of fact and questions of logic" (Bambrough (5), 72). Pascal and Nietzsche, on the evidence we have considered, would agree. Again, the sorts of arguments Philo and Cleanthes consider in Hume's *Dialogues* have also been plausibly described as cumulative; such argument

is not comparable with a chain whose strength is precisely that of its weakest link; it is comparable rather with a piece of chain-armour. And this can the better be seen if the relevant facts be presented again so as to display especially their connexions and their gradually increasing suggestiveness (Tennant, ii. 104).

Wisdom's analysis, therefore, points at least prima facie to types of cases of the sort we saw were needed in Chapter 1 if we are to follow Mitchell in invoking the practice of building cumulative cases in critical exegesis and historical controversy when exploring philosophical argument. If paraduction applies equally, as Bambrough insists, in "critical discussion and philosophical discussion", then the hermeneutic principles of critical exegesis are relevant to finesse. We have seen that Nietzsche, through characterizing philosophical theses as 'interpretations', makes just this move: 'Forgive me as an old philologist who cannot desist from the malice of putting his finger on bad modes of interpretation: but "nature's conformity to law" . . . exists only owing to your interpretation and bad

---

notion embodied in Pascal's *esprit de finesse* or Newman's illative sense" (20–1). However this is presented as a mode of supplying philosophical ideas "with a different kind of support from that provided by standard philosophic reasoning". That Cartesian assumptions lie behind Quinton's conception of this latter form of reasoning is perhaps suggested by his characterization of the Pascalian procedure as "unmethodical".

"philology"' (Nietzsche (7), 22). His tracing of so much philosophy
to its roots in grammar encourages him to give philology a prominent place among those elements of "scholarship" he characterizes
as essential to the "new philosopher". Similarly, in Chapter 5 we
noted Pascal's use, in his "proofs of memory", of hermeneutic
principles very close to those Dame Helen Gardner finds in literary
criticism:

> If it is a passage which we are interpreting, the final test is always the
> consistency of the interpretation of the passage with the interpretation of
> the work as a whole. If we are attempting the interpretation of a single
> complete work, the test is the reverse of this: does our interpretation of the
> whole make sense of all the parts? (Gardner, 53)

Once again we have a case-by-case procedure, to which Bambrough's instancing of "Virgil's half lines" could well be relevant; it
has structural parallels to that "Hermeneutic Circle" which, as we
saw, Rorty regards as debarring a hermeneutically conceived
philosophy from "representing things as they really are" (Rorty (1),
319 and 334), but in the context of finesse the circle no longer looks
threatening. Hume's *Dialogues* indeed, following Ciceronian principles, are designed to be read hermeneutically, but there can
certainly be "bad modes of interpretation" here; Demea, for
example, is certainly not "the Hero of the Dialogue".

Wisdom's three fundamental operators are only in the loosest
sense "formalizable", and they apply in a collaborative dialectic
which aims at resolving disagreement; as it is also claimed that
"deduction itself is a case-by-case procedure" (Yalden-Thomson,
62), it is not surprising to find the most Wisdomesquely exuberant
character in his extended series of dialogues exemplifying the
technique remarking that "There is no sharp line between logic and
philosophy. Logic is rhetoric, proof persuasion, and philosophy
logic played with especially elastic equations" (Wisdom (2), 86).
Even when speaking more soberly in his own voice, as we saw in
Chapter 1, he is prepared to describe the technique of reasoning by
parallels "rational persuasion" and add "only this mixture is critical
proof and the name of it is rhetoric" ((1), 246). The Platonic divorce
between philosophy and rhetoric has repeatedly been re-enacted
(see, for example, Ijsseling), especially by those committed to the
geometric model of rationality, but from the point of view of finesse
Cicero's wish to heal the breach is congenial. The danger, of course,

is that in paying attention to the role of persuasion in dialectical discussion the qualifier "rational" will be evacuated of content; thus Aristotle, as we saw in Chapter 2, was content to advise the dialectician to find a partner who is a trained thinker prepared to participate in a serious co-operative enquiry—and leave it at that. But Augustine's perception that even in such a context some of the considerations adduced in Aristotle's *Rhetoric* remain relevant ((1), *Soliloquies*, II. vii. 14) points to the need for Rylean "persuasions of conciliatory kinds"; persuading, certainly, cannot properly be characterized as 'valid' or 'invalid', but from this truism it is a mistake "to jump to the conclusion that there can be *no* question of validity where persuasion is involved, and that persuading cannot therefore be rational" (Garver, 173).

This is a matter which has been widely canvassed in the field of theology and, as so often, the essential point has been neatly summed up by Dr Farrer:

Without the readiness of faith, the evidence of God will not be accepted, or will not convince. This is not to say that faith is put in the place of evidence. What convinces us is not our faith, but the evidence; faith is a subjective condition favourable to the reception of the evidence (Farrer (3), 22).

Pascal, of course, while he would have certain reservations about the implied definition of 'faith', used a very similar perception as the foundation of the rhetorical strategy for his proposed *Apology*;

Order. Men despise religion. They hate it and are afraid it may be true. The cure for this is first to show that religion is not contrary to reason, but worthy of reverence and respect.
    Next make it attractive, make good men wish it were true, and then show that it is (L.12, B.187, S.46).

In more general terms, when a reasoner is involved in the "presenting and re-presenting of those features of the case which severally co-operate . . . in favour of calling the situation by the name by which he wishes to call it" (Wisdom (1), 157), it is often appropriate to prepare the mind of one's partner to perceive the crucial connections. For example, we have seen that Wittgenstein suggests that when we come to believe "a whole system of propositions" an appropriate metaphor is "Light dawns gradually over the whole" (Wittgenstein (3), 141), but he has written extensively elsewhere of what is involved in the "dawning" of an aspect and the way that a "duck-rabbit surrounded by rabbits" may be seen differently from one surrounded by ducks ((2), II. xi); for light to dawn over a "whole" the rhetorical presentation of the appropriate background may well be in place, as when Hume uses Demea's "strong imagery" to help "root out a whole vision of reality" (Morrisroe (2), 967) and replace it with one closer to that of Philo. Here especially attention to Nietzsche's "totality" can be important.

For Aristotle the eristic is not a fit partner in dialectic. Pascal aims his rhetoric at "good men" who genuinely seek the truth, for "There is enough light for those who wish to see, and enough darkness for those of a contrary disposition" (L.149, B.430, S.182). Similarly Professor Perelman, with his analysis of rational argumentation in terms of "adherence of minds", ultimately appeals to the "élite" audience which is partially defined—as we saw in Chapter 1—by its preparedness to assess the strength of arguments on the principle, "that which was capable of convincing in a specific situation will appear to be convincing in a similar or analogous situation" (464); it must observe, that is, the basic rules of paraduction. Many rhetorical procedures are concerned to handle audiences less principled than these, and persuasions in such cases are likely to be less than rational; but, as Cicero saw, this fact does not show that all rhetorical procedures are irrelevant in dialectical enquiry. Where there is no question of arguing in eristic fashion only to win, but rather a serious co-operative investigation to discover the truth through obedience to Perelman's "rule of justice", the rhetorical model of argumentation fits into place within finesse's quest for *rational* persuasion through a combination of the Classical insistence on method and the Biblical aspiration after authenticity.[6]

4. The Aesthetics of Argument

> All structures in words are partly rhetorical, and hence literary, and . . . the notion of a scientific or philosophical verbal structure free of rhetorical elements is an illusion.
>
> (Frye, 350)

---

[6] It should be clear by now why I have included no Kantian case-study in my account of finesse. Kant's insistence on excluding rhetoric from the field of philosophical reasoning (see ch. 2 n. 54) keeps his approach distinct from that of finesse, though he is certainly well aware of many of the pitfalls of the Cartesian model.

So far as philosophical verbal structures are concerned, Professor Frye's contention has received perceptive support from William Righter. The latter criticizes

the habit of mind which sees feelings and attitudes, framed necessarily in some imaginative sort of way, as separate in kind from the world of evidence and argument. . . . This separation is not only unnecessary, but is in fact a misrepresentation of the way in which philosophy is done; . . . the modes of argument and imagination are interdependent (211).

This interdependence can take many forms, including that of the philosophical novel which is Righter's main concern, but even in less imaginatively extended forms of philosophizing

there will be a minimal sense of this interdependence where argument is contained in the imaginative forms that 'act it out'. . . . All reasoning about human affairs is dependent on some picture of actions, events, relationships, with which argument may be concerned. Human actions and their consequences, the working out of situations, the wish to become clear about problems in the philosophy of morals or society, depend upon a sequence where 'arguing' and 'imagining' are inseparable. There must be someone to borrow books, and someone to whom promises are made. There must be varying circumstances in which intentions, moral or otherwise, choices and decisions, have one or another kind of sense. And it is by altering the picture, by setting different terms or conditions, or telling a different kind of 'story' that arguments become relevant or irrelevant, have force, look foolish—and even, persuade or fail to persuade. This lowest level may contain several kinds of pictures of states of affairs, or of narrative which may or may not be extended. And our pleasure or excitement in what we think to be an argument of consequence is often in the ingenuity with which some such picture is altered, or the perfection or finesse with which the case is reinvented, the telling example found. Perhaps I am suggesting that even at the minimum level the imaginative demand is connected with some kind of aesthetic of argument.

The connection of 'aesthetic' with 'persuade' matches Frye's 'literary' with 'rhetorical'; poetics and rhetoric cannot be finally divorced, even in a "philosophical verbal structure".

Righter's stress on the varying circumstances in which items "have one or another kind of sense", and on the argumentative relevance of "altering the picture", is reminiscent of the rhetorical presentation of appropriate background we noticed in connection with Hume and Wittgenstein; the instances of borrowing books and keeping promises remind us that such considerations apply even in such apparently non-literary debates as those among Professor Geach's "Objectivists" and "Oxford Moralists" (Geach 35–7).[7] If "all reflection comes in the end to a case-by-case procedure" (Yalden-Thomson, quoting Wisdom, 62), this is not surprising; even Spinoza is a favourite subject of study in the humanities for reasons other than his pretensions to "geometric" austerity. Professor Hepburn has suggested that

we may have to admit the presence here of a spectrum of language-use. At one end of it will be poetry which satisfies the symbolists' demands: its mid-positions will contain those writings that use poetic language-devices and yet lack the 'insulation' of pure poetry: at the opposite end will be located pure philosophy, 'demythologised' and free of every poetic device (Hepburn, 343).

However he immediately concedes, not only that "it may turn out that little or no poetry *completely* satisfies the symbolist criteria at their strongest", but also that "no philosophy may be altogether free of metaphor and analogy". Hackforth's dichotomy between "scientific proof" and "imaginative discourse" together with its analogues, which we have repeatedly encountered since Chapter 3 in the work of commentators influenced by "geometric" assumptions, represents an absolutizing of the two ends of this spectrum; but not only is philosophical finesse conducted in its "mid-positions", where the opposition is actively misleading, but its ends are no more than ideal limits.

One reason it has often appeared otherwise has been the hold of the geometric ideal. Ever since the seventeenth-century language reforms associated with the Royal Society and the project of a universal language or "character", there have been recurrent aspirations after Hepburn's "pure philosophy". According to those programmes, each word should relate to a distinct idea and the syntax should be transparent, so that controversies expressible in it should in principle be capable of being settled by calculation (see Cohen (1) and Slaughter). Leibniz's logical work was in part intended as a contribution to the syntax of the universal character, and although the semantics proved intractable, the present cen-

---

[7] For an influential example of the interdependence between argument and imaginative demand within the field of epistemology, consider the role of Quine's image of a field with periphery and interior in the total economy of his 'Two Dogmas of Empiricism'.

tury's logical positivist movement with post-Leibnizian logical syntax providing the framework within which the verification principle did its semantic work was its lineal descendant. From this point of view philosophical argument is to be assessed by reference to the logical content of the various propositions involved, mapped in the context of a formalizable logical system. In the absence of any existing universal character, the actual language used is liable to be misleading—grammatical form can be misleading as to logical form. Thus a gap opens up between the style in which a philosophical argument is presented and its content, and we find commentators like Gallop assuming that "philosophic study" of the *Phaedo* —for example—can be adequately carried out with only perfunctory reference to the dramatic style and context of Plato's arguments. But once we acknowledge the severe limitations of the geometric model, much of the attraction of this approach evaporates.

The case studies we have explored help reinforce this conclusion. If we attempt to treat the *Phaedo* as an integrated whole, treating form and content as indissolubly connected, we find that—even at a philosophical level—it is more to be taken seriously than is usually recognized. Similar considerations apply in the other cases; the alternative to close reading of such authors is likely to be the imposition of contemporary categories on them which distort the interpretation and hence the assessment of their value even in the contemporary context. Righter's considerations suggest that analogous considerations may apply even where the imaginative dimension is minimal.

Style is not everything in the text, but there is nothing that is not touched by it—and this means that unless we read for style consciously, with the awareness of its role in shaping the process of reading, we shall be reading style anyway, but as nature—our *own* nature. Bacon named a "crime of the mind" the tendency of a mind "to identify its own sense of order with the cosmic order". This is exactly what the presumption of neutrality or stylelessness in philosophical discourse does (Lang, 43).

But the literary critic's characteristic questions about style and tone, about how (and how well) a work is made, and about what qualities of the imagination its language exhibits appear to have a direct bearing on Righter's "aesthetic of argument". Arnold, notoriously, argued that "The superior character of truth and seriousness, in the matter and substance of the best poetry, is inseparable from the superiority of diction and movement marking its style and manner" (Arnold, 22). Arnold, however, is not alone. John Casey has pointed out the ways in which those practices of close reading known as "practical criticism" with their attention to minute particularity lend him support, at least where the detection of seriousness and sincerity of emotion is concerned, adding that

> The refusal to separate form and content which is characteristic of both Arnold and Leavis is certainly right for this sort of criticism, because the quality of emotion is indeed bound up with the language in which it is expressed, in exactly the way they say it is. In this sense the form does guarantee the content (Casey, 184).

To the extent that emotion plays a significant role in that "totality" of which Nietzsche wrote, any such contention has important implications for finesse.

Leavis, indeed, is committed to some such totality; for him "emotional quality" and "thought" are typically interdependent, and it is a mark of distinguished achievement when "feeling is not divorced from thinking" (Leavis (2), i. 216). Thus he is able in his critical practice to display an almost Biblical concern for authenticity of the sort we have found to be characteristic of finesse;

> in the examination of [Shelley's] poetry the literary critic finds himself passing, by inevitable transitions, from describing characteristics to making adverse judgements about emotional quality; and so to a kind of discussion in which, by its proper methods and in pursuit of its proper ends, literary criticism becomes the diagnosis of what, looking for an inclusive term, we can only call spiritual malady ((2), i. 219).

It is hardly surprising that we found his methodology apt for comparison when we discussed that of Pascal in Chapter 5. For Leavis, it will be remembered,

> The critic's aim is, first, to realize as sensitively and completely as possible this or that which claims his attention; and a certain valuing is implicit in the realizing. As he matures in experience of the new thing he asks, explicitly and implicitly: 'Where does this come? How does it stand in relation to . . . ? How relatively important does it seem?' And the organization into which it settles as a constituent in becoming 'placed' is an organization of similarly 'placed' things, things that have found their bearings with regard to one another, and not a theoretical system or a system determined by abstract considerations (Leavis (1), 213).

Dr Pole has been notably severe about Leavis's use of the term 'theoretical' here, with the implied contrast between 'theory' and 'organization', but even he has endorsed the "admirable positive depiction of an 'organization', not as static but emerging; . . . the process of creative thought" (Pole (1), 182), and, to the extent that Leavis's conception of "theory" is of a "system" which provides geometric "norms" in terms of which one "measures every poet", his contrast is not without its point. The recommended procedure is, as we have seen, that of the case-by-case procedure, with interpretation and evaluation very closely interconnected,[8] and the characteristic question "This is so, isn't it?" is no mere rhetorical flourish, but an invitation to debate—where the response "Yes, but . . ." must be accompanied by reasons, examples, new perceptions, and discriminations.

Such "practical criticism" is today somewhat dated. But it is not clear that the fashionable criticisms fatally undermine the claims for some such method in the practice of philosophical finesse. Marxist critics, of course, take issue with the notion that literary value can be sustained outside a narrow range of "ideological" contexts;

Literary value is a phenomenon which is *produced* in that ideological appropriation of the text, that 'consumptional production' of the work, which is the act of reading. It is always *relational* value: 'exchange value'. The histories of 'value' are a sub-sector of the histories of literary-ideological receptive practices (Eagleton, 166–7).

But of course the term 'ideology' itself is not wholly value-free, and to justify this reductive mode of thought with its rebarbative vocabulary the "perspective" that sustains it needs to be itself sustained through a form of "dialectic"; and in this dialectic, the close reading of texts by Marx and others may well play a significant role.

More radically, Derridean deconstruction has put in question the whole practice of interpreting texts, including Marxist ones, in ways which take seriously their surface meaning.

---

[8] Casey (ch. 8) characterizes and defends the interconnections between the descriptive and evaluative elements in Leavis's criticism as criteriological, though conceding that at certain points Leavis topples over into treating them as deductively related. For an extended and sophisticated attempt, in similar spirit, to sort out some of the similarities and differences between descriptive and evaluative discourse, and hence of the possibilities of inferential movement between items in the different ranges, see Bambrough (5).

The good writing has . . . always been *comprehended*. Comprehended as that which had to be comprehended: within a nature or a natural law, created or not, but first thought within an eternal presence. Comprehended, therefore, within a totality, and enveloped in a volume or a book. The idea of a book is the idea of a totality, finite or infinite, of the signifier; this totality of the signifier cannot be a totality, unless a totality constituted by the signified preexists it, supervises its inscriptions and its signs, and is independent of it in its ideality. . . . If I distinguish the text from the book, I shall say that the destruction of the book, as it is now under way in all domains, denudes the surface of the text (Derrida (3), 18).

Nietzsche is invoked as a major inspiration behind this "destruction of the book". Rorty, in his turn, invokes Derrida as supporting his own form of pragmatism;

Derrida regards the need to overcome "the book"—the notion of a piece of writing as aimed at accurate treatment of a subject . . .—as justifying his use of any text to interpret any other text. . . . Derrida does not want to comprehend Hegel's books; he wants to play with Hegel. He doesn't want to write a book about the nature of language; he wants to play with the texts which other people have thought they were writing about language. . . . *He is suggesting how things might look if we did not have Kantian philosophy built into the fabric of our intellectual life* (Rorty (2), 96–8).

But of course it is not just Kantianism that Derrida is assaulting, but styles of reading invited by all the pre-Kantian texts we have considered;

Derrida's claim seems to be that philosophy conceives of itself as fundamentally a kind of unmediated speech that seeks access to a mythical fullness beyond language called "being". Derrida's project involves redefining philosophic utterance as a special sort of writing, a play of signifiers that seeks vainly to fulfil the promise of such a language and to deliver the signified in all its concrete fullness or "presence" (Richetti, 8).

It aspires, in other words, to a secular analogue of the epiphany that marks the climax of the Book of Job.

The paradoxes inherent in this position have often been pointed out. In what is probably their most sophisticated exploration in the literature they are summarized in the aphorism, 'Derrida has the problem of saying what he means without meaning what he says' (Wood, 225). If his own writings are to be taken seriously as he intends them, then he cannot wholly set aside the intentions of the authors of the texts he reads as a matter of principle; 'It is not possible for Derrida to dismiss such considerations as too much concerned with what the writer intended, because he too is obsessed with having his intentions properly read' (233). More generally, as with the logical positivists, the anti-metaphysical position is itself metaphysical. Derrida is

committed to a science of the structures of metaphysical writing in the same way in which Husserl was committed to phenomenology as a descriptive science of experience. The belief in the existence of structures of presence is a form of textual realism. On what other basis does he claim such a privilege for his readings? And yet such realism is utterly metaphysical (235).

Perhaps more seriously, for Derrida is well aware that his position is paradoxical, the attempt to deconstruct a whole tradition of intellectual culture is itself narrowly culture-bound. The tell-tale vocabulary of "signifiers" and "signifieds" is that of the Saussure-inspired Structuralists, but the accompanying focus on the "sign" as the unit of meaning already seems curiously archaic. Nevertheless, it determines and distorts his reading of the very Nietzsche whose authority is invoked. Derrida's classic treatment of philosophical reading, 'White Mythology', makes great play with the early Nietzsche's appeal to "metaphor" in place of the concept of truth as "adequate expression", but shows no awareness of the way the more mature Nietzsche's replacement of the literal/metaphorical opposition with the fact/interpretation one represents a philosophical advance linked both to a more sophisticated analysis of "truth" and to a rejection of the referential theory of language (see ch. 7.1 and n. 8) within analogues of which Saussure—through the role given to the "associative" or "paradigmatic" order—was to remain entangled. The diagnosis of "Metaphor in the Text of Philosophy" (Derrida (2), 207) appears to depend in considerable part on the assumption that the only alternative to a sign's giving "adequate expression" to the signified "in all its concrete fullness or 'presence'" is its diagnosis as a "metaphor".

Further, in similar fashion to that in which the celebration of "metaphor" represents a reaction against an overly rigid, somewhat Cartesian, conception of "truth", so the practice of deconstruction represents the reverse pole of Cartesian aspirations after a form of "knowledge" which should "attain a certitude equal to that of the demonstrations of Arithmetic and Geometry" (Descartes (1), i. 5), and hence be justifiable by reasoning construed on such principles.

Like the account which he indicts, Derrida's account presupposes a disjunction: either knowledge—and thus criticism, as a form of knowing—must, like its objects, be clear and distinct, or it cedes any claim to knowledge (so, we might say, the dream of Descartes is still dreamt). The idea of criticism as subordinate commits itself to the first term of this disjunction: insofar as critical judgment is clear and transparent, it reveals the equally clear and distinct outlines of its objects. It is thus mimetic, representational. Derrida rejects this argument with the counterclaim that critical judgment, *all* judgment, is opaque. But in then concluding that criticism fails as knowledge, he accepts the original disjunction: a candidate for knowledge must be clear and distinct, or it has no claim to the title (Lang, 231).

Derrida's preparedness to accept paradox, it would appear, is a function of over-rigid conceptions of knowledge and rationality —perceived as being unattainable. As in the case of Rorty discussed in Chapter 1, reasonable assurance is traded for near total scepticism, out of a misguided desire for "a certitude equal to that of the demonstrations of Arithmetic and Geometry". It is little wonder that Rorty claims Derrida as a kindred spirit.

Deconstructive principles would preclude reading, say, the *Phaedo* with the kind of seriousness displayed in Chapter 3.[9] In this they are representative of one pole of a tendency that has been endemic in much advanced literary criticism of the last two decades. With all its faults, the practical criticism tradition at its best held together the possibility of learning from a text, or otherwise having one's sensibilities enlarged, with that of using it for self-scrutiny or self-interrogation, a two-way process of which Pascal's 'see if you do not find' (L.149, B.430, S.182)—looking both inward and at the specifications given in the text—is an example. Many of the more recent approaches have resolved this potentially creative tension by abandoning one or both of the two elements, thereby rendering themselves less suitable as models for finesse.

In part these tendencies may have developed out of a misplaced search for "geometric" rigour, or an equally misplaced despair at its

---

[9] Deconstructive principles apply, of course, to all texts. To point out that a particular text (for example this one) can be "deconstructed" is not, therefore, to express adverse criticism. Indeed, one might argue that the more extensively it proves possible in practice to "deconstruct" a text, the more valuable—because "richer"—that text turns out to be; such a value judgement might well, however, be at odds with those proposed within the text in question.

In a Pascalian perspective, deconstruction represents an aspect of man's *misère*, whereas the Cartesian aspiration after geometric "certitude" arises out of his *grandeur*; finesse provides the requisite third term.

unavailability.[10] But the older tradition was not thus misled, and its working principles have been well summed up by Professor Abrams in a way that brings out their relevance to finesse:

When critical discourse engages with its objects, it is controlled in considerable part by norms that we call good sense, sagacity, tact, sensibility, taste. These are terms by which we indicate that, though we are operating in a region where the rules are uncodified and elusive and there is room for the play of irreducible temperamental differences, yet decisions and judgements are not arbitrary, but are subject to broad criteria such as coherent –incoherent, adequate–omissive, penetrating–silly, just–distorting, revealing–obfuscatory, disinterested–partisan, better–worse. Although such a mode of discourse is rarely capable of rigidly conclusive arguments, it possesses just the kind of rationality it needs to achieve its own purposes; and although its knowledge is not, judged by an alien criterion, certain, it must satisfy an equivalent criterion in its own realm of discourse, for which, in lieu of a specialized term, we use a word like valid, or sound (Abrams, 53).

These, of course, are the same family of criteria to which those of Righter's "aesthetic of argument" belong—relevant–irrelevant, have force, look foolish—and their employment can help guide argument even at the "minimal" level of interdependence between imaginative and argumentative modes. One example of this level instanced by Righter is that of Moore's presentation of the existence of his own hand as a foundation for his "Proof of an External World", but it also is associated with "more extended imaginings" such as Sartre's nausea and Pascal's prison. Of the latter (L.434, B.199, S.686) he writes,

The men in chains suggest a picture which is not visually developed. Nor is it part of a complex demonstration or argument, but simply poses in itself the whole of man's condition and dilemma. You may draw your conclusions, and there is no doubt from the wider context what sort of conclusions Pascal

[10] The concern of Arnold and Leavis with "seriousness" in literary criticism has been replaced in a good deal of more recent work with a celebration of "play". There is an analogy here with Descartes's rejection of the Aristotelian conception of dialectic as "a process of criticism wherein lies the path to the principles of all inquiries" ((1), i. *Topics*, 101a–b), and relegation of it to "polemics" where it may "give practice to the wits of youths and, producing emulation among them, act as a stimulus" (Descartes (1), 1, *Regulae* ii. 4). If serious reasoning is only to be found where there is "a certitude equal to that of the demonstrations of Arithmetic and Geometry", and a criterion of such certitude is use of the geometric type of reasoning in a "demonstration", then dialectical reasoning may quite properly be relegated to mental gymnastics and literary criticism to game playing.

wishes us to draw. Yet in itself the picture simply confronts us with a kind of directness and simplicity, an ostensive feel to it, like the 'nausea' itself—or for that matter, Moore's hand (Righter, 212).

But while there is certainly this similarity, there are also differences; the hand is exemplary, the nausea and the prison symbolic. Moore's hand could, without loss of either argumentative or imaginative force, be replaced by Moore's finger; but Sartre's nausea cannot, with equal facility, be replaced by dyspepsia. These categories may not, however, be mutually exclusive; it remains to be seen whether an example which is sufficiently telling and precise may attain to that universality we associate with the symbol,[11] and if so what light this throws on the relations between Righter's instances, and on the ways in which we may properly regard them as revealing or obfuscatory, penetrating or silly, and the rest.

In such ways as this, comparing case with case, employing the full range of critical vocabulary which has been precisely developed to handle works in the "mode of imagination", and with scrupulous attention to tone, style, and nuance we may begin to articulate and develop Righter's "aesthetic of argument" in ways which bear significantly on the rational persuasiveness of works of finesse, and the power to illuminate experience they purport to provide.

5. The Scope of Finesse

> By his understanding of the constituent antagonisms of any human reality, by his demands for syntheses and for a knowl-edge of individuals, Pascal's vision of reality marks the turning point in the transition from atomistic rationalism to genuine dialectical thought.
>
> (Goldmann (1), 252)

Professor Goldmann defines the latter in terms of Hegel and Marx, but he is fully alive to the fact that Pascal's dialectical aspirations are different from those of his nineteenth-century successors. 'It is only by indicating the resemblances between Pascal, on the one hand,

---

[11] This use of 'symbol' is, of course, to be distinguished from that of the "symbolists" discussed by Professor Hepburn. In terms of the latter's spectrum, Sartre's *La Nausée* is to be located at some distance from "pure poetry".

and Hegel and Marx, on the other, that one can remain fully aware of the immense gulf which lies between them.' In part this gulf is exaggerated by Goldmann's perverse reading, noted in Chapter 5, of Pascal in terms of the dimension of *misère* without adequate attention to the aspect of *grandeur*; but he is certainly correct to distinguish between the conceptions of dialectic. Repeatedly in Pascal

two contradictory truths about man are presented, in each case the contradiction can only be reconciled by admitting a third truth, containing and superseding the other two . . . But it . . . has nothing to do with the now familiar dialectic of thesis, antithesis, synthesis. In the order of exposition, Christianity comes last, but in the order of truth and reality it always comes first (Krailsheimer (2), 45).

The Hegelian tradition is wedded to a complex interconnection between the *ordo essendi* and the *ordo cognoscendi* whereby the structure of reality is itself dialectical. Pascal is innocent of this metaphysic, and within the Aristotelian tradition he inherited dialectic has no antecedent commitment to any given ontology (the *Topics* is prior to the *Metaphysics*). Similarly, finesse as I have characterized it is a mode of testing any proposed ontology— religious or secular—rather than itself being an aspect of a particular representation of the world. Thus although there are many and intriguing interconnections between the work of Hegel and that of the authors we have considered, it has seemed best not to burden the characterization of finesse with any of the intellectual baggage that is today specifically associated with the Hegelian tradition.

Pascal's concern with "the constituent antagonisms of any human reality" draws, as we have seen, both on the specifically intellectual ἀπορίαι characteristic of the Classical tradition and on the broader, more "personal" range found in the Biblical; his "demands for syntheses" similarly incorporate both approaches. It is the manner in which this integration has proved seminal for subsequent opponents of the use of the geometric model as definitive of rationality, not least among those who have opposed his own religious perspective, that most firmly grounds Pascal's claim to mark an important intellectual "turning point"—as significant in its context as that represented by Descartes for the geometric tradition.

In several ways, appropriately, this book itself bears the imprint of Pascalian *finesse*.[12] To the degree that the latter is the descendant of Aristotelian dialectic it can incorporate deductive (and indeed inductive) elements (see ch. 5, n. 15), and deduction at least has been repeatedly employed. But more distinctively, the abductive element in *finesse* is present in the suggestion that the contemporary perplexities outlined in Chapter 1 "would be a matter of course" if a "dialectical" structure were more fundamental to rationality than that of geometry. Again, the comparison of various works and schools with each other not only strongly represents the hermeneutic strain to be found throughout *finesse*, but is also reminiscent of Pascal's flexible "digressive" manner of "ordering" (L.298, B.283, S.329) which is itself closely related to Wisdom's paraductive "case-by-case procedure". Finally, this overall strategy of displaying the workings of *finesse* through the cumulative interconnection of cases, rather than resting content with providing a "geometric" definition in terms of necessary and sufficient conditions, itself exemplifies that Perelmanesque "rhetoric" which depends for its rational persuasiveness on recognition of the authority of his "rule of justice"; (for further defence of such preference for example over definition, see 'Literature and Philosophy' in Bambrough (4)).

More importantly, finesse appears to have a relevance to modern

[12] From a Nietzschean point of view this book can also be seen as aspiring after that perspective's ideal of objectivity: "There is *only* a perspective seeing, *only* a perspective 'knowing'; and the more . . . eyes, different eyes, we can use to observe one thing, the more complete will our 'concept' of this thing, our 'objectivity' be" (Nietzsche (7), *Genealogy of Morals*, iii. 12). I have not hesitated, any more than did Nietzsche or Pascal, to avail myself of types of argument whose home lies within the geometric perspective I am criticizing; to fail to incorporate the geometric perspective into my own would be to reduce the latter's claim to Nietzschean "objectivity".

From an epistemological point of view the salient features of finesse are that its rejection of an *assiette* distinguishes it from pure Foundationalism while the concern with authenticity (Pascal's "observe yourself, and see . . .") raises problems for attempting to classify it as a type of Coherentism. Perhaps it is best to borrow a term from Professor Haack and describe it as a form of "Foundherentism", for it assumes that experience (though not necessarily just sense experience) should play "an important role in the justification of a person's beliefs" while recognizing that the "justification of more secure beliefs may depend on less secure beliefs, as well as vice versa" (Haack (4), 156 and 151); while some beliefs are sustained largely by experience, it is always possible that further beliefs which are less directly related to experience may be relevant to their justification. The standing problem of Foundationalism remains: how to relate a causal story of how beliefs are sustained to a logical one about the likelihood of their being true. Haack (6) provides a highly promising account of the required "Causical Foundherentism" which takes account of introspective as well as sensory experience; the term, like the theory, is Professor Haack's.

P H I L O S O P H I C A L F I N E S S E

sensibility of wider scope than that with which this book has been
concerned.

The great novels of the twentieth century, its essential books, are without
exception *terminal* books, apotheoses of the narrative form. . . . Each, in
theme, is an inventory of our spiritual holdings, a moral, aesthetic, and
metaphysical reckoning-up of our human estate; some of them, in form,
carry abstraction to a point beyond which further evolution seems impossible. A deep, ultimate seriousness runs through them all, a seriousness
which their ever-present irony increases rather than diminishes (Kahler,
109).

Working at the limits of their form, it is suggested, the irony
represents an aspiration to pass beyond their own categories, "a
chain reaction of transcendence", hence the term 'apotheosis'. This
is not a purely "formal" matter, for the available categories set
bounds to the possibilities of drawing up such "inventories". Nor is
it limited to the narrative form; not only his *Zarathustra* but also his
Götzen-Dämmerung, both works which foreshadow twentieth-
century sensibility, exemplify Nietzsche's consciousness that he was
working at the limits of available categories—'Our language . . . is
the constant advocate of error. . . . We enter a realm of crude
fetishism when we summon before consciousness the basic presuppositions of the metaphysics of language, in plain talk, the presuppositions of reason' (Nietzsche (6), iii. 5). He opposes the
traditional, geometric, canons of "reason" with his own, and to the
extent that the vocabulary available to him is thoroughly permeated
with the former uses the complex range of literary strategies we
explored in Chapter 7, including irony, in an attempt to transcend
them and point to the "apotheosis" represented by Dionysus. And
notoriously that seminal twentieth-century text, Wittgenstein's
Tractatus, welding reason and language together in a quasi-
geometric structure, represents itself—if without irony—as a "terminal" or limit text with respect both to form and content; its
propositions are presented as "definitive" ('Preface'), and as for
what they point to but cannot state, "Whereof one cannot speak,
thereof one must be silent" (Wittgenstein (1), prop. 7).

For Nietzsche and Wittgenstein the limits are in large part set
by reason, construed geometrically, in its reciprocal relationship
to language; their works represent at once the urge to attempt
to transcend these limits and the self-defeating nature of this
aspiration;

My propositions are elucidatory . . . he who understands me finally recognizes them as senseless (Wittgenstein (1), prop. 6.54).

"Reason" in language—oh, what an old deceptive female she is! I am afraid we are not rid of God because we still have faith in grammar (Nietzsche (6), iii. 5).

But similar conceptions of reason often appear to be playing a role in those "terminal" novels and other works of literature that are our time's "essential books" and seek an analogous "apotheosis". The same also appears to be increasingly the case in forms of contemporary criticism more "serious" than that of Deconstruction discussed above. For example, Professor Fish's influential category of the "self-consuming artifact" is defined in terms of a distinction between "rational" and "antirational" which places dialectic on the latter side of the line.

A dialectical presentation . . . is disturbing, for it requires of its readers a searching and rigorous scrutiny of everything they believe in and live by. It . . . asks that its readers discover the truth for themselves, and this discovery is often made at the expense not only of a reader's opinions and values, but of his self-esteem (Fish, 1–2).

Thus far he might be writing of the *Pensées*, though the analysis is in fact directed to a wide range of literary genres and Pascal is not considered. However, we are soon told that "in a dialectical experience . . . the motion of the rational consciousness is stilled", and it is argued that "a dialectical presentation succeeds at its own expense; for by conveying those who experience it to a point where they are beyond the aid that discursive or rational forms can offer, it becomes the vehicle of its own abandonment" (3); it becomes, that is, a "self-consuming artifact".

The pervasive influence in our culture of texts that thus become the vehicle of their own abandonment is becoming increasingly apparent, a process in which Professor Fish's excellent studies have played a significant role. But the underlying conception of "reason" consigns many works of great imaginative potency, whether or not they count as "terminal books", to the "antirational" category, and thus helps to fuel the contemporary disparagement of rationality. It can also help blind us to the subtle rational structures that are actually there. The self-consuming drive to transcend the forms of understanding available to us was long ago epitomized in a Biblical image by Pascal:

Nothing stands still for us. This is our natural state and yet the state most contrary to our inclinations. We burn with desire to find a firm footing, an ultimate, lasting base on which to build a tower rising up to infinity, but our whole foundation cracks and the earth opens up into the depth of the abyss (L.199, B.72, S.230).

But this very recognition, that the Cartesian ambition to build with deductive certainty on the secure foundation of "the intuitive apprehension of . . . the absolutely simple" (Descartes (1), i. 14) is misplaced, was used by Pascal to develop a more "dialectical" conception of the "reasons of the heart"—or *finesse*—to complement the demonstrative, "geometric", conception of rationality. To the extent that contemporary sensibility recognizes as authentic Pascal's characterization of "our natural state", it also suggests that finesse is more appropriate than geometry in our rational endeavours to test and improve our representations of the world.

Bibliography

Because a variety of languages are involved, where practicable references have normally been made to published English translations of items not originally written in English.

ABRAMS, M. H., 'What's the Use of Theorising about the Arts?', in M. W. Bloomfield (ed.), *In Search of Literary Theory* (Ithaca and London: Cornell University Press, 1972).

ACHINSTEIN, P., *Law and Explanation: An Essay in the Philosophy of Science* (Oxford: Clarendon Press, 1971).

AIKEN, H. (ed.), David Hume: *Dialogues Concerning Natural Religion* (New York and London: Hafner Press and Collier Macmillan, 1948).

ALDERMAN, H., *Nietzsche's Gift* (Columbus: Ohio University Press, 1977).

ALLISON, D. B. (ed.), *The New Nietzsche: Contemporary Styles of Interpretation* (New York: Dell, 1977).

ANDERSON, R. F., *Hume's First Principles* (Lincoln, Nebr.: University of Nebraska Press, 1966).

ANNAS, J., 'Plato's Myths of Judgement', *Phronesis*, 27 (1982).

AQUINAS, St Thomas, *Summa Theologiae*, tr. T. Gilby and others, 60 vols (London and New York: Blackfriars, Eyre & Spottiswoode, McGraw-Hill, 1964–81).

ARISTOTLE (1), *The Works of Aristotle translated into English*, ed. W. D. Ross, 12 vols (Oxford: Clarendon Press, 1908–52).

—— (2), *The Rhetoric of Aristotle*, ed. E. M. Cope, 3 vols (Cambridge: The University Press, 1877).

—— (3), *Posterior Analytics*, tr. J. Barnes (Oxford: Clarendon Press, 1975).

ARNAULD, A., *The Art of Thinking: Port-Royal Logic*, tr. J. Dickoff and P. James (Indianapolis, New York, Kansas City: Bobbs-Merrill, 1964).

ARNOLD, M., *Essays in Criticism: Second Series* (London: Macmillan, 1888).

AUGUSTINE (1), *Writings of Saint Augustine*, ed. L. Schopp, 14 vols (Washington, DC: The Catholic University of America, 1947–68).

—— (2), *The Trinity*, tr. S. McKenna (Washington, DC: Catholic University of America Press, 1963).

—— (3), *The City of God*, tr. R. V. G. Tasker, 2 vols (London: Dent (Everyman's Library), 1945).

AUSTIN, J. L., *Sense and Sensibilia*, ed. G. J. Warnock (Oxford: Clarendon Press, 1962).

AYER, A. J., *The Concept of a Person and Other Essays* (London: Macmillan, 1963).

BACON, F., *The Philosophical Works of Francis Bacon: Reprinted from the Texts and Translations, with the Notes and Prefaces, of Ellis and Spedding*, ed. J. M. Robertson (London: George Routledge, 1905).

BAMBROUGH, J. R. (1) (ed.), *New Essays on Plato and Aristotle* (London: Routledge & Kegan Paul, 1965).

—— (2), *Conflict and the Scope of Reason* (Hull: University of Hull, 1974).

—— (3), 'How to read Wittgenstein', in G. Vesey (ed.), *Understanding Wittgenstein*, Royal Institute of Philosophy Lectures, vii (London: Macmillan, 1974).

—— (4), (ed.), *Wisdom: Twelve Essays* (Oxford: Basil Blackwell, 1974).

—— (5), *Moral Scepticism and Moral Knowledge* (London: Routledge & Kegan Paul, 1979).

BARKER, S. F., 'Must Every Inference be either Deductive or Inductive?', in M. Black (ed.), *Philosophy in America* (London: George Allen & Unwin, 1965).

BARNES, J. (1) (tr.), *Aristotle's* Posterior Analytics (Oxford: Clarendon Press, 1975).

—— (2), SCHOFIELD, M., and SORABJI, R. (eds) *Articles on Aristotle*, 4 vols (London: Duckworth, 1975–9).

—— (3) 'Aristotle's Theory of Demonstration', *Phronesis*, 14 (1969).

BARR, J., 'The Book of Job and its Modern Interpreters', *Bulletin of the John Rylands Library*, 54 (1971).

BATTERSBY, C. (1), 'The *Dialogues* as Original Imitation: Cicero and the Nature of Hume's Scepticism', in Norton (2).

—— (2), 'Hume, Newton and "The Hill Called Difficulty"', in Brown (2).

BAYLE, P., *Dictionnaire historique et critique*, ed. Des Maizaux, 4th edn, 4 vols (Amsterdam and Leiden: Brunel and Luchtmans, 1730).

BECK, L. J., *The Method of Descartes: A Study of the Regulae* (Oxford: Clarendon Press, 1952).

BERKELEY, G., *The Works of George Berkeley, Bishop of Cloyne*, ed. A. A. Luce and T. E. Jessop, 9 vols (London and Edinburgh: Thomas Nelson, 1948–57).

BILLINGS, G. H., *The Art of Transition in Plato* (New York and London: Garland Publishing, 1979; original private edn 1920).

BLANCHET, A., 'Pascal est-il le précurseur de Marx?', *Études*, 292 (1957).

BLUCK, R. S. (tr.) *Plato's* Phaedo: *A Translation of Plato's* Phaedo *with Introduction, Notes and Appendices* (London: Routledge & Kegan Paul, 1955).

BOSTOCK, D., *Plato's* Phaedo (Oxford: Clarendon Press, 1986).

BREAZEALE, D. (tr.) *Philosophy and Truth: Selections from Nietzsche's Notebooks of the Early 1870's* (New Jersey and Sussex: Humanities Press and Harvester Press, 1979).

BRICKE, J., 'On the Interpretation of Hume's *Dialogues*', *Religious Studies*, 11 (1975).

BROOME, J. H., *Pascal* (London: Edward Arnold, 1965).

BROWN(1), G., 'A Defence of Pascal's Wager', *Religious Studies*, 20 (1984).

BROWN(2), S. C. (ed.), *Philosophers of the Enlightenment*, Royal Institute of Philosophy Lectures, xii (Sussex and New Jersey: Harvester Press and Humanities Press, 1979).

BROWNE, Sir T., *The Religio Medici & Other Writings*, ed. C. H. Herford (London: Dent (Everyman's Library), 1906).

BRUNSCHVICG, P. G., BOUTROUX, P., and GAZIER, F. (eds), *Œuvres de Blaise Pascal*, 14 vols (Vaduz: Kraus Reprint, 1965).

BUCKLEY, M. J., 'Philosophic Method in Cicero', *Journal of the History of Philosophy*, 8 (1970).

BURNET, J. (ed.), *Plato's* Phaedo (Oxford: Clarendon Press, 1911).

BURNYEAT, M. F., 'Aristotle on Understanding Knowledge', in E. Berti (ed.), *Aristotle on Science*: The Posterior Analytics (Padua: Editrice Antenore, 1981).

BUTLER(1), J., *The Works of the Right Reverend Father in God, Joseph Butler, Late Lord Bishop of Durham*, ed. S. Halifax, 2 vols (Oxford: Oxford University Press, 1849–50).

BUTLER(2), R. J., 'Natural Belief and the Enigma of Hume', *Archiv für Geschichte der Philosophie*, 42 (1960).

BUXTON, R. G. A., *Persuasion in Greek Tragedy: A Study of Peitho* (Cambridge: Cambridge University Press, 1982).

CAPALDI, N., *David Hume: The Newtonian Philosopher* (Boston: Twayne Publishers, 1975).

CARNAP, R., *The Logical Structure of the World and Pseudoproblems in Philosophy*, tr. R. A. George, 2nd edn (London: Routledge & Kegan Paul, 1967).

CASEY, J., *The Language of Criticism* (London: Methuen, 1966).

CASTAÑEDA, H.-N., *On Philosophical Method* (Bloomington, Ind.: Nous Publications, 1980).

CICERO(1), *De Natura Deorum; Academica*, tr. H. Rackham (London and Cambridge, Mass.: Loeb Classical Library, 1933).

——(2), *De Inventione; De Optimo Genere Oratorum; Topica*, tr. H. M. Hubbell (London and Cambridge, Mass.: Loeb Classical Library, 1949).

——(3), *De Oratore: I–II*, tr. E. W. Sutton and H. Rackham (London and Cambridge, Mass.: Loeb Classical Library, 1942).

CICERO (4), *De Oratore: III; De Fato; Paradoxa Stoicorum; De Partitione Oratoria*, tr. H. Rackham (London and Cambridge, Mass.: Loeb Classical Library, 1948).

——(5), *Brutus; Orator*, trs G. L. Hendrickson and H. M. Hubbell (London and Cambridge, Mass.: Loeb Classical Library, 1971).

——(6), *De Republica; De Legibus; Somnium Scipionis*, tr. C. W. Keyes, (London and Cambridge, Mass.: Loeb Classical Library, 1928).

——(7), *De Finibus Bonorum et Malorum*, tr. H. Rackham (London and Cambridge, Mass.: Loeb Classical Library, 1914).

——(8), *Tusculan Disputations*, tr. J. E. King (London and Cambridge, Mass.: Loeb Classical Library, 1945).

——(9), *De Senectute; De Amicitia; De Divinatione*, tr. W. A. Falconer (London and Cambridge, Mass.: Loeb Classical Library, 1923).

——(10), *De Officiis*, tr. W. Miller (London and Cambridge, Mass.: Loeb Classical Library, 1947).

——(11), *Letters to Atticus*, tr. E. O. Winstedt, 3 vols (London and Cambridge, Mass.: Loeb Classical Library, 1912–18).

——(12), *The Speeches: In Catilinam I–IV; Pro Murena; Pro Sulla; Pro Flacco*, tr. L. E. Lord (London and Cambridge, Mass.: Loeb Classical Library, 1946).

——(13), *Letters to Quintus, Brutus, and others*, tr. W. G. Williams and others (London and Cambridge, Mass.: Loeb Classical Library, 1972).

——(14), *M. Tulii Ciceronis de natura deorum libri tres*, ed. J. B. Mayor and J. H. Swainson, 3 vols (Cambridge: Cambridge University Press, 1880–5).

——(15), *M. Tulli Ciceronis De Natura Deorum*, ed. A. S. Pease, 2 vols (Cambridge, Mass.: Harvard University Press, 1955–8).

CIOFFI, F., 'Intention and Interpretation in Criticism', *Proceedings of the Aristotelian Society*, 64 (1963–4).

CLARKE(1), D. M., *Descartes' Philosophy of Science* (Manchester: Manchester University Press, 1982).

CLARKE (2), S., *A Discourse Concerning the Being and Attributes of God, The Obligations of Natural Religion, and the Truth and Certainty of the Christian Revelation*, 9th edn (London: Printed by W. Botham for J. and P. Knapton, 1738).

CLINES, D. J. A., 'Job: A Deconstruction', in Warner.

COHEN, L. J.(1), 'On the Project of a Universal Character', *Mind*, 63 (1954).

——(2), *The Implications of Induction* (London: Methuen, 1970).

——(3), *The Probable and the Provable* (Oxford: Clarendon Press, 1977).

COLLI, G., and MONTINARI, M. (eds), Nietzsche, *Werke, Kritische Gesamtausgabe*, 30 vols (Berlin: de Gruyter, 1967–78).

COLLINGWOOD, R. G., *An Essay on Metaphysics* (Oxford: Clarendon Press, 1940).

COLLINS, A. (tr.), Friedrich Nietzsche, *The Use and Abuse of History*, 2nd edn (Indianapolis: Bobbs-Merrill, 1957).

COLVER, A. W., and PRICE, J. V. (eds), David Hume, *The Natural History of Religion and Dialogues Concerning Natural Religion* (Oxford: Clarendon Press, 1976).

COPE, E. M. (ed.), *The Rhetoric of Aristotle*, 3 vols (Cambridge: The University Press, 1877).

COPLESTON, F. (1), *A History of Philosophy*, 9 vols (London: Burns Oates & Washbourne (i–viii); London: Search Press (ix), 1947–75).

——(2), *Frederich Nietzsche: Philosopher of Culture*, 2nd edn (London and New York: Search Press and Barnes & Noble, 1975).

CRENSHAW, J. L., *Old Testament Wisdom: An Introduction* (London: SCM, 1981).

CROMBIE, I. M., *An Examination of Plato's Doctrines*, 2 vols (London: Routledge & Kegan Paul, 1963).

CROSS, R. C., 'Category Differences', *Proceedings of the Aristotelian Society*, 59 (1958–9).

DANNHAUSER, W. J., *Nietzsche's View of Socrates* (Ithaca and London: Cornell University Press, 1974).

DAVIDSON (1), D., 'On the Very Idea of a Conceptual Scheme', *Proceedings and Addresses of the American Philosophical Association*, 47 (1973–4).

DAVIDSON (2), H. M., *The Origins of Certainty: Means and Meanings in Pascal's* Pensées (Chicago: University of Chicago Press, 1979).

DELEUZE, G., *Nietzsche and Philosophy*, tr. H. Tomlinson (London: The Athlone Press, 1983).

DE MAN, P., 'Pascal's Allegory of Persuasion', in Greenblatt.

DE QUINCEY, T., *The Collected Writings of Thomas De Quincey*, ed. D. Masson, 14 vols (London: Black, 1896–7).

DERRIDA, J. (1), *Spurs: Nietzsche's Styles*, tr. B. Harlow (Venice: Corbo e Fiore, 1976).

——(2), 'White Mythology', in his *Margins of Philosophy*, tr. A. Bass (Brighton: Harvester Press, 1982).

——(3), *Of Grammatology*, tr. G. C. Spivak (Baltimore and London: Johns Hopkins University Press, 1976).

DESCARTES, R. (1), *The Philosophical Works of Descartes*, trs E. Haldane and G. R. T. Ross, 2 vols, 2nd edn (Cambridge: Cambridge University Press, 1931).

——(2), *Regulae ad Directionem Ingenii*, ed. G. Crapulli (The Hague: Martinus Nijhoff, 1966).

DIXON, P., *Rhetoric* ((London: Methuen, 1971).

DONNE, J., *The Satires, Epigrams and Verse Letters*, ed. W. Milgate (Oxford: Clarendon Press, 1967).

DONNELLAN, B., *Nietzsche and the French Moralists* (Bonn: Bouvier Verlag Herbert Grundmann, 1982).

DORTER, K., *Plato's* Phaedo: *An Interpretation* (Toronto, Buffalo, and London: University of Toronto Press, 1982).

DOUGLAS, A. E. (1), 'Platonis Aemulus?', *Greece and Rome*[2], 9 (1962).

——(2), 'Cicero the Philosopher', in T. A. Dorey (ed.), *Cicero* (London: Routledge & Kegan Paul, 1965).

DRIVER, S. R., and GRAY, G. B., *The Book of Job* (Edinburgh: T. & T. Clark, 1921).

DRYDEN, J., *Essays of John Dryden*, ed. W. P. Ker, 2 vols (Oxford: Clarendon Press, 1900).

DUERLINGER, J., 'The Verbal Dispute in Hume's *Dialogues*', *Archiv für Geschichte der Philosophie*, 53 (1971).

DUMMETT, M., 'Can Analytic Philosophy be Systematic, and Ought it to Be?', in his *Truth and other Enigmas* (London: Duckworth, 1978).

DUNS SCOTUS, J., *Opera Omnia*, ed. L. Wadding *et al.*, 12 vols (Lyons: Laurence Durand, 1639).

EAGLETON, T., *Criticism and Ideology: A Study in Marxist Literary Theory* (London: Verso, 1978).

EDWARDS, P. (ed.), *The Encyclopaedia of Philosophy*, 8 vols (London and New York: Collier Macmillan, 1967).

ELIOT, T. S., *Poetry and Drama* (London: Faber & Faber, 1951).

EVANS, J. D. G., *Aristotle's Concept of Dialectic* (Cambridge: Cambridge University Press, 1977).

FANN, K. T., *Peirce's Theory of Abduction* (The Hague: Martinus Nijhoff, 1970).

FARRER, A. (1), *Finite and Infinite: A Philosophical Essay*, 2nd edn (London: Dacre Press, 1959).

——(2), *The Glass of Vision* (London: Dacre Press, 1948).

——(3), *Saving Belief: A Discussion of Essentials* (London: Hodder and Stoughton, 1964).

——(4), 'The Christian Apologist', in J. Gibb (ed.), *Light on C. S. Lewis* (London: Geoffrey Bles, 1965).

——(5), *Interpretation and Belief*, ed. C. C. Conti (London: SPCK, 1976).

FEYERABEND, P., *Against Method: Outline of an Anarchistic Theory of Knowledge* (London: Verso, 1978).

FISH, S. E., *Self-Consuming Artifacts: The Experience of Seventeenth-Century Literature* (Berkeley, Los Angeles, and London: University of California Press, 1974).

FOOT, P. (1), 'Nietzsche: The Revaluation of Values', in Solomon; reprinted in Foot (2).

——(2), *Virtues and Vices and Other Essays in Moral Philosophy* (Oxford: Basil Blackwell, 1978).

FOSTER, M., *Mystery and Philosophy* (London: SCM, 1957).

FRANCE, P., *Rhetoric and Truth in France: Descartes to Diderot* (Oxford: Clarendon Press, 1972).

FRIEDLÄNDER, P., *Plato*, tr. H. Mayerhoff, 3 vols (Princeton, NJ: Princeton University Press, 1958–69).

FRYE, N., *Anatomy of Criticism: Four Essays* (Princeton, NJ: Princeton University Press, 1957).

GADAMER, H.-G., *Truth and Method*, ed. W. Glen-Doepel, 2nd edn (London: Sheed and Ward, 1979).

GALILEO, G., *Dialogue Concerning the Two Chief World Systems— Ptolomaic & Copernican*, tr. D. Drake, 2nd edn (Berkeley and Los Angeles: University of California Press, 1967).

GALLOP, D. (tr.), *Plato*: Phaedo (Oxford: Clarendon Press, 1975).

GARDNER, H., *The Business of Criticism* (Oxford: Clarendon Press, 1959).

GARVER, J. N., 'On the Rationality of Persuading', *Mind*, 69 (1960).

GASKIN, J. C. A. (1), 'Hume's Critique of Religion', *Journal of the History of Philosophy*, 14 (1976).

——(2), *Hume's Philosophy of Religion* (London: Macmillan, 1978).

GEACH, P. T., 'Good and Evil', *Analysis*, 17 (1956).

GENUNG, J. F., *The Epic of the Inner Life* (London: Clarke, 1891).

GILL, C., 'The Death of Socrates', *The Classical Quarterly*, 23 (1973).

GLATZER, N. N. (1), 'The Book of Job and Its Interpreters', in A. Altmann (ed.), *Biblical Motifs: Origins and Transformations* (Cambridge, Mass.: Harvard University Press (Brandeis University: *Studies and Texts*, 3), 1966).

——(2), 'A Study of Job', in N. N. Glatzer (ed.), *The Dimensions of Job* (New York: Schocken Books, 1969).

GOLDMANN, L. (1), *The Hidden God: A Study of Tragic Vision in the Pensées of Pascal and the Tragedies of Racine*, tr. P. Thody (London: Routledge & Kegan Paul, 1964).

——(2), and others, 'Le Pari est-il écrit pour le libertin?', in *Blaise Pascal: l'homme et l'œuvre*, (Paris: Les Éditions de Minuit (Cahiers de Royaumont; Philosophie, 1), 1956).

GORDIS, R., *The Book of God and Man: A Study of Job* (Chicago and London: The University of Chicago Press, 1965).

GOSLING, J. C. B., *Pleasure and Desire: The Case for Hedonism Reviewed* (Oxford: Clarendon Press, 1969).

GRANIER, J., 'Perspectivism and Interpretation', in Allison.

GRASSI, E., *Rhetoric as Philosophy: The Humanist Tradition* (Pennsylvania: Pennsylvania State University Press, 1980).

GRAVE, S. A., 'Hume's Criticism of the Argument from Design', *Revue Internationale de Philosophie*, 30 (1976).

GRAY, G. B., and DRIVER, S. R., *The Book of Job* (Edinburgh: T. & T. Clark, 1921).

GREEN, T. H., and GROSE, T. H. (eds), *The Philosophical Works of David Hume*, 4 vols (London: Longman, Green & Co., 1874–5).

GREENBLATT, S. J. (ed.), *Allegory and Representation: Selected Papers from the English Institute*, New Series, no. 5 (Baltimore and London: John Hopkins University Press, 1981).

GREIG, J. Y. T. (ed.), *The Letters of David Hume*, 2 vols (Oxford: Clarendon Press, 1932).

GRIMALDI, W. M. A., *Studies in the Philosophy of Aristotle's* Rhetoric (Wiesbaden: Franz Steiner Verlag (*Hermes Zeitschrift für Klassische Philologie*, 24), 1972).

GRIMM, R. H., *Nietzsche's Theory of Knowledge* (Berlin and New York: de Gruyter, 1977).

GUILLAUME, A., 'The Arabic Background to the Book of Job', in F. F. Bruce (ed.), *Promise and Fulfilment* (Edinburgh: Clark, 1963).

HAACK, S. W. (1), 'Equivocality: a Discussion of Sommers' Views', *Analysis*, 28 (1967–8).

——(2), 'The Justification of Deduction', *Mind*, 85 (1976).

——(3), 'Dummett's Justification of Deduction', *Mind*, 91 (1982).

——(4), 'Theories of Knowledge: An Analytic Framework', *Proceedings of the Aristotelian Society*, 83 (1982–3).

——(5), Review of N. Rescher, *The Strife of Systems: An Essay on the Grounds and Implications of Philosophical Diversity*, *Philosophy and Phenomenological Research*, 48 (1987).

——(6), 'Causical Foundherentism' (unpublished paper: versions read at University of Warwick and Moral Sciences Club, Cambridge, in 1986, and at University of Rochester and Brown University in 1987).

HABEL, N. C., *The Book of Job* (London: SCM, 1985).

HACKFORTH, R. (1) (tr.), *Plato's* Phaedrus (Cambridge: Cambridge University Press, 1952).

——(2), (tr.), *Plato's* Phaedo (Cambridge: Cambridge University Press, 1955).

HACKING, I. (1), 'The Logic of Pascal's Wager', *American Philosophical Quarterly*, 9 (1972).

——(2), *The Emergence of Probability: A Philosophical Study of Early Ideas about Probability, Induction and Statistical Inference* (Cambridge: Cambridge University Press, 1975).

HALDANE, E., and ROSS, G. R. T. (trs.) *The Philosophical Works of Descartes*, 2 vols, 2nd edn (Cambridge: Cambridge University Press, 1931).

HAMILTON, E. and CAIRNS, H. (eds), *The Collected Dialogues of Plato, Including the Letters* (New York: Bollingen Foundation, 1963).

HAMMOND, N. G. L., and SCULLARD, H. H., *The Oxford Classical Dictionary*, 2nd edn. (Oxford: Clarendon Press, 1970).

HATHAWAY, R., 'Explaining the Unity of the Platonic Dialogue', *Philosophy and Literature*, 8 (1984).

HEIDEGGER, M., *Nietzsche*, 2 vols (Pfullingen: Neske, 1961).

HENDEL, C. W., *Studies in the Philosophy of David Hume* (Indianapolis and New York: Bobbs-Merrill, 1963).

HEPBURN, R. W., 'Literary and Logical Analysis', *The Philosophical Quarterly*, 8 (1958).

HILLMAN, D. J., 'On Grammars and Category-Mistakes', *Mind*, 72 (1963).

HINMAN, L. M., 'Can a Form of Life be Wrong?', *Philosophy*, 58 (1983).

HINTIKKA, J., and REMES, U., *The Method of Analysis: Its Geometrical Origin and Its General Significance*, Boston Studies in the Philosophy of Science, xxv (Dordrecht and Boston: Reidel, 1974).

HOBBES, T. (1), *Thomae Hobbes Malmesburiensis: Opera philosophica quae latine scripsit omnia*, ed. Sir W. Molesworth, 5 vols (London: Bohn, 1839–45).

——(2), *The English Works of Thomas Hobbes of Malmesbury*, ed. Sir W. Molesworth, 11 vols (London: Bohn, 1839–45).

HOLLEY, D. M., 'Argument and Rhetoric in Philosophy', *Philosophy Today*, 26 (1982).

HOLLINGDALE, R. J. (1) (tr.), Friedrich Nietzsche, *Daybreak: Thoughts on the Prejudices of Morality* (Cambridge: Cambridge University Press, 1982).

——(2) (tr.), *A Nietzsche Reader* (Harmondsworth: Penguin Books, 1977).

——(3), *Nietzsche* (London and Boston: Routledge & Kegan Paul, 1973).

HOWELL, W. S. (1), 'Nathaniel Carpenter's Place in the Controversy between Dialectic and Rhetoric', *Speech Monographs*, 1 (1934).

——(2), Logic and Rhetoric in England, 1500–1700 (Princeton, NJ: Princeton University Press, 1956).

HUBERT, M. L., *Pascal's Unfinished Apology: A Study of his Plan* (New Haven and Paris: Yale University Press, 1952).

HUME, D. (1), *The Philosophical Works of David Hume*, ed. T. H. Green, and T. H. Grose, 4 vols (London: Longman, Green & Co., 1874–5).

——(2), *The Letters of David Hume*, ed. J. Y. T. Greig, 2 vols (Oxford: Clarendon Press, 1932).

——(3), *New Letters of David Hume*, ed. R. Klibansky and E. C. Mossner (Oxford: Clarendon Press, 1954).

——(4), *A Letter from a Gentleman to his friend in Edinburgh*, ed. E. C. Mossner and J. V. Price (Edinburgh: Edinburgh University Press, 1967).

——(5), *Hume's Treatise of Human Nature*, ed. L. A. Selby-Bigge (Oxford: Clarendon Press, 1888).

——(6), *Enquiries Concerning the Human Understanding and Concerning the Principles of Morals*, ed. L. A. Selby-Bigge, 2nd edn (Oxford: Clarendon Press, 1902).

HUME, D. (7), *Hume's Dialogues Concerning Natural Religion*, ed. N. Kemp Smith, 2nd edn (London and Edinburgh: Nelson, 1947).

——(8), *Dialogues Concerning Natural Religion*, ed. H. D. Aiken (New York and London: Hafner Press and Collier Macmillan, 1948).

——(9), *Dialogues Concerning Natural Religion*, ed. N. Pike (Indianapolis and New York: Bobbs-Merill, 1970).

——(10), *The Natural History of Religion*, ed. H. E. Root (London: Adam & Charles Black, 1956).

——(11), *The Natural History of Religion and Dialogues concerning Natural Religion*, ed. A. W. Colver, and J. V. Price (Oxford: Clarendon Press, 1976).

——(12), *Hume on Religion*, ed. R. Wollheim (London and Glasgow: Collins (Fontana Library), 1963).

HUNT, H. A. K., *The Humanism of Cicero* (Carlton: Melbourne University Press, 1954).

HURLBUTT, R. H. (1), 'David Hume and Scientific Theism', *The Journal of the History of Ideas*, 17 (1956).

——(2), *Hume, Newton and the Design Argument* (Lincoln, Nebr.: University of Nebraska Press, 1965).

HUTCHINS, R. M. (ed.), *Pascal* (Chicago, London, Toronto: William Benton, 1952).

IJSSELING, S., *Rhetoric and Philosophy in Conflict: An Historical Survey* (The Hague: Martinus Nijhoff, 1976).

IRWIN, W. A., 'Job', in Peake (2).

ISOCRATES, *Isocrates*, tr. G. Norlin and L. van Hook, 3 vols (London and Cambridge, Mass.: Loeb Classical Library, 1928–45).

JACKSON, B. D., 'The Prayers of Socrates', *Phronesis*, 16 (1971).

JANSENIUS, C., *Augustinus*, 3 vols (Louvain: Jacob Zegerus, 1640).

JEFFNER, A., *Butler and Hume on Religion: A Comparative Analysis* (Stockholm: Diakonistyrelsens Bokförlag, 1966).

JONES (1), E., *The Triumph of Job* (London: SCM, 1966).

JONES (2), P., *Hume's Sentiments: Their Ciceronian and French Context* (Edinburgh: Edinburgh University Press, 1982).

JOWETT, B. (tr.), *The Dialogues of Plato*, 4th edn, 4 vols (Oxford: Clarendon Press, 1953).

JUHL, P. D., *Interpretation: An Essay in the Philosophy of Literary Criticism* (Princeton, NJ: Princeton University Press, 1980).

JUNG, C. G. (1), *Psychological Types* (London: Routledge & Kegan Paul, 1944).

——(2), 'Answer to Job' in his *Collected Works*, xi, tr. R. F. C. Hull (London: Routledge & Kegan Paul, 1958).

JUNKER, H., *Jobs Leid, Streit und Sieg* (Freiburg im Breisgau: Herder, 1948).

KAHLER, E., 'The Devil Secularised: Thomas Mann's Faust', tr. F. C. Golffing, in H. Hatfield (ed.), *Thomas Mann: A Collection of Critical Essays* (Englewood Cliffs, NJ: Prentice-Hall, 1964).

KAHN, J., *Job's Illness: Loss, Grief and Integration: A Psychological Interpretation* (Oxford: Pergamon, 1975).

KALLEN, H. M., *The Book of Job as Greek Tragedy* (New York: Hill & Wang, 1918).

KANT, I. (1), *Critique of Pure Reason*, tr. N. Kemp Smith (London and New York: Macmillan and St Martin's Press, 1933).

——(2), *Critique of Judgement*, tr. J. C. Meredith (Oxford: Clarendon Press, 1952).

——(3), 'The Failure of All Philosophical Attempts Towards a Theodicy', in G. Rabel (tr.), *Kant Selections* (Oxford: Clarendon Press, 1963).

KAPP, E., 'Syllogistic', in Barnes (2), i.

KAUFMANN, W. (1) (tr.), *The Portable Nietzsche* (New York: The Viking Press, 1954).

——(2), (tr.), *Basic Writings of Nietzsche* (New York: The Modern Library, 1968).

——(3), (tr.), Friedrich Nietzsche, *The Gay Science: with a Prelude in Rhymes and an Appendix of Songs* (New York: Vintage Books, 1974).

——(4), and HOLLINGDALE, R. J. (trs.), Friedrich Nietzsche, *The Will to Power* (New York: Vintage Books, 1968).

——(5), *Nietzsche: Philosopher, Psychologist, Antichrist*, 3rd edn (New York: Vintage Books, 1968).

KEMP SMITH, N. (1) (ed.), *Hume's Dialogues Concerning Natural Religion*, 2nd edn (London and Edinburgh: Nelson, 1947).

——(2), *The Philosophy of David Hume: A Critical Study of its Origins and Central Doctrines* (London: Macmillan, 1941).

——(3), (tr.), *Immanuel Kant's Critique of Pure Reason* (London and New York: Macmillan and St Martin's Press, 1933).

KENNEDY, G. A. (1), *The Art of Persuasion in Greece*, (Princeton, NJ: Princeton University Press, 1963).

——(2), *Classical Rhetoric and Its Christian and Secular Tradition from Ancient to Modern Times* (London: Croom Helm, 1980).

KENNY, A., *Action, Emotion and Will* (London: Routledge & Kegan Paul, 1963).

KIERKEGAARD, S. (1), *Repetition: An Essay in Experimental Psychology*, tr. W. Lowrie (London: Oxford University Press, 1942).

——(2), *Purity of Heart is to Will One Thing: Spiritual Preparation for the Office of Confession*, tr. D. Steere (London and Glasgow: Fontana, 1961).

KISSANE, E. J., *The Book of Job* (Dublin: Browne & Nolan, 1939).

KITTEL, G. (ed.), Theologisches Wörterbuch zum Neuen Testament, 6 vols (Stuttgart: Kohlhammer, 1950–5).

KLIBANSKY, R., and MOSSNER, E. (eds), *New Letters of David Hume* (Oxford: Clarendon Press, 1954).

KNEALE, W., and KNEALE, M., *The Development of Logic* (Oxford: Clarendon Press, 1962).

KÖRNER, S., *Metaphysics: Its Structure And Function* (Cambridge: Cambridge University Press, 1984).

KOSMAN, A., 'Explanation and Understanding in Aristotle's *Posterior Analytics*', in E. N. Lee and others (eds), *Exegesis and Argument: Studies in Greek Philosophy Presented to Gregory Vlastos* (Assen: Van Gorcum (*Phronesis*. suppl. vol. 1), 1973).

KRAELING, E. G., *The Book of the Ways of God* (London: SPCK, 1938).

KRAILSHEIMER, A. J. (1) (tr.), *Pascal*: Pensées (Harmondsworth: Penguin, 1966).

——(2), *Pascal* (Oxford: Oxford University Press, 1980).

KUHN, T. S., *The Structure of Scientific Revolutions*, 2nd edn (Chicago: University of Chicago Press, 1970).

LAFUMA, L. (1) (ed.), Pascal, *Œuvres complètes* (Paris: Seuil, 1963).

——(2) (ed.), Blaise Pascal, *Pensées sur la religion et sur quelques autres sujets*, 3 vols (Paris: éditions du Luxembourg, 1951).

——(3) (ed.), *La Manuscrit des Pensées de Pascal: 1662* (Paris: Les Libraires Associés, 1962).

——(4), and ANGERS, J. E. d', 'A propos d'une thèse marxiste sur Pascal', *Études franciscaines*, 7 (1956).

LAIRD, J. (1), *Hume's Philosophy of Human Nature* (London: Methuen, 1932).

——(2), 'The Present-Day Relevance of Hume's *Dialogues Concerning Natural Religion*', *Proceedings of the Aristotelian Society (Supplementary Volumes)*, 18 (1939).

LAKATOS, I., and MUSGRAVE, A. (eds), *Criticism and the Growth of Knowledge* (Cambridge: Cambridge University Press, 1970).

LAKE, F., *Clinical Theology* (London: Darton, Longman and Todd, 1966).

LANG, B., *Philosophy and the Art of Writing: Studies in Philosophical and Literary Style* (Lewisburg, Pa.: Bucknell University Press, 1983).

LAPORTE, J., *La Doctrine de Port-Royal*, 2 vols (Paris: Presses Universitaires de France, 1923).

LAUDAN, L., 'Two Dogmas of Methodology', *Philosophy of Science*, 43 (1976).

LEA, F. A., *The Tragic Philosopher: Friedrich Nietzsche*, 2nd edn (London: Methuen, 1977).

LEAVIS, F. R. (1), *The Common Pursuit* (Harmondsworth: Penguin, 1962).

——(2) (ed.), *A Selection from* Scrutiny, 2 vols (Cambridge: Cambridge University Press, 1968).

LEE, H. D. P., 'Geometrical Method and Aristotle's Account of First Principles', *Classical Quarterly*, 29 (1935).

LEIBNIZ, G. W., *New Essays on Human Understanding*, tr. P. Remnant and J. Bennett (Cambridge: Cambridge University Press, 1981).

LESHER, J., 'The Role of *Nous* in Aristotle's *Posterior Analytics*', *Phronesis*, 18 (1973).

LEVI(1), A., *French Moralists: The Theory of the Passions, 1585 to 1649* (Oxford: Clarendon Press, 1964).

LEVI(2), A. W., 'Wittgenstein as Dialectician', *The Journal of Philosophy*, 61 (1964).

LEWIS, C. S., *The Problem of Pain* (London: Geoffrey Bles, 1940).

LIVINGSTON, D. W., and KING, J. T. (eds), *Hume: A Re-Evaluation* (New York: Fordham University Press, 1976).

LOCKE, J. (1), *The Works of John Locke*, 11th edn, 10 vols (London: W. Otridge and others, 1812).

——(2), *An Essay Concerning Human Understanding*, ed. A. C. Fraser, 2 vols (New York: Dover, 1959).

LUCRETIUS, *De Rerum Natura*, tr. W. H. D. Rouse and M. F. Smith (London and Cambridge, Mass.: Loeb Classical Library, 1975).

LUGG, A., 'Feyerabend's Rationalism', *Canadian Journal of Philosophy*, 7 (1977).

MACDONALD, D. B., 'The Original Form of the Legend of Job', *Journal of Biblical Literature*, 14 (1895).

McGREGOR, C. P. (tr.), Cicero, *The Nature of the Gods* (Harmondsworth: Penguin, 1972).

MacINTYRE, A., *After Virtue: A Study in Moral Theory* (London: Duckworth, 1981).

McKAY, J. W., 'Elihu: A Proto-Charismatic?', *The Expository Times*, 90 (1979).

McKENZIE, J. L., Review of R. Gordis, *The Book of God and Man: A Study of Job*, *Interpretation*, 20 (1966).

MACKIE, J. L., *The Miracle of Theism: Arguments for and against the Existence of God* (Oxford: Clarendon Press, 1982).

MADDEN, E. H., 'The Enthymeme: Crossroads of Logic, Rhetoric and Metaphysics', *Philosophical Review*, 61, (1952).

MAIMONIDES, M., *The Guide of the Perplexed*, ed. S. Pines (Chicago: The University of Chicago Press, 1963).

MAYOR, J. B., and SWAINSON, J. H. (eds), *M. Tulii Ciceronis de natura deorum libri tres*, 3 vols (Cambridge: Cambridge University Press, 1880–5).

MEADOR, P. A., 'Rhetoric and Humanism in Cicero', *Philosophy and Rhetoric*, 3 (1970).

MESNARD, J. (1) (ed.), Blaise Pascal, *Œuvres complètes*, 2 vols (Paris: Desclée de Brower, 1964–70).

MESNARD, J. (2), *Pascal et les Roannez*, 2 vols (Bruges: Desclée de Brower, 1965).

—— (3), *Les Pensées de Pascal* (Paris: Société d'Édition d'Enseignement Supérieur, 1976).

MEYER, M., 'Dialectic and Questioning: Socrates and Plato', *American Philosophical Quarterly*, 17 (1980).

MIDDLETON, C. (tr.), *Selected Letters of Friedrich Nietzsche* (Chicago and London; The University of Chicago Press, 1969).

MIEL, J. (1), *Pascal and Theology* (Baltimore and London: Johns Hopkins University Press, 1969).

—— (2), 'Pascal, Port-Royal, and Cartesian Linguistics', *Journal of the History of Ideas*, 30 (1969).

MILL, J. S., *A System of Logic: Ratiocinative and Inductive*, 3rd edn, 2 vols (London: J. W. Parker, 1851).

MILLER (1), A. B. and BEE, J. D., 'Enthymemes: Body and Soul', *Philosophy and Rhetoric*, 5 (1972).

MILLER (2), D. W., 'A Critique of Good Reasons', in J. Agassi and I. C. Jarvie (eds), *Rationality: The Critical View*, (Dordrecht: Nijhoff, 1987).

MITCHELL, B. (1), 'The Justification of Religious Belief', *The Philosophical Quarterly*, 11 (1961).

—— (2), *The Justification of Religious Belief* (London: Macmillan, 1973).

MOFFATT, J. (tr.), *A New Translation of the Bible* (London: Hodder & Stoughton, 1935).

MONTAIGNE (1), *Essais de Montaigne*, ed. M. Rat, 2 vols (Paris: Éditions Garnier Frères, 1962).

—— (2), *The Complete Essays of Montaigne*, tr. D. M. Frame (Stanford: Stanford University Press, 1965).

MONTINARI, M., 'The New Critical Edition of Nietzsche's Complete Works', tr. D. S. Thatcher, *Malahat Review*, 24 (1972).

MOORE, G. E. (1), *Philosophical Papers* (London: George Allen & Unwin, 1959).

—— (2), *The Philosophy of G. E. Moore*, ed. P. A. Schilpp (La Salle, Ill. and London: Open Court and Cambridge University Press, 1968).

MORAUX, P., 'La Joute dialectique d' après le huitième livre des *Topiques*', in Owen (5).

MORGAN, J. (1), 'Pascal, Concupiscence, and "La Machine"', *The Modern Language Review*, 71 (1976).

—— (2), 'Pascal's Three Orders', *The Modern Language Review*, 73 (1978).

MORICE, G. P. (ed.), *David Hume: Bicentenary Papers* (Edinburgh: Edinburgh University Press, 1977).

MORRISROE, M. (1), 'Rhetorical Methods in Hume's Works on Religion', *Philosophy and Rhetoric*, 2 (1969).

—— (2), 'Hume's Rhetorical Strategy: A Solution to the Riddle of the *Dialogues Concerning Natural Religion*', *Texas Studies in Literature and Language*, 11 (1969–70).

—— (3), 'Characterisation as Rhetorical Device in Hume's *Dialogues Concerning Natural Religion*', *Enlightenment Essays*, 1 (1970).

MOSSNER, E. C. (1), 'The Enigma of Hume', *Mind*, 45 (1936).

—— (2), *The Life of David Hume* (London and Edinburgh: Nelson, 1954).

—— (3), 'Hume and the Legacy of the *Dialogues*', in Morice.

—— (4), and PRICE, J. V. (eds), David Hume, *A Letter from a Gentleman to his friend in Edinburgh* (Edinburgh: Edinburgh University Press, 1967).

MOULTON, R. G., *The Modern Reader's Bible* (New York and London: Macmillan, 1922).

MUNDLE, C. W. K., *A Critique of Linguistic Philosophy* (Oxford: Clarendon Press, 1970).

MURRAY, G., *Aeschylus: The Creator of Tragedy* (Oxford; Clarendon Press, 1940).

NATHAN, G. J., 'The Existence and Nature of God in Hume's Theism', in Livingston.

NEB: *The New English Bible with the Apocrypha* (Oxford and Cambridge: Oxford and Cambridge University Presses, 1970).

NEHAMAS, A., 'The Eternal Recurrence', *The Philosophical Review*, 89 (1980).

NELSON, R. J., *Pascal: Adversary and Advocate* (Cambridge, Mass. and London: Harvard University Press, 1981).

NEWTON, I., *The Correspondence of Isaac Newton*, ed. H. W. Turnbull and others, 7 vols (Cambridge: Cambridge University Press, 1959–77).

NICOLE, P., *Essais de morale, contenus en divers traités sur plusieurs devoirs importans*, 14 vols (Paris: G. Desprez, 1755–67).

NIETZSCHE, F. (1), *Werke, Kritische Gesamtausgabe*, ed. G. Colli and M. Montinari, 30 vols (Berlin: de Gruyter, 1967–78).

—— (2), *Philosophy and Truth: Selections from Nietzsche's Notebooks of the Early 1870's*, tr. D. Breazeale (New Jersey and Brighton: Humanities Press and Harvester Press, 1979).

—— (3), *The Use and Abuse of History*, tr. A. Collins, 2nd edn (Indianapolis: Bobbs-Merrill, 1957).

—— (4), *Daybreak: Thoughts on the Prejudices of Morality*, tr. R. J. Hollingdale (Cambridge: Cambridge University Press, 1982).

—— (5), *The Gay Science: with a Prelude in Rhymes and an Appendix of Songs*, tr. W. Kaufmann (New York: Vintage Books, 1974).

—— (6), *The Portable Nietzsche*, tr. W. Kaufmann (New York: The Viking Press, 1954).

—— (7), *Basic Writings of Nietzsche*, tr. W. Kaufmann (New York: The Modern Library, 1968).

NIETZSCHE, F. (8), *The Will to Power*, tr. W. Kaufmann and R. J. Hollingdale (New York: Vintage Books, 1968).

—— (9), *Selected Letters of Friedrich Nietzsche*, tr. C. Middleton (Chicago and London: The University of Chicago Press, 1969).

—— (10), *A Nietzsche Reader*, tr. R. J. Hollingdale (Harmondsworth: Penguin Books, 1977).

NORTON, D. F. (1), *David Hume: Common-Sense Moralist, Sceptical Metaphysician*, (Princeton, NJ: Princeton University Press, 1982).

—— (2), CAPALDI, N., and ROBISON, W. L. (eds), *McGill Hume Studies* (San Diego: Austin Hill, 1979).

NOXON, J., 'Hume's Agnosticism', *The Philosophical Review*, 73 (1964).

NOZICK, R., *Philosophical Explanations* (Oxford: Clarendon Press, 1981).

NUSSBAUM, M. C., 'Saving Aristotle's Appearances', in Schofield.

ODEGARD, D., 'Absurdity and Types', *Mind*, 75 (1966).

OED: *The Compact Edition of the Oxford English Dictionary*, 2 vols (Oxford: Oxford University Press, 1971).

OESTERLEY, W. O. E., and ROBINSON, T. H., *An Introduction to the Books of the Old Testament* (London: SPCK, 1934).

OLDING, A. (1), 'The Argument from Design: A Reply to R. G. Swinburne', *Religious Studies*, 7 (1971).

—— (2), 'Design: A Further Reply to R. G. Swinburne', *Religious Studies*, 9 (1973).

OTTO, R., *The Idea of the Holy: An Inquiry into the Non-Rational Factor in the Idea of the Divine and its Relation to the Rational*, tr. J. W. Harvey, 2nd edn (London: Oxford University Press, 1950).

OWEN, G. E. L. (1), 'The Platonism of Aristotle', in Barnes (2), i.

—— (2), '*Tithenai ta Phainomena*' in Barnes (2), i.

—— (3), 'Logic and Metaphysics in Some Earlier Works of Aristotle', in Barnes (2), iii.

—— (4), 'Dialectic and Eristic in the Treatment of the Forms', in Owen (5).

—— (5) (ed.), *Aristotle on Dialectic: The Topics* (Oxford: Clarendon Press, 1968).

PAP, A., 'Types and Meaninglessness', *Mind*, 69 (1960).

PARENT, W. A. (1), 'Philo's Confession', *The Philosophical Quarterly*, 26 (1976).

—— (2), 'An Interpretation of Hume's Dialogues', *The Review of Metaphysics*, 30 (1976–7).

PARSONS, K. P., 'Nietzsche and Moral Change', in Solomon.

PASCAL, B. (1), *Œuvres de Blaise Pascal*, ed. P. B. Brunschvicg, P. Boutroux, and F. Gazier, 14 vols (Vaduz: Kraus Reprint, 1965).

—— (2), *Œuvres complètes*, ed. L. Lafuma (Paris: Seuil, 1963).

—— (3), *Pensées sur la religion et sur quelques autres sujets*, ed. L. Lafuma, 3 vols (Paris: Éditions du Luxembourg, 1951).

—— (4), *La Manuscrit des Pensées de Pascal: 1662*, ed. L. Lafuma (Paris: Les Libraires Associés, 1962).

—— (5), *Œuvres complètes*, ed. J. Mesnard, 2 vols (Paris: Desclée de Brower, 1964–70).

—— (6), *Blaise Pascal*, Pensées: *Nouvelle Édition établie pour la première fois d'après la copie de référence de Gilberte Pascal*, ed. P. Sellier (Paris: Mercure de France, 1976).

—— (7), *Pascal*, ed. R. M. Hutchins (Chicago, London, Toronto: William Benton, 1952).

—— (8), *Pensées*, tr. A. J. Krailsheimer (Harmondsworth, Penguin, 1966).

—— (9), Pensées, *Notes on Religion and Other Subjects*, ed. L. Lafuma, tr. J. Warrington (London: J. M. Dent (Everyman's Library), 1973).

PASLEY, M. (ed.), *Nietzsche: Imagery and Thought* (London: Methuen, 1978).

PASSMORE, J., *Philosophical Reasoning* (London: Duckworth, 1961).

PEAKE, A. S. (1), *The Problem of Suffering in the Old Testament* (London: Robert Bryant, 1904).

—— (2), *Peake's Commentary on the Bible: completely revised and reset*, ed. M. Black, and H. H. Rowley (London and Edinburgh: Nelson, 1962).

PEASE, A. S. (1), 'The Conclusion of Cicero's *De Natura Deorum*', *Transactions of the American Philological Association*, 44 (1913).

—— (2) (ed.), *M. Tulli Ciceronis De Natura Deorum*, 2 vols (Cambridge, Mass.: Harvard University Press, 1955–8).

PEIRCE, C. S., *Collected Papers of Charles Sanders Peirce*, ed. C. Hartshorne and P. Weiss, 6 vols (Cambridge, Mass.: Harvard University Press, 1931–5).

PENELHUM, T. (1), 'Hume's Scepticism and the *Dialogues*', in Norton (2).

—— (2), 'Natural Belief and Religious Belief in Hume's Philosophy', *The Philosophical Quarterly*, 33 (1983).

PERELMAN, Ch. and OLBRECHTS-TYTECA, L., *The New Rhetoric: A Treatise on Argumentation*, tr. J. Wilkinson and P. Weaver (Notre Dame, Ind., and London: University of Notre Dame Press, 1971).

PFEIFFER, R. H., *Introduction to the Old Testament* (London: A. & C. Black, 1952).

PIKE, N. (ed.), David Hume, *Dialogues Concerning Natural Religion* (Indianapolis and New York: Bobbs-Merrill, 1970).

PITCHER, G. (ed.), *Truth* (Englewood Cliffs, NJ: Prentice-Hall, 1964).

PLANTINGA, A., *God and Other Minds: A Study of the Rational Justification of Belief in God* (Ithaca and London: Cornell University Press, 1967).

PLATO (1), *The Collected Dialogues of Plato, Including the Letters*, ed. E. Hamilton and H. Cairns (New York: Bollingen Foundation, 1963).

—— (2), *The Dialogues of Plato*, tr. B. Jowett, 4th edn, 4 vols (Oxford: Clarendon Press, 1953).

PLATO (3), *Plato's* Phaedo, ed. J. Burnet (Clarendon Press, 1911).

——(4), *Plato's* Phaedo: *A Translation of Plato's* Phaedo *with Introduction, Notes and Appendices*, tr. R. S. Bluck (London: Routledge & Kegan Paul, 1955).

——(5), *Plato's* Phaedo, tr. R. Hackforth (Cambridge: Cambridge University Press, 1955).

——(6), *Phaedo*, tr. D. Gallop (Oxford: Clarendon Press, 1975).

——(7), *Plato's* Phaedrus, tr. R. Hackforth (Cambridge: Cambridge University Press, 1952).

——(8), *Lysis; Symposium; Gorgias*, tr. W. R. M. Lamb (London and Cambridge, Mass.: Loeb Classical Library, 1925).

PLUTARCH, *Plutarch's* Moralia, tr. F. C. Babbitt and others, 16 vols (London and Cambridge, Mass.: Loeb Classical Library, 1960–9).

POLANYI, M., *Personal Knowledge: Towards a Post-Critical Philosophy* (London: Routledge & Kegan Paul, 1962).

POLE, D. (1), 'Leavis and Literary Criticism', in Pole (2).

——(2), *Aesthetics, Form and Emotion*, ed. G. Roberts (London: Duckworth, 1983).

POLLOCK, S., *Stubborn Soil* (London: Sidgwick & Jackson, 1946).

POPE, A., *The Poems of Alexander Pope: A One-Volume Edition of the Twickenham Text with Selected Annotations*, ed. J. Butt (London: Methuen, 1965).

POPPER, K. R., *Objective Knowledge: An Evolutionary Approach* (Oxford: Clarendon Press, 1972).

PRICE, J. V. (1), 'Empirical Theists in Cicero and Hume', *Texas Studies in Literature and Language*, 5 (1963).

——(2), 'Sceptics in Cicero and Hume', *The Journal of the History of Ideas*, 25 (1964).

——(3), *The Ironic Hume* (Austin: University of Texas Press, 1965).

QUINE, W. V. (1), 'Two Dogmas of Empiricism', in his *From a Logical Point of View* (New York: Harper & Row, 1963).

——(2), 'Epistemology Naturalised', in his *Ontological Relativity and Other Essays* (New York and London: Columbia University Press, 1969).

——(3), and ULLIAN, J. S., *The Web of Belief* (New York: Random House, 1970).

QUINTILIAN, *Institutio Oratoria*, tr. H. E. Butler, 4 vols (London and Cambridge, Mass.: Loeb Classical Library, 1921–2).

QUINTON, A. M., *The Divergence of the Twain: Poet's Philosophy and Philosopher's Philosophy* (Coventry: University of Warwick, 1985).

RANDALL, J. H., 'The Development of Scientific Method in the School of Padua', *Journal of the History of Ideas*, 1 (1940).

RAPAPORT, W. J., 'Unsolvable Problems and Philosophical Progress', *American Philosophical Quarterly*, 19 (1982).

RAPHAEL, S., 'Rhetoric, Dialectic and Syllogistic Argument: Aristotle's Position in *Rhetoric I–II*', *Phronesis*, 19 (1974).

REICHENBACH, H., *The Rise of Scientific Philosophy* (Berkeley and Los Angeles: University of California Press, 1951).

RESCHER, N., *The Strife of Systems: An Essay on the Grounds and Implications of Philosophical Diversity* (Pittsburgh: University of Pittsburgh Press, 1985).

RICHARDS, I. A., *Beyond* (New York: Harcourt, 1974).

RICHARDSON, A. (ed.), *A Theological Word Book of the Bible* (London: SCM, 1950).

RICHETTI, J. J., *Philosophical Writing: Locke, Berkeley, Hume* (Cambridge, Mass.: Harvard University Press, 1983).

RICŒUR, P., *Freud and Philosophy; An Essay on Interpretation*, tr. D. Savage (New Haven and London: Yale University Press, 1970).

RIGHTER, W. H., 'Some Notes on "Acting it out" and "Being in it up to the nose"', in Pole (2).

ROBINSON, R. (1), 'Analysis in Greek Geometry', *Mind*, 45 (1936), repr. in Robinson (2).

—— (2), *Essays in Greek Philosophy* (Oxford: Clarendon Press, 1969).

—— (3), *Plato's Earlier Dialectic*, 2nd edn (Oxford: Clarendon Press, 1953).

RODIS-LEWIS, G., *Descartes et le rationalisme* (Paris: Presses universitaires de France, 1966).

ROOT, H. E. (ed.), David Hume, *The Natural History of Religion* (London: Adam & Charles Black, 1956).

RORTY, R. (1), *Philosophy and the Mirror of Nature* (Oxford: Basil Blackwell, 1980).

—— (2), *Consequences of Pragmatism (Essays: 1972–1980)* (Brighton: Harvester, 1982).

ROSEN, S., *Plato's Sophist: The Drama of Original and Image* (New Haven and London: Yale University Press, 1983).

ROSS, W. D. (1), *Aristotle*, 5th edn (London: Methuen, 1949).

—— (2), *The Works of Aristotle translated into English*, 12 vols (Oxford: Clarendon Press, 1908–52).

ROWE, W. L., *The Cosmological Argument* (Princeton, NJ: Princeton University Press, 1975).

ROWLEY, H. H. (1), *Submission in Suffering* (Cardiff: University of Wales Press, 1951).

—— (2), *Job* (London: Nelson, 1970).

RSV: *The Holy Bible: Revised Standard Version* (London: Nelson, 1952).

RV: *The Holy Bible Containing the Old and New Testaments and the Apocrypha Translated out of the Original Tongues: Being the Version Set Forth A.D. 1611 Compared with the Most Ancient Authorities and*

Revised, commonly known as the 'Revised Version' of the Bible (Oxford: The University Press, 1898).

RYLAARSDAM, J. C., 'Hebrew Wisdom', in Peake (2).

RYLE, G. (1), *The Concept of Mind* (London: Hutchinson, 1949).

—— (2), *Collected Essays, 1929–1968* (London: Hutchinson, 1971).

—— (3) (ed.), *The Revolution in Philosophy* (London: Macmillan, 1963).

—— (4), 'Dialectic in the Academy', in Bambrough (1).

—— (5), *Plato's Progress* (Cambridge: Cambridge University Press, 1966).

SAINT-CYRAN, Jean Duvergier de Hauranne, Abbé de Saint-Cyran, *Lettres chrétiennes et spirituelles*, 3 vols (Paris: A. Lyon, 1674).

SARTRE, J.-P., *La Nausée* (Paris: Gallimard, 1938).

SAYERS, D. L., *The Poetry of Search and the Poetry of Statement* (London: Gollancz, 1963).

SCHACHT, R. (1), *Nietzsche* (London: Routledge, 1983).

—— (2), 'Nietzsche and Nihilism', in Solomon.

SCHELER, M., *Ressentiment*, ed. L. A. Coser, tr. W. W. Holdheim (New York: The Free Press of Glencoe, 1961).

SCHILPP, P. A. (ed.), *The Philosophy of G. E. Moore* (La Salle, Ill. and London: Open Court and Cambridge University Press, 1968).

SCHOFIELD, M., and NUSSBAUM, M. C. (eds), *Language and Logos: Studies in Ancient Greek Philosophy Presented to G. E. L. Owen*, (Cambridge: Cambridge University Press, 1982).

SCOFIELD, R. (tr.), 'Pascal's Scientific Treatises', in Hutchins.

SEIGEL, J. E., *Rhetoric and Philosophy in Renaissance Humanism: The Union of Eloquence and Wisdom, Petrarch to Valla* (Princeton, NJ: Princeton University Press, 1968).

SELBY-BIGGE, L. A. (1) (ed.), *Hume's Treatise of Human Nature* (Oxford: Clarendon Press, 1888).

—— (2) (ed.), David Hume, *Enquiries Concerning the Human Understanding and Concerning the Principles of Morals*, 2nd edn (Oxford: Clarendon Press, 1902).

SELLIER, P. (1) (ed.), *Blaise Pascal, Pensées: Nouvelle Édition établie pour la première fois d'après la copie de référence de Gilberte Pascal* (Paris: Mercure de France, 1976).

—— (2), *Pascal et Saint Augustine* (Paris: Armand Colin, 1970).

SHEPHERD, J. J., *Experience, Inference and God* (London: Macmillan, 1975).

SLAUGHTER, M. M., *Universal Languages and Scientific Taxonomy in the Seventeenth Century* (Cambridge: Cambridge University Press, 1982).

SMART, J. J. C., 'A Note on Categories', *The British Journal for the Philosophy of Science*, 4 (1953–4).

SMETHURST, S. E., 'Cicero and Isocrates', *Transactions of the American Philological Association*, 84 (1953).

SMITH, P., *A History of Modern Culture*, 2 vols (London: G. Routledge & Sons, 1930–4).

SNAITH, N. H., *The Book of Job: Its Origin and Purpose* (London: SCM, 1968).

SOLOMON, R. C. (ed.), *Nietzsche: A Collection of Critical Essays* (New York: Anchor Books, 1973).

SOMMERS, F., 'Predicability', in M. Black (ed.), *Philosophy in America* (London: Allen & Unwin, 1965).

SPINOZA, *The Chief Works of Benedict de Spinoza*, tr. R. H. M. Elwes, 2 vols (New York: Dover, 1951).

STENZEL, J., *Plato's Method of Dialectic*, tr. D. J. Allan (Oxford: Clarendon Press, 1940).

STEPHENSON, R. H., 'On the Widespread Use of an Inappropriate and Restrictive Model of the Literary Aphorism', *The Modern Language Review*, 75 (1980).

STERN, J. P., *A Study of Nietzsche* (Cambridge: Cambridge University Press, 1979).

STEVENSON, W. B., *The Poem of Job* (London: Oxford University Press, 1947).

STEWART, M. A., 'Dead-Born from the Press', *Philosophical Books*, 18 (1977).

STONE, R., 'Ratiocination not Rationalisation', *Mind*, 74 (1965).

STRAHAN, J., *The Book of Job Interpreted* (Edinburgh: T. & T. Clark, 1913).

STRAWSON, P. F. (1), *Individuals: An Essay in Descriptive Metaphysics* (London: Methuen, 1959).

—— (2), 'Categories', in O. P. Wood and G. Pitcher (eds), *Ryle* (New York and London: Doubleday and Macmillan, 1970).

SUTHERLAND, S. R., 'Penelhum on Hume', *The Philosophical Quarterly*, 33 (1983).

SWINBURNE, R. G. (1), 'The Argument from Design', *Philosophy*, 43 (1968).

—— (2), 'The Argument from Design: A Defence', *Religious Studies*, 8 (1972).

—— (3), *The Existence of God* (Oxford: Clarendon Press, 1979).

TAIT, M. D. C., 'A Problem in the Method of Hypothesis in the *Phaedo*', in M. E. White (ed.), *Studies in Honour of Gilbert Norwood* (Toronto: University of Toronto Press, 1952).

TEMPLE, W., Archbishop of York, *Thoughts on Some Problems of the Day: A Charge Delivered at his Primary Visitation* (London: Macmillan, 1931).

TENNANT, F. R., *Philosophical Theology*, 2 vols (Cambridge: Cambridge University Press, 1928–30).

TERENCE, *Phormio; The Mother-in-Law; The Brothers*, tr. J. Sargeaunt (London and New York: Loeb Classical Library, 1912).

TERRIEN, S., *Job: Poet of Existence* (Indianapolis: Bobbs-Merrill, 1957).

THOMPSON, M., 'On Category Differences', *The Philosophical Review*, 66 (1957).

TOPLISS, P., *The Rhetoric of Pascal: A Study of his Art of Persuasion in the Provinciales and the Pensées* (Amsterdam: Leicester University Press, 1966).

TRILLING, L., *Sincerity and Authenticity* (London: Oxford University Press, 1972).

UNGER, P., *Philosophical Relativity* (Oxford: Basil Blackwell, 1984).

VERDENIUS, W. J. 'Notes on Plato's *Phaedo*', *Mnemosyne*, 11 (1958).

VLASTOS, G. (1), 'Reasons and Causes in the *Phaedo*', *The Philosophical Review*, 78 (1969).

—— (2), 'The Paradox of Socrates', in his *The Philosophy of Socrates* (New York: Anchor Books, 1971).

—— (3), *Exegesis and Argument: Studies in Greek Philosophy Presented to Gregory Vlastos*, ed. E. N. Lee *et al.* (Assen: Van Gorcum (*Phronesis*. suppl. vol. 1), 1973).

WADIA, P. S. 'Philo Confounded', in Norton (2).

WAISMANN, F., 'How I see Philosophy', in H. D. Lewis (ed.), *Contemporary British Philosophy: Third Series* (London: George Allen & Unwin, 1956).

WARNER, M. M. (ed.), *The Bible as Rhetoric* (London & New York: Routledge, forthcoming).

WARNOCK (1), G. J., *English Philosophy since 1900* (London: Oxford University Press, 1958).

WARNOCK (2), M., 'Nietzsche's Conception of Truth', in Pasley.

WARRINGTON, J. (tr.), *Blaise Pascal: Pensées, Notes on Religion and Other Subjects*, ed. L. Lafuma (London: J. M. Dent (Everyman's Library), 1973).

WEIL (1), E., 'The Place of Logic in Aristotle's Thought', in Barnes (2), i.

WEIL (2), S., *Waiting on God*, tr. E. Craufurd (London: Routledge & Kegan Paul, 1951).

WEISS, P., 'God, Job, and Evil', *Commentary*, 6 (1948).

WETSEL, D., *L'Écriture et le reste: The Pensées of Pascal in the Exigetical Tradition of Port-Royal* (Columbus: Ohio State University Press, 1981).

WHEELER ROBINSON, H., *The Religious Ideas of the Old Testament* (London: Duckworth, 1913).

WILAMOWITZ-MOELLENDORFF, U. von, *Platon*, 2 vols (Berlin: Weidmann, 1920).

WILLIAMS (1), B., *Descartes: The Project of Pure Enquiry*, (Harmondsworth: Penguin, 1978).

WILLIAMS (2), C., *He Came Down From Heaven and The Forgiveness of Sins* (London: Faber & Faber, 1940).

—— (3), *The Descent of the Dove: A Short History of the Holy Spirit in the Church*, 2nd edn (London: Faber & Faber, 1950).

WILLIAMS (4), C. J. F., 'Dying', *Philosophy*, 44 (1969).

WILLIAMS (5), W. D., 'Nietzsche's Masks', in Pasley.

WISDOM, J. (1), *Philosophy and Psycho-Analysis* (Oxford: Basil Blackwell, 1953).

—— (2), *Other Minds* (Oxford: Basil Blackwell, 1956).

—— (3), *Paradox and Discovery* (Oxford: Basil Blackwell, 1965).

—— (4), *Wisdom: Twelve Essays*, ed. R. Bambrough (Oxford: Basil Blackwell, 1974).

WITTGENSTEIN, L. (1), *Tractatus Logico-Philosophicus*, tr. C. K. Ogden (London: Kegan Paul, Trench & Trubner, 1922).

—— (2), *Philosophical Investigations*, tr. G. E. M. Anscombe (Oxford: Basil Blackwell, 1958).

—— (3), *On Certainty*, ed. G. E. M. Anscombe and G. H. von Wright, tr. D. Paul and G. E. M. Anscombe (Oxford: Basil Blackwell, 1969).

—— (4), *Philosophical Remarks*, ed. R. Rhees, tr. R. Hargreaves and R. White (Oxford: Basil Blackwell, 1975).

WOLLHEIM, R. (ed.), *Hume on Religion* (London and Glasgow: Collins (Fontana Library), 1963).

WOOD, D. C., 'Derrida and the Paradoxes of Reflection', *Journal of the British Society for Phenomenology*, 11 (1980).

WRIGHT, J. P., *The Sceptical Realism of David Hume* (Manchester: Manchester University Press, 1983).

YALDEN-THOMSON, D. C. 'The Virginia Lectures', in Wisdom (4).

YANDELL, K. E., 'Hume on Religious Belief', in Livingston.

ZASLAVSKY, R., *Platonic Myth and Platonic Writing* (Washington, DC: University Press of America, 1981).

Index

abduction 25n., 345–7, 366
Abrams, M. H. 363
aesthetic 258, 271, 281, 285, 288–9,
354–64, 367
Alderman, H. 283n.
analogical reasoning 21, 26–7, 52–3,
213–15, 220, 227, 231, 247, 257,
346–54
analytic method 1, 7n., 9–10, 16–18,
42n., 94n., 188–9
Annas, J. 97n., 305
aphoristic form 187–8, 198, 307, 316, 318
Aquinas, St Thomas: *see* Thomas
Aquinas, St
Arcesilas 57–8, 227
Aristotle 2–3, 6n., 7n., 8, 25n., ch. 2.2
passim, 54–5, 58–9, 64, 94n.,
103–4, 105–6, 150, 154, 204–5, 207,
209, 226n., 238, 309, 310, 327,
334–6, 340, 343, 345, 346n., 347,
353, 354, 363, 366
Arnauld, A. 6n., 10, 12
Arnold, M. 357–8, 363n.
artist: *see* aesthetic
Asklepios 98, 100
assiette 169, 324, 326, 337, 340, 366n.
Augustine, St 54n., 125, 160–2, 166,
170–1, 172, 178–9, 189, 193, 197, 204,
336–7, 353
Austin, J. L. 16
authenticity 2, 144n., 175, 182, 204,
308, 336, 354, 358, 366n., 369
Ayer, A. J. 18–19, 21, 22, 26, 29, 63,
340

Bacon, F. 10n., 164, 187, 357
Bambrough, J. R. 185n., 348–52,
359n., 366
Barker, S. F. 25n.
Barnes, J. 43n., 47
Barr, J. 105n.
Battersby, C. 219, 232n., 250n.
Bayle, P. 234, 247–8, 250n., 260
Beck, L. J. 8–9
Berkeley, G. 231, 237, 239, 260n.,
263n.

Bible 2, 5, 96, ch. 4 *passim*, 158–9,
161, 167, 171, 172–5, 186n., 197,
202, 204, 295, 311, 322, 331, 334–5,
354, 365, 368
Billings, G. H. 69
Bluck, R. S. 68–70, 72, 98
Bostock, D. 66n.
Broome, J. H. 197–8
Brown, G. 192n.
Browne, T. 1n.
Brunschvicg, P. B. 152n., 188
Buckley, M. J. 56n., 60
Burnet, J. 78, 81, 83n., 98
Burnham, H. D. 88n.
Butler, J. 239
Butler, R. J. 254n.

Cantor, G. 207n.
Capaldi, N. 256n.
carelessness 230–2
Carnap, R. 16, 343
Carneades 57–8, 227
Cartesian: *see* Descartes, R.
case-by-case procedure 26–7, 205, 283,
346–52, 359, 364, 366
Casey, J. 358, 359n.
Castañeda, H.-N. 341–5
Cicero 34, 41n., 50, ch. 2.3 *passim*, 64,
65n., 208, 219, 221, 224–30, 233–4,
242–3, 249n., 250, 255n., 256, 258–9,
334, 335, 336, 340, 343, 352, 354
Cioffi, F. 107
Clarke, D. M. 7n.
Clarke, S. 223n., 235, 238, 241n.
Clines, D. J. A. 146n.
Cohen, L. J. 23, 25–6, 351, 356
Collingwood, R. G. 20n.
Colver, A. W. 251n., 264
common sense 17, 211, 280
Copleston, F. 161–2, 166, 194, 311,
325
Crombie, I. M. 94–5
cumulative argument 5, 25–6, 27, 176,
204, 329, 337, 347, 350–1, 366

Dannhauser, W. J. 268